Oklahoma Treasures and Treasure Tales

University of Oklahoma Press : Norman

OKLAHOMA TREASURES AND TREASURE TALES

BY STEVE WILSON

Library of Congress Cataloging in Publication Data

Wilson, Steve.
    Oklahoma treasures and treasure tales.

    Bibliography: p.
    1. Treasure-trove—Oklahoma. 2. Legends—Oklahoma.
3. Oklahoma—Gold discoveries. I. Title.
F694.W54   917.66'03   74-15912
ISBN: 0-8061-1240-9

The paper in this book meets the guidelines for permanence and durability of the Committee on Production Guidelines for Book Longevity of the Council on Library Resources, Inc.

To Linda, who spurred my interest when it tired, who knows the stories herein as well as I do, who followed me over hill and dale while on the trail of lost treasure

Preface

On the Trail of Lost Treasure

I do not maintain that the legends told in the following pages are fact. I do maintain that those who told them believed them to be true. My purpose has been to record each tale while someone was still living to tell it. When that was no longer possible, the only alternative was to seek the story from earlier published sources. In both these endeavors I feel that I have been successful.

I must admit that often the origin of the story interested me more than the story itself. No one has successfully explained why legends of buried treasure are pandemic throughout the Southwest. It is more difficult to understand the multitude of tales in Oklahoma, because this state experienced no gold rush of the magnitude of western states. It had no documented Spanish forts or missions or permanent settlements, and yet its legends are no less in number than those of states that had a more auriferous magnetism.

While compiling *Legends of Texas* for the Texas Folklore Society in 1924, J. Frank Dobie observed that no one particular area of his state had more legends than another, and, "moreover, instead of diminishing in number, these legends are constantly increasing."[1] The reason is not a simple one, but perhaps Dobie answered it best when he said that, because "the Spanish found immense wealth in America, they became credulous of mythical wealth. Later ages and folk, failing to inherit their wealth, inherited their credulity."[2]

Early in this century the father of Oklahoma geology, Charles N. Gould, spent more than twenty years traveling over the Plains and throughout Oklahoma. In that time he made more than a thousand night camps, during which he was often entertained by legends of buried treasure.

As revealed in an early article, "Hidden Treasure on the Plains," for *Sturm's Magazine*, Gould observed that the stories shared a common form. Wherever he went, he said, "from the Dakotas to the Gulf and from the Mississippi to the Rockies, the legend of buried treasure is omnipresent. There is probably not a county in any one of the states of the plains where the story is not told and believed."[3]

Almost always the story concerned Mexicans who were attacked by Indians and forced to bury their gold. All were massacred except for one or two, who escaped. Then, years afterward, one—now an old man—returned to refind the treasure hidden so long before. Always there were mysterious signs and symbols left to lead him back to the lost fortune, and almost always he found the prescribed etching of a cross or triangle or arrow, which placed him at the brink of the treasure. But, alas, he returned to his native land unsuccessful in his final attempt to find the gold. Wrote Gould:

> How much of the truth there may be in these various legends, no one may venture to guess. It would be folly to assert that all of the tales are false, but certainly still greater folly to believe that all are true. As a person travels over Oklahoma and the surrounding states, however, and listens to these various tales, he is forced to one of the following conclusions: Either there is a wonderful amount of treasure hidden on the plains, or the world is full of deluded people, or there are a tremendous lot of liars.

I have tried to determine the historical reasons for the prevalence of treasure tales in Soonerland. For the most part historians have turned a deaf ear to tales of lost gold. But, if given a chance, the treasure legend—oral tradition—can often paint a picture that history has failed to record. Not everything is to be found in the documents. Sometimes when history has failed, tradition has succeeded. In the case of the "Great Spanish Road to Red River" tradition—not history—has preserved its route, a trail sprinkled with tales of lost Spanish gold all the way from Santa Fe to New Orleans. The legends alone virtually mark this long-forgotten ancient trail down the North Fork of Red River and its mainstream.

The Spanish conquistadors blazed the trail for less official treasure quests, many of which history failed to record. But how can one ignore the signs, the documents written not on paper but in ancient ruins, crumbled smelters, crudely worked mines, and, yes, the bleached bones of those forgotten, unknown explorers? Perhaps the multitude of legends can never be fully explained, but might it be that the countless quests in every area of Oklahoma reveal that both Spaniards and Mexicans searched this part of his empire far more than we have heretofore believed? The search goes on.

I have never been a pothunter, because at a very early age I was in the field with archaeologists and saw how sickened and horrified they were by the destruction wreaked by treasure seekers. Not only had irreplaceable artifacts been destroyed but also the place and depth at which they were found had been obliterated. In many instances what nature had preserved for centuries man had destroyed in a few careless, thoughtless moments.

A pothunter—there are other names for him— is a selfish person who damages or robs an old Indian campsite, an ancient burial ground, the remains of a prehistoric animal, or a historic ruin and scoops up all the pottery, arrow points, or artifacts for loot. In short, he is a pirate—a ravager, not a researcher, not a hunter of history, not a preserver of the past. He refuses to report his discovery, and consequently artifacts are destroyed or lost forever. The story that a relic might have told an archaeologist or a historian has been lost to everyone who might have gained knowledge from it.

If one happens onto the ruins of a fort or an Indian campsite or a burial ground, he is enjoying something he cannot monopolize. The archaeologists know how to excavate scientifically and preserve their findings. In one's own field research he might very well contribute to a historic discovery and thereby help piece together the story of man's past. Because most states have strict laws against damaging or digging into historic sites, one should leave the meticulous job of excavation to the professional, whose tools are designed for that purpose and whose knowledge has prepared him to restore and preserve.

Whenever one finds artifacts, he should report the site to the nearest museum, university, or historical society. Only then will this historically precious material be saved for study and evaluation. The professional can be of immense help,

both to the researcher and to the amateur archaeologist.

Finally: one must respect the other man's property. I know one man who learned to do that the hard way. He was digging a hole, when suddenly he was gazing into the barrels of a double-gauge shotgun. Luckily he was a good talker. I know many ranchers and farmers who would allow treasure and history buffs onto their property if only someone before them had not left a gate open or torn down a fence. It is always wise to obtain permission before entering private property. The treasure hunter should assure the landowner that he will respect his land and will check with him before leaving. Only then will he be confident that everything is left as it was found.

Buried treasure is constantly being discovered. Discoveries occur almost daily in this archaeologically rich state. The treasure seeker should not alienate the professional by allowing himself to be called a pothunter. Once destroyed, historic sites, like rare books, are irreplaceable—gone forever.

In this book I have attempted to include every part of the state and believe that I have culled the oldest and most popular legends from every section. I am convinced that I have amassed the most exhaustive bibliography of treasure legends of Oklahoma ever published, though I have not attempted to compile herein all the legends.

The garnering of these stories began just over fifteen years ago, and I must credit the late J. Frank Dobie for sparking that interest—an interest that has always led me on in quest of a story. Dobie's monumental *Coronado's Children* fired that interest in my early years.

The Wichita Mountains of southwestern Oklahoma provided me with more tales than I ever thought possible for a mountain range of its comparatively small extent, but, it provided the setting for innumerable gold expeditions, both ancient and recent.[4] I spent the better part of ten years seeking its stories—and even yet I yearn to know more.

I have devoted as many hours, days, and weeks to the archives as I have to the field. Many an exciting story lay waiting to be released from the records. The discovery of the lost city of Cascorillo was such a story, as were many others of its kind, not to be found on index cards. I think such discoveries have always been *my* greatest treasure.

I owe much to many. First, I must thank my parents, George and Marie Wilson, who had the wisdom to let me seek my own adventure at a very early age. Mrs. Julia B. Russell, of Lawton, spurred my desire and nourished it in her American literature class. I would not forget Foster-Harris, Professor Emeritus of English in the University of Oklahoma, writer, freethinker, teacher of the old school, who has been more than generous with his time. My deepest gratitude to him.

Certainly I owe much to Joe Christy, of Lawton, whose specialty is writing about aviation. I never left his home uninspired. My gracious instructor of history, Thomas Reynolds, of Oklahoma State University, was always eager to lend me his ear and wisdom. Berlin B. Chapman, also of that school, was never so busy that he could not share enthusiasm.

Historian and author Glenn Shirley, of Stillwater, always was eager to give advice. Historian Arthur Lawrence, of Lawton, proofread many of my early works and guided me to sources. Gillett Griswold, Director of the Fort Sill Museum, and his former Assistant Director, Jimmy Marler, were always eager to share their knowledge. Dale Durham, curator of the museum, gladly gave of his time on many occasions to seek out both information and photographs, finding them when I thought the trail had grown dim.

Stan Hoig, of Central State University, often gave helpful criticism. Jack Haley, Assistant Curator of the University of Oklahoma Western History Collections, led me to material hidden deep in the documents. Henry Johnson, Jr., who compiled tales for his map, *Oklahoma's Buried Treasures*, assisted freely with sources I might have otherwise overlooked.

Certainly my research would never have been complete without the kind and generous cooperation of Mrs. Louise Cook, Curator of the Newspaper Collection of the Oklahoma Historical Society, and Mrs. Rella Looney, Archivist of the Indian Archives Division of the society. The society librarians, Mrs. Alene Simpson and Mrs. Manon Atkins, never failed to go out of their way to help. William H. Stewart, of the Muskogee Public Library, F. R. Blackburn, Research Director of the Kansas State Historical Society, and Judith A. Schiff, of the Yale University Library, were equally helpful.

My deepest appreciation to LaVere Anderson, who freely allowed me to quote from her tales of forty years past—tales she often obtained only after she had "climbed cliffs and rowed down rivers with some old-timer who had a place to show." Certainly these tales would not be complete without the stories of the participants, the discoverers, the seekers, who shared with me some of their own adventures. For each one listed in the Sources, there were ten more who furnished leads, an obscure detail, or fragments of information. No words can express my appreciation to each of them. My gratitude to the editors of *Argosy* and *Saga* magazines for permission to incorporate my earlier articles for them. Robert Webb prepared the maps.

STEVE WILSON

Lawton, Oklahoma

Contents

Preface: On the Trail of Lost Treasure .... Page vii

1. They Found Buried Treasure 3
2. The Secrets Spanish Fort Tells 39
3. Quests for Red River's Silver Mines 69
4. Oklahoma's Forgotten Treasure Trail 89
5. Ghosts of Devil's Canyon and Their Gold 111
6. Jesse James's Two-Million-Dollar Treasure 129
7. The Last of the Old Prospectors 149
8. Skeletons, Jewels, and Platinum 189
9. Gold the Stagecoaches Never Delivered 201
10. The Lost Cave with the Iron Door 209
11. The Frenchmen's Gold at Sugar Loaf Peak 215
12. The Mystery of Cascorillo—A Lost City 227
13. Cartloads, Jack Loads, and an Aztec Sun God 233
14. The Treasures the Arbuckles Guard 241
15. Tales of the Indian Nations 249
16. Gold the Outlaws Never Spent 279
17. Lost Indian Treasure 287
18. The Treasure the Spaniards Keep Hunting 297
    Notes 303
    Sources 313
    Index 319

Maps

Landforms of Oklahoma	*Page* 6
Oklahoma trails	90
The Texas and Oklahoma Panhandles	100
Seventeenth-century Spanish exploration east of New Mexico	102
Eighteenth-century Spanish exploration of Oklahoma and Texas	103
Southwestern Oklahoma	112
Devil's Canyon	116
The Wichita Mountains	150
Landmarks for the Frenchmen's gold in Cimarron County	217
Northwestern Oklahoma	234
Indian Territory, 1855--66	252
Northeastern Oklahoma	253
Indian Territory, 1866--89	255
Colton's Map of Indian Territory, 1873	257
Johnson's Map of Indian Territory, 1883	258
Cram's Map of Indian Territory, 1883	259
Southeastern Oklahoma	300

Oklahoma Treasures and Treasure Tales

A panoramic view of the Wichita Mountains from the top of Mount Scott in the Wichita Mountains Wildlife Refuge. Photographs are by the author or are from his personal collection unless otherwise indicated.

1. They Found Buried Treasure

Early one brisk morning in January, 1913, George Hardsook, laborer, went to work. The day started like any other. He would be digging a ditch to lay an oil pipeline. This morning he was working near Oglesby, a wide place in the road in northeastern Oklahoma.

Painfully Hardsook picked at the hard clay soil, little by little. He was making good progress with the trench, when, not yet two feet down, his pick hit a metallic object. Surely there was not another pipeline here, he thought. He knelt down on the damp earth to wipe away the covering. Coins! Gold coins! He had unearthed a buried treasure!

Frantically he picked up the scattered gold pieces, not one or two or three but hundreds of them. It was evident that someone years before had placed several cloth bags full of gold and silver here, for the sacks had almost entirely rotted away.

Wild with joy, Hardsook gathered up all the money, filling his pockets and everything else he could find to cram a coin into. He managed to carry his discovery to Rodecker's Store in Oglesby, where he counted it, as a wide-eyed, bewildered crowd looked on. The golden stacks of coins grew higher and higher. When proud Hardsook had counted his last coin, his treasure totaled $37,500, most of which was in $20 gold pieces; $200 was in silver. It weighed in at more than one hundred pounds, reported the Claremore paper on January 3.[1]

George Hardsook, ditch digger, had become rich in one day. His is just one of many similar success stories that come from the gentle rolling plains and rugged hill country of Red Man's Land—Oklahoma.

Oklahoma is little known for its tales of fabulous lost treasure, but that is only because the state has had the least publicity of any in the Southwest. Oklahoma, too, had its Spanish conquistadors, clad in heavy, shiny armor. Its French forts are documented. Its Spanish forts are founded on more than legend. It has had its share of gold rushes—virtually every county has had one—land

rushes, and oil-boom towns. Last and most, it has had more than its share of ruthless outlaws and gunmen, all the way from Jesse James to Pretty Boy Floyd.

The timbered hills of Oklahoma have provided a haven for countless outlaw bands. The rugged Wichitas, the eroded Keechis, the desolate Black Mesa, the rolling Antelopes, the cavern-laden Arbuckles, the densely timbered Kiamichis and Cookson and Osage hills—all have their tales of booty—booty lost and booty found.

Between the Civil War and the turn of the century cutthroats, renegade Indians, moonshiners, whisky peddlers, gunrunners, and hard-bitten ruffians of all kinds holed up in dark caves and secluded cabins in what was then Indian Territory. The Jameses, the Youngers, Quantrill and his guerrillas, the Dalton and Doolin gangs, Red Buck, Zip Wyatt, Cherokee Bill, the reckless female desperado Belle Starr and her crew, and countless others had their secret hideaways in these hills.

For years the Indian nations of the region were in such lawless turmoil that editorials criticizing the deplorable conditions were commonplace. A typical sentiment was expressed by Fort Smith's *Western Independent*, August 28, 1873:

We have lived in and around the Indian country since the spring of 1834, but have never known such a state of terror. Now it is murder throughout the length and breadth of the Indian country. It has been the rendezvous of the vile and wicked from everywhere, an inviting field for murder and robbery because it is the highway between Texas, Missouri, Kansas and Arkansas.

People were calling Indian Territory the "Robbers' Roost," and the "Land of the Six-Shooter." Depredations were so common that people were saying, "There is no Sunday west of St. Louis—no God west of Fort Smith."[2]

Wherever there are tales of outlaws there are tales of buried loot. The evidence is convincing that much of that loot still lies beneath the veneer of sod in the state, and the odds are good that in just about any hill one picks in the Soonerland, he will discover that it bears a tale of buried treasure—all the way from the Black Mesa in the Panhandle to the Ozarks on the Arkansas border.

Landmarks alongside old trails have always proved to be veritable treasure depositories. The ancient Spanish and Indian trails, military routes, stage roads, and cattle trails are likely sites for hidden treasure. A treasure of five thousand dollars found alongside one such route in 1895 proves that hidden caches can be found—if the hunter knows where to look.

The Elm Tree Cache

Near the end of April, 1895, a stranger showed up at a farm five miles south of Guthrie. He obtained the owner's permission to search for a hidden cache and even went so far as to locate the stump of an elm tree near which the treasure was supposed to be buried. But there his search ended. He offered the landowner nine hundred dollars for his farm—a more than fair price—but at that offer the owner decided that there just might after all be something to the yarn about the elm tree. He would hold onto his land.

In a few days the stranger checked out of the Guthrie hotel. What his mission had been was no secret for long, however, for he had lost his all-telling pocketbook. Inside was found a letter dated March 25, 1895, written by John Litchfield, of Santa Fe, to his cousin, Joe Litchfield, of Tishomingo. In the letter John revealed that he had discovered a document among his father's papers stating that in 1869, while crossing the Indian Territory bound for New Mexico, he had buried a pot of money amounting to forty-five hundred dollars in gold and five hundred dollars in silver. Details of how it could be found were given.

Banker Joseph McNeal soon became custodian of the letter, and he with others persuaded the landowner to allow them to search for the cache. They paced off the prescribed distance from the stump, sank their spades into the soft earth, and soon struck an iron pot, filled to its brim. The money was "placed in the vault of the Guthrie National Bank until the courts or the finders shall decide what disposition to make of it," reported the Guthrie paper on April 22.[3]

Digging Wells and Cellars

It would be interesting to know just how many persons have found treasures while digging wells. One such incident occurred in early 1895 northeast of the Glass Mountains, near the small settlement of Cleo Springs. Farmer Alfred Abrams found his pot of gold at the end of the rainbow when his shovel unearthed such a vessel a few feet down. The gold pieces were dated in the early 1850's. The cache amounted to more than two thousand dollars, reported the *Hennessey Clipper*.[4]

Little has been written about Oklahoma's treasure trail, the subject of a subsequent chapter, in which the following incident is but one of many similar discoveries. When the Kiowa-Comanche-Apache country of southwestern Oklahoma was opened to white settlement in August, 1901, Corwin Adams took a farm on the banks of Otter Creek, about nine miles northeast of Tipton. Adams had no knowledge of the ancient Spanish trail that had once passed near his farm, down the east bank of the North Fork of Red River. Nor did he take much stock in the legend that a Spanish packtrain had met its doom along Otter Creek. But when one day an employee of Adams discovered that a human skeleton had been exposed by high water at the base of a large tree on the creek bank, Adams' curiosity got the better of him. It was not long before he convinced himself that he had stumbled onto the grave of a lone Spaniard who obviously had been interred with some of his loose change, for among his bones were found several antiquated Spanish coins and an iron stiletto, or dagger.[5]

Some years later Adams was digging a cellar near the former discovery and unearthed two more human skeletons. No document substantiated the Spanish battle site, but bones do not lie. Spanish gold is still being sought along the banks of Otter Creek.

Civil War Loot

Just southwest of Tulsa lies a small red butte known as Turkey Mountain. In 1902 a small community called Red Fork thrived nearby. In September of that year Red Fork had a visitor, and when he left, he took over $700 in gold with him.

The old gentleman had come from the East and had given the ready-made excuse of "seeing the country" for being in town. He checked into the Field Hotel and employed the liveryman, Bill Barnett, to drive him to Turkey Mountain.

The stranger asked Barnett whether he had ever seen a rock up Turkey Mountain with a cross cut on it. Barnett recalled having seen such a rock and believed that he could take the stranger to it. After some hunting the two men found the stone. On its smooth surface had been carved a cross and the numbers 64, which, even though badly weathered, were still visible. The stranger pulled a compass and tape measure from his coat pocket and placed the compass on the rock. When he got his bearing, he gave one end of the tape to Barnett and told him to walk seventy feet south. From there Barnett was to walk east, turn south a few steps, and then drive a stake.

The stranger then sent Barnett to the buggy for a shovel and directed him to dig beneath the stake. After twenty or thirty minutes Barnett began to doubt whether the old man was "in his right mind." He stopped work and demanded to know what the old-timer was up to. The stranger told him to keep digging and assured him that he would be "amply rewarded." Barnett complied.

When Barnett had reached a depth of about two feet, his spade struck something solid. When he cleared away the dirt, he saw he had uncovered a rust-eaten kettle. Both men tried to lift the pot to the surface, but its weight proved too much for the decayed vessel. Its bottom crumbled, and out poured fistfuls of glittering gold coins.

"The old gentleman [the mysterious stranger] was in the service during the Civil War and was scouting in the Indian Territory," stated a reporter.[6] "On one occasion he carried a large sum of money with him. It seems that he found himself at this time hard pressed by Pierce's army and buried the money. He claims to know of other buried treasure near here and says he will return and try to unearth more of the yellow metal in a few days."

The Indian Mummy

The sprawling, granite-clad Wichita Mountains, which rise like islands from a sea of plains, have spawned more treasure stories for a range its size—and often much larger—than perhaps any similar range in all the West, as subsequent chapters will verify. Perhaps best known for its turn-of-the-century gold rush and Jesse James's $2 million treasure, certain discoveries among its boulder-strewn peaks have given rise to more questions than the answers that have been provided.

One such find was stumbled onto by prospectors in the summer of 1902. While searching up Spanish Canyon in what is now the Wichita Mountains Wildlife Refuge, the gold seekers discovered a curious cave in an otherwise solid granite mountain. The cave had served as a tomb for an Indian child who appeared to be six or seven years old at death and who was mummified. A legend said that he was the son of an Indian chief, for "his leather dress and moccasins are more elaborate than those worn by the ordinary Indian."[7] His costume was richly ornamented with beads, a half-dozen rings, an elaborately carved bracelet, a pearl talisman, and other articles. Found sitting in an upright position, the mummy was wrapped in three thick Navajo blankets, and, the report said, "War paint shows upon the face, while the hair which covers the small head is bleached almost white with the long entombment."

Also found with the mummy were a handful of Spanish and Mexican coins, the latest dated 1821; a bag holding tubes of war paint and three spools of thread; and a package of needles and buckskin thongs. In still another leather bag were marbles, a bear claw, strings of beads, and "a stick of black root, for the little boy to chew should he become thirsty upon his long trip to the happy hunting ground."

Thenceforth the mountain tomb became known as Spanish Cave.[8] Situated about a mile southwest of Treasure Lake and facing south on the side of the granite knoll, the cave has long been studied for its pictographs, believed by some to represent hidden Spanish treasure. Faded almost beyond identification, the paintings appear to represent a cross and a sun.

The unexplained mummy was later procured by E. C. Brewer, of Lawton, who in turn sold it to an eastern traveling show. It was returned to Law-

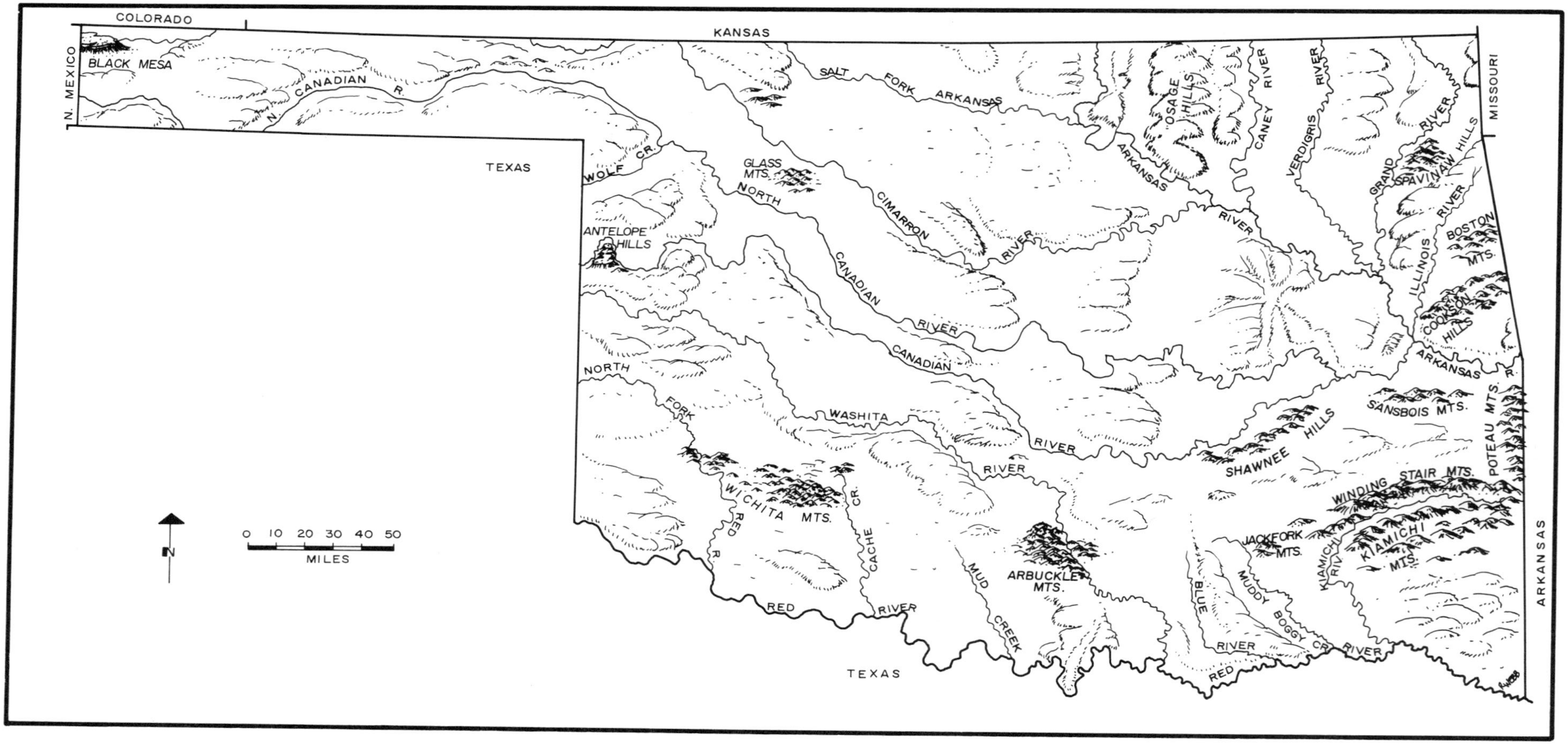
COLORADO
KANSAS
MISSOURI
ARKANSAS
N. MEXICO
TEXAS
TEXAS
BLACK MESA
CANADIAN R.
N.
WOLF CR.
ANTELOPE HILLS
GLASS MTS.
NORTH
SALT FORK ARKANSAS
CIMARRON RIVER
CANADIAN RIVER
CANADIAN
NORTH FORK
WASHITA RIVER
RIVER
WICHITA MTS.
RED R.
CACHE CR.
RED RIVER
MUD CREEK
ARBUCKLE MTS.
BLUE RIVER
RED
MUDDY BOGGY CR.
RIVER
JACKFORK MTS.
KIAMICHI RIV.
KIAMICHI MTS.
WINDING STAIR MTS.
SHAWNEE HILLS
SANSBOIS MTS.
POTEAU MTS.
ARKANSAS R.
COOKSON HILLS
BOSTON MTS.
ILLINOIS RIVER
GRAND RIVER
SPAVINAW HILLS
VERDIGRIS RIVER
CANEY RIVER
OSAGE HILLS
ARKANSAS
RIVER
0 10 20 30 40 50
MILES
N

Landforms of Oklahoma

Erwin E. Fancher, who believed that he had found the lost tomb of Sequoyah when in 1903 he discovered the grave containing the Jefferson peace medal. Courtesy Museum of the Great Plains.

ton in 1908, only to be sold to a large Indian curio firm in New York City.[9]

Sequoyah's Tomb

In the late fall of 1903 two or three thousand gold seekers in the boulder-clad Wichita Mountains were grubbing out rocks with "color" in their quest for fast wealth. Erwin E. Fancher owned land and worked a claim eight miles north of Snyder, in Kiowa County.

Late in the evening of November 26, Fancher was walking home, when he spied a rabbit run into a crevice of rocks piled on the northeast side of a small hill. Thinking that the animal would make a juicy supper, Fancher pulled back the strange stones, placed together in the form of an A. The rabbit was forgotten when the miner discovered the long rusty barrel of a big fifty-bore flintlock rifle. Since it was already late, Fancher put back the stones but took his prize discovery home to study for the night.

Early the following morning Fancher returned with his brother, Logan, and two attorneys, Mitchell and Hayes. Together they removed the rocks of the cairn until finally they exposed a human skull and then an entire skeleton that had been buried facing west.

The old flintlock had been placed near the head of the grave. Because the breech pin was bent upward, Fancher believed that the gun had been used as a club and broken. The brass trimmings of the stock lay near the feet. With the skeletal remains were found an old-fashioned English hoe, an ax, a clay pipe, a frying pan, a knife, a file, a whetstone, a powder horn, three handmade bars of lead, some bullet molds, and some bullet ladles.

Midway between the head and feet were pieces of coarsely woven wool cloth, a belt buckle, seven flints, a nugget of copper and gold, and—the object that attracted nationwide attention to the secluded mountain tomb—a large silver medallion that many believed had belonged to the great Cherokee Sequoyah, inventor of the Cherokee syllabary.

Four inches in diameter, the silver medal was perfectly round. Embossed on the face was a bust of President Thomas Jefferson, and around the border appeared the inscription: "TH. JEFFERSON PRESIDENT OF THE U.S. A.D. 1801." On the reverse side appeared a tomahawk and a pipe with crossed handles; below were two clasped hands and the words: "PEACE AND FRIENDSHIP."[10]

The gold-speckled nugget began to steal the show when mining engineer Henry Hallett, owner of the Rattlesnake Mine, assayed the nugget and reported that it ran 70 per cent copper and $800 to $1,000 to the ton in gold. Instantly the rich nugget gave rise to a lost mine, and many believed that it would be found right in the Wichitas.

Further investigation of the skeleton showed it to have been of a man about five feet, eight or ten

Among the many personal articles Fancher found in the grave in the Wichitas was this presidential peace medal, four inches in diameter, given to the Cherokee chief Thomas Chisholm by President Thomas Jefferson in 1809. Courtesy Oklahoma Historical Society.

inches. The left leg had been broken between the hip and knee and had knit together for about four inches. The right leg bone had been burned off. One hand, both feet, some of the vertebrae, and the lower right side of the skull were missing. The teeth were perfect except for the absence of the middle molar of the right half of the lower jaw. A hole in the skull about the size of a silver dollar above and behind the left ear told the story of death.

Speculation about the mystery grave ran rampant. Fancher believed that the presidential peace medal had been given to Sequoyah for forming the Cherokee alphabet and claimed to have examined a book sent to him from England stating that Sequoyah was crippled in the left leg and had died in the Wichita Mountains while hunting a band of lost Cherokees.

"The skeleton I found shows that the left leg had been affected and was probably shorter than the other," Fancher reported.[11] It was known, too, that Sequoyah's English name was George Guess. Fancher had found the initials G. G. stamped on the silver medal on the right of Jefferson's bust.

Fancher claimed that Mrs. Lucy Keys, of Vinita, a relative of Sequoyah, had examined the medal and believed that it was Sequoyah's. "She is positive that the remains are his and has made me large offers for the things I have in my possession," Fancher stated, "but it will take five hundred dollars to get them."

No one could prove the mountain tomb was not that of Sequoyah, the great Cherokee who had never learned to read, write, or speak English but who had given his people the first written Indian language. Sequoyah's place of death had been unknown since his disappearance in 1842. Three years later Cherokees reported that he died in August, 1843, in San Fernando, Mexico. Although a two-hundred-dollar reward was offered for the recovery of his body at that early date, it was never found.

When the *Washington Evening Star* picked up the story of the strange tomb in the Wichitas, one excited reader was convinced that the grave was not Sequoyah's and was prepared to prove it.[12] Mrs. Narcissa Owen, mother of Oklahoma Senator Robert L. Owen, insisted that the silver medal found in the mystery grave was the same medal given to her father, Thomas Chisholm, the last hereditary chief of the Western Cherokees, who was presented the peace medal by President Jefferson in January, 1809. (Thomas Chisholm was a lineal descendant of Occonostota, who, with other Cherokee chiefs, was received in Dover, England, in June, 1730, as a native American prince.[13])

When Thomas Chisholm died in November, 1834, Mrs. Owen's brother, Alfred, inherited the peace medal. He died at Fort Gibson in 1862, and an Indian trader present at his death procured the medal. He attached a ring to it and used the medal as a dangling ornament on his belt. The peace medal Erwin Fancher found in the Wichitas had a small silver ring fastened to a post atop the medal. Narcissa Owen was convinced that it was the same medal.[14]

When finally Fancher gave the medal to Mrs. Owen in 1905, there was no doubt that it was the same heirloom long handed down in her family. But Fancher never flagged in his belief that he had found Sequoyah's long-lost tomb. Nor did his brother, Logan, who as late as 1958 showed the small hill on which the grave had been exhumed to his niece, Mrs. Charles A. Paul, of Lubbock, Texas.[15]

Today Mrs. Paul laments that all the relics have disappeared, except for the presidential peace medal, which Senator Owen presented to the Oklahoma Historical Society in 1945.[16] Mrs. Paul recalls clearly her uncle Logan telling of the initials G. G. on the face of the medal, adding that "a clay pipe exactly like the one in the famous painting of Sequoyah was found in the grave."[17] Might it be that the G. G. initials were the coincidental initials of the unknown Indian trader from Fort Gibson?

Out of disgust Erwin Fancher later reburied the bones in an unmarked grave near the mountain tomb. No one ever explained the story of the Indian trader's death or strange burial. Local miners still wondered where the rich nugget came from that assayed almost one thousand dollars to the ton. The mystery has remained unsolved.

A Buried Tombstone

Far too often the archaeologist and the historian have failed to be at the right place at the right time. Even worse are the discoveries that have gone uninvestigated. The route that Francisco de Coronado and his daring Spanish cavaliers followed through the Southwest more than four centuries ago has long been debated. Today few believe that the swashbuckling adventurers passed through what is now southwestern Oklahoma when they sought the fabled golden cities of Quivira. Yet the discovery of a strange tombstone in August, 1907, two miles east of Grandfield, in southern Tillman County, has never been explained. While excavating a right of way, railroad workers unearthed the tombstone near the old Eschiti townsite about ten feet below the surface. The rough-hewn gravestone consisted of a granite base about ten inches high, six inches wide, and three feet long, in which sat the diamond-shaped stone, almost two feet square, its vortex pointing skyward.[18]

The chiseled inscription perplexed its discoverers. Above an indiscernible Spanish message appeared the name Don Juan Valeréz el Padre, Madrid Señor de la Bonito Señorito. Below was inscribed the date, 1542, the year after Coronado's army crossed the Great Plains. If the strange tombstone was not carved by one of Coronado's men, might it have been the work of Luis de Moscoso's three-hundred-man expedition in the Red River country? It is believed that this lost Spanish army, almost without horses, reached the present site of Wichita Falls, Texas, one hot August day in 1542.[19]

The *Temple Tribune* reported that the railroad removed the tombstone to Fort Worth for safekeeping. However, since then all attempts to find it have failed.[20] Ah, if only historians could examine that strange tombstone today. What mysteries might it unveil?

The Confederate Cave

The storied Wichita Mountains never ceased surprising its new inhabitants, once they were opened to legal settlement. The strange makeshift graves, the mountain tombs, bleached skeletons with rust-eaten sidearms came to be almost a yearly occurrence.[21] Few answers were provided, but it required little imagination to fill in the missing details.

The Wichita Mountains, with their deep, narrow canyons, furnished Spaniards

Such was the case one day in 1915, when W. M. McDaniels happened upon a cave not far northwest of Mount Roosevelt, near the old mining camp of Meers. McDaniels had prospected the area for years and had never seen this cave. Something compelled him to investigate it. He crawled inside and was aghast at what lay on the floor between him and the back of the cave.

Four human skulls and scattered bones greeted him. Pieces of rotted Confederate uniforms convinced him of the victims' identity. The Confederates had not died without means, for partly buried in the debris of the cavern floor was a large bundle of Confederate notes that McDaniel apparently failed to count because of their worthlessness.

of past centuries and latter-day outlaws lairs in which to hide their booty.

The large bundle made curious gift items over the years until only three remained, said Mrs. Lola McDaniel, of Lawton, who now possesses those few bills.[22] One fragile paper bears the words, "J. M. Hills has deposited in this bank ONE DOLLAR payable in currency or Confederate notes, Augusta, Ga., Dec. 9, 1861." A $20.50 note reads, "The State of Alabama, Montgomery, Jan. 1, 1863." The third bill, for five cents, bears the mark of "The Marine Bank of Georgia." Of course, McDaniel had no idea then that his stash of Confederate treasure might ever be worth anything. Had that partly concealed cache been gold, it would have been a different story.

Gold in an Earthen Bank

Such luck followed Robert and Elmo Randolph and Tim Casey one morning in October, 1905, when they shouldered their guns and followed a choice embankment while hunting a few miles outside Wilburton in the dense timberlands of southeastern Oklahoma.[23] As the three black men walked along, something showed brightly in the clay ahead of them.

One of them knelt down to brush away the dirt and glimpsed a gold piece. Immediately the threesome began digging out the embankment, and, after some effort, they found the proverbial pot, almost filled with five-, ten-, twenty-, and fifty-dollar gold pieces. The trio rushed back to Wilburton to exhibit their treasure and excitedly "declared themselves to be Rockefellers and Vanderbilts," reported the *Wilburton News*.[24] "The Negroes exhibited about $400 of the money, and some of it has been sent to New York to determine its real value, as it is supposed that there are premiums on the coins."

The coins were somewhat larger than regular twenty-dollar gold pieces with scalloped edges. One fifty-dollar piece was dated 1821; others, a year later. It was believed that the premiums on the gold coins would increase their value to several thousand dollars. Who had buried the cache was never determined.

Gold in a Garden

Sometime in 1852 an Indian woman received her share of a large government annuity at Fort Gibson. When she returned to her farm, fourteen miles east of Pryor Creek, she alone knew where she had buried her gold in the family garden. When she died some years later, she had told no one the secret. Fifty-four years later, in 1906, the woman's five grandsons were digging in the family garden. Their spades struck the gold their grandmother had buried so long before. It was all there, one thousand dollars in twenty-dollar gold pieces.[25]

Discovery of a Lost Fort

When Bert Moore settled his farm near the west bank of the Arkansas River, not far south of the Kansas line, in 1893, he knew nothing about the lost French fort of Ferdinandina. Historians knew little more about the trading post that flour-

ished on the Arkansas sometime between 1720 and 1750 and then mysteriously vanished without a trace. Were it not for the preservation of early maps printed in England and Scotland, the French post might never have been known to exist, and its relics, which had decayed in the earth's surface for almost two hundred years would have puzzled historians who chanced upon them. But the ancient maps showed that Ferdinandina existed somewhere on the Arkansas and was important enough to have been placed on those obscure trade routes.[26]

The settlement of the Cherokee Outlet allowed Moore to make his discovery of an ancient Wichita Indian village at the mouth of Deer Creek, about five miles northeast of Newkirk, in Kay County. When Indian artifacts led to French ones, historians began to take notice. Finally, in the summer of 1926, Joseph B. Thoburn, of the Oklahoma Historical Society, began excavating and proved beyond a doubt that the long-lost site of Ferdinandina had at last been found. His digging yielded more than five thousand fragments of iron, brass, copper, lead, flint, stone, bone, glass, and potsherds.[27] Among the relics were pieces of flintlocks, axes, knives, scissors, copper bells, locks, glass beads, bridle bits, pottery, and tomahawks. Many French designs were dated before 1637, while others came into use about 1720.

Ancient chronicles tell that, as early as 1719, French explorer Claude-Charles Dutisné visited a Wichita village along the Arkansas, perhaps the same village as the one discovered on Deer Creek. On September 27, Dutisné planted his French flag, claiming the land for his king.[28] Many French traders penetrated into northeastern Oklahoma in the 1740's, and about the time that Colonel Diego Ortiz Parilla (or Parrilla) led his Spanish army of five hundred against the Taovaya (Wichita) Indian fortress, which was flying a French flag, on Red River, it was reported that the French had established five trading posts between that Red River fortification and Santa Fe.[29] None of these ruins have been found, but the discovery of their relics might well bring them to light.

It was some of these French traders who built Ferdinandina on the Arkansas, ferrying their goods up the river in canoes and flat-bottomed

An artist's conception of Ferdinandina, the French trading post on the Arkansas River northeast of present Newkirk. Oklahoma's first white settlement, it flourished sometime before 1750. Sketch by L. P. Thompson. Courtesy Oklahoma Historical Society.

Metal artifacts are often only inches beneath the surface. This French trade ax from the Ferdinandina site was buried eight inches deep. Photograph by William Mahan.

With the permission of the landowner, William Mahan, of Garland, Texas, examined the site of Ferdinandina and found French trade axes, hoes, gun barrels, and assorted gun parts. Photograph by William Mahan.

This painting of Spiro Mound, in the Stovall Museum at the University of Oklahoma, illustrates the earthworks left by prehistoric man in eastern Oklahoma. Courtesy Stovall Museum.

This diorama of a probable Spiro Mound structure depicts the ornate ceremony of the Mound Builders. Courtesy Stovall Museum.

boats, docking their vessels at the mouth of Deer Creek. Through excavation it has been shown that Oklahoma's earliest white settlement consisted of a large round stockade of upright logs firmly implanted in an earthen embankment 250 feet in diameter. A deep moat encircled the palisade on the outside, a customary protection for the day. Inside a blockhouse served as a bastion, or gun-tower, in which a musket-armed sentinel could keep a close vigil on the outside, where hundreds of Indians were usually camped. Digging also revealed the sites of log cabins occupied by traders and a garrison of soldiers, as well as a blacksmith shop and related buildings.

Just how long Ferdinandina flourished on the Arkansas no one is sure. It may have been destroyed by warring Osages.[30] It took an observant settler to rediscover it more than 150 years later, just as other ancient forts may yet be found.

The Treasure of Spiro Mound

It goes without saying that Oklahoma's greatest treasure has been Spiro Mound, also known as the Great Temple Mound, a conical earthwork towering 34 feet above the surface and 112 feet in diameter. The central chamber within that mound held the tombs of two important figures of the Mound Builders, who thrived there from about A.D. 800 to 1400.

With those two graves was found one of the rarest archaeological treasures ever uncovered in the United States—a treasure hidden for more than five hundred years—that proved to be from the most advanced culture north of the Río Grande. The inventory of that tantalizing discovery of only four decades ago is enough to send chills up one's back: axes of copper, a gallon of pearl beads, human masks carved of wood, ornate effigy pipes of human and animal figures, perhaps half a ton of shell beads, breastplates of copper—centuries-old artifacts that would rival the awesome treasures of the Aztecs.

Spiro Mound is the largest of four mounds rising south of the Arkansas River, about six miles northeast of Spiro, in Le Flore County. One mile northwest was Fort Coffee, where in 1832 the Choctaw Indians were resettled from their southeastern lands. Only ten miles northeast lies Fort Smith, Arkansas.

For many years Spiro Mound was singular in both its archaeological treasures and its virtual disregard. Though it was known in 1838, the first surviving photograph was not made of the spectacular mound until 1914 or 1915. Oddly enough, it was not until 1934 that the mound was dug into. Its spectacular treasures—one of the great discoveries of the century—is a story both exciting and pitiful, owing to then-nonexistent antiquity laws, disinterested landowners, and a seemingly timid scientific community.

Its lessons were many and tragic. The five-hundred-year-old records of an extinct race—records carved into stone and wood and ornately painted onto shell, depicting a highly advanced culture—were ransacked and scattered in a period of a few months, destroying forever the life and culture of centuries past. It was a crime accomplished by a few dollar-minded individuals. "At no other known site north of Mexico has so extensive a record of prehistoric ceremonies, uses, and customs been preserved," wrote one archaeologist.[31] It has been termed "a tragedy comparable to the burning of the Aztec Codices."[32] At few times in our past has a prehistoric race told its story so majestically, for so much of it to be destroyed in a few careless, profit-minded moments. Such is the tragedy of Spiro Mound.

The discoverers of Spiro Mound saw three additional conical mounds abutting the Temple Mound on the south, each smaller and less elevated than the last. Within a quarter-mile radius are still smaller mounds, about fifteen feet in diameter and four feet high. Long before the pot-hunters came, many of these mounds became part of cultivated fields.

The Indians and their black slaves who lived around Spiro Mound had become familiar with similar ancient burial grounds in their native Mississippi and Alabama. Superstitions about them protected the treasure-laden mounds well after the turn of the twentieth century. About 1905, Rachel Brown's allotment took in Spiro Mound. Once, she said later, she was mysteriously awakened, and when she looked out her window to the great mound, "shimmering sheets of blue flame" covered it, and in the blue fire appeared "a team of cats harnessed tandem-fashion to a small wagon which they were pulling around and around the summit."[33]

Between 1933 and 1935, Spiro Mound was gutted and robbed of its priceless, irreplaceable archaeological treasures. What ancient man had carefully preserved for the ages modern man destroyed or scattered. What happened here has been termed "a tragedy comparable to the burning of the Aztec Codices." Courtesy Stovall Museum. Pages 17, 18, and 19.

The tale of a blue fire appearing over hidden treasure—a widespread legend throughout Oklahoma—caused the local populace to avoid the great mound. Tales of animals that became frightened upon approaching the strange ground and weird noises on dark nights further prevented the molestation of the ancient burial ground.

One wonders why the professional historian and archaeologist so long neglected Spiro Mound. For twenty years before its ravage by pothunters, intermittent digging turned up some tantalizing artifacts. The professionals did not take notice until December, 1933, about a month after six relic hunters had leased the mound from the

18

Little remained of the centuries-old Spiro Mound and its smaller auxiliaries once pot-hunters had looted the mounds of their contents. Courtesy Stovall Museum.

Large quantities of conch shells and shell beads were uncovered within the mounds, many of which were carelessly crushed and destroyed forever by the untrained pot-hunter. Courtesy Stovall Museum.

landowner for the purpose of exhuming its hidden treasure. When spectacular artifacts began appearing in commercial markets, Spiro Mound became the focus of nationwide attention. Had there been antiquity laws—and perhaps a better understanding between the trained archaeologist and the amateur—many more of the mound's irreplaceable records of man's prehistoric past might have been saved—preserved for all, not a few.

The artifact was not the only matter of impor-

tance here, but how it was found, its depth, its location, the soil around it, its size, its relationship to other artifacts—all dovetail in piecing together a story that can never now be told. In his own way prehistoric man preserved his story for us. Nature protected it for more than six centuries. A few individuals destroyed it in a few months.

The six lessees began tunneling into the great mound, gutting it for anything they could find of value. Historically priceless objects were thrown

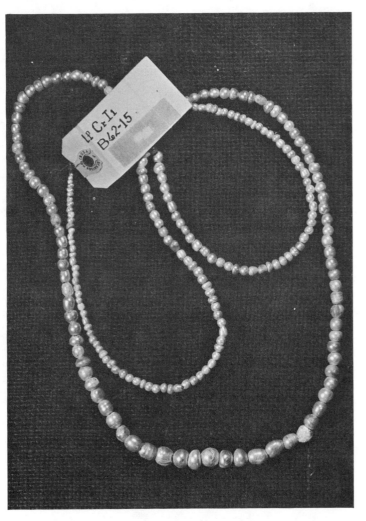

Some of the pearl beads found among the treasures of the Spiro Mound people. Courtesy Stovall Museum.

Many fragments of sheet copper with embossed designs were found at Spiro Mound. Courtesy Stovall Museum.

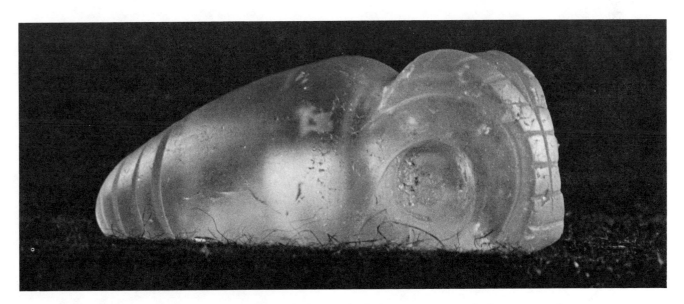

The Mound Builders left this effigy of a locust, made from quartz crystal, about two and one-half inches long and one inch wide. Courtesy Stovall Museum.

A shell gorget with cut and incised designs. Note the raccoon in the top center, a popular motif in engraved Spiro shells. Courtesy Stovall Museum.

A shell pendant fashioned in the form of a human face, found at Spiro Mound. Courtesy Stovall Museum.

A human-effigy pipe made from catlinite, a stone possibly obtained in Minnesota. The tobacco bowl is in the top of the head; the hole for the pipestem is in the back. The effigy is eight and one-half inches tall. Courtesy Stovall Museum.

One of the finest human-effigy pipes found at Spiro Mound. It was used by the Mound Builders for ceremonial occasions. It is nine and one-half inches tall. Courtesy Stovall Museum.

aside and tramped on. The relic hunters called their venture the Pocola Mining Company. The name fit their technique. When the state legislature finally acted in the spring of 1935, making it necessary to obtain an official permit to excavate, the Spiro Mound lessees thumbed their noses. At the last moment, when officialdom could have prevented the complete gutting of the Temple Mound, law-enforcement officers looked the other way.[34] By the end of the summer the mound had been tunneled in such haste that fragments of artifacts and textiles were strewn about the area. "It was impossible to take a single step in hundreds of square yards around the ruined structure without scuffing up broken pieces of pottery, sections of engraved shell, and beads of shell, stone, and bone," wrote an observer.[35]

One newspaper heralded the story "King Tut Tomb in the Arkansas River Valley." It failed to state that the "tomb" had been raped beyond telling the story it had so long preserved. "The quantity of material discovered was so great as temporarily to break the market for such objects," wrote one, who spent years tracing the lost artifacts.[36]

A pen-and-ink drawing of the human-effigy pipe. Courtesy Stovall Museum.

a jaguar, a turtle, an owl, a lizard, and a frog were found (similar frog effigies have been unearthed in Mississippi, Louisiana, Tennessee, Ohio, and Virginia).[37]

As many as forty human effigy masks carved from red cedar, with eyes and teeth inlaid with shell, were reported found at Spiro Mound. Two masks were complete with a carved set of antlers. There were bowls of cedar and a wood-duck head, its eyes and beak inlaid with mother-of-pearl, while a carved wildcat ornamented another.

Pottery vessels; chipped stone maces and stone blades; projectile points; celts; hoes; copper axes with wooden handles; decorated stone plummets; effigies of rock crystal, pearl, shell, stone, and bone; wooden and copper beads; hairpins; needles; and embossed plates of copper were all part of that tantalizing prehistoric treasure. There were pulley-shaped earspools, perhaps as many as four hundred, carved from stone, shale, and cedar, most of them decorated.

The people of Spiro had engraved their life story on large marine shells, used as bowls or dippers. Brought to Spiro Mound from the Gulf of Mexico, the engraved shells revealed their commerce, mythology, religion, and ceremonial life—recorded five centuries before the Europeans set foot on this land. The cultural remains of Spiro showed a distinguishable and consistent resemblance to artifacts found near Etowah, Georgia. And the many "representations of jaguars, plumed or feathered serpents, and the use of speech symbols in the shell engravings may indicate at least some contact to the south, in Mexico."[38]

Remains of the Spiro culture have been found along the Arkansas River from western Arkansas to the Grand River north of Muskogee, Oklahoma, and along that river north and east to Missouri. Still other remains are found on the Illinois River near Tahlequah and the Poteau River south of Spiro and westward on the Canadian River near Eufaula, all tributaries of the Arkansas.[39]

Fortunately, not all was lost at Spiro Mound. In the summer of 1936 the Oklahoma Historical Society and the University of Oklahoma began archaeological salvaging of the mounds. The tens of thousands of fragments and artifacts recovered are now housed and exhibited in the Oklahoma

No one will ever know what was found in the mound's central treasure chamber. A stone alligator effigy pipe has never been traced. Each of the altars on the sides of the inner room are said to have supported a blanket with about one hundred pounds of shell beads. A "somewhat mummified" body found a few feet inside the mound was moved outside, where curious onlookers observed it for months until it disintegrated forever. About five hundred pounds of galena balls and one thousand pounds of unworked lead ore were unearthed, along with many quartz crystals.

The many large human effigy pipes carved from stone exhibited the superb craftsmanship of the Spiro people. Similar effigy pipes have been found at other mounds in southern states. A group of animal effigy pipes of stone and clay, representing

In 1957, Elmer Craft discovered this burial site at Quartz Mountain State Park. Subsequent careful excavation proved it to be the grave of a young soldier killed accidentally in 1869. Objects in the grave were percussion caps, United States Army buttons, boot nails, legging hooks, a bone pipestem, and a bootstrap (below). Courtesy Oklahoma Historical Society.

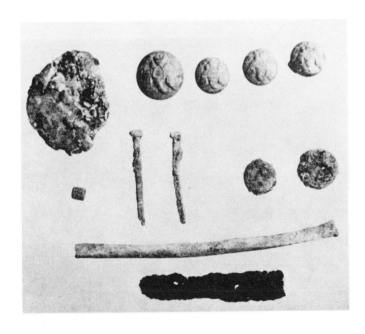

State Historical Museum, the university's Stovall Museum in Norman, and Woolaroc Museum, near Bartlesville. Other collections of the ancient culture—many of the pieces bought back from private collectors—are found at the University of Arkansas Museum, in Fayetteville, and the Museum of the American Indian, in New York City.

The study of Oklahoma's ancient race of Mound Builders is not completed and perhaps will not be for years to come. Archaeologists are still piecing together the fragments surviving from the wanton destruction of forty years ago—ancient shards that reveal stories prehistoric man left us.[40]

A Forgotten Soldier

It does not take a professional archaeologist to find a historic treasure, as one man in southwestern Oklahoma has proved time and again. Elmer C. Craft, Jr., of Eldorado, has made such discoveries for years while prowling the canyons and hills of his country. A serious-minded collector since 1952, Craft has one of the largest private collections of arrowheads and stone tools found in Oklahoma, many of which he has loaned to professionals to study.[41]

Craft's accidental discovery of an unusual grave made it possible for historians to solve a frontier mystery that might have remained a puzzle had he not acted cautiously. In the spring of 1957 he was searching for Indian artifacts north of Quartz Mountain State Park Lodge, on the western edge of the Wichita Mountains. The eroding action of waves from adjacent Lake Altus had exposed the hillside and the toe bones of a presumed Indian burial. But very unlike an Indian were the remains of boot nails. Craft knew that the only way to excavate was with professional supervision. He notified James B. Shaeffer, then salvage archaeologist for the Department of Anthropology at the University of Oklahoma. In April they began excavating with all the care and pain of dentists working on patients. Soon their meticulous digging showed that the head lay only about six inches under the surface.

Then their digging tools exposed a bird bone—later identified as the stem of a wooden or corncob pipe placed in a breast pocket. They also found a small, round metal box, which when later opened in the laboratory was found to contain corroded percussion caps. Leather fragments, legging fasteners, buttons, and a hook were revealed as the skeleton was carefully exposed.

All the evidence indicated that the grave was that of a white soldier, for the body had been laid

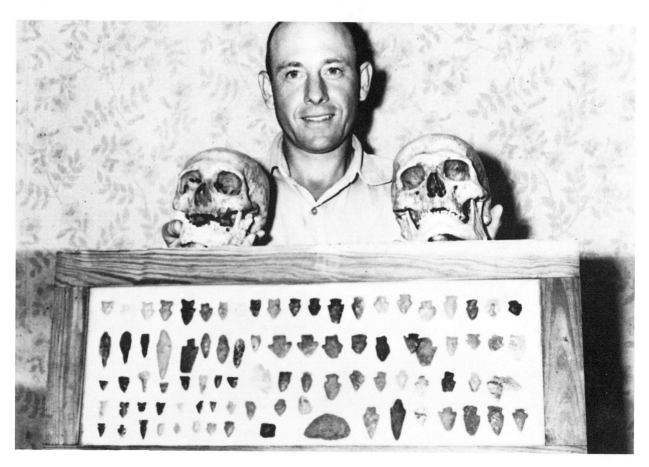

An amateur archaeologist, Elmer Craft has found many Indian campsites and burial sites throughout southwestern Oklahoma.

Among Craft's many Indian artifacts are these granite metates, once used to grind grain.

Craft's collection includes reconstructed pottery vessels and a Clovis point found in a sand dune on Red River.

While collecting these arrow points in southwestern Oklahoma, Craft has found and reported many archaeological sites to professional archaeologists for further research and excavation.

on its back with the arms folded across the chest. A hole in the left temple of the skull indicated that his death had been caused by a large-caliber weapon or by one of small caliber fired at close range. Because of the pistol caps and buttons, it was assumed that the soldier had been buried between 1861 and 1874. The victim had evidently been eighteen to twenty years old.[42]

Several months of research followed the excavation, and finally the diary of one of General George Custer's troopers, kept on an expedition from Fort Sill soon after that frontier post was established, solved the mystery of the lone soldier's grave. According to the diary, on Friday, March 5, 1869, Private William Gruber, chief bugler of the nineteenth Kansas Volunteers, was shot and killed in a hunting accident. Before daybreak the next morning the soldier was buried beside the trail "with honors of war."[43] It was the way of the frontier.

Only weeks after that historic excavation the

gravesite was once again covered by the waters of Lake Altus. Craft had probably saved it from being lost forever.

The Contents of a Wash Kettle

Perhaps the most mysterious of treasure recoveries occurred fourteen miles northwest of Vinita one evening in February, 1935. A farmer, A. J. Lee, his wife, and their neighbors, Mr. and Mrs. Duncan Snider, had just finished dinner when a car sped up to the Lee home. Out jumped three men brandishing pistols.[44] The couples were told to remain in the house and were assured that no harm would come to them. The bewildered people obeyed the orders, wondering what the gunmen were after.

They watched from the windows as the trio of gunmen turned their car around so that the headlights shone on a large cottonwood tree at the edge of the driveway. For some time the men consulted a piece of paper, holding it up to a headlight. Then they paced out from the tree trunk. With a crowbar they probed the ground, as if searching for something buried. Finally, about six feet from the tree, just inside the roadbed, they went to work with pick and shovel.

A large tree root grew over what they were seeking. At first they dug around it. Then they cut the huge root in two, removing a section about eight inches in diameter and three feet long. After more digging the trio lifted out a large iron wash kettle, which they slowly carried to the trunk of the car. In moments they had sped away.

When the strangers had gone, the Lees and the Sniders ran out to examine the hole. The big imprint was there. Whatever the kettle contained, it was heavy, they knew. If only they had graded that road one more time, the Lees thought. . . .

Treasures in Peculiar Places

Treasure is found in the strangest places—or are they perhaps the most obvious places? An old Cherokee named Ed Walkingstick once unearthed "a large amount" of Spanish gold while plowing the Laura B. Ketcher farm near Peavine, in Adair County. No one ever knew just how much he found. And there was a Dr. Bailey, whose big

house seven miles southwest of Hugo, in Choctaw County, had three large fireplaces. The hearth of one was a solid slab of stone. Bailey was murdered for his money, but it was years later before anyone looked under the large rock, where $16,000 reposed. No one ever knew just how much money was found in the Tom Patton Cave, west of Courtney on Red River in Love County, but Kate Davenport believed that it was more than what its finders would ever admit.[45]

Messages of the Vikings

Spanish cryptographers cannot take credit for all the stone carvings shrouded in mystery and scattered throughout Soonerland. Evidence has been amassed in recent years—and is still being found—that might well prove that Viking voyagers sailed up the Arkansas River and left their "marks"—scattered runic inscriptions—carved on stones in today almost inaccessible regions of the Arkansas Valley and its tributaries.

The first and most impressive of these runestones, aged Indians say, was found by Choctaws in the 1830's, when the Indians were removed from their native lands to what is now eastern Oklahoma. The antiquated rune characters were probably not known to white men until about 1898, when Luther Capps, of Heavener, chanced upon them. The stone came to be known as Indian Rock, and no one questioned that the carvings were Indian.

Now known as the Heavener Runestone, the rock is a vertical slab of stone twelve feet high, ten feet wide, and eighteen inches thick. It lies halfway up the west side of Poteau Mountain, less than two miles northeast of Heavener, in Le Flore County. Five feet above the surface, facing west, eight runic characters stretch more than five feet across the face of the stone. The left character, carved into the hard sandstone rock, measures six inches high. Each succeeding character becomes slightly larger, and the last is almost nine inches high.

Some have scoffed at theories that the runes are authentic. Renowned historians, runologists, and cryptographers the world over have offered translations. Who carved them, and when they were carved, are questions yet to be answered.

Ghost towns are rich sites for the "heavy change" of westerners of yore. These few remaining buildings of Cold Springs, in Kiowa County, were removed forever in 1973.

Mrs. Gloria Farley with her sons, Scott and Mark, examine the Heavener Runestone high on Poteau Mountain near Heavener, Oklahoma. Some believe that the eight runes, translated, are the date November 11, 1012. Courtesy Gloria Farley, Heavener, Oklahoma.

The characters appear to be from two runic alphabets centuries apart. Transliterated from runic characters to Latin letters, the inscription was believed by some to read: GNOMEDAL, translated to mean Sun Dial Valley, or Valley of the Boundary Marker.[46]

Were it not for the curiosity of a young girl who saw Indian Rock one day in 1928 and years later recognized its strange carvings as those similar to a runic alphabet published in a Sunday School paper, the runestone might yet remain entangled in the brush upon Poteau Mountain and its cryptic message obscured to the legion of scholars who have studied it.

That girl is now Mrs. Gloria Farley, of Heavener, who never put the runic inscription out of her mind. When she returned to the eastern Oklahoma hill country in 1950, she climbed Poteau Mountain to begin a quest for answers to the puzzle—and that of other runestones—that has not ended to this day. Gloria Farley's passion for clues was every bit as strong as that of a gold seeker, for she sought an ancient treasure—not of metal but of carvings in stone, a trail that seemingly has not ended but lengthens with each discovery.

Soon hunting runestones in the Heavener area became a pastime for others—one that yielded a wealth of runes. In 1954, Ed Baker recalled that fifty years before he had found a peculiar carved stone that he had used as a stepping stone over a fence near Morris Creek. The stone was almost a mile and a half northwest of the Heavener runestone, and carved on its surface was what appeared to be a three-pronged turkey track but was later said to be a twelve-inch rune, weathered through the centuries. On the stone's side appeared a smaller symbol, or bindrune. For the sake of identification the discovery was dubbed Heavener runestone No. 2.[47]

Five years later a third discovery was made. A mile and a half southeast of the Heavener runestone, on a slope of Poteau Mountain, Wes Thomas pointed out a stone that he had found forty-five years before. It bore three letters six to nine inches long: the proverbial turkey track, a cross, and an arrow—all forms of runes in the runic alphabet. It was called runestone No. 3.

In 1967, Henry McBride (left) and Mike Griffeth discovered the Poteau Runestone on Terry Hill, ten miles from the Heavener Runestone. It is said to read November 11, 1017. Courtesy Gloria Farley.

Old settlers in the region recalled having seen similar carvings about the area. In 1889, J. R. Faulkenberry found such a stone in Kitchen Canyon. Ed Wilson described a four-line inscription that he had found in that canyon. About the turn of the century markings were observed on the west side of Poteau Mountain. T. V. Morris once saw turkey tracks carved on High Top Peak of Poteau Mountain. Still others saw similar markings over the mountain.

Frederick J. Pohl was drawn to the runestones in 1959, and he offered possible translations in his *Atlantic Crossings Before Columbus*. By this time scholars over the world were poring over

In 1965, Jim Shipley discovered the Tulsa Runestone. Believed to be another Viking rune, it has been deciphered as the date December 2, 1022. Courtesy Gloria Farley.

The Shawnee Runestone. It is said to read November 24, 1024. Courtesy Gloria Farley.

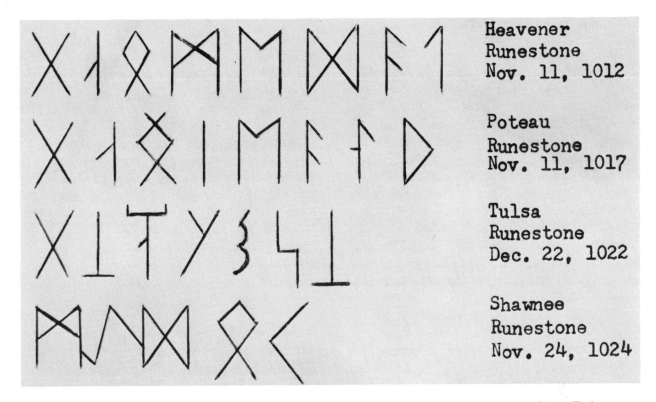

Drawings of the four runic inscriptions found in central and eastern Oklahoma. Courtesy Gloria Farley.

ancient alphabets, attempting to unravel the mystery of the Heavener runestones. In 1967 scholars came forth with evidence that sought to establish that Norsemen voyagers had landed in Oklahoma 480 years before Columbus.

Californians Alf Monge, a retired United States Army cryptographer, and O. G. Landsverk, a Norse specialist, revolutionized rune analysis. Making a major breakthrough in rune deciphering, they concluded that the Heavener runestone was not a message but a coded date, a cryptogram that read eight different ways to verify the date November 11, 1012. The mystery scribe, whoever he was, had substituted "runes for numbers, according to their place in his runic alphabets."[48]

This mystery carver of more than nine centuries ago left no message or name, but he may have left a trail of dates. Heavener runestone No. 2 was translated into December 25 (New Year's Day for ancient Norsemen), 1015. Runestone No. 3 was deciphered as December 30, 1022.

In September, 1967, still another accidental discovery came to light—more runes on the runestone trail. One afternoon, after a hard rain, thirteen-year-olds Henry McBride and Mike Griffeth were hunting arrowheads on Terry Hill just west of Poteau, about ten miles northwest of the large Heavener runes. On a stone ledge near the hilltop they found another runic inscription with eight characters, many of them the same as those on the Heavener runestone.

Later it was discovered that the Heavener runestone, stones No. 2 and No. 3, and the Poteau find had all been found along a straight line stretching for ten miles northwestward. Monge, elated, declared that the same mystery man who had carved the Heavener rune had also punched the inscription at Poteau. Its date: exactly five years after the Heavener carving, November 11, 1017.

In 1965, Tulsan Jim Shipley and his son were climbing the highest peak in Tulsa County—Bull Dog Hill—northwest of Turley, when they spied seven six-inch-high runes.[49] When cryptanalyst Monge examined the symbols, he was astonished to discover that the inscription also contained two bindrunes. And just as if signed by the mystery runesmith himself, it was obvious that whoever carved this stone had also chiseled the Heavener and Poteau runes. Another cryptopuzzle, the Bull Dog Hill runes, were deciphered as December 2, 1022.[50]

Two years after the Poteau runestone was found, another incredible find was made by Jim Estep. In August, 1969, he was hiking along a tributary of the North Canadian River near Shawnee— 150 miles west of the Heavener-Poteau discoveries—when something moved him to turn over a small slab of red sandstone. Although Estep did not realize it at the time, the stone bore five runic symbols. Later it proved to be one of the latest dated runestones yet found in Oklahoma, carved on November 24, 1024, exactly twelve years and thirteen days after the great Heavener runestone. Today both it and the Poteau runestone rest on exhibit at the Kerr Museum near Poteau.

The enigma of the Viking explorers is yet unsolved. Many believe that they were not Vikings at all but early German colonists who explored the Arkansas and its tributaries some time after 1720—colonists who were led by a Swedish captain capable of carving runes from two widely separated alphabets.[51] If only the stones could talk. . . .

Whoever the stone carver, or carvers, were, they—like the Spaniards who also made their mark in the state—left a long trail of "runes." The end to that trail has not yet been found. Fifty miles from the Heavener discoveries a stone has turned up with twenty-nine characters, some of which appear to be runic, some Latin. To date rune buffs have failed to find a cliff near Wewoka that is said to yield others or those seen along the Arkansas River between Ponca City and Ralston. Reports have also sent seekers to the Poteau River near Wister and downstream near Arkoma and up Poteau Mountain above Forrester. At the confluence of the Poteau and Arkansas rivers near Fort Smith old settlers recall four lines of strange carvings on the face of a cliff.

Other, similar carvings have been sought on Spring and Winding Stair mountains. Runes have been reported in neighboring Arkansas, on a creek in the Cossatot Mountains and at the base of Mount Magazine. One carving, too faint to verify, was found near the Dardanelle Rapids on the Arkansas River and now lies in the Geology Museum at Arkansas Technological College. One inscription which appears to be runic has even turned up as far west as the Texas Panhandle. Regrettably, some inscriptions have been wantonly destroyed.

No one knows where the ancient trail of the "Norsemen" will end. Mrs. Farley believes that ten authentic runestones have been discovered in Oklahoma. She sums it up thus: "All these bits and pieces of an ancient jigsaw puzzle are falling into place. The completed puzzle may take many more years of research. We already have enough pieces to say with certainty, 'The Vikings Were Here.'"[52] Meanwhile, the quests for runes continues.

Treasure in Trash

Hugo resident Charles Coker proved that treasure finding is not a thing of the past. In April, 1971, he unearthed a hoard of gold and silver coins with a face value of $2,532. No, Coker was not looking for treasure. He was digging for old bottles.

The coins had apparently been wrapped and placed in an old bucket, although the bucket and wrappers had long decayed until nothing remained but the bail. Coker had found the usual amount of trash in his quest when his metal detector gave a low groan. That weak signal yielded a total of seventy-nine $20 gold pieces, $202 in silver dollars, fifty-three $10 gold pieces, forty-three $5 gold pieces, and two $2.50 gold pieces with dates ranging from 1850 to 1881.[53]

Yes, Oklahoma is a land of tantalizing treasures—lost and found. Not all of Oklahoma's treasure recoveries have been listed here, their telling better suited for later: the brass cannon and twenty-five thousand dollars in Spanish gold found in a cave near the old Indian fortress of San Bernardo on Red River, the discovery of the Spanish town and fort of Cascorillo on Turkey Creek, the ruins of the Mexican mining settlement in Devil's Canyon, the five hundred dollars in gold near an outlaw's grave near Mount Scott, the silver dollars from an Indian massacre in Cutthroat Gap, the six thousand dollars in outlaw treasure that Frank James retrieved while he lived in the shadow of the Wichita Mountains, the silver ingots from

Old settlers' private "banks" were often lost with the death of their owners. One such cache was unearthed by a modern-day Oklahoma prospector. Photograph by William Mahan.

Standing Rock—all are stories of treasure found— and, in many instances, more treasure yet lost.

One old-timer summed it up aptly: "Son, there's more treasure buried right here in Oklahoma than in the rest of the whole Southwest."[54]

While digging for old bottles, Charles Coker, of Hugo, found a twenty-five-hundred-dollar cache of gold and silver coins dating from 1850 to 1881. Collectors' premiums on the 379 coins will bring several times their face value. Photograph by William Mahan.

35

Bill Mahan and Charles Coker display a day's find of flintlock side plates and hammers, a muzzle-loading Colt revolver, and pieces of exploded cannon balls. Photograph by William Mahan.

Bill Mahan has spent a lifetime searching for hidden caches of Spanish gold ingots and outlaw booty, both shown here. Photograph by William Mahan.

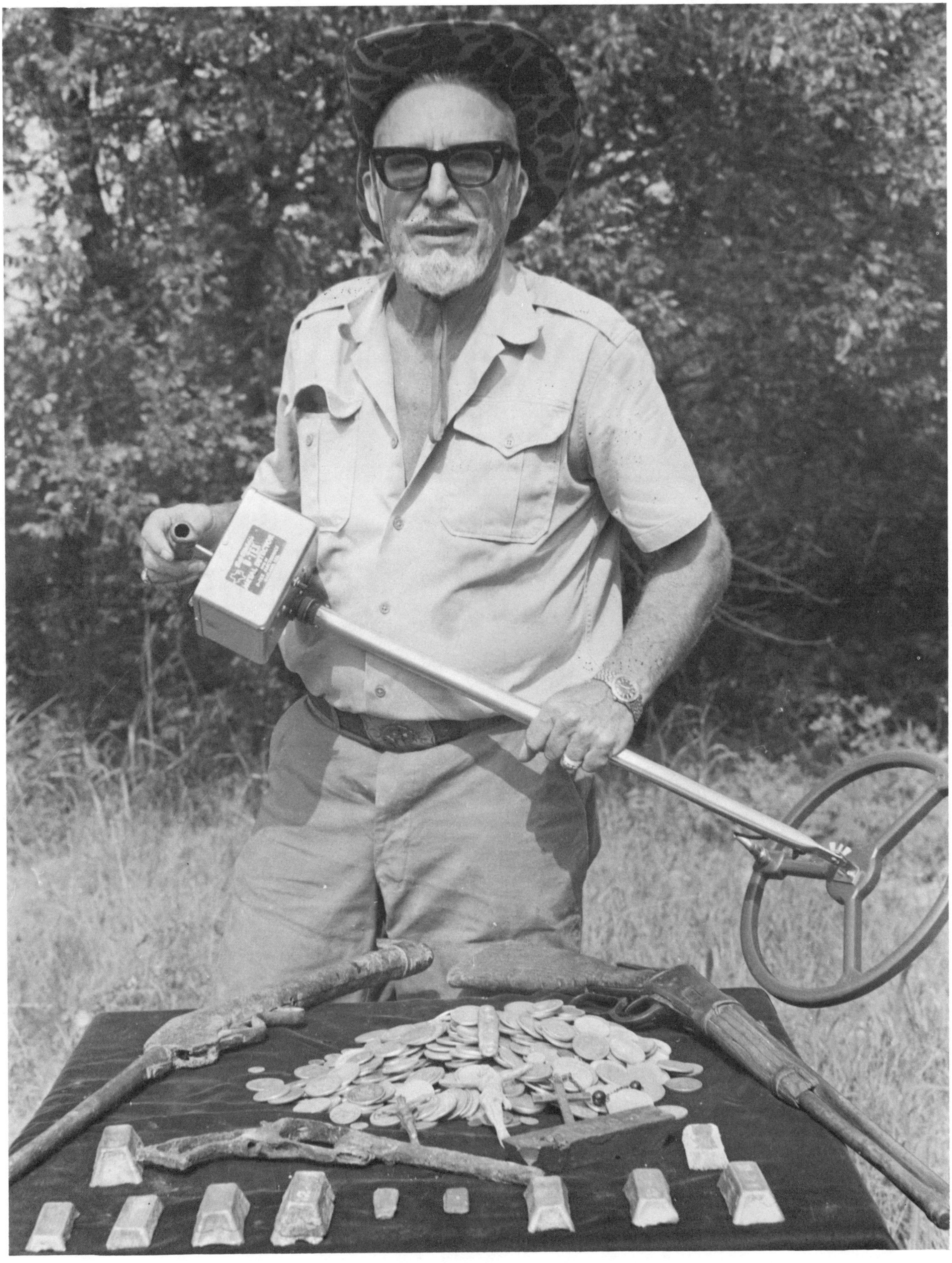

Presidio San Luis de las Amarillas, near Menard, Texas.

2. The Secrets Spanish Fort Tells

An aura of mystery greets you as you approach the sandy banks of Red River where it twists from its eastward course and runs almost southward, carving out a half-circle channel known today as Spanish Fort Bend, named for the small north-Texas settlement that sprang up there before the Civil War. Those Montague County pioneers did not choose the name Spanish Fort without reason.

In 1859, when Captain W. A. "Bud" Morris settled nearby, portions of circular stockades still remained south of the river. Morris found six such palisades, running north and south 150 yards apart, each containing portholes about 4 feet above the ground. The artifacts exposed when the settlers broke sod were myriad—European pottery, pieces of flintlocks, Spanish musketry, brass cannon balls, swords, knives, Indian artifacts.

What else could this have been but an old Spanish fort, where tales were already afloat of lost Spanish gold, both up and down the river, on one side or the other? Only ten years earlier, in 1849, an expedition had been mounted to find such a treasure hidden at the mouth of the Little Wichita just inside Clay County a few miles to the west. And eastward into Cooke County where Red River shifts again to a southward course, then northward, carving out a veritable horseshoe called Sivells Bend—the largest of its kind in the entire river course—strange symbols carved on rocks and trees were found: turtles, snakes, even a fish on the face of a boulder. Across from Sivells Bend in Oklahoma, Spanish treasure has been sought for years. Back on the Texas side west of Dexter near Walnut Bend the story was repeated.

While treasure failed to reveal itself, relics were never in short supply. A one-pound brass cannon ball was turned up a mile northwest of Burns City, and a brass spearhead, near Dexter. "Where the river turns south" seems to have been a traditional landmark for the Spaniard seeking a place to hide his golden wares. At Spanish Fort Bend, where the river turned south and skirted a bluff on which grew a lone tree were the clues dictated by an old Mexican map. In fact, similar clues "are

essentials of all the Red River legends of buried treasure," observed one local resident.[1]

Actually, there was no Spanish fort on upper Red River, but instead an Indian fortress—a palisaded village on the plains where once lived perhaps as many as three to five thousand Taovayas, or Wichita, Indians on both sides of Red River, indeed where Spaniards fought and died but lived almost always only as captives.

And, contrary to what heretofore has been believed, the Indian fort was not in Texas but across the river in Oklahoma, in present Jefferson County.[2] In 1778 it came to be known as San Bernardo, and its twin village, on the south side of the river, San Teodoro. They figured prominently in Southern Great Plains history, a story well documented in Spanish, French, and Anglo-American records.

The Spaniards called the Indians Taovayas. The French knew them as Panis, or so as not to confuse them with the Pawnees farther north, referred to them as Panis Noirs or Panis Piqués, the former meaning black Pawnees and the latter, tattooed, or pricked, Pawnees—referring to their dark skin and the tattooing of their bodies from the waist up. Later the Anglo-Americans called them Tawehash, Panis or Pawnee Picts, and, finally, Wichitas.

They had not always lived on the upper Red River, at the eastern edge of the Great Plains. The French found them in the Arkansas River valley in 1719. In the 1740's they lived near a French post, a traders' rendezvous on the Arkansas that French *voyageurs* knew as Ferdinandina, east of present Newkirk in Kay County, Oklahoma—rediscovered in this century.[3]

About 1757 the Taovayas migrated to Red River, where they erected a fortification of their own of split logs complete with an outside moat filled with water diverted from Red River. There they settled on New Spain's northern frontier and carried on a lucrative trade, serving as middlemen between their Comanche allies and French traders from Louisiana. The Spaniards would refer to the

Coinciding with the location of the palisaded Indian fortress attacked in 1759 by Colonel Parilla's Spanish army, in the spring of 1967 deep plowing revealed an oval-shaped fortification ditch about 262 feet by 393 feet, shown near the center of this aerial photograph. An exploratory trench revealed a buried ditch almost 12½ feet across and 4 feet deep. The wooded gully west of the outline may have served as an entrance leading from Red River. Courtesy Museum of the Great Plains.

Taovayas and their allies as the Norteños—Nations of the North—and dread their might for the remainder of the eighteenth century.

The Lipan Apaches lived on upper Red River before the Taovayas drove them away, and with their Comanche allies, relentlessly pursued them throughout south Texas, even into the Spanish settlements. The Taovayas had found themselves a paradise on the edge of the Plains. Springs furnished their drinking water and irrigated their fenced fields of corn, beans, pumpkins, watermelons, and tobacco—commodities bartered to the Comanches for horses, mules, Apache and Spanish captives, and war booty, and in turn traded to the French for guns, shot, and powder.[4]

Vast herds of buffaloes were easily accessible, and deer roamed at will, although neither they nor the boundless fish in the river were eaten by the Taovayas. Black bears and wild boars lived in the Cross Timbers on the east. A river-salt deposit

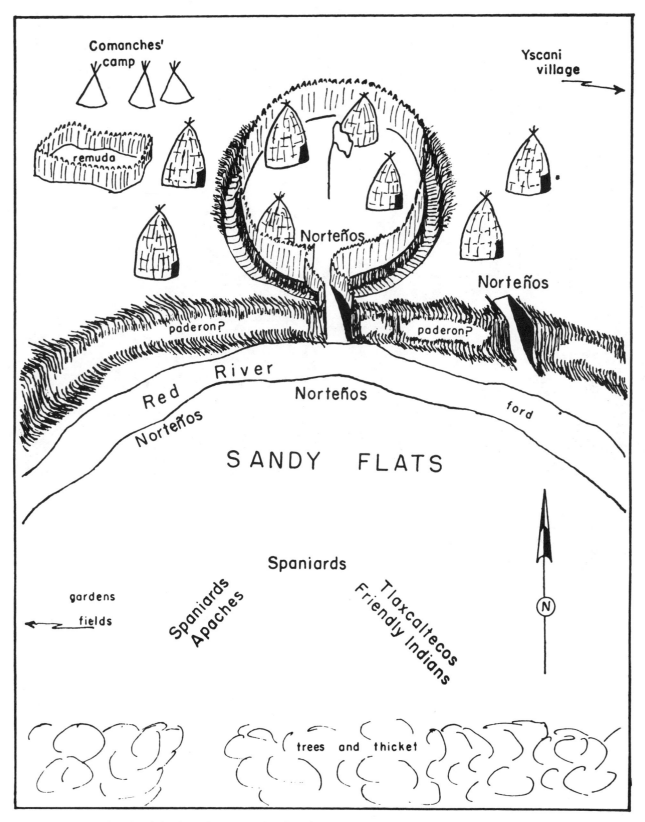

Comanches' camp

Yscani village

remuda

Norteños

Norteños

paderon?   paderon?

Red   River

Norteños

Norteños   ford

SANDY   FLATS

gardens
fields

Spaniards

Spaniards
Apaches

Tlaxcaltecos
Friendly Indians

N

trees   and   thicket

A sketch of the heavily manned Indian fortress on Red River that surprised Colonel Parilla and his Spanish army in October, 1759. Courtesy Museum of the Great Plains.

Presidio San Luis de las Amarillas, near Menard, Texas. From this fortress, 250 miles southwest of the Red River Taovaya Indians, the five-hundred-man Spanish army marched northward to punish the Nations of the North. Although early settlers used all the original stone of the presidio, it was rebuilt during the Depression much as it appeared in the 1700's, when it was the largest Spanish garrisoned outpost in Texas. Pages 42 and 43.

furnished the Taovayas' needs, as well as providing a valuable trading item. Their twin villages on either side of Red River—in one of which they could fortify themselves from their enemies—served as the first and most important trading post on upper Red River, a crossroads linking Spanish New Mexico and French Louisiana.

About the same time the Taovayas settled on Red River, the Spaniards founded their northernmost mission on the San Sabá River and erected a fort three miles upriver, near present Menard, Texas, roughly 250 miles southwest of the Red River villages. While Colonel Diego Ortiz Parilla guided the erection of his stockaded fort—Presidio San Luis de las Amarillas—the missionaries built

their church of logs and adobe, around which they erected a tall wooden stockade. They christened it Mission Santa Cruz de San Sabá.

The Spaniards knew virtually nothing of the Nations of the North, but rumors began to spread that the Indians were mounting an offensive against the isolated Spanish outposts that had become the protectorate of the Apaches. Colonel Parilla begged the priests to move into the fort, but they steadfastly refused. He left eight soldiers at the mission, where lived the three padres, Indian servants and their families, and the wives and children of the soldiers. Two cannons were there if needed.[5]

The spring day of March 2, 1758, brought the

42

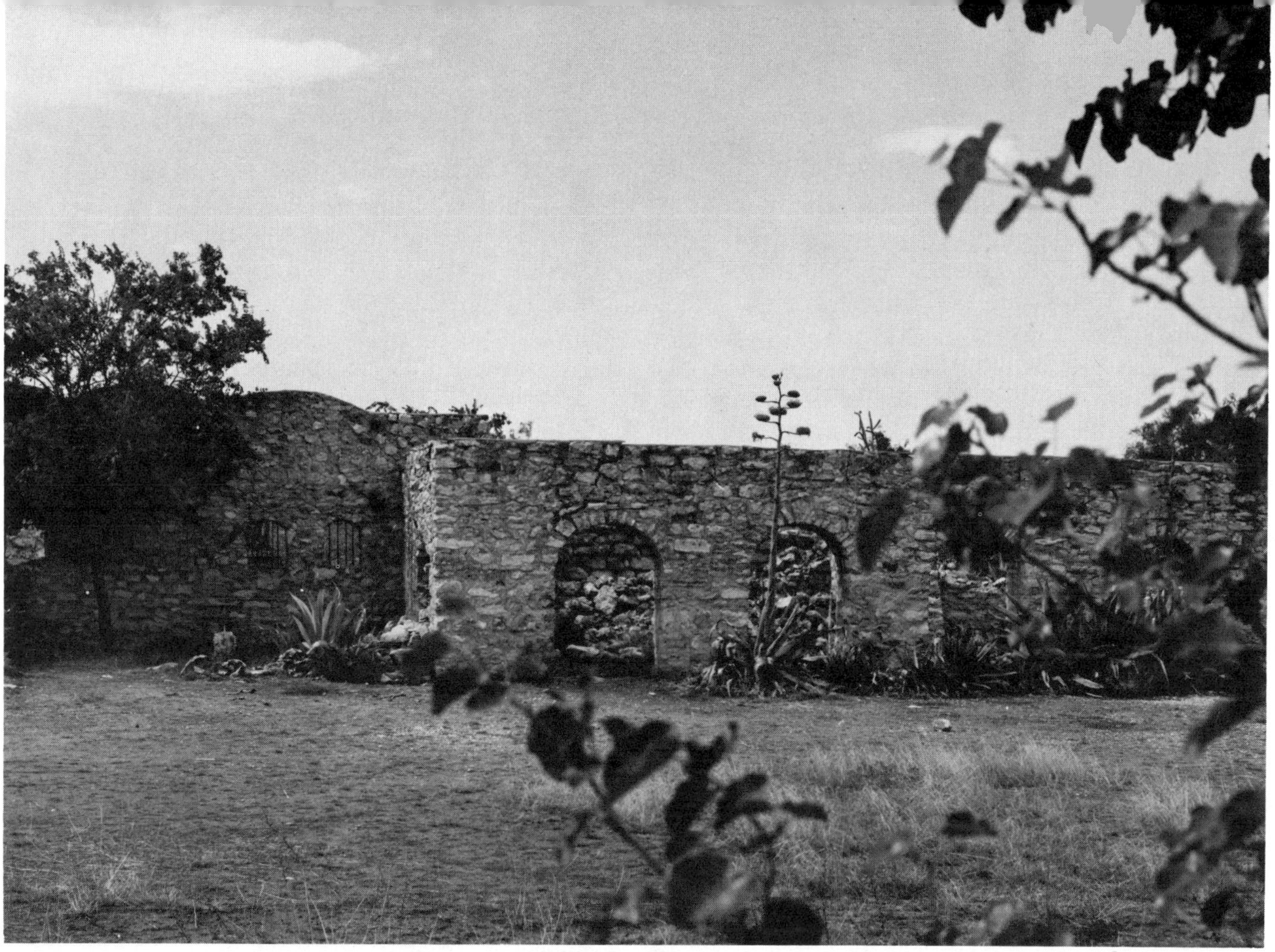

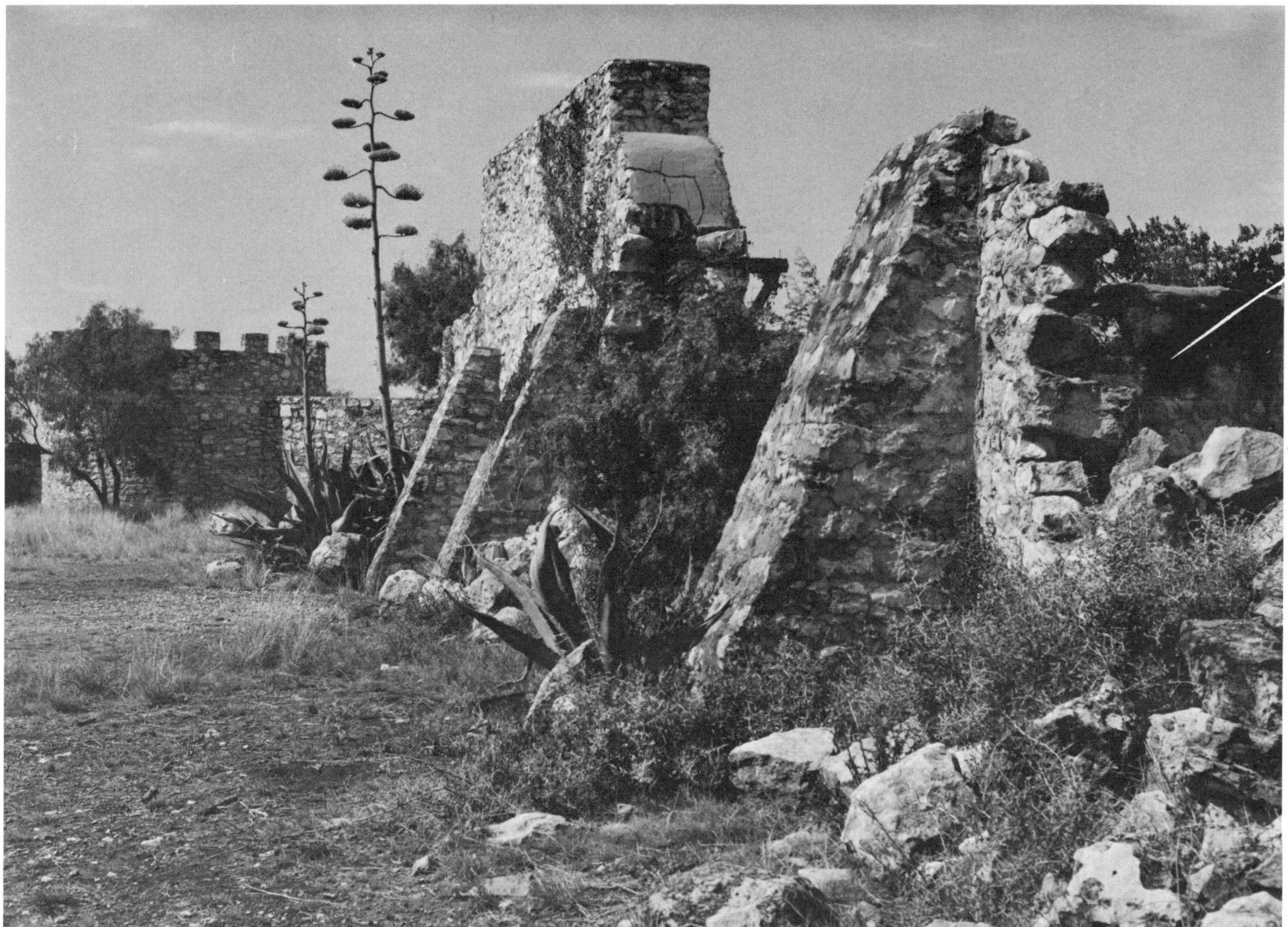

first war party of Indians from the north. They raided the presidial ranch, stealing away with sixty-two animals. Little did the Spaniards realize that from within a fort of their own—250 miles as the crow flies—the Indians were laying plans for a major attack on the isolated mission.

That onslaught came in the early-morning hours of March 16, when two thousand mounted warriors encircled the mission with faces painted black and crimson. Comanches, Taovayas, and their northern allies were clad in the skins of wild beasts, some wearing buffalo horns, and armed with French muskets, sabres, and spears, with powder horns and bullet pouches dangling from their waists.

A horde of Indians dismounted, clambered up the stockade, and removed the bars from the gate. Hoping to pacify them, the padres quickly ordered tobacco and presents to be given to them. One, Fray Molina, approached a Comanche chief with handfuls of the weed. Clad in a soiled French uniform, the Indian grabbed the tobacco, wrinkling his face with a smile as his warriors began pilfering the mission storerooms.

After stealing everything within reach, the Indians demanded to visit the fort but said that they were afraid of its commander. Fray Alonso scrawled a note of introduction. A few minutes passed, and a Tejas chief galloped back into the mission, exclaiming that he had been welcomed with a volley of gunfire. Fray Alonso knew that he had not had time to reach the fort, three miles upstream. Fray Alonso agreed to accompany the Indians to the fort and, with a mission soldier, proceeded to ride outside the mission to join the Tejas chief. As they rode through the mission gate, a musket blast knocked the friar to the ground. A fusillade of fire followed, and two thousand Indians rushed into the mission, shooting, lancing all in their path, and setting the still-green logs ablaze. Fray Santiesteban, found kneeling at the foot of the church altar praying, was beheaded. Fray Molina, suffering a broken arm, managed to seek refuge with twenty-five others in a mission room.

When mission servants reached the fort, Colonel Parilla dispatched a handful of soldiers to make a reconnaissance, but they were turned back under a barrage of fire that knocked three from their saddles, killing two.

The holocaust raged all day. When the burning logs drove the survivors from the mission to an adjoining building, that too was set afire. At night, the Nations of the North, satisfied that no one could have survived the charred, smoldering hull, relaxed and celebrated their victory. The survivors crept out, one by one. Fray Molina struggled into the fort two days later, where the Spanish garrison of 59 soldiers and 237 women and children kept vigil.

On the second day after the siege, the victors having gone northward, Colonel Parilla took a force of soldiers to investigate. Buzzards circled the charred ruins where lay the stripped bodies—lanced, desecrated, scalped. The two priests and four others were buried in the mission cemetery. Two soldiers were interred where they had fallen. The San Sabá mission was never to be rebuilt.

The attacks on the Spanish outpost and its supply trains, nine days' journey from San Antonio, were not to end, although they were few the winter of 1758–59. In the meantime, Colonel Parilla was laying plans for a war of his own—one of vengeance. He would lead an army to punish the Nations of the North. He had already learned that most of the booty from the besieged mission was in the villages of the Taovayas. Parilla would need a drove of more than 1,600 horses, mules, and cattle; a train of 200 mules alone to carry supplies of maize, biscuits, and frijoles; four thousand pounds of shot and powder; and two brass cannons. With five hundred men, Parilla, a seasoned soldier of many campaigns, was convinced of victory.

By mid-August of 1759, Parilla was ready to ride. He reviewed his makeshift army, if it could be called that. He had at his command 360 presidial soldiers and 176 Indian allies as the long caravan struck northward from San Sabá. His soldiers of "cowboys, tailors, laborers, cigar-dealers, hatters, peons from the mines, and persons of similar occupations," began to grumble. They sought a dreaded enemy in an unknown land, at an unknown destination.[6]

Finally, on October 2, the Spaniards spied a Tonkawa village just beyond the Clear Fork of the Brazos near present-day Fort Griffin. The Spanish cavalry struck in force, slaying 55 of the enemy and taking another 149 men, women, and children prisoner—without the loss of a single Spaniard.

Encouraged, Parilla led his army onward, his shackled captives pointing the way to the Taovayas on Red River, where he arrived four days later, on October 7, at a site that a century later would be called Spanish Fort.

As Parilla's forces neared Red River about one o'clock in the afternoon, sixty or seventy Indians charged from the timber, sending the Spaniards into swift action. Parilla formed his men into a line, sending the stock and the prisoners to the rear. After a brief skirmish the Indians fled back into the timber, and the Spaniards followed to the edge of the sandy bank.

The attackers had crossed the river to the opposite bank, where stood something none of the Spaniards were accustomed to seeing—an Indian fortress with a well-built, circular stockade made of split logs and placed apart so that its occupants could fire their muskets from within, from which flew a large French flag. Surrounding the palisade on the outside was an earthen rampart "a vara and a third in height," which served as an intrenchment, and four paces beyond that a moat several yards wide and more than three feet deep filled with water from Red River on its front. A gate opened toward the river, and that road was also protected by a palisade.

Within the river fortification Parilla could see the many straw-thatched houses of the Wichitas, and farther beyond the large corrals for their horses, and nearby the camps of the Taovayas' allies the Comanches, their tipis extending far into the distance.

Upstream on the south bank were the irrigated fields of corn, beans, pumpkins, and watermelons. Below the fortification was the river crossing, guarded by a large force of Indians. The entire stockade fronting the river was crawling with a mass of musket-armed warriors. Women and children perched themselves in advantageous seats atop their grass houses.

The Spaniards had not counted on the Nations of the North banding together. Their numbers were estimated at between two and six thousand, with perhaps five hundred mounted. Colonel Parilla organized three hundred of his troops into a line of battle, placing the Spaniards in the center, flanked on the right by mission Indians and on the left by Apache allies. They trained their two brass cannons on the Indian stronghold. Parilla believed that he could rush his enemy and force his way into their fortress. For a seasoned commander used to victory, he grossly underestimated his enemy.

As Parilla ordered the assault, many of the Spaniards' horses sank knee-deep into the loose river sand. From the fort stormed an onslaught of mounted warriors riding swiftly toward the Spaniards as warriors from within the stockade kept up a heavy fire. As the Indians retreated to the fortress, they were met by swift footmen, who handed them loaded muskets for empty ones.

Parilla's enemy was better armed, better trained, and better disciplined than his own troops. He counted fourteen Frenchmen among the Taovayas, seemingly employing the Indians in tactics used by European troops.

Perhaps most surprising to the Spaniards was that the Indians were directed by a gallant chief clad in a spotless white doeskin uniform with white hat and plume of bright red horsehair and mounted astride a lightning-fast, dark-red horse "with flowing black mane and tail."[7] With incredible horsemanship he recklessly surged into the midst of battle, as if no bullet could penetrate him, leading his warriors. Over the battlefield he rode, brazenly exposing himself until finally a Spaniard's bullet felled him.

To the mind-racking pounding drums and blowing fifes from within the palisade Parilla added the fire of his two cannons, but to little avail. After eleven volleys the Indians taunted the Spaniards with laughter. As the Indians continued their assaults, Parilla's Indian allies broke rank, leaving the Spaniards' flanks exposed to the enemy. Under orders to remain steadfast, the Spaniards began retreating to the timber, abandoning the two cannons. Perhaps darkness alone saved Parilla's scattered forces from annihilation.

Considering the disadvantages of the Spaniards, they had fought an undaunting battle. When

Parilla's horse was killed under him, he caught a riderless steed and charged his enemy again. Before he withdrew, his cuirass was twice shot and he was wounded in the left arm and side. Several other officers had narrow escapes. One lieutenant escaped death when "one bullet knocked the leather shield from his hand, another left him hatless, a third hit the large pommel of his saddle, and a fourth whizzed through the lapel of his coat."[8] One captain had been shot nine times, each ball sailing through his clothes without touching him.

All considered, the Spaniards' losses were not heavy. Sixteen Spaniards and three Indian allies had been killed, another thirteen Spaniards and one Apache had been wounded, and nineteen were missing.[9] Parilla believed that his forces had killed about fifty Indians. That night a demoralized Spanish army dressed its wounds and tallied its losses.

On the opposite bank of the river the Taovayas and their northern allies danced in triumphant victory around their blazing campfires. The reflection of the fires told the Spaniards that the stockade was still heavily guarded — and reinforcements continued to ride in. At first eager to continue battle the next day, Colonel Parilla conceded to the wishes of his officers to return to San Sabá.

Two cannons; many muskets, weapons, and saddles; and more than one thousand horses and mules had been lost. The ill-fated expedition had cost the Spanish government sixty thousand pesos. Parilla struck a more direct course homeward, where the disheartened Spaniards arrived in a little over two weeks, on October 25.

In 1765 the Spaniards received their first eyewitness account of their bitter enemy on the north from one who had lived among them. Lieutenant Antonio Treviño, captured when his patrol from San Sabá skirmished with a Taovaya party, had sustained four bullet and two spear wounds. Treviño's bravery so greatly impressed the Taovaya chief that he was taken to the Red River fort to recover.[10] There he lived as a member of the tribe for six months; finally he was escorted safely to Nacogdoches.

Treviño told his superiors that the Red River fort could sustain a far greater attack than any

that the Spaniards could muster. Four massive subterranean houses within the fort would hold the villagers who were not fighting. Too, the Indians had mounted the two captured cannons in their fort and had learned to operate them from the French.

It was almost twenty years after the Spanish fiasco at Red River that the two cannons were retrieved, not by the Spaniards but by a Frenchman in their employment, Athanase de Mézières, the lieutenant-governor of Natchitoches. When he visited the Taovayas in 1778, De Mézières named the twin villages San Bernardo and San Teodoro, honoring Bernardo de Gálvez, governor of Louisiana, and Teodoro de Croix, commandant-general of the Interior Provinces.[11]

The fieldpieces were removed to San Antonio, but even today the legend prevails that two brass cannons remain lost somewhere about the Indian fort. Cannonballs of three different sizes have been found on the banks of Red River and have turned up downriver in Cooke County, Texas.

Wherever the Spaniards traveled, they left their stories behind — stories very much a part of Red River's heritage. Firmly implanted along the old Spanish road later blazed down Red River, the tales persist equally on both sides. It is said that, when the nights are still and the moon full, the clank of their silver spurs and the beat of their horses' hooves can still be heard about old Spanish Fort.

Such stories prevail some distance west of the village once called San Teodoro. On the Texas side of Red River near present Stanfield were reportedly buried fifteen jack loads of Spanish gold. The burros hauling that precious cargo were driven off the side of a bluff and the rim sloughed off onto the gold-laden animals.[12]

And a few miles downstream, west of Terral, survives a more than century-old tale that twenty-seven mule loads of golden cargo were hidden near the mouth of the Little Wichita River "by a large boulder."[13] As early as 1849, Texans sought it under a veil of secrecy. Once fallen adobe ruins were found there and, not far away, an old copper mine with smelter works.[14] The occupants of this Red River town remain a mystery, but many have seen the ruins.

There are similar tales of lost treasure on the Oklahoma side, but, according to a story published in the Fort Worth *Gazette* on November 3, 1884, not all of the legendary treasure there is buried; some $25,000 of it may have been found. A special correspondent for the *Gazette* who visited Spanish Fort dispatched to his paper this intriguing story:

Your correspondent arrived in this usually quiet village this evening from Gainesville to find considerable excitement on account of the discovery of a large cave in the bluff on Red River, containing a vast treasure and many old Spanish relics.

The sites of the old forts are yet to be seen in the valley, and many old relics, such as crude hoes, picks, copper kettles, etc., have been found, and in one case a piece of an old brass cannon was ploughed from the soil.

After supper at the Inman house, I wended my way to the Cowboy Saloon, the proprietor, Mr. Jno. Shrock, being one of the party that made the discovery of the cave. I found quite a large number of men present to hear the story told by Mr. Shrock:

"On late Friday evening, Wm. Shackelford, Walton Crain, W. F. Cole, Sherman Jones and I went over Red River into the Indian territory to hunt a couple of panthers which had been seen a few days previously on South Mud Creek. While returning on Sunday evening, our dogs jumped a cat in the thicket about two miles above here on the river. After a lively chase of half an hour, the cat took refuge in a cave at the base of a cliff about 50 feet high which fronts the lower valley of the river.

"We had little hope of getting the cat as we had treed a cat in this place before. The cat had entered between a mass of large rocks which had evidently fallen from the face of the cliff. We decided that by a united effort we might remove a large stone so that the dogs might enter after the cat. We succeeded in removing the large stone, after which we found the hole passing through a mass of small stones. These we soon removed and found a large opening into the cliff, which the dogs entered and to our surprise, we heard them fighting the cat far back in the rocks.

"We hastily gathered some dry rosin wood, from which we constructed a torch, which by replenishing would serve us several minutes. We proceeded into the cave but a short distance when we found a solid rock wall in our front. But here the opening bore to our left into a passage, triangular in shape, about 50 feet high, and 10 feet wide. We followed this about 20 feet, when the passage bore off at right angles to our right a few feet and then opened.

"I was attracted by an exclamation from Shackelford, who was rattling some kind of metal between his feet.

This we found to be old pieces of copper, which we decided afterwards had been the bindings for an old packsaddle. We then found that the object which had caused me to stumble was nothing more or less than an old brass howitzer about three and a half feet long.

"We hastily secured the cat, which was near at hand, and retraced our steps, for our light was nearly out. On emerging we decided to come back to town and get lanterns to explore the cave. We agreed to tell no one of our discovery and go back after dark. We secured a lantern apiece and arrived back at the cave about 9 p.m. We soon got to the old cannon, which we found to be about one-third buried in the ground. The extent of the cave we found to be about 40 feet wide and about 130 feet long.

"As we proceeded, the ceiling gradually approached the floor, and here we found a considerable number of bones which we believed to be those of buffalo and deer. We also found several pieces of charred wood and two old copper kettles. This had probably been the kitchen, the smoke escaping through a rift in the rock here, which probably passed out to the face of the cliff. From this point we passed to the rear of the cave where we made our find, which consisted of a considerable number of old packsaddles and agricultural implements and a few old wick baskets which were badly decayed.

"But the thing which attracted our attention at once was the sight of six large boxes all of the same size and shape. They were about five and one-half feet long, two feet wide and 18 inches deep, the lids being fastened by crude copper hasps. We found little trouble in prying up the lids. We found quite a lot of old arms such as swords and blunderbusses and stilettoes, some old quilted coats of mail, many old Spanish books and a complete wardrobe for an old convent.

"But the contents of the third box which we opened was the one which excited us. This one had a partition which cut off about two feet from one end and in this we found two bushels of Spanish money and bullion. The gold consisted of old Spanish doubloons and was contained in five leather sacks. The silver coin was principally in Spanish Rex dollars. There was also three silver bricks and two golden crucifixes of considerable value."[15]

The *Gazette* correspondent estimated that the treasure was worth twenty-five thousand dollars and said that its five discoverers planned to exhibit their find at New Orleans. A fanciful tale? Perhaps so, but very much believed by many, and a direct result of the legendary atmosphere about old Spanish Fort.

Just how long the ruins of the Indian fortress remained is not known. The Red River villages were probably abandoned in the early 1820's. The

Stone relics greet visitors at the private museum of Mrs. Joe Benton, east of Nocona, Texas. Most of the Benton collection was found at the twin Taovaya Indian villages near present Spanish Fort on Red River.

Above: Indian pipes found by archaeologists at Longest Site, the Wichita village on the Oklahoma side of Red River. Below: a brass ornament representing a maned lion for a gunstock and a miquelet flintlock cock jaw, both of probable Spanish design, unearthed in a cache pit at the nearby eighteenth-century town of San Bernardo. Courtesy Museum of the Great Plains.

circular stockades that Captain W. A. Morris found there in 1859 may have been built later.[16] But the countless relics found at both San Bernardo (Longest Site, in southeastern Jefferson County, Oklahoma) and San Teodoro (in Texas) attest to the more than half-century of Indian and French occupation there.

Mrs. Joe Benton, of Nocona, Texas, maintains a private museum not only of Indian artifacts but of French ornaments, dinner ware, Spanish cannon balls, silver bells, and a rosary cross inlaid with turquoise, as well as of parts of French and Spanish muskets and flintlock pistols collected by her late husband along the banks of Red River.[17]

For more than thirty years Gene Wilson, of Ringgold, Texas, found early relics up and down both sides of Red River. Among his finds are hundreds of beads, barrels from flintlock guns, military buttons worn by French and Spanish troops, musket balls, metal and flint arrowheads, gun flints, stone pipes, and crosses, stars, and other figures fashioned from metal.

Once, about forty years ago, Gene recalled, several graves were found near the confluence of Beaver Creek and Red River northeast of Ringgold on what was known as the McNott Ranch. He distinctly remembered that each grave yielded large rowel spurs of early Spanish design.[18]

To the archaeologist and the historian the Taovaya villages are two of the most important sites in the Southern Great Plains, so important that the National Science Foundation awarded a $77,200 grant to the Museum of the Great Plains, the Southern Methodist University, the University of Oklahoma, and the University of Texas to excavate and research the sites, a project which began in November, 1965. The result was a myriad of relics, each telling a separate story to the expert.

Perhaps uppermost in the excavators' minds was finding the exact ground on which the Indian fortress was situated, which proved to be on the Oklahoma side, contrary to what most had believed theretofore. Nothing exists of the ancient Taovaya villages today, although both the Oklahoma and the Texas historical societies have erected a monument near the two-hundred-year-old sites.

The Spanish trail across the plains that led down Red River was blazed almost thirty years after the Spanish fiasco on that river. Ironically enough, it required the expertise of a Frenchman, commissioned by the Spanish governor of Texas, to explore a route from San Antonio to Santa Fe. Pedro Vial was that Frenchman. A man of mystery, he was a paladin on the plains, often a lone navigator in a vast, uncharted wilderness.

A native of Lyons, France, Vial lived in Spanish Illinois in the early 1770's. From St. Louis he migrated to Texas and was "for many years a captive of the Comanches" before he began living with the Taovayas, perhaps as early as 1779. A gunsmith by trade, he was said to have repaired arms for the Indians. His knowledge of them was profound, and the Spaniards wisely decided to capitalize on that knowledge when he offered his services at Bexar (present San Antonio) in 1786.[19]

Vial could not write Spanish, and his French was poor. But his journals, even though often scanty, reveal his incredible voyages in an unknown land filled with Indians who constantly held the Spaniards in terror. Vial made not one but several expeditions over the Red River country. Those expeditions were completely unlike the armor-clad, sword-carrying, well-mounted Spanish *entradas* of his time.

His first journey began from San Antonio on October 4, 1786. Riding at his side as his sole companion, was Cristóbal de los Santos. By mid-December they had arrived at the Taovaya villages on Red River where twenty-seven years earlier Colonel Parilla and his Spanish army had been defeated—and where Vial himself had no doubt lived and traded with the Indians.[20] Unlike the Spaniards, the French had never had trouble with the Taovayas, and Vial and his companion remained with the tribes for several weeks and then wintered upstream, near present Burkburnett, Texas.

In early spring, 1787, they again headed westward into the Texas Panhandle and followed the Canadian River into New Mexico. After seven and one-half months and a journey of eleven hundred miles, Vial and Santos rode into Santa Fe on May 26, having blazed a trail covered by no other white man and for the first time in the history of

While excavating the Wichita Indian sites, archaeologists from the Museum of the Great Plains and the University of Oklahoma unearthed this skeleton of a forty-year-old Wichita woman. The site is on the north side of Red River, near what may have been the palisaded fortification of the Taovayas. Courtesy Museum of the Great Plains.

The excavation at the Red River site revealed this skeleton of a thirty- to forty-year-old woman. Around the lower right leg were thirty-three small blue glass beads. Courtesy Museum of the Great Plains.

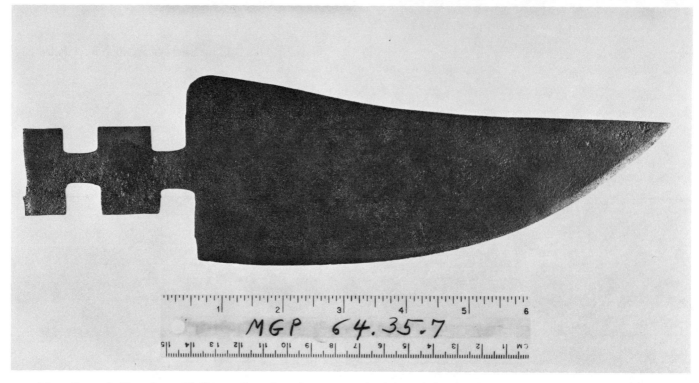

Many Spanish, French, and Indian artifacts have been unearthed during the past century near Spanish Fort, Texas, on Red River, where Colonel Parilla's Spanish army was defeated by the Indians in 1759. This iron knife is one of many such relics. Courtesy Museum of the Great Plains.

A brass cup, probably of French origin, found near San Bernardo. Courtesy Museum of the Great Plains.

T. A. Youngblood, of Bowie, Texas, found these iron arrow points, parts of flintlocks, axheads, and assorted artifacts near Spanish Fort. Courtesy Museum of the Great Plains.

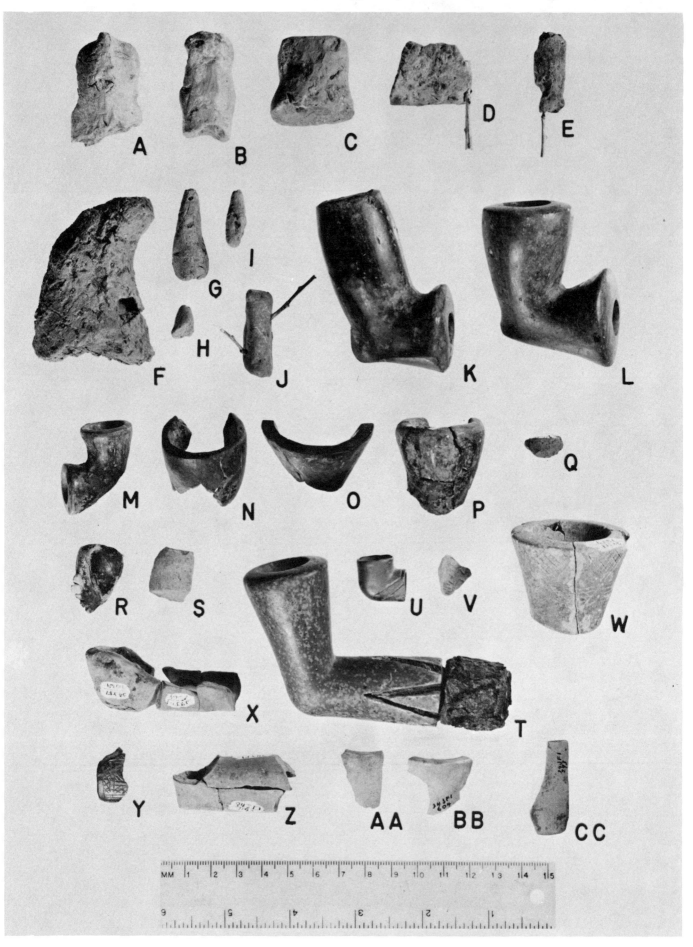

Longest Site yielded many figurines and pipes. A–J: figurine fragments; K–Q: Indian clay pipes; R: a Euro-American kaolin pipe; S–CC: Indian stone pipes. Courtesy Museum of the Great Plains.

This grave at Longest Site yielded the skeletal remains of a twenty- to twenty-five-year-old male Indian. An ear ornament of glass beads and a perforated shell disk was found on each side of the skull. Courtesy Museum of the Great Plains.

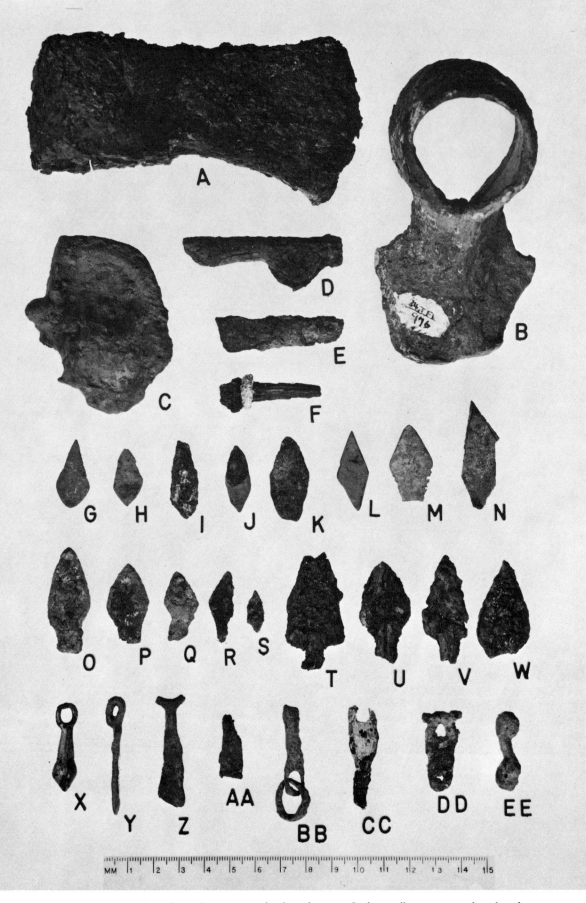

Many metal artifacts have been unearthed at the twin Indian villages on each side of Red River. Excavations from the Oklahoma side produced the ones shown here. A: an ax; B: a hoe; C: a flesher (?); D: a hammer; E–F: knives; G–N: diamond-shaped points; O–W: stemmed points; X–EE: horse trappings. Courtesy Museum of the Great Plains.

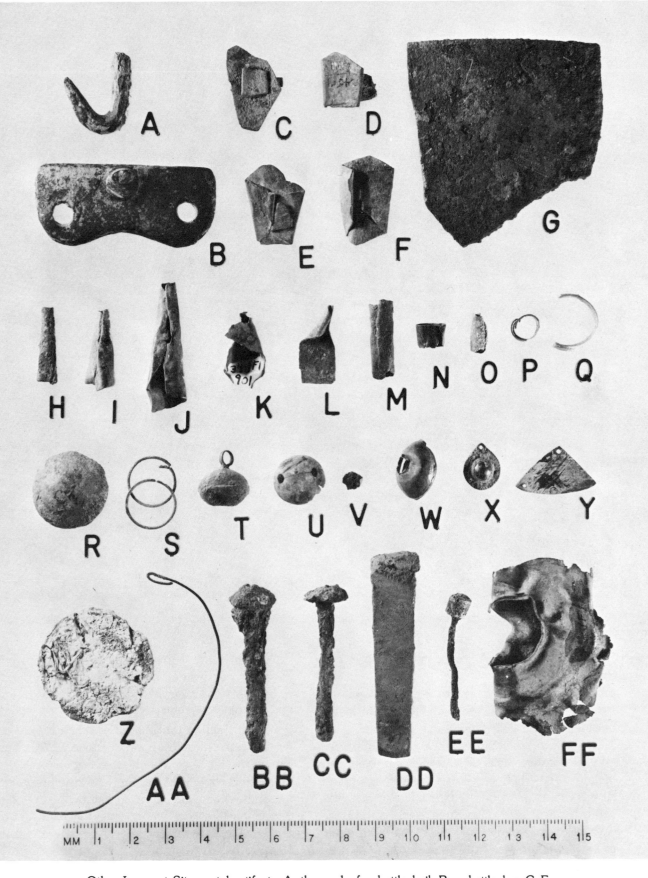

Other Longest Site metal artifacts. A: the end of a kettle bail; B: a kettle lug; C–F: rivets of sheet metal; G: a kettle rim; H–L: tinklers; M–O: beads; P, Q, S: rings; R: a button; T, U, W: hawk bells; V: a bell clapper; X–Y: pendants; Z: a lead seal (?); AA: wire; BB–CC: nails; DD–EE: pins; FF: the base of a candlestick holder (?). Courtesy Museum of the Great Plains.

Archaeological workers carefully excavate and clean, measure, and photograph each discovery while seeking

Santa Fe and San Antonio, linking those two Spanish cities.[21]

Desiring an even more direct route between the two settlements, the Spaniards launched still another expedition in July of the same year. José Mares, Vial's companion, Santos, and a Comanche interpreter, Alejandro Martín rode east and by late August had struck the headwaters of Red River, Prairie Dog Town Creek. Following the south bank of Red River, they reached the Taovaya villages in early September. Mares appears to be the first to report a French post, known as El Comercio de los Franceses, about three leagues

southwest of the Taovayas "on a high point between two very small mesas" which French *contrabandistas* had established for trade with the Comanches.[22]

After traveling more than 930 miles, Mares arrived at San Antonio in early October, 1787, but, like his predecessor, Vial, he had not followed the most direct route.[23] Mares lost little time preparing for another journey back to Santa Fe and departed for that destination the following January 18, 1788. After wintering on the Double Mountain Fork, in present Stonewall County, Texas, the party struck north through the Palo

58

to reconstruct the twin Wichita Indian villages on Red River. Courtesy Museum of the Great Plains.

Duro Canyon country, reaching Santa Fe at the end of April, 1788, after measuring a route of about 845 miles.[24]

Because the Taovayas on Red River were eager to trade, and because the Spaniards wanted to establish trade relations with the French in Louisiana, the Spaniards launched still another expedition across the plains. Once again hired to blaze that trail was the intrepid Pedro Vial, whose job was now to find the shortest route from Santa Fe to Natchitoches, Louisiana.

Vial lost no time, leaving Santa Fe on June 24, 1788, accompanied by Francisco Xavier Fragoso,

three Indians, and Santiago Fernández, who commanded a squad of three soldiers who would escort the party to the Taovaya villages. Once on the plains they followed Red River downstream through rugged Palo Duro Canyon and crossed into Oklahoma near present Grandfield and noted in their diary the looming Wichita Mountains on the north.[25] Continuing downstream on the north side of the river, they crossed Beaver Creek near present Ryan, and near modern Fleetwood were met by three chiefs, who escorted them to their rancheria of 372 tents on Red River.

Vial, Fragoso, and Fernández camped in the

59

Excavators at Longest Site meticulously remove overlying strata while uncovering artifacts, storage pits, hearths, and post holes marking the once circular, beehivelike grass houses of the Wichitas. Courtesy Museum of the Great Plains.

Taovaya villages until July 24; then the captain and his soldiers returned to Santa Fe, while Vial and Fragoso continued eastward the following day. They followed Red River downstream and near present Gainesville, Texas, struck southeast. By August 20 they had reached Natchitoches, where they were welcomed by the commander of the French fort. Once again Vial had opened the first communication between the far-distant provinces of New Mexico and Louisiana. A night of celebration followed.

Ten days after their arrival Vial and Fragoso were bound for San Antonio. After a two-month rest at the Spanish settlements of San Augustine and Nacogdoches they arrived at the presidio in San Antonio on November 18. Shortly afterward Fragoso fell sick with fever and was bedridden for

more than three months.

Finally, on June 25, 1789, the explorers were once again charting the wilderness to Santa Fe. They arrived at that old settlement on August 20. They had tallied 361 leagues from Santa Fe to Natchitoches, 51 to Nacogdoches, 154 to San Antonio, and 348 back to Santa Fe, to complete a route of 914 leagues, or about 2,300 lonely miles across an empty land virtually unknown to other white men.

"The dangers braved by these explorers are comparable to those of Lewis and Clark, and the fund of information obtained is no less important," rightfully wrote Carlos E. Castañeda.[26] Certainly history should call Pedro Vial the unsung hero of the plains.

But Vial's travels across the plains were not yet

While excavating the Longest Site in 1965–66, archaeologists uncovered the remains of a beehive-shaped grass house about thirty-three feet in diameter, including trash-filled storage pits, post holes, and, in the center, a basin-shaped fireplace. Courtesy Museum of the Great Plains.

completed, for in May, 1792, he blazed a trail from Santa Fe to St. Louis that one day would become a well-traveled highway known as the Santa Fe Trail. His path led down the Canadian River, across the Texas Panhandle, through the Antelope Hills of western Oklahoma, and thence northeastward through Kansas. For the first time in the six years of his indomitable travels, Vial encountered a hostile band of Indians. They stole his horses, slashed off his clothes, and threatened to butcher him. By a sheer streak of luck an Indian who recognized Vial demanded that his life be spared. Even so, he was held prisoner for more than two months. Finally, on October 6, he reached St. Louis in good health after traveling 1,185 miles between the New Mexican capital and St. Louis

(one day soon to be the Gateway to the West).

As epoch-making as Vial's travels were, the Spaniards made little use of his vast knowledge. Unfortunately, Vial did not keep journals (or none has been found) of other *entradas*, of which we know very little. About 1797 he went to live with the Comanches. Two years later he was living just north of St. Louis. About 1800 he discovered and worked a lead mine near St. Geneviève, Missouri.[27] In 1805 the Spaniards employed him to intercept the Lewis and Clark expedition known to be penetrating Spanish territory. Three years later William Clark issued Vial a license to trap on the Missouri, and it may be that Vial was the first white man on the headwaters of that river, after spending "considerable time in Canada."[28]

The small amount of pottery found at the two Wichita Red River sites indicates that Indian-made containers were replaced with metal pots introduced by early traders. The artifacts shown here are of native origin. A–C: undecorated, straight-rim shards; D–F: undecorated rim shards with outturned lips; G–T: engraved rim and body shards; U: a basal shard; V–W: brushed shards; R–S: large decorated shards. Courtesy Museum of the Great Plains.

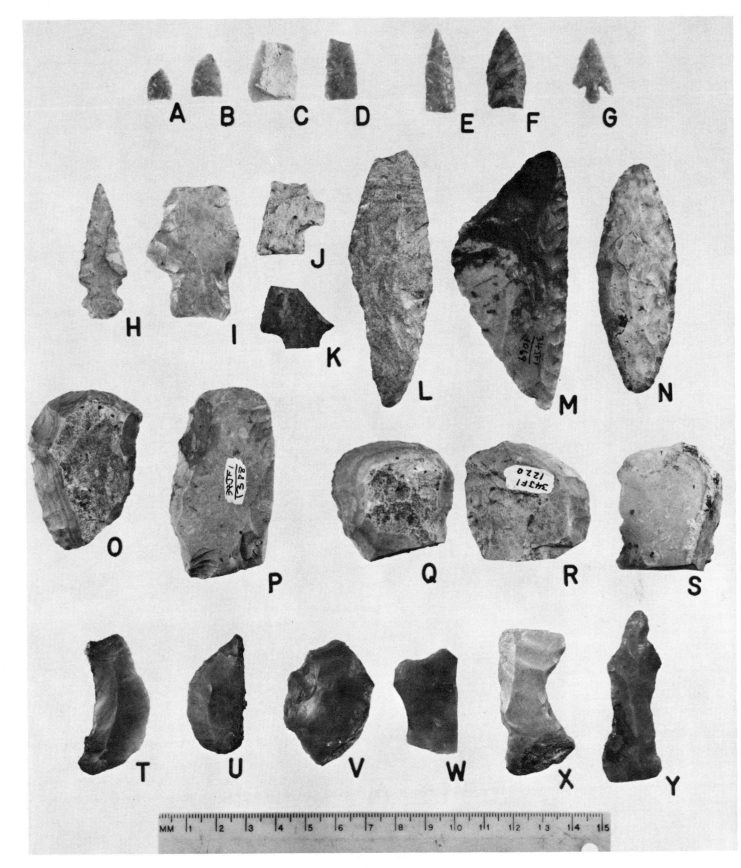

Chipped-stone artifacts from Longest Site. A–D: small, unnotched, triangular points;
E–F: small, unnotched pentagonal points; G: a small, corner-notched point; H–K:
large points; L–N: knives; O–S: large end scrapers; T–Y: flake scrapers. Courtesy
Museum of the Great Plains.

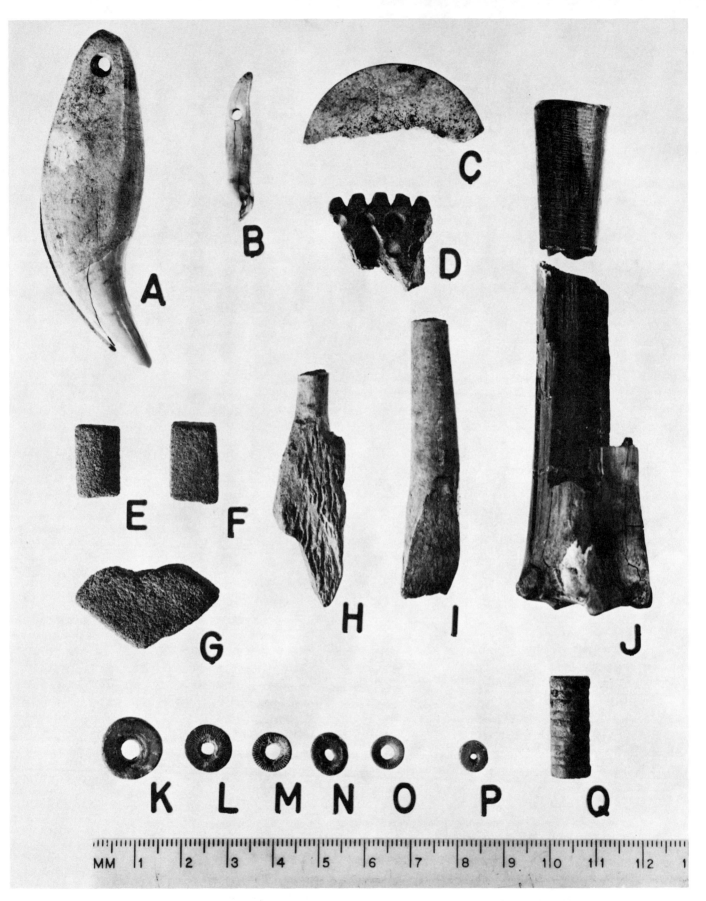

Bone and ground-stone artifacts from Longest Site. A–B: pendants; C–J: objects of unknown function; K–P: beads; Q: bead stock. Courtesy Museum of the Great Plains.

In the grave of an adult male at Longest Site was unearthed this Indian-made, shell-tempered pottery vessel, which was later restored in the laboratory. Courtesy Museum of the Great Plains.

He had blazed the roads from San Antonio to Santa Fe, from there to Natchitoches, and later from Santa Fe to St. Louis, traveling more than 4,500 miles when his life depended on his finesse with the Indians. How many miles he traveled during the time he kept no records remains unknown. It is known that he did keep a number of diaries that have never been found. In 1814, after twenty-six years of service to Spain, the unsung frontiersman, "who had by himself covered more ground than any other man of his era," died in Santa Fe of natural causes.[29]

WICHITA INDIANS

From contact with Coronado in 1541, the Wichita slowly drifted south across Oklahoma to Spanish Fort on the Red River by 1750. In 1834, a small group lived at Devil's Canyon.

Wichita hunting and gardening was a successful life for an environment marked by cyclic droughts. However, with the addition of the horse to the plains the advantage of their ~~enemy waned. Inroads of mounted Indians and~~ ~~...by Europeans~~

This diorama at the Museum of the Great Plains, Lawton, Oklahoma, depicts a Wichita Indian village as it looked when French and Anglo-American traders arrived on upper Red River. Courtesy Museum of the Great Plains.

The probable site of the Wichita Indian fortress on Red River as it appears today. Courtesy Museum of the Great Plains.

A Pawnee Pict Wig-Wam and Family in Western Texas (George Catlin, 1852). This grass house was similar to those found by Anthony Glass and John Maley on upper Red River. Courtesy Thomas Gilcrease Institute of American History and Art, Tulsa, Oklahoma.

3. Quests for Red River's Silver Mines

Thomas Jefferson was President when a wealthy Natchez, Mississippi, merchant, Anthony Glass, conceived the idea of leading an unprecedented expedition far up Red River's hinterlands in quest of a lost silver mine. Little is known about Glass. He was often seen at the notorious King's Tavern, where famous persons—as well as ruffians and assorted riffraff—converged to swap tales or plot ill-conceived deeds.

Anglo-American traders and trappers who had been on the uncharted headwaters of Red River were few, but they brought back tales of a rich silver mine far up the stream. By chance Glass may have even learned from French records that a Spanish soldier had deserted his post in Texas and defected to the French at Natchitoches, Louisiana, where in 1725 he revealed that the Spaniards worked a "silver mine near the Trinity."

In short time a force of almost five hundred Frenchmen and friendly Indians marched into Texas and "explored the country for ninety leagues to a point beyond the Trinity in search of the silver mine."[1] Although the expedition was unsuccessful, it is interesting to ponder what might have occurred if the French cavaliers had met the Spaniards during their quest for silver.

Glass may have been familiar with the expeditions of French explorer De Mézières, who reported in 1772 that, at a site about forty leagues southwest of the Taovayas on Red River, "besides having in its territory red ochre beds, which persons versed in mining suppose to be deposits of greatest richness, is only a short distance from a mass of metal which the Indians say is hard, thick, heavy, and composed of iron. They venerate it as an extraordinary manifestation of nature; . . . there is not a person in the village who does not tell of it."[2]

Traditions might well have told also of a mysterious expedition in February, 1774, when three Frenchmen accompanied twenty Spanish soldiers and seven civilians from San Antonio "to look for a rich mine" near the Taovaya villages.[3]

Anthony Glass had so often involved himself in shady dealings around Natchez that he had been dubbed "the fence and informer of bandits" operating on the Natchez Trace, particularly of the infamous Samuel Mason, noted scourge of the Trace, who was brought to trial in 1803.[4]

It is probable that the stories of two seasoned Red River traders, who, with four or five others, had in 1806–1807, traveled four hundred miles overland to trade with the Taovayas—referred to by this time as the Panis Nation, or the Wichitas—prompted Anthony Glass to raise an expedition of his own, allowing him to cash in on a lucrative trade with the Indians, as well as to pursue the tale he had obviously heard of a rich silver mine near Red River's upper waters.

Those two traders, of whom little is known, and both of whom would accompany Glass and no doubt guide his expedition, were William C. Alexander and an interpreter named Joseph Lucas, the former of North Carolina and a relative of its former governor.

Although neither man would ever intimate as much, Glass no doubt was told those stories by the United States Indian agent, Dr. John Sibley, of Natchitoches, who had migrated to that border outpost in 1803 and had become the surgeon's mate for the United States troops stationed there and later Indian agent.

In June, 1807, John S. Lewis and Jeremiah Downs, two traders who had accompanied Alexander, Lucas, and two others to the Panis Nation the December before, returned to Natchitoches with a Panis chief and eight warriors. Lewis reported to Dr. Sibley that he had seen specimens of silver ore that he believed to be rich and were "found in great quantities on the N East side of Red River above the Panis Nation."[5]

Two months later Dr. Sibley held a "Grand Council" of the chiefs at Natchitoches. The chiefs represented eight tribes, among whom were the Comanches, allies of the Panis, or Wichitas, of upper Red River. During the parley Dr. Sibley made note of John Lewis' discovery, saying that the Indians could always trade their horses, mules, robes, and silver ore for such articles as they may desire.[6]

When both the Panis and the Comanches arrived at Natchitoches in mid-October, 1807, Dr. Sibley presented them with gifts of blankets, shirts, hats, plumes, guns, powder, balls, presidential medals, and, to the Panis chief, a handsome Philadelphia saddle and officer's uniform coat, among other utensils and knickknacks. The Indians were impressed, and a Comanche chief in return stated that they "knew where there was Silver Ore plenty."[7]

When the Comanche requested more guns and some picks or mattocks to dig out the silver ore, Dr. Sibley promised them all the guns and mattocks they desired if they would return with "plenty of Horses, Mules, Buffalo Robes & Silver ore."[8]

The stories of silver on Red River's headwaters coincided with and reinforced Dr. Sibley's own knowledge, for only two years before he had received firsthand information about those beckoning silver mines. Sibley had talked with an old French trader named Brevel, who forty years earlier (about 1765) had traveled Red River's upper waters on his way to Santa Fe.

Several days' travel above the Panis Nation (the site of the fortified village near present Spanish Fort) Brevel told Sibley that they had struck a mountain range containing an ore that his Indian allies said was the "white people's treasure" and he later learned was silver. In those "mountains of mines," Brevel recounted, "we often heard a noise like the explosion of cannon, or distant thunder, which the Indians said was the spirit of the white people, working in their treasure."[9] It may be assumed that Glass was armed with that knowledge when he launched his overland expedition.

In the spring of 1808, Sibley received a message from the Panis chief that during the summer neighboring tribes of friendly Indians would assemble "at or near his village" for a trading fair and invited traders from Natchitoches to attend. Agent Sibley in turn informed Anthony Glass, who put up a bond of one thousand dollars and was thereby granted a license to trade with the Panis Nation, known to be about 800 to 1,000 miles up Red River from Natchitoches or about 350 to 400 miles overland. The license, however, stipulated that Glass was to travel by way of the northeast side of Red River, within the territory of the United States, for crossing to the south side would place him in Spanish territory, in violation of its laws.

The governor of the Territory of Orleans, William C. C. Claiborne, did not look with favor upon Sibley's licensing Glass and expressed strong reservations about Glass's motives. In reporting to the secretary of war, Claiborne charged that Glass had given himself the title of captain and procured from army officers an epaulet, sword, belt, and military coat, boasting that he held a commission so that "the Spaniards could not touch him." Moreover, Glass had revealed that his real intention "was to visit a silver mine." Claiborne believed that Glass's motive was probably "nothing more than a plundering or silver mine expedition," suggesting that it smacked of filibustering.[10]

In further letters penned after Glass was well under way, Claiborne referred to Glass's enterprise as the "Silver Mine Expedition" and to Secretary of State James Madison once again questioned Sibley's authority to license Glass, adding, "and I should Suppose, that the conduct of Mr. Sibley, will furnish on the part of the Spanish authorities just cause for complaint."[11]

In defense of granting Glass the license, Dr. Sibley wrote Secretary of War Henry Dearborn that William Alexander was "a Man of great Sobriety, discretion, and a very honest Character" and that Glass and his men were "all of them Characters that I knew & approved of, . . . There never has to my knowledge, so respectable a trading party taken their departure from this place, nor one on whose prudence I had Such Confidence, knowing them all well Attached to Our government. I have always calculated that good would result from it."[12]

No doubt had Governor Claiborne known in time he would have done all in his power to stop Glass. But the self-made Captain Glass and ten of his cohorts left Natchitoches on June 20, 1808, with two thousand dollars' worth of merchandise tied to their mounts. Glass carried with him a small United States flag and a scarlet uniform coat promised to the Panis chief by Dr. Sibley.

But Glass's shady past still pursued him, probably not entirely without cause, for word of his quest for a silver mine had circulated among the Spanish officials, and the rumors of Glass's numbers had multiplied. Not long after he left Natchitoches, the Spanish agent there, Juan Cortés, notified the Nacogdoches commander that Antonio Glass had set out with one hundred men with the intention of prospecting for mines and establishing trade with the Taovayas and Comanches and might go as far as Santa Fe, for a party was to join him in New Mexico. They were "desperate characters and well armed," he stressed.[13]

Some days later more details of Glass's "true motives" surfaced. From Nacogdoches, commandant Simón de Herrera reiterated Glass's intention of discovering silver mines, as shown by the tools he carried, and believed the party to number sixty men, but still another group of twenty-eight, enforced by one hundred more from New Madrid, were to join them. Expressing fear that they might raid Spanish settlements, Herrera suggested that the Texas governor send an army to intercept Glass and hang the intruders. Texas Governor Manuel María de Salcedo did not dispatch his army but instead instructed friendly Indians at San Antonio to bring him Glass's head, a danger that Glass would later confront far out on the Plains.

In his saddlebags Glass kept his daily journal, a long-obscure and little-known record of one of the earliest Anglo-American expeditions to the upper waters of Red River, made forty-four years before Captain Randolph B. Marcy would officially explore that stream. Unlike the Spaniards' estimate, Glass did not have 188 men, only 10.

Accompanying him were George Schamp, Stephen Holmes, Ezra McCall, Jacob Low, John Davis, James Davis, Peter Young, Joseph White, William C. Alexander, and his interpreter, Joseph Lucas. As mentioned above, the last two men had journeyed to the Panis Nation more than a year before and brought back a recounting of the legendary silver mine far onto the plains, which if only in a clandestine way now spurred the Anthony Glass of King's Tavern onto a one-thousand-mile, eleven-month journey into a hostile land whose Indians had greeted few Anglo-Americans, obscure traders all of whom before

Glass had kept no written record of their journeys.

Glass began his journal on July 6, 1808.[14] At no time did he mention his search for a silver mine. If it was on his mind, apparently he thought it best not to record it. His journal, virtually unknown to historians, shows that Glass was an observant traveler, educated for his day, and a chronicler of the flora, fauna, and ethnology of upper Red River.

Glass daily noted significant events, landmarks, animals (even noxious flies), vegetation, course of direction, weather, miles covered, and Indians encountered. However, Glass and his men lost little time breaking the stipulation of keeping to the northeast bank of Red River, for on July 15 about 120 miles north of Natchitoches they crossed that stream traveling north-northwest. On July 24 the traders crossed the road made almost two years before by Francisco Viana's Spanish force of about two hundred soldiers who had stopped the first officially authorized expedition up Red River under Thomas Freeman near the southeast corner of present-day Oklahoma.

On August 1, Glass and his men covered twenty-six miles, heading west-northwest across a lush prairie and crossing two creeks on which grew an abundance of bois d'arc, trees resembling apple trees and bearing orangelike fruit. A hard, elastic wood long prized by the Indians for making bows, the French named the tree "bois d'arc," and the Red River tributary through present central Fannin County, Texas, yet bears that name.

Forty miles west-northwestward, on August 7, the adventurers "stopped at twelve O'Clock to dine at an old Camp" made the previous fall by two of their men—no doubt Alexander and the interpreter Lucas. This camp they knew to be "about 50 miles from the Panie Villages."

By August 10 they were within five miles of the Panis villages. Glass and his men probably had no idea that only two months before the amazing Pedro Vial had been hunting near the Canadian River in the present Texas Panhandle, where he met Captain Francisco Amangual and his two hundred Spaniards, who were seeking a northern route between San Antonio and Santa Fe.[15]

According to trading custom, Glass dispatched a messenger to notify the Wichitas of his approach.

Early the following morning the messenger returned with an Indian escort, and some distance outside the Indian villages fifty mounted warriors met and accompanied the eleven traders into their village. By Glass's reckoning they had covered a distance of about 365 miles to the twin villages San Bernardo and San Teodoro, situated on either side of Red River. Glass camped on the south side of the river at San Teodoro.

Glass devoted considerable space in his journal to visiting the chief of the Panis, who lived on the north side of the river, to trading with the Indians—almost always for horses—and to the Indians' lifestyle, sexual practices, and even folklore. The Wichita village on the Texas side of the river maintained about 150 acres of their land in corn, beans, pumpkins, and muskmelons, Glass observed. The Indians kept his men furnished with an abundance of vegetables, in addition to buffalo meat. And although deer were plentiful, they were "tame like Domestic Animals," wrote Glass, for the Wichitas did not harm them.

The village on the Oklahoma side of the river contained sixty-five thatched houses and its inhabitants cultivated about three hundred acres. Glass noted that the Panis were "great libertines, both men and women." They were "not addicted to Jealousy and nothing is more common than for a man to lend or hire out his Wife, particularly to Strangers who visit the nation." There were "many more women than men" among them, completely unlike the Comanches with whom he would soon trade. Glass estimated the Panis to number about three hundred warriors among a population of two thousand.

The Wichitas had long been subjected to raids by the Osages, several of which occurred while Glass lived among them. That they showed no mercy to prisoners is shown by Glass's description of their methods:

The Panies are singular in their mode of putting their prisoners to Death. They have a post planted in the ground about two hundred yards from the village. They strip the prisoner naked and tie him to the post. They remain some time and all the people come to see him, after [which] the women and children with sticks fall to beating him and beat him till he expires under their blows. They then cut the flesh from the Bones and hang it up in pieces in different parts of the village.

Glass had been among the Panis more than a month when he was told of "a remarkable piece of metal" several days' journey south on the Brazos River. On September 19 he wrote that the Indians "attributed singular virtues" to the metal in curing diseases. When he sought permission to examine it, "this they would not listen to." Such were the "magic stones" so carefully guarded by the aborigines.

While among the Wichitas, Glass became a good friend of a Spaniard with the Indian name Tatesuck, who had been taken prisoner as a child. A distinguished warrior, "subtle & intrepid," he was "the first Leader of war parties." Glass remarked that the Spaniard's wife, "a Panie woman," was "as remarkable for her address and intrigue." It was from them that Glass obtained a promise to show him the sacred stone held in such high veneration and ascribed with wondrous healing powers.

Glass's eagerness to see the mass of metal, and obviously procure it if possible, was spurred by his belief that "it might be Platina or something of great value," something "no white man at this time had seen." The possibility of platinum on the Plains perhaps overshadowed his desire for that long-reputed silver lode.

Finally, on October 3, after fifty-two days among the Wichitas, Glass and his men packed their gear and set off southwestward to trade among the Comanches, whom Glass called Hietans. They readily spoke of the magic stone but just as readily objected to showing it. The Comanches were in agreement that the Panis, who had found the metallic mass, "had the best right to it," but the land on which it was found belonged to them.

After some heated debate among the Comanches, it was decided that, if their sacred stone was valuable, it should be divided between them and the Panis. Although the Indians had reported the supernatural metal to the French as early as 1772, one Wichita now with Glass claimed to be its finder. He obviously had second thoughts about revealing it to Glass, for, as Glass wrote in his journal, "I was obliged to flatter and bribe him to go on."

Whether interested in trading horses for the two thousand dollars in goods Glass carried or in-

and three times that number of Horses & Mules, most of them
were tied with Ropes made of Buffaloe skins every night. — It was
impossible to remain at the same place but a short time on account of
the Grass being soon Eaten up.

9th to 14th Moving slowly on to the west through a hilly broken Country
which is fit only for pasturage — crossing the river Brasos
about fifty Miles we approached the place where the metal
was; the Indians observing considerable ceremony as they approached
we found it resting on its heaviest end and leaning towards one
side and under it were some Pipes or Trinkets which had been placed
there by some Indians who had been healed by visiting it. the mass
was but very little bedded in the place we found it — there is no
reason to think it had ever been moved by man; it had the colour of
Iron, but no rust upon it — the Indians had contrived with
Chisels they had made of old files to cut off some small pieces which
there had hammered out to their fancy. there has been no other found
near it nor any thing resembling it. the surrounding country is
barren, Hilly. no timber but dwarf Musquitte, filled with grey
and reddish granite Rock; not having the means of ascertaining
its precise Quality only. that it was Obedient to the magnet
very Malable would take a brilliant polish and give fire with a
flint. I had some small scales cutt off and left it. the Indians
informed me they knew of two others smaller pieces of the same kind
of metal one about thirty miles distant and the other fifty, —
about twenty miles distant west of it there is a great appearance of Iron Ore and the country exhibits Strata of Shells which
were pronounced to be Cokle Shells by all of our Party —
The country entirely Prarie. we have not seen a spring since
we left the Panie Towns many of the streams do not run but
there is an abundance of standing water — not being able to purchase
Horses of these Hietans our Party became discontented and they all
Except Peter Young and Joseph Lucas the Interpreter Left me taking
some of the goods and went in search of a large horde of Hietans
of whom they expected to Purchase what Horses and Mules they wanted

In October, 1808, Anthony Glass wrote in his journal about being shown the singular
mass of metal about fifty miles southwest of the Wichita Indian villages on Red River.
Yale University Library.

In 1810, after a four-hundred-mile journey into Spanish Texas, traders found one of the Indians' sacred stones. Believing that it was platinum, they hauled the meteorite, which weighed more than a ton, to Red River and boated it downstream to Natchitoches, Louisiana.

sisting that their sacred metal must be protected, the Comanches' numbers had now grown to nearly one thousand, with three times as many horses and mules, making it necessary for the traders to move on for grass.

About October 14, roughly fifty miles southwest of the Red River villages, Glass and his large Indian following crossed the Brazos to where the venerated mass of metal lay. As the Indians approached the metallic chunk, they observed "considerable ceremony." Perhaps the first white man ever to lay eyes on the magic stone, Glass "found it resting on its heavist end and leaning towards one side." It measured 3 feet 4½ inches long, 2 feet 4 inches wide, and 16 inches high. Though Glass and the Indians could not know it, it weighed more than one ton.

Glass continued:

Under it were some Pipes and Trinkets which had been placed there by some Indians who had been healed by visiting it. The mass was but very little bedded in the place we found it. There is no reason to think it has ever been moved by man. It had the colour of iron, but no rust upon it.

The Indians had used files converted into chisels to cut off small pieces of the metal "which they had hammered out to their fancy." Glass further observed that "it was obedient to the magnet, very malable, would take a brilliant polish and give fire with a flint. I had some small scales cutt off and left it."

To the Wichitas and Comanches, who had long revered the metal, each visitation to the lone metallic mass had become a sacred ceremony in which everyone who passed it offered a stone of his own by placing it on the mound of rocks that had accumulated nearby. Perhaps contributing to that reverence was the fact that the metal "talked." With the tap of an object or snap of a finger against it, the more than three-foot-long metal rang "like a church bell."[16]

Glass noted that the surrounding country was "barren, hilly," and had "no timber but dwarf musquette, filled with grey and reddish granite." Twenty miles to the west Glass noted large quantities of iron ore, "and the country exhibits strata of Shells." Glass learned, too, that the metal was not the only such in this wilderness. The Indians

74

told of two smaller pieces of the metal, "one about thirty miles distant and the other fifty."

Dollar signs shot through the trader's mind, for if the metallic masses were platina, that platinum would bring handsome prices in the trading markets of New Orleans. But Glass's hands were tied for lack of a cart in which to carry away the treasure.

Glass and his men continued their journey southwestward in search of more bands of Comanches with whom to trade for horses. On October 20 they arrived at a large branch of the Colorado. He wrote in his journal that day, "We gathered as many Pecans as we pleased, the ground was covered with them, being no other timber on the creek bottom."

Shortly after he changed his course back northeast toward the Wichita villages, two Lipans from near San Antonio visited Glass's camp and called all the chiefs together. Glass was present to hear their message. They had been sent by the Spanish governor to find Glass and carry his head back to San Antonio. The Spanish captive Tatesuck rose to his feet and turned to the Lipan who had reported the governor's instructions:

"You want a Head do you? To carry to the Spanish governor? If you do I advise you to get your own cutt off and have it sent to him. I further tell you that this American is my friend, and if you offer the least harm to him, I will soon cutt your head off."

Tatesuck seated himself, and "There was not another word said on the subject, and the governor's messengers disappeared in a few minutes," Glass observed.

Glass remained in camp over Christmas and by December 30 had left the branches of the Colorado and returned to the Brazos. He estimated that he was now about one hundred miles southwest of the Panis villages. The weather was cold and the water frozen an inch thick. "Here we attempted to pen some wild Horses which are seen by thousands and finished a strong Pen for the purpose, but the Buffalo were so plenty and so much in the way we succeeded badly in several attempts."

Snow covered the plains six inches deep, and Glass's men suffered continuously from the Co-

manches' thefts of their horses. On February 8 a Comanche chief returned some of the stolen animals, and Glass awarded him with a blanket, some powder, and lead. On about the twentieth of that month the traders arrived back at the Wichita villages on Red River. Glass recorded that, all told, the "Lower Hietans" had stolen forty-one horses from him.

On March 21, Glass and his party began their downstream journey to Natchitoches with horses so poor that they were forced to travel slowly. Apparently thinking his return to civilization was of little consequence, Glass devoted the final pages of his ethnologically rich narrative on the life-style of the Comanches, whom he had often compared with the Panis; he obviously liked the latter more.

By May 10, 1809, Glass and his men had returned to Natchitoches. The captain lost no time reporting to Indian Agent John Sibley and exclaiming about the possible value of the "Singular Kind of Mineral" whose "colour resembles Iron but whiter," was "hard as Steel," and "is obedient to the Magnet, but less so than Iron."[17]

Sibley took specimens of Glass's metal to the blacksmith, where it was fired and was proved "not Flexible in the greatest heat that Can be produced in a Blacksmith's furnace." Nor did nitric sulphuric acid or muriatic acid react to it, but it "receives a polish as Brilliant as a diamond & of a quicksilver colour. . . . If it is not Platina, I do not know what it is," Sibley wrote Secretary of War Samuel Eustice immediately upon Glass's return. Sibley said that Glass believed 100,000 pounds of the metal could be obtained if it proved valuable and sent a piece of the metal to Philadelphia for assaying.

Glass's stories of his odyssey on the plains—and the mass of supposed platinum that he had been shown—stirred no small amount of excitement in the border town of Natchitoches during that summer of 1809. Glass returned to Natchez, but the men who had accompanied him had ideas of their own for retrieving the potentially valuable metal. Obviously those plans did not call for sharing the metal among them, for in the spring of 1810 two rival expeditions were mounted, each led by a former member of Glass's trading party.

It was reported that Agent Sibley believed so strongly in the reputed platina that he offered the men who would launch another expedition back upriver to retrieve the large mass all the rifles, ammunition, and blankets the Indians demanded for it and promised that each man would share equally in its value.[18]

At Natchitoches, George Schamp put together a party of ten, most of whom had been with Glass. Joining him were Ezra McCall, William C. Alexander, Peter Young, William M. Williams, John Smith, Jacob Low, James Davis, William Piper, and Jourdon Dungeon.[19]

From Nacogdoches, John Davis, a Glass-party member who had plans of his own, left with an equal party of men consisting of Edward Robinson, Edward Juirk, William Skinner, William McClestar, William Knowlton, John Cochran, James White, and two or three others for the four-hundred-mile trek overland into Spanish territory. Bent on overtaking Schamp's party, which was prepared to trade for the metal, Davis' men arrived at the metal first. They had made no preparations for hauling away the mass, perhaps not realizing its true weight.

Now aware of their predicament, they proceeded to hide the hunk of metal, and with cut poles rolled the oval chunk some distance away, where they had found a flat stone. They removed the rock, dug out a hole large enough to bury their treasure, planted grass around it, and replaced the flat stone. After concealing all traces of their ruse, they hurried off for wheels and draft horses.

Meanwhile, Schamp's Natchitoches party pawned off their trade goods to the Wichitas and were accompanied to the metal by representatives of the Red River villages. But no metal was to be found—nor a trace of where it had gone. Finally, after a two-day search, they detected the dry grass planted around the flat stone and discovered that its roots were unnaturally loose. Pulling the flat stone aside, they found the hidden "god of platinum."

Armed with the proper tools and wheels, Schamp's men contrived a truck wagon and with ropes, crowbars, and brawn, hauled the more than one-ton mass onto their cart and harnessed it with six horses. They set off for Red River while the Indians returned to their villages.

Pulling the wagon and its heavy cargo over a trackless wilderness proved no small ordeal. They crossed the Brazos with some difficulty and on the third day were trailed by "a company of Spaniards" (they may have been Indians), who did not attack but waited until that night, when they made off with all the horses. The next morning not a single steed could be found. Alone on the Plains, George Schamp and his men gathered around their truck wagon and its heavy treasure and pondered what to do.

Schamp and William Piper returned to the Wichita villages on Red River and traded them two more rifles for horses. (One account says that they journeyed afoot four hundred miles overland back to Natchitoches.[20]) Once again Schamp was moving his metallic prize—cumbersome though it was—toward Red River. At the mouth of the Bois d'Arc Bayou in present northeast Fannin County, Schamp's men hollowed out a pirogue from a large black walnut tree and manhandled the heavy metal into the boat—a feat that surely must have been the first of its kind in the wilderness. Perhaps instead it was a raft they built, but once launched and headed downstream, the traders were soon compelled to "halt and wait for the water to rise." While several of the men ferried the metal almost a thousand miles downriver to Natchitoches, the others returned overland with the horses.

How long Schamp's men had to wait for the water to rise is not recorded, but some months later they arrived safely in Natchitoches, where the metal proved to be a curio unlike any the border settlers had glimpsed before. "The people crowded in from all quarters to see this wonder" and hear it ring "like a church bell."[21]

At Natchitoches the metal weighed in at 2,300 pounds, considerably more than the 1,635-pound piece scientists would later examine. Merchants offered the traders "great prices" for their share, "but they refused selling at any price," observed one.[22] None of the local artisans could ascertain its composition. Even though it was the color of iron, no blacksmith's forge would touch it.

After keeping it in Natchitoches for almost a year, Sibley sent the Indian's "magic stone" downriver to New Orleans, where again no one could make a true identification. Still later he sent it to

Dec 19th   Journal continued

the six Indians have taken my drove of Horses entirely under their care
...untill as I sell off for home — two Indians who live near St. Antonio
(Lepans) arrived in our Camp and called the chiefs together in (Council)
I was present, one of the strangers then informed them that they were
sent by the governor of St. Antonio to cut off my head and carry it
to him — after a minute or two Tatesuck my friend the great Panie
warrior arose and addressed himself to the one who last spoke as
follows — You want a Head do you? to carry to the Spaniish
governor? if you do I advise you to get your own cutt off and have
it sent to him: I farther tell you that this american is my friend
and if you offer the least harm to him I will soon cutt your
head off — there was not another word said on the subject —
and the governors messengers disappeared in a few minutes. — a
Hietan from some of the upper hordes arrived and says that
some of his nation have lately been to St. Antonio and stolen a
Large number of Horses and Mules and says that the spaniards and
his own people are on bad terms and that at the coming of new
grass something will be done: they understand likewise that the
spaniards and United States are going to war. I advised them
in case it should happen, to have Nothing to do in the quarrel. —
On Hietan this morning caught his wife in bed with a man of
his party. he immediately shott him dead and then deliberately
loaded his gun and shott his Wife also. some of the relations
of those killed cried for a short time and all was over. this would
not have happened among the Panies they are more generous to
one another. the Hietans often kill their wives so that in their
camps there are more men than women — but with the Panies
the contrary —

Dec 30th the Hietans this day stole twenty three head of my Horses and say
they lost that number when at Nackitosh. the Panies

a friend in New York, where later it was ruefully pronounced as only iron.

Although Sibley may have been convinced, apparently he did not show the report to any of the traders who had braved the wilds for months to retrieve the ore. Many of them believed the metal to be platinum, and apparently ill feeling had developed between the frontiersmen and Sibley.

It was at about this time that one John Maley arrived in Natchitoches, on February 24, 1812.[23] Maley, who perhaps fancied himself as a swash-buckling adventurer, was educated and observant enough to keep a diary and had some time earlier planned on ascending Red River to its headwaters. It was not his first visit to Natchitoches. He had come earlier, in December, 1810, had joined a band of Texas filibusters, and had been lucky to escape with his life.

Virtually nothing is known about John Maley the traveler. Perhaps he had hopes that his journal of adventures would one day be published. He was termed "an erratic adventurer," a man with a "roving disposition" who "possessed a strong and inquiring though uncultivated mind."[24]

His journal reveals that he had some time earlier traveled up the Arkansas River, if he knew his geography. By his own admission he was not an experienced trapper and had spent little if any time among Indians. He never hinted about his home, although he had known William Johnson, of Charleston, South Carolina, a United States jurist who looked upon Maley as a "wanderer."[25]

Maley knew something about minerals and mining and even carried crucibles and assaying equipment. While he prepared for his journey up Red River, several of the traders who had dealt with Sibley—and had a bone to pick with him—told Maley of their overland journey for the platina and Sibley's subsequent strange behavior. They agreed to share all their knowledge of the country if Maley would make his own assay of a sample of the metal that Sibley still possessed. But when Sibley was approached, he vehemently turned the men away, claiming to have none of the metal and that it was nothing more than iron.

While the men attempted to find other small pieces cut from the ore, Sibley summoned Maley to his quarters and told him that the metal was not worth his attention and that he "would receive no thanks for it after telling them." Sibley stressed that he was the Indian agent and that, "without his assistance, I could not trade with the Indians," Maley wrote in his journal. Sibley offered Maley a free license to go among the Indians if he would "shun" the men, "otherwise, none at all." Ten years later Sibley would claim that he never knew John Maley.[26]

"I was then bound so to do," Maley wrote. "I kep myself out of their way." Sibley arranged for Maley to travel upriver with a party of twelve "Cashotoo" Indians in five pirogues who were homeward bound five hundred miles upstream.

On March 5, 1812, John Maley was at last on his way up Red River to explore the stream he called the "garden of the world." With him went two companions named William Cox and one Bradley, about whom nothing is known other than that the former was an old hunter. Maley carried a dozen steel beaver traps, a supply of bacon and hard bread, some whisky, a rifle, a tomahawk, knives, cooking utensils, and his "small laboratory with a good set of crucibles to make assays on ore." The three whites and twelve Indians divided themselves, three climbing into each canoe. It was ten o'clock in the morning by Maley's timepiece.

Like his predecessor Glass, Maley was keen in his observation of the flora and fauna and Indian life along the river. Supplementary and complementary to Glass's overland expedition, Maley's trip by canoe sheds light on the river life during this period found in no other journal. Almost like a schoolboy, Maley meticulously recorded each encounter with the Indians, noting each new experience with them—from eating to pipe smoking.

On the fifth day they encountered alligators that "roared like great bulls." The men lived off raccoons, deer, turkey, and wild cattle. On the tenth day they found "fresh signs of beaver," "otter slides," and, for the first time on the river, "signs of bufaloe." Later they trapped six beavers and two otters, which they skinned and braced on bows.

On the sixteenth day Maley shot a female bear and then found her two young cubs. His Indian guides adopted the cubs and took them aboard, but the bears died shortly later for want of milk.

For the first time mosquitoes became so noxious that the men "had to keep a brisk smoke to keep them away" at night.

On the seventeenth day of their journey they struck the great bend of Red River where it turns westward near what later would be Fulton, Arkansas. The next morning they had five beavers and one otter in their traps. A short distance upstream Maley and his men were surprised to meet a man named Hardy with his wife who had been upriver for fifteen months and were now canoeing downstream with their cargo of beaver, muskrat, otter, and raccoon skins, beeswax, buffalo tallow, and bear oil. It was Hardy's third trip upriver and the one before had profited him one thousand dollars. He believed that this cargo would nearly double that amount. It was his wife's first trip, and "she appeared as rugged as a bear and full as greasy when skined," Maley observed.

On their twentieth day they passed the mouth of Little River, where they spied their first buffaloes. After chasing one through the brush, Maley wrote that he was "crawling alive with ticks."

Shortly before arriving at the Cashotoo village, about ninety miles below the mouth of the Kiamichi River where lived the dozen Indians whom Maley had accompanied upriver, the Indians halted to don the new regalia they had had made at Natchitoches. Their costumes consisted of red-stripped calico shirts and scarlet leggings trimmed with blue ribbons. Silver bands ornamented their arms. They wore headbands, their faces were painted assorted colors, and they wore half-moon-shaped breastplates.

On March 29, twenty-four days out from Natchitoches, they reached the Cashotoo village, of about 1,800 Indians, on the south side of Red River. Although the young men were away on a hunt, the oldsters and women hastened to greet them. That evening a great feast was prepared for the returned members of the band and their three white travelers. Dumplings boiled and wrapped with corn shucks, hominy soup, and dried buffalo meat dipped in bear oil made up the menu.

While in the Cashotoo camp, Maley and his men prepared themselves for their long journey upriver into a land none of them had ever seen. They dressed deerskins to make themselves hunt-

ing shirts, leggings, and moccasins. Maley distributed his last two quarts of whisky among the Indians, gaining himself "great favours," and presented to the young women beads and handkerchiefs. The Indians demanded two of Maley's steel traps in trade for one of their pirogues for their journey upriver.

On the morning of April 6, Maley and his two companions bade good-by to the Cashotoos. The villagers brought them ground parched corn, hominy, white beans, and dried buffalo meat. They cautioned Maley that "it would be six days before we could find any game."

Forty miles above the Cashotoos' village they passed the village of the Caddoes, a tribe Maley estimated to number about thirty-five hundred persons. Two days later they reached the mouth of the Kiamichi River, famous for its beaver, Maley had been informed.

If Maley had been told anything about the reported silver mines on the Kiamichi by Sibley, who had written about them and had said that the French called the stream Mine River, Maley did not mention it in his journal. After two days' travel up the Kiamichi, Maley left his companions to trap beaver while he explored inward. With rifle, tomahawk, and side knife, he left early on the morning of April 12, traveling north.

On that sojourn he lived off wild turkey and even shot a buffalo. After several days' journey up that country Maley discovered a large bed of coal. One night he hung a piece of venison in a bush and was later awakened to see something jumping at the meat. He fired and downed the animal, to discover that it was a male panther. He cut off an ear to show his companions. After twelve days, Maley returned to his partners' camp, where they waited with thirty-five beaver skins and seven otter skins.

After three days' travel up Red River from the mouth of the Kiamichi the traders hid their canoe alongside the river and made a shelter for their skins. While Bradley remained at the camp, Maley and Cox journeyed overland toward the southwest. Some distance away "we found an extensive ridge of Iron ore," Maley wrote in his journal. On a high ridge they could view the country for thirty miles, and on the horizon they spied a sugar-loaf

19 stone seemed to be a soap stone I could cut
them with my knife without receiving any dam
age I made some elagant pipes out of them when
we came on the top of the mountain again I was
then particular in viewing this shaft in looking
down by laying on my belly I discovered the bottom
and also a drift out from the main shaft
not more then half the way down I supposed the
shaft to be about leo feet I was curious enough
to contrive a way to get down I cut an Indian ladder
long enough to reach down to the drift which after
putting it down I descended it without much diffi
culty got safe into the drift it was dark in there
did not venture in any distance it had a bad
scent much like burnt sulphur I was not satisfied

In 1812, five days' journey from Red River, atop a sugar-loaf peak, John Maley discovered an abandoned mine that he believed to be rich in silver. This page from Maley's long-obscure journal describes the mine he found in 1812. Yale University Library.

peak rising among a range of mountains toward the west-southwest. "I could not be satisfied till I had seen this Magnificent cone," Maley wrote.

They crossed a creek that ran rapidly toward the northeast and later that day killed a buffalo and "feasted on his marrow bone." Five days after leaving Red River, Maley and Cox reached the foot of their sugar-loaf peak, a mysterious mountain well into Spanish territory. As they climbed the mountain, they found "stone that were tumbled on heaps and of a light substance, burnt as it were like unto a honey comb." Then, he wrote "I discovered stone crusted over with virgin copper, and the red Iron ore in vast bodies." At the summit the mountain formed "a perfect point," where Maley, with a prospector's eye, discovered a mine

shaft six by ten feet square, so deep that he could not see the bottom. On one side a large mound of tailings showed that the mine had been sunk deep into the mountain. It was nearly sunset when Maley and Cox made their discovery—an ancient mine somewhere in the northern reaches of Spanish Texas. In need of water, they descended the opposite side of the mountain, where they found "virgin copper which was almost as mealable and soft as lead." Halfway down the mountain they found a spring of water with "a sweetish taste" and there camped for the night in a stand of oak, hickory, and pine.

The next morning they climbed the mountain on another side and stumbled onto the burned stone of a furnace, but "so much decayed and tumbled down" that no form remained of the ancient smelter abandoned by miners long before. Now more than ever Maley was determined to explore the mine shaft atop the peak.

Lying spread-eagled at the mouth of the shaft, he could make out the bottom and, halfway down, a drift into the mountain. He guessed the mine to be about sixty feet deep. Bent on getting into it, Maley "cut an Indian ladder long enough to reach down to the drift" and on that pole descended into the mine. Smelling a "bad scent much like burnt sulpher," he hurriedly climbed out of the mine to make a torch of splint pine and descended back into the hole. At the top of the shaft he found a vein of multicolored ore eighteen inches wide that made a forty-five degree angle to the drift, where it became a four-foot-wide vein of "solid ore of a red colour and very heavy, not hard."

Maley could see that the drift penetrated only about ten feet. He hacked off samples with his tomahawk and then climbed out of the shaft. He recorded that, like the white earth above the ore vein, the mine tailings outside tasted like alum. It would be some days before Maley would assay his discovery to find that he had chanced upon an almost pure vein of silver to which he would give the name New Potosí, after the famous Bolivian mountain of ore discovered by the Spaniards centuries before.

"After spending a half a day, I then began to think of a return," Maley wrote in his journal. "I took a full view of the country around me. The sight was delightfull. I could see as far as my eyes would let me."

Reluctantly the traders left their New Potosí and returned to Red River, where they arrived five days later and found Bradley with ten skinned beavers and an otter. He had killed a buffalo and "had all the meat handsomely dried." It would suffice them for another week.

On May 14 they loaded their furs into the canoe and renewed their journey up Red River. Several days upstream they viewed the two-mile-wide path of a tornado that had leveled or uprooted every tree in its path. The region harbored great numbers of bears.

In June they reached what they called the Salt

Branch (perhaps the Blue River) and traveled up it for two days. Cox remained in camp, while Maley and Bradley explored upstream traveling north-northwest. There they found numerous salt licks, where "the bufaloe had eaten away the clay in great gullies and the salt was perceiveable on the ground like a white frost." Acres of bleached bones of various animals, primarily buffaloes, covered the ground around the salt licks. Maley believed the animals had gone there to die of old age.

Two days' travel farther up the stream they reached the mountain that Maley believed they had spotted from atop New Potosí on the southeast. The rocks there "seemed as if the mountain had shook them all out of its bowels and thrown them on piles." Near the top Maley could view his New Potosí across Red River—"a very majestick appearance." While gathering samples of rocks, he found beds of iron ore. Three days later the men arrived back at camp and on June 24 again reached Red River.

Four days above the Salt Branch the trio spied a large force of Indians riding mules. The Indians rode down to the river and appeared eager to parley. Since they were armed only with bows and arrows, Maley and his companions pulled their canoe to shore. The natives ran to greet the whites, "shaking hands, slaping on their breasts, crying out Hyatan" (Comanche). About fifty men, women, and children greeted the trio. The tribe was well ornamented with silver—arm and headbands and breastplates. "They have more silver than they know what to do with which they have taken from the Spaniards by way laying them in the wilderness," Maley noted. The Indians told Maley that the Panis were two moons away, which he knew would be about two months at twenty miles a day.

The headwaters of Red River beckoned, as did those two additional chunks of supposed platina venerated by the Indians. The trio continued upstream for six weeks. The water level became so shallow that in places they were forced to pull their canoe. When it became impossible to proceed farther, they hid the pirogue in the brush, concealed their steel traps, and placed their furs on a scaffold ten feet high, covered for protection from the weather.

16 their is a good growth of timber here different kinds of oak and hickery mixt with some pine we rested comfortable that night and next morning I took a view of the branch that run from the spring and descending it I found in its bed earths of all denominations fullis [?]earth especially very plenty paints of all colours this will be of use some day this shews the riches that may be obtained in the bounds of the united states after taking something to eat we started to ascend the mountain again but took a different direction took a little round the mountain their we discovered an old works apparently a furnace built of a peculiar kind of stone such as would stand the fire but it was so much decayed and tumbled down that I could not see the form of it the

On a side of the sugar-loaf mountain, Maley reported finding the remains of an ancient smelter. Yale University Library.

Packing the remainder of their gear, they headed westward overland to the Panis villages upstream, where Anthony Glass had first learned of the magic stones that rang like a bell four years before. Traveling on the north side of the river, they encountered large herds of buffaloes. Five days' travel brought them to a boundless open prairie, where soon they were approached by a band of Panis riding "elegant fat horses." In sign language Maley told them that he wanted to trade. The Indians agreed to escort them to their village two days distant. Maley believed the village would be about three hundred miles above their pirogue, twelve hundred miles upriver from Natchitoches.

The Panis packed Maley's gear on their horses and insisted that he and his companions ride. The next day, on August 10, they reached the Wichita village just above the Illinois Bend where Red River runs almost north and south, on the opposite bank across from present Spanish Fort, Texas. Upon their arrival the villagers flocked "from all parts of the town" to eye the white visitors. Maley estimated that the village numbered about fifteen hundred persons.

Maley and his men were escorted to the chief, who lived near the center of the town. That evening the trio was entertained as the Indians blew their flutes and played a drum made from a "small hollow log" with "a raw deer skin stretched over one end." Then they feasted on "tompulla," fresh buffalo stew, and cornbread baked in ashes.

That night they slept in the chief's house, their beds of buffalo rugs atop a mat of interwoven cane. The next morning Maley presented to the

82

chief a gift of wampum, vermilion paint, and a small looking glass. He gave the young women beads, "which seem to please them very highly."

Maley communicated solely by sign language. While being escorted through the town by the chief, he noted the large numbers of both horses and mules. Perhaps owing to the lack of the good interpreter that Glass had had, Maley was not as impressed by the Panis as Glass had been. Noting that the Indians were "generally very nasty" and "their wigwams not so commodious as those of the other nations," he admitted, however, that "their mode of lodging is much better and also their cookery."

Through signs Maley inquired about mines in their country. The chief gestured that there had been others who had visited his village for that purpose and told of the two magic stones they possessed in the land southwest, but he demanded more goods for them than Maley by now possessed.

The chief agreed to show Maley and his companions the metal and dispatched five warriors to guide them. They crossed Red River and traveled three days southwestward "through an open broken country," where they found "large ledges of limestone but no signs of mineral." A few miles from a mountain they found the metal. When Maley expressed a desire to examine the mountain, "the Indians made signs that there was nothing there, but higher up Red River was plenty silver." Again those mysterious silver mines beckoned.

Upon returning to the Wichitas, Maley could not entice any of the Indians to guide him upriver for fear of the Osages. He left his goods with the chief, and the trio departed for Red River's headwaters, traveling up the north side of the stream. After three days' travel they reached a "very broken country, lands very poor, and timber scrubby."

When Maley spotted "some high knobbs at a distance," he steered his course in that direction and, on the fourth day from the Panis, reached a high ground, where he "had fair view of that shining mountain that I once made an attempt to get too when I was up the Arkansas." Maley was now viewing the Wichita Mountains, which he would spot from near Red River. His "shining

mountain" may have been Mount Scott, the conspicuous granite-clad peak of the Wichitas, roughly seventy-five miles due northwest of the Wichita Indian villages in southwestern Oklahoma.

Maley shifted his course "due west and struck the waters of Red River which I crossed over in several small branches." He was probably now on the North Fork of Red River, which for another forty years was believed to be the headwaters of Red.

"Now came in this mountain that I mentioned before," Maley continued. "It crowded the waters of Red River much to the north." Maley may have approached Navajoe Mountain, just west of the North Fork, or he may have been farther up, perhaps even at the mouth of Devil's Canyon, where the ruins of a Mexican mining settlement would later be found, for Maley recorded: "After traceing along the mountain for two days and examining every curriossity, I found some workings that I was not aquainted with. It was on a small creek that came out of the mountain, altho it formed a deep hollow with a flat of 100 yards." Was it the mouth of Devil's Canyon, the site where twenty years later traders would find Mexican miners? If so, the Spaniards had worked the streams earlier.

"I found piles of gravel and sand as if it had been washed," Maley noted in his journal. Just what kind of workings he had found Maley did not know until he discovered "a small flat dish made out of wood and also a shovel that they had made use of for digging up the gravel."

The pieces of the puzzle began to fall together. The diggings obviously had been abandoned not long before Maley arrived. He dug out some of the gravel and began washing it in the bowl in the fashion of a miner but detected nothing. He continued washing, shaking the sand away until "behold, then in the bottom, I discovered several particles of pure gold."

The threesome dug and washed in earnest the remainder of that day and all the next, collecting fifty pennyweights of gold dust and one small nugget weighing seven pennyweights. "I thought my fortune made," Maley wrote. Even though his efforts yielded only two and one-half ounces of gold—not unusual for panning in the right streams in the Wichitas—Maley was understandably optimistic in his belief in its potential yield: "Every branch or run of water we tried for gold, and found more or less in every place we took on the mountain. It abounds in minerals beyond anything I had seen yet."

Maley continually speaks of "the mountain," not disclosing that there were many mountains—a range sixty miles long. Probably intentionally, too, he failed to disclose the composition of these granite hills—a spectacular range rising like islands in a vast sea of prairie that would beckon gold seekers for almost the next one hundred years.

"After tracing on the top of the mountain," Maley wrote, "we found old diggings in abundance where the Spaniards had dug silver ore, but they now have avacuated and gone on their own boundaries."

Had Maley now found the silver lode boasted about for years by the Wichitas and Comanches? Had he found the ancient silver workings the French trader Brevel had seen when he heard "the thunder like cannon" while passing the region in 1765? Were these the silver mines clandestinely sought by Glass? Decades later old Mexicans would tell of a silver mine on Navajoe Mountain and, a few miles to the north, ancient workings in the Devil's Canyon region—old mines that would be found before and after the turn of the twentieth century.

Maley was so impressed by his discovery that he immediately made plans to return downriver and come back the next spring with sufficient supplies and mining tools. With Cox and Bradley he returned to the Wichita villages on Red River, traded their goods for mules, and traveled downstream to their pirogue and cached furs. Maley had not forgotten the two chunks of supposed platina on the plains and agreed with the Indians to return with suitable goods to make a trade the next spring.

Finding their cache of pelts safe, they packed them on their mules, leaving their pirogue and beaver traps behind to retrieve the next season. Traveling away from the river, they struck a course almost due east and held it for two months, when they struck an Indian trail that within a week took them to a settlement only seventy-five miles north of Natchitoches. Then, on November 10, nine

months and five days after leaving, they arrived at the frontier border settlement.

Maley sold his mules and journeyed downriver to Natchez, where he and his companions wintered. If he met the infamous Glass there, he made no mention of it. In Natchez, Maley told his own stories of gold and interested others in his return expedition. By spring none were yet outfitted to go, but agreed to follow later by river.

With fifteen hundred dollars' worth of trade goods for the Wichitas and mining tools and supplies, Maley and his two companions returned to Natchitoches, bought six Spanish horses, packed three of them, and on March 3, 1813, headed overland. They had traveled several weeks when they met three hunters killing buffaloes and robbing bees of their wax. The hunters warned Maley that the Osages were dangerous at that time of year. Though realizing the peril, Maley decided to risk the nearest route to the Wichita villages and set out across a vast prairie. It was now summer, and once, for want of water, the men shot a buffalo, cut its throat, and caught its blood in cups to drink.

Three days after Maley and his men left the hunters, a party of well-armed Indians rode up to them, dismounted, and pulled Maley and his men off their horses, crying, "Ozaazee!" (Osage). The Osages robbed the whites of everything they possessed except their knives, which were hidden on their bodies, and Maley's pocketbook. Maley judged they were then about six hundred miles from the nearest white inhabitants.

For four days they struggled back to the camp of the three hunters, with nothing to eat or to "moisten our throats." There they drank turkey soup, ate dried buffalo meat, and departed with a kettle and a hatchet. They traveled northeast ten days to the Ouachita River bottomlands of southern Arkansas, where they became lost in the wilderness and survived on root herbs, bark, and rattlesnakes. On the nineteenth day Cox was bitten by a copperhead and was left to die alone in cypress swamps alive with alligators. But he miraculously managed enough strength to continue on.

On the twenty-second day they found an Indian trace that led them to a Choctaw village fifteen miles from Ouachita Post, near present Monroe,

54 for digging up the gravel I took this bowl or dish and made an experiment I dug up some of the gravel where I ~~saw~~ discovered that they had dug and I washed it by shaking it about in the water after the mud was washed off I then took off the top gravel ~~with my hands~~ and examined it very closely but found nothing ~~then~~ I keep washing and (shaking of it till I had all the sand washed away behold then in the bottom I discovered several particles of pure gold then I thought my fortune made we then went to work knowing then what it was for we found several penny w weight we searched there that day and all next and we accumalated 50 dwt of pure gold one piece of 7 dwt the remainder in small grains then we were for seeing the country more extensively we took our apparatus for washing

Four days' journey northwest of the Wichita Indian villages Maley and his two companions discovered the placer diggings of Spanish miners. His journal reveals their excitement when they found fifty pennyweights of gold dust. Yale University Library.

Louisiana. They arrived on August 16, 1813, counting themselves lucky to be alive. Shortly afterward Cox and Bradley went their separate ways, while Maley joined a party boating up the Ouachita three hundred miles to the Hot Springs, where he explored the country alone for twenty-one days. He returned to Natchez on October 10, and from there traveled with a party to Nashville, Tennessee, where he wintered and virtually disappeared from the pages of history.

John Maley, the wanderer, had written a classic 180-page account of his odyssey on the plains. Perhaps all he had to show for his amazing adventures among the Indians was the five hundred dollars he received from a New York bookdealer for his incredible journal. The mystery is that his odyssey never saw printer's ink. Were it not for a scientist's inquiry about Red River's uncanny "magic stones" some years later, perhaps neither Maley's nor Glass's journal would have survived. Their long obscurity attests to their virtual concealment from the historian.

It is safe to assume that Maley's own stories of his bizarre Red River discoveries would lure adventurers up Red River for years to come. Had he not left stories of lost silver mines, even a Spanish gold placer far onto the Plains—perhaps Oklahoma's first lost gold mine?

It was some years after Glass's men retrieved the metallic mass that any reports were published on it. Not until 1824 did its complete story become known. In that year Benjamin Silliman, professor

Perhaps near what years later would be known as Devil's Canyon, Maley recorded that he and his partners found "old diggings in abundance where the Spaniards had dug silver ore." Yale University Library.

of chemistry and natural history at Yale College (now Yale University), reported it in the *American Journal of Science*, stating that, instead of platinum, the 1,635-pound metal was an iron meteorite.[27] A later analysis showed that it contained 90.02 per cent iron and 9.67 per cent nickel. From the Museum of the Lyceum of New York the meteorite traveled to Yale, where it was donated in 1835. The *American Journal of Science* that year reported that the meteor was "the largest piece in any collection in the world."[28] Today it rests in the university's Peabody Museum of Natural History.

Even so, two more meteorites beckoned hunters on the Plains, and the reports of platina did not cease, nor did those of silver mines. As late as 1819, George Schamp still believed that his prize,

retrieved almost a decade before, was platinum. Stories were afloat of a still "much larger" mass of precious metal to be had—a veritable "god of platinum" worshiped by the Comanches. So believed one party of early Texans, who had found a Comanche trader who had seen the metallic mass and agreed to guide them but died in 1824, before their expedition could get underway.[29]

In that year, too, Texan Daniel Shipman and several others fell in with "an old Red River hunter who told us he could take us to an inexhaustible silver mine."[30] Upstream from the Cross Timbers they forded Red River and after four days' travel southward reached the Brazos, but Indian sightings prevented them from reaching the mine.

As early as 1830, another Texan, David Edward, heard of the mass of metal on the headwaters of

86

the Brazos, "said to be several tons in weight, malleable and bright."[31] And in 1839, Mrs. Rachel Plummer, who had been held captive by the Comanches, revealed that she had seen the "large lump of platina" near the Brazos where "every year, the chiefs collect sacrifices, and offer them to this their God."[32]

At least one of the lesser masses of metal reported to Glass in 1808, and perhaps seen by Maley in 1812, was retrieved by Indian Agent Robert S. Neighbors in May, 1856. From Fort Belknap, in present Young County, Texas, Neighbors sent a government wagon to obtain the meteorite. It was found about sixty miles north of the Comanche Reserve, not far from Red River itself in present Wichita County, at latitude 33° 12' north and longitude 98° 40' west.

The Indians' high veneration for the metal had not lessened in the almost fifty years since Glass had visited the region. Believing the stone "possessed extraordinary curative virtues," they called it variously Ta-pic-ta-car-re (Standing Rock), Po-wisht-car-re (Standing Metal), and Po-a-cat-le-pi-le-car-re (Medicine Rock). "It was the custom of all who passed by to deposit upon it beads, arrowheads, tobacco, and other articles as offerings," Neighbors observed.[33]

The Comanches told Neighbors that the Spaniards had discovered the metal and "made several ineffectual attempts to remove it on pack mules." The Indians had attempted to melt the metal by building fires around it and, failing, "attempted to break it in pieces." It was believed to be "a kind of 'fetich' or object of worship . . . by the Indians who revered it as foreign to the earth and coming from the Great Spirit." Several Indian trails converged at the site, which indicated periodical visits to the transcendent wonder.

Elongated and pearlike, the meteorite measured two feet long, one foot wide, eight inches thick at the larger end, and four inches thick at the smaller. Into that relatively small volume was compacted 320 pounds of iron. Although it presented "a dark somewhat oily appearance," a freshly cut surface displayed "a bright silvery gray hue."

When the meteorite was hauled into the fort, the Comanches gathered in large numbers around their sacred stone, "manifesting their attachment by rubbing their arms, hands, and chests over it," begging Neighbors not to take it away from them. But, considering it of scientific importance, Neigh-

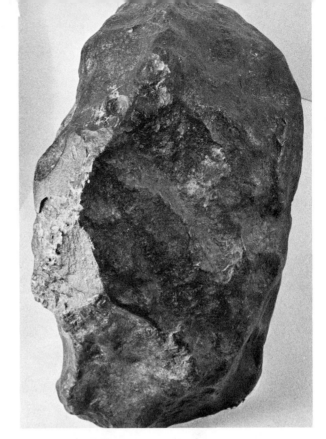

One of the two smaller venerated stones, first shown to Anthony Glass in 1808, was retrieved from near Red River in 1856. The 320-pound meteorite measures two feet long and one foot wide. Courtesy Texas Memorial Museum.

bors took it with him to San Antonio and shortly later presented it to the state capitol building, where it rested until the capitol burned in 1881.

Two years later, undamaged by the fire, the pear-shaped chunk of iron was turned over to the University of Texas, where today it is displayed in the Texas Memorial Museum. Similar in composition to Yale's specimen, it contains 89.99 per cent iron, 10 per cent nickel, and a trace of cobalt. It is believed that the meteorites formed a separate portion of the same meteoric fall at some time immemorial, unrecorded even in ancient Indian tradition.

Whether or not the third meteorite, reported to Anthony Glass in the wilderness over 160 years ago, yet remains to be found cannot be determined. It is known that sometime before 1860 a forty-pound meteorite was found in Denton County, Texas, so malleable that a blacksmith in McKinney wrought pieces of it into cane heads and other implements.[34]

Perhaps the third "magic stone" yet remains hidden somewhere on the plains. Its discovery would be a treasure in its own right.

Coronatto 1541. Photograph by William Mahan.

4. Oklahoma's Forgotten Treasure Trail

Even if there were no historical documentation mapping the ancient Spanish trail that led east from Santa Fe across western Oklahoma and down Red River to the Louisiana settlement of Natchitoches—over which treasure-laden packtrains and ox-drawn *carretas* once traveled—legends of lost gold would pinpoint the route of this treasure trail. It is by far Oklahoma's oldest highway of commerce.

Documentation does not always lie in dusty archives—assuming that all archival records can be believed. Human skeletons clad in rust-eaten armor, ancient weapons unearthed in plowed fields, a strange circle of eighteenth-century swords buried to their hilts, adobe and stone ruins of long-abandoned settlements, discarded ox yokes—all these testify to this ancient Spanish road that once crossed the parched plains and meandered down the Red River. All of the above and much more have been discovered alongside Oklahoma's treasure trail—and dead men's bones do not lie.

Oklahoma's oldest highway was noted on early maps as the Great Spanish Road to Red River and was called such by Major Stephen H. Long, who during his expedition of 1819–20 made the first map that charted the route.[1] Voluminous notes of a court case heard before the turn of the century and legends of lost gold agree on the route the ancient trace took as it led eastward from Santa Fe, down the north bank of the Canadian River, and across the Texas Panhandle into Oklahoma, where it dropped southward and struck the North Fork of Red River, passing down the east bank through the Wichita Mountains and by the mouth of Devil's Canyon—where both stories and ruins reveal that Spanish or Mexican miners once lived.

Crossing to the south bank of Red River just below the mouth of the North Fork, the Spanish road meandered its way downstream to the historic Red River settlement of Natchitoches, Louisiana, where all expeditions up the Red River once began. Not a few of those expeditions were in quest of lost Spanish mines—both gold and silver—reputedly lying somewhere up the Red River.

The trail that Pedro Vial blazed down Red River to Natchitoches in 1788 was not entirely the same route followed in later years by traders and treasure-laden packtrains, especially through Oklahoma, as eyewitness accounts show. Were it not for the famous Greer County court case of the 1890's, perhaps nothing would be known about Oklahoma's forgotten treasure trail down Red River—known to the earliest settlers as the Santa Fe–Natchitoches Trail.

The case upheld the claim of Oklahoma Territory to Greer County, which had also been claimed by Texas. In the two volumes of depositions taken during the case, *The United States* v. *The State of Texas*, are found the eyewitness testimony of early traders, soldiers, muleteers, miners, buffalo hunters, and, yes, the earliest treasure hunters, who acknowledged the ancient Spanish trail down Red River, the strings of packtrains that traveled it—and the bones of those found alongside it. As Grant Foreman correctly stated, in this "printed record of 1400 pages filed in the United States Supreme Court is compressed more historical material concerning Oklahoma otherwise unpublished and unknown than is to be found in any other printed document."[2]

These too-little-known and too-often-ignored chronicles are veritable mines of untapped information concerning the earliest travels through what was once Greer County, Texas—in present southwestern Oklahoma—as well as the Spanish road down Red River. "This testimony was offered for the purpose of showing that as the Mexicans had used this road through the future Greer County, it had long been considered part of New Spain and then Texas."[3] Before the United States Supreme Court decided in favor of Oklahoma in 1896, all the land west of the North Fork of Red River was encompassed in Greer County. All or part of four Oklahoma counties form that piece of land today.

One of the many who testified to having seen Mexican packtrains on the old Red River–Santa

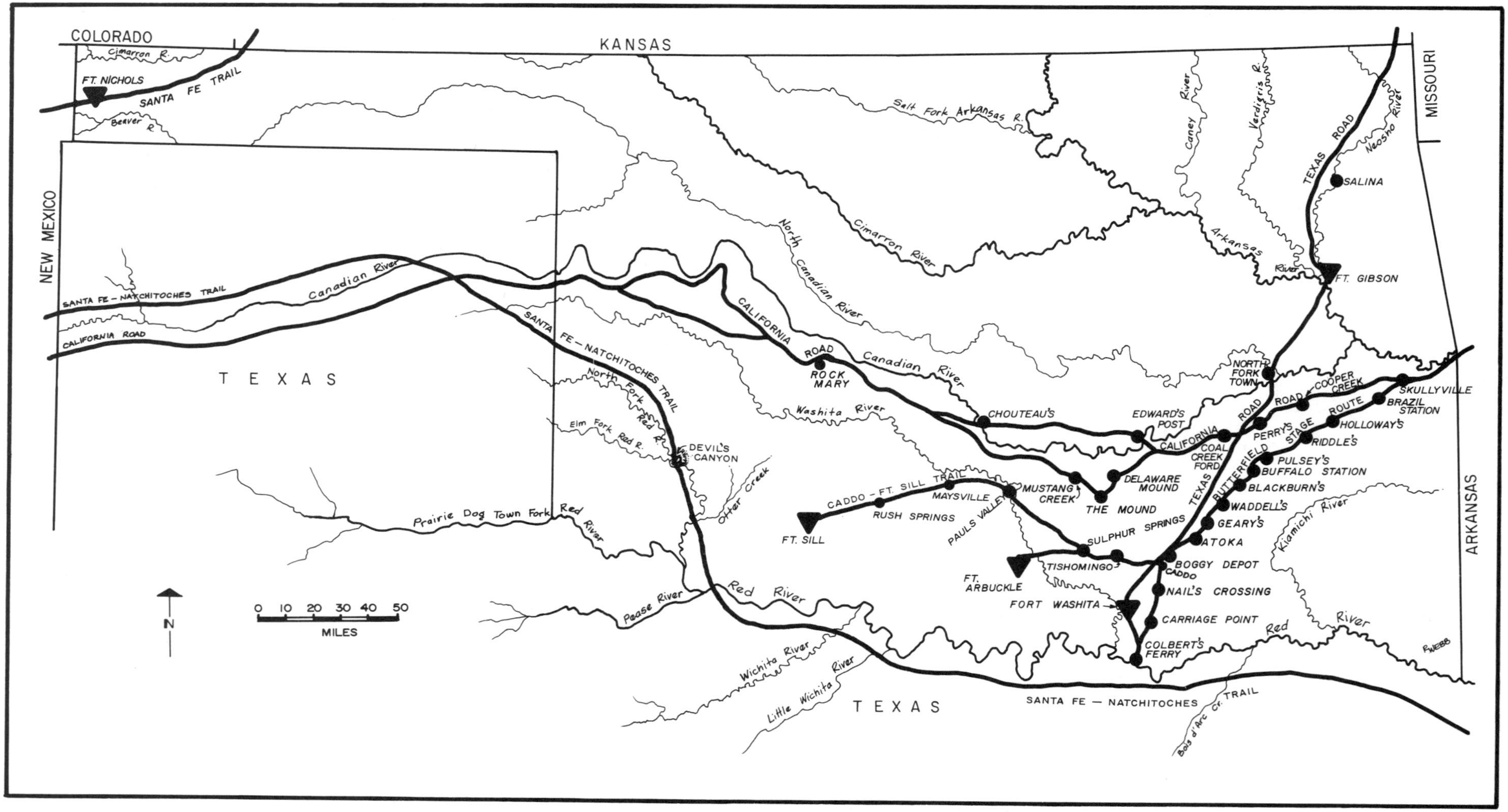
COLORADO
KANSAS
MISSOURI
NEW MEXICO
ARKANSAS
TEXAS
TEXAS
FT. NICHOLS
SANTA FE TRAIL
Cimarron R.
Beaver R.
Salt Fork Arkansas R.
Cimarron River
North Canadian River
Canadian River
Caney River
Verdigris R.
Neosho River
Arkansas River
TEXAS ROAD
SALINA
FT. GIBSON
SANTA FE – NATCHITOCHES TRAIL
CALIFORNIA ROAD
CALIFORNIA ROAD
ROCK MARY
Washita River
North Fork Red R.
Elm Fork Red R.
DEVIL'S CANYON
Otter Creek
Prairie Dog Town Fork Red River
Pease River
Red River
Wichita River
Little Wichita River
CHOUTEAU'S
EDWARD'S POST
NORTH FORK TOWN
COAL CREEK FORD
DELAWARE MOUND
MUSTANG CREEK
THE MOUND
CADDO – FT. SILL TRAIL
MAYSVILLE
RUSH SPRINGS
FT. SILL
PAULS VALLEY
SULPHUR SPRINGS
TISHOMINGO'S
FT. ARBUCKLE
FORT WASHITA
BOGGY DEPOT
CADDO
NAIL'S CROSSING
CARRIAGE POINT
COLBERT'S FERRY
ATOKA
GEARY'S
WADDELL'S
BLACKBURN'S
BUFFALO STATION
PULSEY'S
RIDDLE'S
HOLLOWAY'S
BRAZIL STATION
SKULLYVILLE
COOPER CREEK
PERRY'S
TEXAS ROAD
BUTTERFIELD STAGE ROUTE
Kiamichi River
Bois d'Arc Cr.
SANTA FE — NATCHITOCHES TRAIL
N
0 10 20 30 40 50
MILES
R. WEBB

Oklahoma trails

Fe Trail was seventy-nine-year-old Martin H. Ragsdale, a Paris, Texas, resident in 1893, when his deposition was recorded.[4] Ragsdale had first observed the ancient trace "in about 1819," when his family migrated from Tennessee to a farm three miles downstream from Jonesborough, in Red River County, Texas, only about fourteen miles or so from Fort Towson, in Indian Territory. At that early date, Ragsdale recalled, only seventeen families lived in the Red River country—in what later became Bowie, Red River, and Lamar counties. At that time the country was within the jurisdiction of Miller County, Arkansas.

Jonesborough and nearby Pecan Point—Texas' first Anglo-American settlements—became prominent centers for Red River traders. Jonesborough, founded just above the mouth of Lower Pine Creek and across Red River from Doaksville in the Choctaw Nation, became the county seat of Miller County in 1832, and for eleven years afterward reputedly served as the final destination for steamboat traffic on Red River.[5]

Ragsdale testified that there were actually two roads "called the Mexican trail from Santa Fe to Natchitoches." One almost paralleled the south bank of Red River near the Ragsdale farm, while the other was about thirty miles south of the river, although Ragsdale never saw Mexicans traveling the latter route.

He recalled seeing a large company of Mexican traders on the Red River Trail in 1824. They camped and watered their large remuda of mules and ponies at a water hole near their farm. "I learnt to count a hundred from them in Spanish," Ragsdale told attorney G. R. Freeman, who was questioning witnesses for the state of Texas. The Mexicans made the journey two or three times a year, he said, usually in the spring, when water was most plentiful.

Ragsdale was convinced that at least one bullion train from Santa Fe met its doom on Red River in present northwest Lamar County, Texas. It had become common knowledge that, sometime in 1816, a band of Osage or Comanche Indians had massacred a party of Mexicans and Frenchmen leading eleven mules with gold bullion from Santa Fe to Alexandria, Louisiana. Old settlers hunted the site for years. No one knew just where the

massacre had occurred until one Judge Rutherford moved to Texas in 1835 and cleared his land along Red River, about twenty-two miles from Paris. His plowing yielded eight musket barrels—all empty. Afterward many others were found, Ragsdale testified, along with "plenty of human bones." It had been believed that there were no survivors, but was later learned that three had escaped. A group of hunters formed a company and went to Louisiana, where they found the uncle of one of the survivors. He revealed that his nephew had died soon after the Indian attack and gave the men a copy of a "diagram" showing where the eleven mule loads of gold had been hidden, but no one had any luck following it.

Ragsdale himself first visited the massacre site about 1879, after having been told the story and given a copy of the diagram by George Wright, a member of the company who found the survivor's uncle—and probably the same George W. Wright who founded Paris in 1839.

Old-timers along Red River long told of a Mexican army officer who once camped in the region in later years, seeking the gold with a map he had received from a survivor of another such ill-fated party.[6] As late as 1900, Paris resident L. B. McDaniel found relics and human bones near Palmer Lake on the Crain farm northwest of Forest Chapel. And former Paris *News* editor Judge A. W. Neville knew of several human skeletons and gun barrels that had been plowed up in the area of Palmer Lake, once a slough of Red River, where many believed that buckskin bags of Mexican gold and silver were hidden.[7]

In still later years Horseshoe Lake drew similar search parties. Paris settler Ross Braden, who had sought the treasure for more than forty years, believed that seven burro loads of gold had been dumped into Horseshoe Lake near Ragtown, in northwest Lamar County.[8] During the 1920's he and other farmers in the area searched for two summers, but the quicksand in the shallow lake proved to be too great an obstacle. From thirty-one feet down they brought up a piece of buckskin in which Braden believed the gold was hidden, but no amount of fervor overcame the mud and quicksand.

Sixty-five-year-old J. M. Fort, also of Paris, was

another Tennessean who had migrated with his family to Texas. They arrived in the fall of 1836, settling in present Bowie County. He recollected the old trace paralleling Red River "known as the Santa Fe road," and recalled seeing Mexicans traveling it.[9] Fort stated that his family had traveled the "Santa Fe road" after they crossed Red River at Fulton, Arkansas, and had reached the highlands about twelve or fifteen miles from the Fulton crossing.

Thomas F. Roberts settled in Fannin County, Texas, in 1836. Roberts, another eyewitness who recalled seeing Mexican traders on the Red River Trail, was seventy-three when he added his story to the testimony in the Greer County case in 1893.[10] The year he entered Texas, Roberts observed the old road, "known as the Natchitoches and Santa Fe trail," up and down Red River across Fannin and Lamar counties. Roberts later traveled the old trace westward from Paris through Montague County. He remembered that the trail turned north to within about two miles of Red River as it approached the present western border of Fannin County and then led upstream.

The trail showed all the signs of "quite an old road," he recalled, for often it was washed out, and at many stream crossings it could no longer be used. On the prairie "it was considerably worn—beaten down," while through the timber it had left roots bare and often the bark worn away.

Roberts continued:

In '38, some twenty or twenty-five Mexican traders came down from Santa Fe, . . . down Red River into this section of country. They . . . went East and bought goods and shipped them up Red River to the mouth of Kiameshi, where they put them upon wagons and carried them across the plains to Chihuahua. The distance from Santa Fe to Chihuahua is something like 600 miles, and by going directly to Chihuahua they could cut off that distance. The distance from here to Chihuahua is nearly the same as the distance from here to Santa Fe. They made a new road.

In 1840, Roberts joined an expedition up Red River under the command of Colonel William G. Cooke of the Texas Regulars, who was trying to intercept traders bartering arms and ammunition with hostile Indians. The regulars traveled up the north bank of Red River and were furnished a guide by the well-known trader Colonel Holland Coffee. The guide, a half-blood named Jack Ivey, led the party a day's travel up what was then known as Red River—the present North Fork of that stream—and then crossed the stream and traveled down its south side to Prairie Dog River and then Plum River (which later came to be known as the Pease River).

Roberts pointed out that Indians had long been aware of the "Santa Fe road," for he was with Captain Randolph Marcy in the fall of 1849 when he crossed the Plains from El Paso. When they had traveled just above the mouth of the Clear Fork of the Brazos, above what later became Fort Belknap, a Comanche guide who wanted to return home asked permission to leave the party, stating that "there was an old road on Red river that he could go to from there that led to Santa Fe." Other Indians would tell them about that old road, which few frontiersmen had any knowledge of.

Richard Boren, of Montague County, Texas, sixty-eight years old in 1893, recounted settling in Lamar County in the fall of 1835. Almost from that time, he said, he had heard of the "old Santa Fe road" and had traveled it at various points along Red River from Honey Grove, in Fannin County, west to China Creek, due north of Harrold, in Wilbarger County.[11] He recalled that the road ran past Spanish Fort, the site of the ancient Taovaya villages, and within three or four miles of the mouth of the Big Wichita.

"It looked to be powerful old," Boren noted, adding that, three-quarters of a mile from his farm, where the ancient road crossed Belknap Creek, mesquite trees as large as stovepipes grew from the roadbed and that scarred ruts on either side showed plainly. "Mesquite, you know, is mighty slow growth," he commented.

Boren went on to tell of a group of more than one hundred who "called themselves Chihuahua traders" who traveled down the Red River road when he was fourteen or fifteen years old, about 1837 or 1838, and camped near the Boren farm in Lamar County, seven miles south of present Paris. Women were among the group, he recalled, some riding mules and others in carts with "great broad tires" pulled by steers and "hitched by what we call yokes, but they were just poles, just tied in front of the horns."

Boren was undoubtedly remembering the expedition of 1839, led by the well-known Chihuahua trader Dr. Henry Connelly, who headed a caravan of more than one hundred men—fifty of them Mexican dragoons—and about seven hundred mules and seven wagons conveying three hundred thousand dollars in gold and silver bullion and supplies. The muleteers blazed what came to be known as the Chihuahua Trail, having traveled from that distant Mexican city across the hostile plains to Red River. Like the Mexicans of 1824, they appear to have headquartered near Jonesborough.[12]

Connelly's Chihuahua traders caused no small amount of excitement in the frontier settlements. Their bullion shipment was announced in the *Arkansas State Gazette* of August 14, 1839, which revealed that the Mexican treasure had just been sold in New Orleans after making the long overland journey.

The traders had left Chihuahua on April 3, 1839. Their return trip began in April one year later. The party had increased to about 225 men, including the dragoon escort, and there were sixty to seventy wagons heavy with merchandise. Perhaps Boren did not remember that what may have been the first American circus to tour Mexico also accompanied that return trip across the Texas plains. The circus riders and Connelly's sprawling caravan must have made an impressive sight to the north Texas settlers of the day.[13]

R. H. Burnett, a Greer County farmer who turned sixty-seven a month before he gave testimony in the famous court case, originally had settled at Pinhook, Texas—later to be known as Paris—in the winter of 1839. Burnett recounted that in the fall of 1848 he had joined a company of sixty or so men under M. T. Johnson, from Dallas County, scouting for Indians.

Burnett had known about "the old Spanish trail" ever since he had lived at Paris, but while he was with Johnson's company, they struck the road near Spanish Fort and followed it almost to the mouth of the Pease River.[14] Burnett was sure that it led no farther west from that point, or farther up the Prairie Dog Fork, for they rode up that stream

some distance before traveling south to a tributary of the Pease, where all of Johnson's men lost their horses when Indians "backed us up into a hollow and we had to leave them."

Burnett pointed out, too, that Mexican traders were traveling the road as late as 1848, for at Spanish Fort they found a Mexican train of ox-drawn carts and mule-drawn wagons. These traders were perhaps the last to traverse the Red River Trail, for in that year all of the Mexican southwest became part of the United States at the conclusion of the Mexican War.

Because of the gold and silver transported over the ancient road, it is little wonder that practically every tributary up and down Red River bears a tale of so many burro or jack loads of gold hidden before an Indian attack. And it is not so surprising that the treasure tales coincide with the eyewitness accounts of the route the Red River Trail took to Santa Fe. The tales alone could virtually trace the path of the long-forgotten trail even if there were no documented knowledge of its existence.

Because of the lucrative trading possibilities with the Plains Indians—and perhaps because of the increase in traffic over the Santa Fe–Natchitoches Trail down Red River—American traders launched expeditions up Red River in 1833 with the purpose of establishing trading posts. Holland Coffee and Silas Colville led the first in the spring of 1833 from Fort Smith, Arkansas. Their party of forty men chose a once-inhabited site just below the junction of the North Fork and Red River in present southwestern Tillman County, Oklahoma.[15] It was evident that nearby had once passed an old trail, its scars from large wooden wheels still plain to the eye. Coffee had not been the first to build a post there, believed Simon N. Cockrell, a hunter in the expedition, for near the site he chose lay the crumbled ruins of a log house and stone chimney.[16] It may have served early Mexican or French traders. Its ruins were not the last to be found.

In the following years Coffee built three more such posts, one on Walnut Bayou, on the north side of Red River in Love County, and another, in March, 1836, at the mouth of Cache Creek, in Cotton County. Both posts later served as trading houses for Abel Warren, whose trading ventures continued until 1848.[17]

Coffee established his fourth and final trading post—sometimes known as Coffee's Fort—in 1836–37 alongside the old Chihuahua Trail on the top of a hill overlooking Red River on the north, about eleven miles northwest of present-day Denison, in Grayson County, Texas. Coffee built his post, enclosed with a high stockade one hundred feet square, near an ancient Indian trail that crossed Red River at Rock Bluff, a natural ford in an otherwise steep bluff that became a major route into central Texas after Colonel William G. Cooke completed a military road across the Texas Republic to that point in 1840. Across the river a few miles to the north Fort Washita was founded in 1842.[18]

Riverboats ferried goods to Fort Towson, downstream, and for a time when there was sufficient water upstream to Preston, near Coffee's Trading House. There Coffee built a plantation of almost four thousand acres and in 1839 brought his bride, Sophia Suttenfield, who was said to have nursed Sam Houston at the Battle of San Jacinto. In time Coffee built his wife a two-story double-log mansion with massive stone chimneys at either end and broad porches at front and back, upstairs and down, running the full length of the house. Known as Glen Eden, the home was frequented by innumerable notables of the day, among them Sam Houston and young officers from nearby Fort Washita, Robert E. Lee, Ulysses S. Grant, and Fitzhugh Lee. The historic site was inundated in 1942 by the man-made Lake Texoma.

In 1836 twenty-two-year-old Abel Warren erected a trading post on the Texas side of Red River in the extreme northwest corner of Fannin County, a mile below the mouth of Choctaw Bayou. Constructed in frontier fashion, his post was surrounded by a strong, heavy wooden palisade—about two hundred feet square—of upright logs fifteen feet high. A two-story bastion, or log tower, about twelve feet square stood at each corner and was furnished with sleeping bunks and a dozen muskets with plenty of buckshot. "On two sides of the enclosure were strong gates for admission of stock and wagon trains," wrote one chronicler.[19] "Sheds and warehouses were on the inside walls . . . and a corral for stock on the prairie outside."

Warren's first trading house was a financial failure. About 1839 he bought the two Coffee posts upstream. Most often referred to as Warren's Trading Post, Coffee's Cache Creek fortification was similar to the first one Warren had built, except that the four gun towers stood at each corner of a large double-log building within the stockade. It was abandoned in the late 1840's. Indians may have burned the post, for its exact location—like that of most of the others—is unknown today.[20]

Like the Spaniards, Mexican traders left their tales of lost gold, and Warren's Trading Post was no exception. Once, in the early 1900's, seekers with a "Mexican map" earnestly hunted the site of the old fort and its supposed hidden cache.[21] Relics may yet reveal the lost site, somewhere in the area ten miles south of Temple.

Even though most of the treasure tales along the old Red River Trail are attributed to the Spaniards or Mexicans—often no distinction made—who traveled this early route before Anglo-American intrusion, not all the legends were a result of Indian forays or massacres. At least one story arose from an 1843 expedition made with the sanction of the government of the Republic of Texas to raid a rich Mexican packtrain traveling from St. Louis to Santa Fe across the upper portion of what was then Texas.

Organized by Colonel Jacob Snively, a staff officer under two Texas presidents, about 180 young adventurers from the north Texas settlements rendezvoused at Fort Johnson, near Coffee's Fort in Grayson County. In April, 1843, Snively's "Battalion of Invincibles" struck west up Red River along the Chihuahua Trail, crossed into present-day Oklahoma below the mouth of the Wichita River, and skirted the western end of the Wichita Mountains. Colonel Snively's planned raid on the Mexican caravans was halted on the Arkansas River when United States dragoons intervened in behalf of the Mexicans. Snively and his men returned to Bird's Fort, on the Trinity River. It was during that return trip to Texas that Snively—probably unknowingly—contributed to the Red River treasure lore.

According to the story told by a veteran Texas Ranger, a rich Mexican caravan was traveling across Texas en route to St. Louis late in the summer when Colonel Snively's army was re-

In 1928 only stone chimneys remained of Fort Towson, established in 1824 near Red River in Choctaw County. Courtesy Western History Collections, University of Oklahoma Library.

turning to the north Texas settlements.[22] A detachment of Texas Rangers accompanied the Mexicans, although they remained almost a day's travel behind the train. At Red River the Mexican train was to be met by United States troops, but when the advance scout reached the river, he spied two riders heading toward him in a most uncustomary manner. Aware of the Snively Expedition and its intent, the scout promptly concluded that the riders were part of the already

branded Snively "land pirates" and galloped back to the train to report as much.

Convinced that the Texas Rangers would support the Snively gang, the Mexicans decided to bury their treasure. Quickly they chose three hills that appeared on a direct line beginning "about a mile south of a cottonwood tree" growing on Red River just below "an old Spanish crossing." On the first hill was buried five hundred dollars in gold. On top of the "next hill south" was buried

An artist's conception of Warren's Trading Post, built at the mouth of Cache Creek in 1836. Similar trading houses were established by Holland Coffee and Abel Warren on both sides of Red River. Drawing by Lee Adams. Courtesy Hugh Corwin.

five hundred dollars more. Both were to serve as shallow markers to the third hill, on which was buried the remainder of the treasure. Afterward the wagons were destroyed, and the Mexicans headed for the Río Grande. Ever since that time many have sought the old Spanish crossing on Red River and the "line of three hills to the south," the first only a mile from the river.[23]

Had Colonel Snively known that he had generated such a treasure burial, he no doubt would have stayed on Red River until he found the spoils, for already he was making plans to find a Spanish silver mine in south Texas reported to him by a Mexican captured near the Arkansas River. Snively was to become one of the Southwest's first lost-mine seekers and further contributed to lost-mine lore by losing a legendary mine of his own in the Eagle Mountains of southwest Texas.[24]

While Colonel Snively was returning from his abortive raid on the Arkansas, another group of Texans was crossing Red River and hunting Comanches in the Wichita Mountains seeking a peace treaty. Hamilton P. Bee, of San Antonio, was a member of that party, and his testimony in the Greer County case in 1893 shed more light on the antiquity of the Red River Trail.[25]

When he gave his testimony, Bee was seventy-

one years old. He had been a Texan since 1837, a member of the legislature, speaker of the House of Representatives, a lieutenant in the Mexican War, and a brigadier general in the Confederacy. In the spring of 1843, Bee accompanied Colonel J. C. Eldredge, commissioner of Indian affairs of the Republic of Texas, on an expedition to make treaties with the tribes on the northern frontier. Guiding the expedition were three Delaware Indians, Jim Shaw, John Conner, and Jim Secondeye, all selected by President Sam Houston himself.

Bee recalled that his party followed for many miles the trail of the Texan–Santa Fe Expedition of 1841, which almost ended in tragedy on the west Texas plains; the survivors were captured by Mexican troops and imprisoned near Mexico City. Bee remembered that the trail was "distinctly marked" by the refuse of its camps, including a blacksmith's forge. He recalled, too, an ironic statement made by the Delaware Jim Shaw, who had watched the 321 "Santa Fe Pioneers" when they mistook the Wichita for the Red River and trudged hungrily westward into the desolate Llano Estacado, where many died of thirst or were killed by Indians. Bee said:

Upon [our] arriving at a commanding hill approaching the valley of the Red river the trail of the Santa Fe expedition turned to the left, in the direction of a strip of timber which we were told was the Wichita River. Jim Shaw remarked to me at that time and at that place, "With two other men I stood in that mott of timber and saw the expedition turn towards the Wichita, and if I had not been afraid I would have gone to their camp and I could have guided them through a road that would have taken them direct to Santa Fe."

Had he done so, the annals of Texas history might have been greatly altered.

Bee revealed that he had kept a daily journal of his 1843 journey, but he declined to present it to the court, "for the reason that it contains other matter of a political and private nature concerning those now dead." Today his journal is a cherished family heirloom.

Bee's party traveled up Cache Creek to just southeast of the Wichita Mountains, where they found a village of Wichita Indians. From there they traveled northwest and for two days and nights were without water. After "some twenty days" on the plains, the party returned to the Wichita encampment and crossed back into Texas at Warren's Trading House, near the mouth of Cache Creek.

What mysteries lie beside the old Santa Fe Trail down Red River? Perhaps the Indians foresaw the advantages of remaining silent about the road to Santa Fe, a road blazed and traveled by foreigners of yore.

Treasure hunting in Oklahoma is not a new avocation. It provided the incentive for many of the earliest expeditions into the region. Texans made what may have been the first search in the Wichita Mountains in 1849. A Mexican War veteran, Thomas K. Carmack, joined a company of eighty men that summer to hunt Mexican gold mines on the upper waters of Red River.[26] A man named Loving had been given a "waybill" to the purported gold mines by a "very old Mexican." Carmack had learned that the Mexican miners had smelted the gold into bars at the Red River mine and were transporting it in bearskins downstream "about sixty miles below the mines" when they were attacked by Indians and forced to dispose of it in a pond or lake on the river.

Men throughout the north Texas settlements joined the treasure hunt, rendezvousing near present Gainesville, Texas, where they elected Robert McFail captain of the company. The party, equipped for a six months' outing, traveled up the Red River Trail, which the men called "the old Santa Fe trail," by now so dim that it was often difficult to trace. Like all Texans of the time, they considered the North Fork the headwaters of Red River and the South Fork, or mainstream, as Prairie Dog River.

Although Carmack was somewhat unclear in his testimony in the Greer County case, it seems that most of the gold seekers did not travel above the confluence of the forks but instead hunted for the mine at a place "where the water ran out of the hill" from which they could see the Wichita Mountains on the north. Although Carmack did not find the mine, nearby were signs that there had been "something like an old furnace there some time, and we decided that that was the place."

Carmack recalled that twenty-one of his party crossed Red River to explore farther up. When they reached the Wichita Mountains, they were taken captive by Indians. They were held four days before being freed, and when they finally rejoined the main body on Red River, the gold seekers abandoned the search and returned home. Carmack was not the last to find what he believed to be a smelter on Red River, nor was his party the last to search for lost gold on that stream.

The summer of 1849 brought considerable gold excitement in the Wichita Mountains, which were then a part of the Choctaw-Chickasaw Nation. In May a party left Clarksville, Texas, en route to the Wichitas. Their agenda included searching for twenty-seven mule loads of gold bullion hidden near the mouth of the Little Wichita River near "a huge boulder,"[27] where in later years the adobe ruins of a settlement were reported found.

The gold seekers returned to Clarksville and left no surviving account of their expedition into the Wichitas. The local paper, the *Northern Standard*, disclosed that much secrecy had shrouded certain Clarksville citizens while they were preparing to depart to search for "gold, pure and in considerable pieces," which had earlier been "brought in from the Wichitas by some Indian or Indians."[28]

Cattleman W. E. Gates was another who had followed what he knew to be called the old Spanish trail—or perhaps a branch of it—through the Wichita Mountains.[29] He remembered that it crossed Otter Creek about six miles upstream from its confluence with the North Fork, skirted Granite Mountain, passed through a gap near the Narrows on Otter Creek, and led northwest up Elk Creek through the mountains to Elm Creek. Gates had traveled the route no farther but had found articles discarded by wayfarers in years past.

It was on Otter Creek that settler Corwin Adams discovered a human skeleton at the base of a large tree on his farm nine miles northeast of Tipton, interred with a stiletto and several Spanish coins. In later years, while digging a cellar, he found two more graves. The legend that a Spanish packtrain was massacred there cannot be scoffed at. Obviously three met their doom.

Other strange ruins of stone and adobe were discovered alongside the old Spanish trace as it meandered through the Texas Panhandle and down the North Fork of Red River and its mainstream. Many are the accounts of the Mexican miners' settlement in Devil's Canyon at its confluence with the North Fork on the western end of the Wichita Mountains (so much that the Cañon Diablo demands a chapter all its own). And in 1895 the discovery of the ruins of a town and fortress drew such excitement that a surveyor's plat of it made the front page of the Cloud Chief (Washita County) *Herald-Sentinel.* These ruins, said to have been the Mexican mining settlement of Cascorillo, also require a chapter. The Greer County testimony, rich with the recollections of those in a position to know, is the only record of these almost forgotten ruins.

Greer County cattleman George W. Briggs came across the ruins when few other white persons lived along the North Fork. As early as 1879 he was herding seventy thousand head of cattle for Dan Waggoner and Sons along the South Fork. Briggs was familiar with the road that he had always heard called "the old Santa Fe trail" leading up the North Fork.[30] He recalled that the trail crossed into Oklahoma about six miles below the junction of the Red and Pease rivers, and then led up the east side of the North Fork, crossed into Greer County

at the mouth of Otter Creek, and skirted the west side of Navajoe Mountain about fifteen miles east of Altus. The road then again crossed the North Fork, led north about eighteen miles, turned westerly, passing "up between Elk creek and the North fork of Red river right along the divide," and crossed the Texas Panhandle "about eighteen to twenty-five miles north of Mobeetie in Wheeler county." From there Briggs had traveled no farther westward.

But he had learned that the Indians had long known about the road to Santa Fe, and had passed that knowledge down from generation to generation. Once, about 1880, Briggs and the celebrated Comanche chief Quanah Parker rode together along part of the trail. "He told me that the trail was made before he could remember anything about it," Briggs reported. "He said he had heard his forefathers talk about when people used to travel there. . . . He did not call it the Santa Fe trail, but said it was the old trail that went into Mexico and went into Texas—he did not know where."

Briggs had heard other stories from old Kiowa Indians, who told of mines in the Wichita Mountains worked for a time by the Spaniards, who would then return whence they came. He had always heard that the old Spanish settlement was at the mouth of Devil's Canyon, four miles below the junction of Elm Creek and the North Fork. When he first found the ruins, only "cedar logs and posts buried in the ground" remained.

Briggs had heard two versions of what became of the last Spanish inhabitants. Indians had told him that "nearly all that colony was killed by the Kiowa and Comanche nearly right north of here, about two miles north of the North Fork, at what is called Cedar Top Mountain," twenty miles or so upstream from Devil's Canyon. Another story had it that "they were killed there near the old mine," Briggs said.

Briggs found the ruins of two stone fortifications up the North Fork, both on the west side of the river. One lay within three hundred yards of his house, about three-quarters of a mile from the river, while the other lay twenty miles upstream, closer to the river, two miles above the mouth of Spring Creek.

The circular fortification near Briggs's home—

about twelve miles west of present-day Hobart—appeared about six feet high and three hundred feet in diameter. "There are a whole lot of old graves there, too, . . . depressions there in the ground about the length and breadth of a grave," he said. "Looks to be from anywhere from fifty to one hundred years old." Briggs recalled having found "lots of pieces of glass, broken plates, Indian spear heads," and even champagne bottles within the stone structure. These ruins would probably have been found about five miles downstream from the storied Cedar Top Mountain (in S.32, T.7N., R.20W.), where the Spanish miners were supposedly massacred. No one knew who had occupied the strange, fortresslike structure.

Briggs was not the last to come upon these mysterious "forts" along the North Fork. S. C. Talley, Sr., who lived near Mangum in 1892, also found crude breastworks "resembling a circus ring, though much larger, on the south bank of North fork about two miles above the mouth of Spring creek."[31] About eighteen miles upstream from the ruins on Briggs's ranch, this strange structure of stone above Spring Creek was probably about three miles south and three miles west of Carter (in S.7, T.8N., R.22W.).

Talley went on to relate that Preston Bell, who lived on Spring Creek, had told him about an old Kiowa Indian who once revealed that his tribe had "fought the white people there for three days" before finally killing them all. The old Indian claimed that "they had shot into his tepee and killed two of his papooses." As nearly as the Indian could remember, the battle had occurred when Lone Wolf, chief of the Kiowas, was only a baby.

Shortly after the turn of the century a farmer named Lee Castillo found more than a dozen bleached skulls on his land about a mile south of the stone ruins above the mouth of Spring Creek (in S.18, T.8N., R.22W.). A mere coincidence? Perhaps. Or perhaps the victims of the Kiowas?

James T. Pollard was another early traveler who testified to having found these mysterious ruins. Fifty-eight years old and a resident of Greer County in 1892, he had made numerous early expeditions into the Wichita Mountains as a Texas Ranger and Indian fighter long before Greer County was settled.[32] Pollard first saw the country in 1859 when

he joined an expedition from Fannin County searching for traces of the ill-fated Ryan and Alexander wagon train that had left Clarksville for California more than ten years before and disappeared up the North Fork of Red River (see Chapter 8). In 1860, Pollard was a member of the Young County militia attached to Ross's Rangers, who scouted for Indians on the Pease, South Fork, and North Fork in the Wichita Mountains.[33] Two years later he again traveled up the North Fork into the mountains with James Buckner "Buck" Barry's regiment of Texas Indian fighters. On his travels up Red River, Pollard found adobe ruins near the mouth of the Little Wichita north of present Ringgold, Texas—the same location at which Texans had searched for lost Spanish gold in 1849. Later he found the ruins at the three sites in Greer County on the North Fork reported by George Briggs.

Some years before, Pollard had been told of the mining settlement in Devil's Canyon by two captives whose families had been killed there. He recalled:

There were two old Mexicans, very old Mexicans, from around Ft. Sill that frequently stopped at Doan's [Store], and they claimed to have been captured by the Indians when they were boys and were raised up by the Indians, by the Comanche Indians, and they said they were living there [Devil's Canyon] and were captured right there at that place by the Indians. That was the first way the people found out, was by the reports of these old Mexicans, who told where they had mined and about the old mining camp. That is what I learned from the people. That is why they went to look at it and found it.

Near the canyon Pollard had found many strange symbols engraved on the trees. "I do not know what they were," he admitted, "but I have seen the same character marks on the Spanish brand of horses."

Two or three miles upstream from Devil's Canyon, on the west side of the North Fork, Pollard had found an old shaft about eighteen feet deep and "some picks and a part of a crucible and several things that showed them to be Mexican miners." The crucible "looked like it had been heated," he recalled. As Pollard testified in the Greer County case in Mangum, he stated that he could see "the mountain from here where the

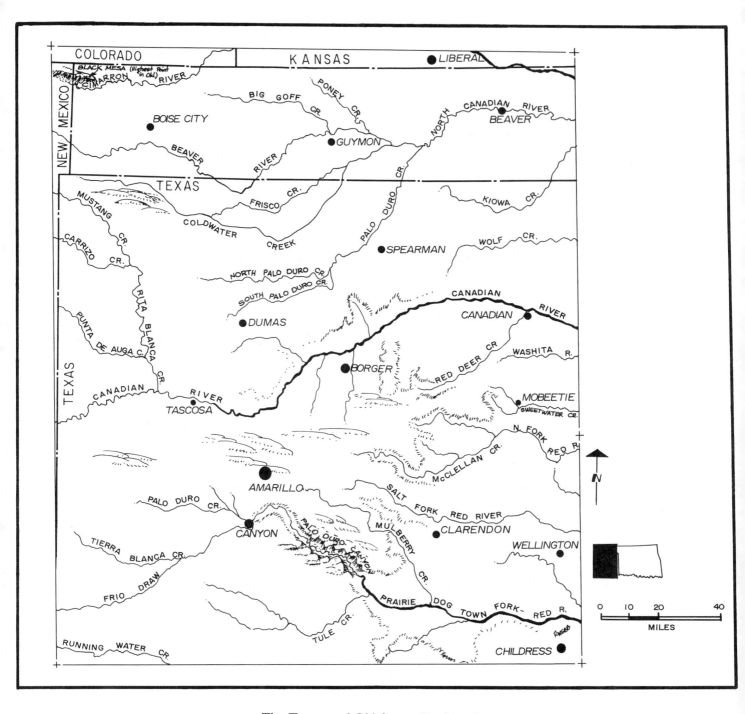

The Texas and Oklahoma Panhandles

shaft is." He had found no signs of a smelter at the old mine but had discovered one on Red River near a copper mine ten or twelve miles upstream from Spanish Fort—perhaps the same mine and smelter ruins found by Thomas K. Carmack in 1849.

When he was a boy living in Hopkins County, Texas, Pollard knew of the ancient road "called the Natchitoches and Santa Fe trail." That trail "is plain and can be seen today," he said, at Cedar Top Mountain, "where it goes over the gravelly point," adding that "there are several graves there," as there were at the fortification on George Briggs's ranch about five miles downstream.

Pollard had examined much of Greer County while he was county surveyor for two years, and,

100

although he had not seen any ruins on the trail where it crossed Red River into Oklahoma, he had heard that "an old Spanish fort" had been found "near old Camp Augur," about nine miles southwest of present Grandfield, Oklahoma. At the time, Pollard testified to the court, he lived within two and a half miles of George Briggs's ranch and had seen the ruins nearby. He believed they were "more of a fort" than a settlement. He had also seen the similar ruins above the mouth of Spring Creek.

Other settlers had come across equally strange ruins alongside the Spanish trail as it led westward across the Texas Panhandle. W. B. Kiser, who settled in Greer County in 1884, had never followed the road across the Panhandle to Santa Fe, but he believed—as did George Briggs—that it was the same trail that he had found in Hemphill County, Texas, about twenty miles northeast of Mobeetie. He recalled, too, having found stone foundation ruins in the brakes of Wolf Creek north of the Canadian:

They appear to be more sand hills at first, but when you come to examine them you find the old stone walls coming and cropping out of the places above the ground. The mounds as they stand now are around in the position that would indicate that there had been a town laid off in a square, with a much larger building than any other near the center of the square.[34]

When Kiser had last visited the ruins in 1885, they appeared to cover an area of more than 150 square yards. He had been told about the ruins some time before, and once, while freighting between Dodge City and Fort Elliott, he lost several cattle near the Wolf Creek brakes and happened upon the forgotten town.

The ruins Kiser chanced upon were not Spanish but those of a Pueblo culture, Indians who constructed multiroomed buildings of stone and adobe and lived in the Canadian River valley some time between A.D. 1200 and 1400. Kiser's discovery, which later became known as the Buried City, was on the Jim Fryer ranch in east-central Ochiltree County, Texas.[35]

Similar ruins have been found throughout the Canadian Valley on promontories, mesa tops, and river terraces. Often they covered several acres or extended along a ridge for a mile or more. The Canadian Valley, archaeologists say, "served as a trade route between Puebloans and Plains Indians."[36] The ancient apartment dwellers had disappeared long before Coronado and his conquistadors crossed the region in 1541. Found only in that part of Texas, the stone and adobe buildings were mortared and caulked with caliche, assuring their survival for centuries to come.

In 1893, E. R. Fletcher testified that he had found the foundations of adobe walls about four and a half miles southwest of old Tascosa, near Parker Creek in Oldham County, Texas.[37] Fletcher recalled finding pieces of broken earthenware among ruins that covered about an acre of ground. Near Fletcher's discovery are still other Pueblo ruins extending westward through the Panhandle. One ruin—perhaps the one that Fletcher found—just south of the Canadian, is known as the Saddleback Ruin. It was built on the top of a saddlelike mesa, with a superb vantage of the land around. Archaeological excavation in one building alone disclosed thirty-three rooms, yielding such artifacts as clay and soapstone pipes, turquoise pendants, shell beads, bone necklaces, and thousands of potsherds.[38]

Many Spanish artifacts have been found along the old Santa Fe–Natchitoches Trail as it wound its way across the scorched Llano Estacado. Indeed, numerous Spanish conquistadors once trod this land—the Canadian Valley provided a natural route across the parched plains. Among those bold cavaliers was Francisco Vásquez de Coronado, who left his name carved in rock near the confluence of Carrizzo Creek and the Cimarron River north of Kenton, in the Oklahoma Panhandle. Although it may have been engraved by an Italian member of the expedition (for it is spelled in the Italian form) the ancient inscription "Coronatto 1541" can yet be seen in a region bearing even older Indian rock art.[39]

Others who marched into this region were the mutineers Francisco Leyva de Bonilla and Antonio Gutiérrez de Humaña in 1594; Vicente de Zaldivar in 1598; Juan de Oñate in 1601; Alonzo Vaca in 1634; Juan Paez Hurtado in 1715; Pedro de Villasur in 1720; and, of course, the members of the expeditions of Vial, Francisco Xavier Fragoso, and José Mares between 1786 and 1789.[40]

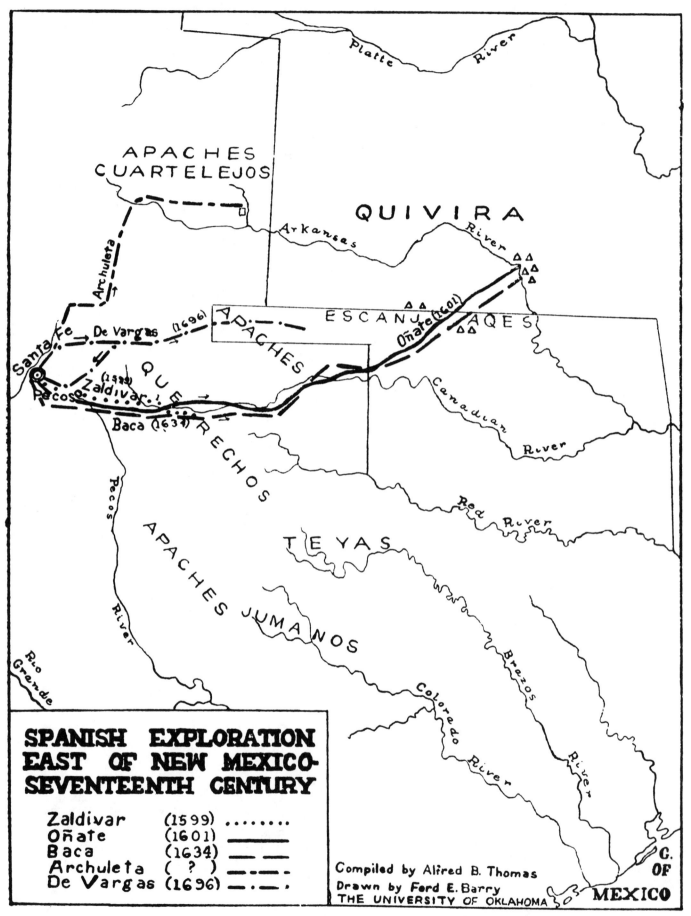

A map of seventeenth-century Spanish exploration east of New Mexico. Courtesy Oklahoma Historical Society.

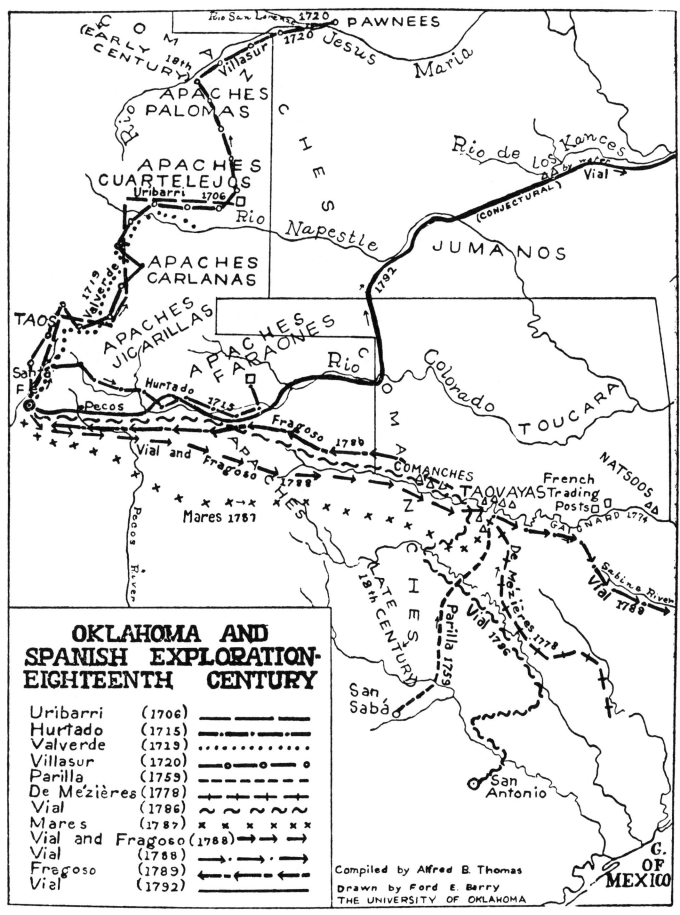

A map of eighteenth-century Spanish exploration of Oklahoma and Texas. Courtesy Oklahoma Historical Society.

Italian in spelling, and probably carved by an Italian member of the Coronado Expedition, the first Spanish conquistador in the Southwest left his "calling card" in a small cave near the Cimarron River in the Black Mesa. The weathered inscription reads "Coronatto 1541." A later explorer carved his initials, "H. G.," below it and the date 1877. Photograph by William Mahan.

The last Spanish army to look upon the plains was that of Captain Francisco Amangual, who in 1810 found the ruins of "a circular palisade of pickets and moat with one small bastion in the center" near the Canadian River north of present Amarillo. Interestingly, Amangual met Pedro Vial while he was once again in that country.[41]

It was along the Canadian River through eastern New Mexico and the Texas Panhandle that other early travelers found remains of the Spanish trail that led to Red River and down that stream to Natchitoches. On his expedition from Bent's Fort to St. Louis in 1845, Lieutenant J. W. Abert encountered the road a few miles below the junction of the Canadian and the Conchos rivers in eastern New Mexico. "Although faint," Abert recorded in his journal, "it could be distinguished by the color of the grass which grew upon it."[42]

Soon afterward Abert found what remained of a crude axletree. "There was also a deep rut curving abruptly," he reported, "which showed that they had locked the wheels for the purpose of descending the hill, when, the chain giving way, the cart had capsized, and the axletree got broken, and the scattered chips explained that it was there that it had been repaired."

Farther eastward at a ford known as Spanish Crossing, where the old trace crossed Ute Creek at its confluence with the Canadian, Abert observed that "two deeply cut ruts gave to the trail the appearance of a wagon road, but their sometimes variable parallelism showed that they were formed principally by the feet of passing animals." Beyond that point he noted that "the road was strewed with the broken axletrees of the Spanish carts which had preceded us." Long used by the Comancheros (Mexicans who traded with the Comanches and other Plains Indians), the route was, according to Abert, "the most feasible road for descending the Canadian."

When Abert reached the present Texas–New Mexico line, he found where the "Spaniards" had cached their *carretas*, secreted there before entering the Indian country, "as the road here changes from a wagon trail to a bridle path." A cart the soldiers found was made with

Joyce Mahan points to Coronado's name carved on the left side of a cave in the Oklahoma Panhandle. Photograph by William Mahan.

Many petroglyphs can yet be seen along the walls of the mesa where Coronado's name was etched four centuries ago. Photograph by William Mahan.

two eccentric wheels, not exactly circular, formed by sawing off the ends of large logs, and rimming them with pieces of timber to increase the diameter. . . . They were perforated in the neighborhood of the centre, to receive an axletree of cotton-wood. A suitable pole, and a little square box of wicker-work, completed the laughable machine.

Several days later, about midway through the Panhandle, Abert and his men met for the first time a party of the "Comancheeros" twenty days out from Taos, New Mexico. Typifying their breed,

They were dressed in conical-crowned sombreros, jackets with the stripes running tranversely; large bag breeches extending to the knee; long stockings and moccasins. They were badly armed, and presented a shabby and poor appearance, though we learned that

they were a good specimen of the class to which they belong.

In 1849, Captain Randolph B. Marcy was well aware of the cart trail. In 1886 he testified before the Texas Boundary Commission:

I was informed in New Mexico that the Mexicans were the only semi-civilized people who for many years ventured into the Comanche and Kiowa country, and they only went there for traffic, transporting their merchandise in ox-carts from Santa Fe along the identical track which I followed in excorting California emigrants from Arkansas in 1849, . . . and upon this route deep Mexican cart tracks, made when the ground was soft many years previous, were observed, showing that the route had been traveled for a long time.[43]

The rust-eaten artifacts may have been dropped

105

On display at the Panhandle-Plains Museum in Canyon are many Spanish artifacts found in the Texas Panhandle.

or discarded by the armor-clad cavaliers or the Mexican traders who followed them. Perhaps the most interesting and mysterious discovery in the Texas Panhandle occurred just north of Clarendon about 1887. Three young boys chanced upon ten to fifteen swords stuck to their hilts in the parched clay, all planted nicely in a small circle or oval. The boys tried unsuccessfully to pull the swords from the sun-baked earth. Finally they freed one sword by loosening it with water, but not until its hilt had been pulled from the long rusty blade. The weapon proved to be a thin-bladed rapier that came into use after 1700. Later each of the boys tried in vain to relocate the lost swords. The mystery of the Spanish rapiers, stuck deeply into the wind-swept earth, has never been unraveled.[44]

In 1925 a Spanish flag standard was plowed up on the Ray Uselding farm, about a mile south of Happy, Texas, as were a halbert lance and a battle axhead. Near Borger an iron cross of the kind used during Coronado's expedition was found. Northwest of Spearman, on Palo Duro Creek, a rusted pair of Spanish handcuffs and bridle bits were found. On Spring Draw three miles north of Canyon still another pair of ancient bridle bits were unearthed. All these relics may be seen today at the Panhandle Plains Museum in Canyon, gateway to the historic Palo Duro Canyon, where daring Spanish explorers camped in centuries past.

Perhaps we will never know the whole story of Oklahoma's treasure trail, but the countless relics, the nameless graves, the adobe ruins all remain as testimonies to the route the ancient trail took and to those nameless explorers and travelers who passed that way, burying their gold in desperate straits up and down the old Santa Fe–Natchitoches Trail on Red River.

This Mexican cart, from Taos (donated to the Panhandle-Plains Museum in Canyon, Texas, by Charles Goodnight), was typical of the ox-drawn *carretas* once used on the Red River Trail from Santa Fe to Natchitoches.

In 1887, in an arroyo about five miles north of Clarendon, in the Texas Panhandle, Henry Taylor, his brother, and a companion discovered this thin-bladed, forty-inch-long Spanish rapier stuck to its hilt in the earth. Ten or more of the early-eighteenth-century swords formed a circle that no one has since rediscovered. On one side of the blade appears the inscription "IN XX SOL ING ON XX X." Courtesy Panhandle-Plains Historical Society.

107

In 1925, Ray Uselding plowed up this fifteen-inch-long Spanish halbert about a mile south of Happy, Texas. Also found were a flag standard and a battle-ax. Courtesy Panhandle-Plains Historical Society.

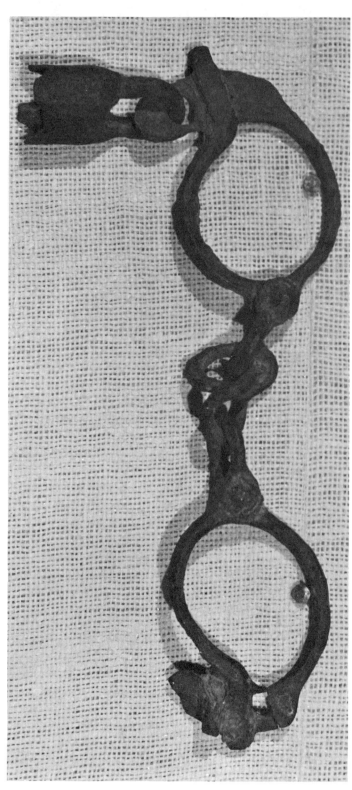

In 1930, while excavating for a vat four feet below the surface on Palo Duro Creek northwest of Spearman, Texas, workmen found these Spanish handcuffs. Locked (and perhaps buried with the victim), they are of a kind used on pirate ships in the 1500's. Courtesy Panhandle-Plains Historical Society.

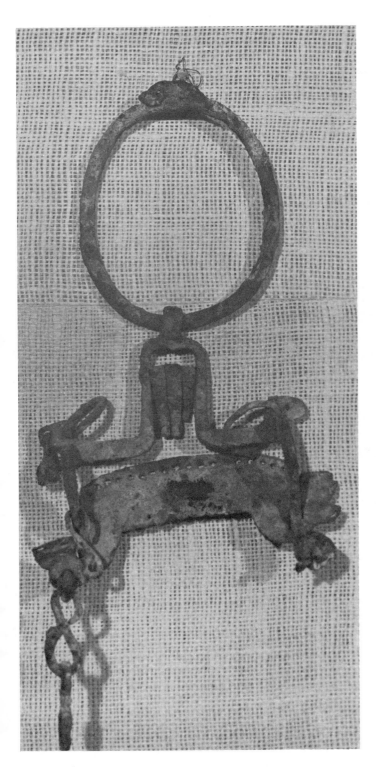

Three miles north of Canyon, Texas, on Spring Draw, this Spanish bridle bit was found. Similar bits have been discovered in Ochiltree County. Courtesy Panhandle-Plains Historical Society.

This 3 1/8-inch-long mid-sixteenth century Spanish iron cross, found near Borger, Texas, may well have been lost by a member of the Coronado expedition in 1541. Courtesy Panhandle-Plains Historical Society.

109

Pawneepic Village (George Catlin). Catlin painted this work from a sketch of the Wichita Indian village at the mouth of Devil's Canyon fronting the North Fork of Red River. Courtesy American Museum of Natural History.

5. Ghosts of Devil's Canyon and Their Gold

Legends of lost mines in the Southwest are many, but for legends per square mile, the Wichita Mountains of southwestern Oklahoma must surpass all other ranges of equal size—and many even larger. I was reared on a farm just south of these rugged granite hills and as a boy spent every spare moment exploring caves, searching for abandoned gold mines and ghost towns, interviewing old prospectors, and seeking every thread of evidence I could put my hands on to add credence to the many legends of lost Spanish gold in the Wichitas, and in particular in the Devil's Canyon country.

When I first became interested in Devil's Canyon—its history, its skeletons, its treasures—I found it difficult to find but fragments of information. But as I searched the archives, government reports, and stacks of yellowed newspaper files, the fragments started piecing together a story that is only now being told.

If Devil's Canyon could speak, perhaps it would tell of Spanish conquistadors clad in shiny armor, of Spanish and Mexican miners who dug for yellow metal, of gold-laden packtrains, of devastating massacres, of buried treasure—and certainly of lost mines. Always it would tell of its crumbled ruins where miners once lived—and perhaps died. Mexicans themselves would tell the tales, and old Indians would verify them.

Once the home of the Wichita Indians, Devil's Canyon cuts a swath a mile and a half long through rugged granite peaks before emptying into the North Fork of Red River in western Kiowa County. Lying between Flat Top and Soldier Spring mountains, the brush-choked Cañon Diablo abounds with tales of lost Spanish gold and the smelters that melted that metal, the foundation ruins of a forgotten, ancient church, a brass cannon—even the treasure of a Spanish ship.

Not all the tales are improbable—for did not many travelers find the ancient ruins of adobe? And one must remember that the highway from Santa Fe passed here on its meandering journey down Red River to Louisiana. The evidence that the Spanish, or more probably the Mexicans, lived here is not lacking. It is only natural that their legends survive.

No one can say when the first armor-clad Spaniards set foot in these mountains, which rise abruptly from the rolling Great Plains. Although no account yet found tells of Spanish exploration in the Wichitas, the evidence is favorable that the Spaniards were there. The evidence is overwhelming that there were early Mexican inhabitants. Mexican *ciboleros* and Comancheros knew these mountains as the Sierra Jumanos. Other early hunters called them the Towyash, no doubt for the Taovaya, or Wichita, Indians who lived there.[1] Whoever came first left their traditions. Others followed and added to those traditions.

Some historians have written that the first Spaniard there was Fray Juan de Salas, who established a temporary mission in 1629, followed by gold seekers such as Captains Hernán Martín and Don Diego del Castillo in 1650.[2] However, it is more probable that these early explorers were on the Concho River near present San Angelo, Texas, where they found not gold but fresh-water pearls.[3]

There were other early trail blazers who explored this jagged mountain range, the first sizable range the Spaniards would see east of Santa Fe after crossing the sun-baked Plains. No Spaniard with an eye to gold-bearing country would have passed up such beckoning hills. Perhaps the first historic reference to the Wichita Mountains was left us by a Frenchman named Brevel, who passed there about 1765. More of him later.

Where history has failed in recording these events, tradition has often succeeded, preserving a story that perhaps history never could. Devil's Canyon, in part, is such a story—a blending of both history and tradition.

As the missionaries crossed the plains to convert the Indians to Christianity, so did the gold seekers. How many dug for gold in the rugged Wichitas in the seventeenth or eighteenth centuries will never be known. But tradition tells that one of the first was in 1657. A Spanish priest,

111

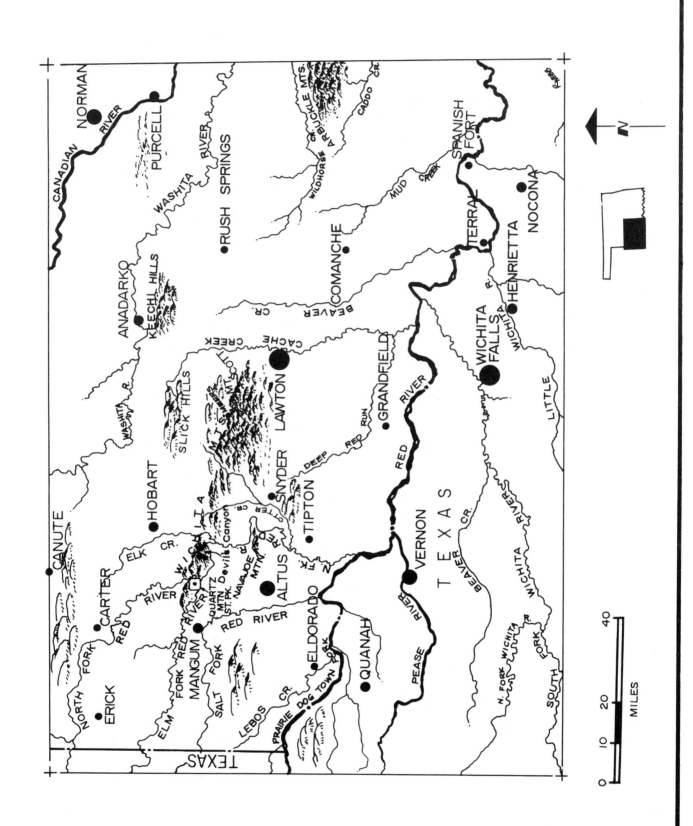

Southwestern Oklahoma

one Father Gilbert, and a well-equipped party of one hundred men are said to have marched into the Sierra Jumanos and dug a shaft one hundred feet deep about nine miles northwest of Mount Scott.[4]

In the 1890's newspapers were urging exploration of the Wichitas for the purpose of discovering old Spanish mines. The *Purcell Register* in the Chickasaw Nation reported some of its findings in 1893. Its source of information is unknown:

... Being entirely satisfied that both gold and silver were buried in the cliffs, canyons and gulches of the Wichita Mountains, and that it was only a question of time when they would be forced to disgorge to the sturdy blows of the pick and shovel as progressive civilization encompassed them, a few weeks ago the paper detailed one of its staff to investigate the subject.

One Spanish expedition landed on the Gulf coast in May 1698, and during the following month, under the guidance of Indians familiar with the country, it came north into the Wichita Mountains where a portion of the miners were put to work prospecting and mining.

Mining was continued in the Wichita Mountains with great success until the fall of 1700, when the miners were driven out by the Comanches and other hostile tribes. The shafts they sunk and the furnaces they constructed for reducing the metals, are yet to be seen.[5]

Such accounts undoubtedly enticed lost-mine hunters during this period, many of whom were bodily removed by Indian police or Fort Sill soldiers patrolling the Kiowa-Comanche-Apache Reservation.

Perhaps the first historical account of mining in the Wichitas was left by the Frenchman named Brevel who passed through about 1765 on his way to Santa Fe. Sibley recorded Brevel's story as he told it years later in Natchitoches:

About forty years ago, I set off on foot, from the Panis nation . . . in company with a party of young Indian men, with whom I had been partly raised, on a hunting voyage, and to procure horses. . . . [Following Red River upstream for several days], . . . the hills rising into mountains, amongst which, we saw a great deal of rock salt, and an ore, the Indians said was my (meaning the white people's) treasure; which I afterwards learnt was silver; and that amongst these mountains of mines, we often heard a noise like the explosion of cannon, or distant thunder, which the Indians said was the spirit of the white people, working in their treasure; which I afterwards was informed, was the

blowing of the mines, as it is called, which is common in all parts of Spanish America where mines exist.[6]

Brevel went on to say that after a short sojourn in Santa Fe, a town of about one hundred houses, he and his party returned to the Panis towns on Red River in eighteen days, three months and twenty days after the time they had left. If his story was true—and Sibley termed him a "reputable old man"—it is probable that Brevel had "heard the noise like the explosion of cannon" while traveling through the western peaks of the Wichita Mountains as he headed up the North Fork of Red River—perhaps the very same region discovered by traveler John Maley when he found abandoned mining operations there in 1812.

No extant record reveals who the mystery miners were. But with Brevel's story in mind, Anglo-Americans would long have good reason to prospect the Wichitas, said to have yielded "specimens of silver ores," according to Josiah Gregg in his classic *Commerce of the Prairies*, first published in 1844.[7]

In the testimony in *The United States* v. *The State of Texas*, Simon N. Cockrell left one of the most interesting accounts of early travel on the upper waters of Red River, and perhaps the only extant account of Mexican miners living in or near Devil's Canyon. The oldest witness to testify in the Greer County case, Cockrell also was among the first white men to enter the Wichita Mountains.

Cockrell, half-brother of Missouri Senator F. M. Cockrell and of Texas Congressman Jeremiah V. Cockrell, was ninety-three years old, a resident of Archer County, Texas, when he gave his deposition. He said that he was a hunter with Holland Coffee's and Silas Colville's party of "twenty-five" when they established a trading fort in May, 1833, about a mile and a half below the confluence of the North and South forks of Red River in present southwest Tillman County, Oklahoma.[8]

Cockrell recalled that from Fort Smith, Arkansas, the traders had traveled in wagons on "the same tracks that we supposed were made by the Mexican carts going to Santa Fe." The old road passed "from three-quarters to a mile above our fort," Cockrell said. "Our wagons followed the ruts. We had a guide with us who was an old man, and I have heard him say that he knew when

Devil's Canyon, in western Kiowa County, abounds in legends of lost Spanish gold. The canyon was once the home of Mexican miners. Adobe ruins, crude shafts, and discarded tools were found here by early hunters.

those ruts were made." It was common knowledge, he said, that the road led on to Nacogdoches and Natchitoches.

Cockrell went on to state that only seven of the twenty-five men remained to build the fort, erected near the ruins of a house. Only its chimney was still standing, its logs having rotted or burned years before. No one among the traders had any knowledge about the mysterious house and its blackened chimney. Perhaps it had been the home for early French traders or Comancheros.

Of the seven men remaining at Coffee's trading post, Cockrell distinctly remembered William Bean, who with a trapper named Harris had traded with the Indians in the Wichita Mountains some time earlier. Bean had been with Harris when he cached his whisky and beaver traps at an Indian village about seventy-five miles up the North Fork.

Bean no doubt had been with John Harris, a Missourian, the leader of a large party of trappers whom Albert Pike joined at Taos in 1832 to trap beaver in the Comanche country. While in west Texas that October, many of the trappers became disgruntled with Harris. Some returned to Taos, while Pike and four of his men continued northeast to Fort Smith. Harris led the remaining thirty or so trappers northward up the North Fork of Red River and reached Fort Gibson in January, 1833.[9]

Bean led Cockrell to a "Kiowa village" about seventy-five miles above Coffee's post in a "valley on the northeast side of the river" which "was very beautiful and stretched out from a mile to a mile and a quarter." Cockrell recalled that the Indians— no doubt Wichitas—"had between 80 to 100 acres in cultivation, which were fenced in with lariats." Bean showed Cockrell the supplies earlier cached by Harris, "and we opened it and found the alcohol and traps ruined," he lamented.

Cockrell was perhaps the first Anglo-American to witness Mexican miners living in the Wichitas, about forty miles up the North Fork from the trading post—probably in Devil's Canyon. "They were miners by profession," he remembered, referring to them as "Spaniards," and added that about five miles upriver on the west side was a sheep ranch where lived "a Mexican boy about 18 years old, whose parents were killed by the Co-

manches." The youngster had a Mexican cart, Cockrell remembered.

Skirting the Mexican settlement, he said, was "this road that ran up the river to Santa Fe. I was there since, and the chimneys had all fallen down," and the town abandoned. The old hunter did not know when the miners left but had understood that "the Indians drove them off."

During the time that Cockrell remained at Coffee's trading post, between May, 1833, and February, 1836, Indians "came there by hundreds to trade." Four miles downstream from the fort at the mouth of a creek, they built a boat to ferry their furs and buffalo hides downriver. Finally, early in 1836, Cockrell left the traders to join Sam Houston's army. No doubt his stories influenced fellow Texans to take up the quest for Mexican gold in the Wichitas.

Cockrell perhaps did not know that, one year after he helped build the Red River trading post, the First Regiment of the United States Dragoons, about 180 soldiers under Colonel Henry Dodge, marched into Devil's Canyon on its first peace mission on the Plains. The soldiers had paid heavily to parley with the Indians, whom they called "Toyash" or Pawnee Picts—the same Wichitas who had left their Red River fortification some years before. When the troops left Fort Gibson on June 21, 1834, they numbered five hundred. As they progressed onto the Plains, the severe summer heat took its toll, and sick camps were set up along the route. Of the sick dragoons more than one hundred would die. George Catlin, the famous painter of Indians, accompanied the expedition almost to the Wichitas' camps but grew too ill to witness the first encounter between United States soldiers and the Taovayas, who had earlier struck terror in the hearts of Spaniards.

Colonel Dodge's troops found the Wichitas in the mouth of Devil's Canyon, where about two thousand of them were living in two hundred grass lodges. Their agricultural abilities had not changed, but they were no longer the well-armed, well-mounted, fortified warriors the Spaniards had known. The dragoons met with the Wichitas on July 21. In the peace council that followed, they traded a captive Wichita girl for a seven-year-old white boy captured some weeks before.

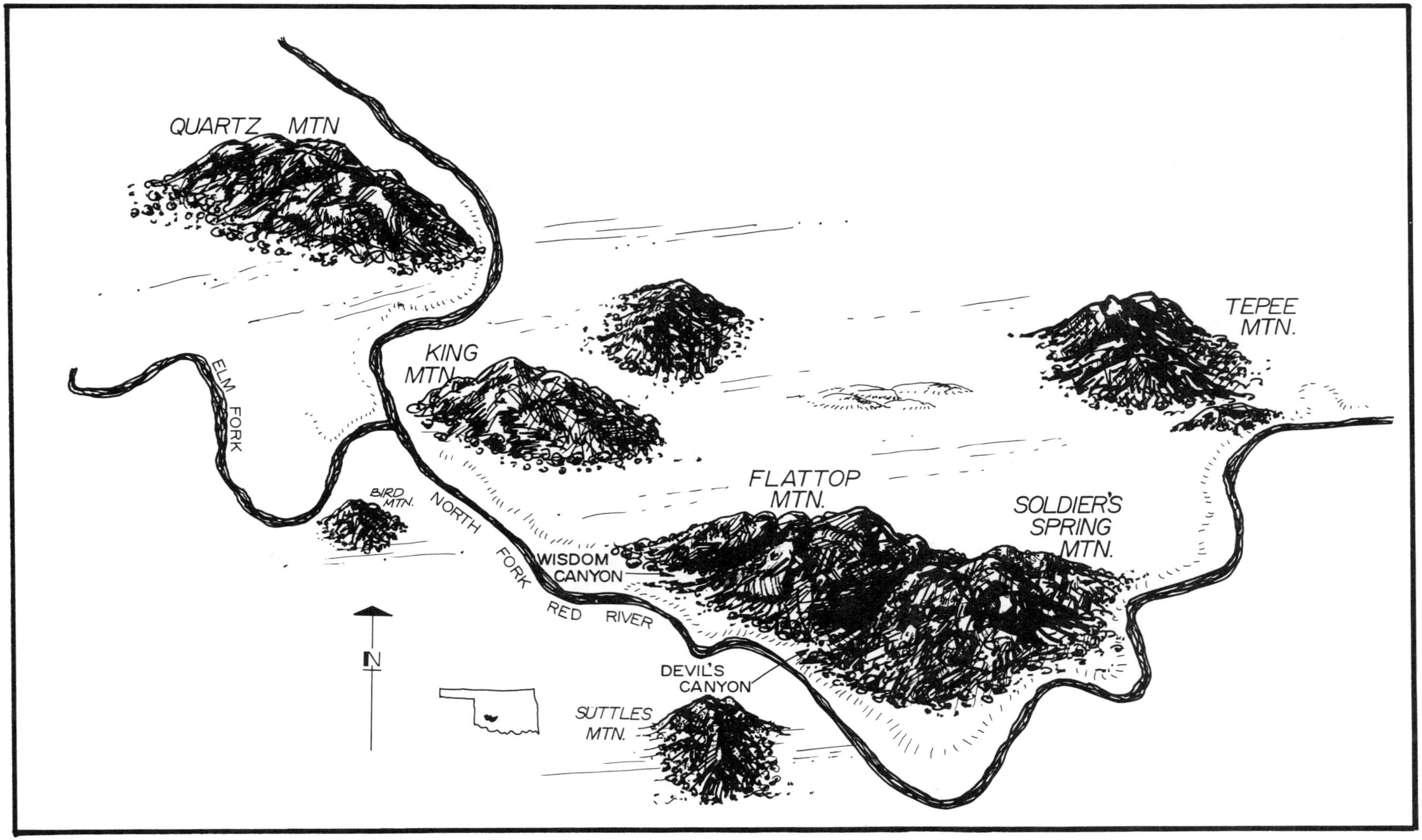
QUARTZ MTN
KING MTN.
TEPEE MTN.
FLATTOP MTN.
SOLDIER'S SPRING MTN.
ELM FORK
BIRD MTN.
NORTH FORK RED RIVER
WISDOM CANYON
DEVIL'S CANYON
SUTTLES MTN.
N

Devil's Canyon

Simon Cockrell's story of observing a party of "Spaniards" in the mountains, though told much later, had already been recorded. When Colonel Dodge asked the Indians whether the Spaniards had come there to trade, the chief replied that they had done so and had left "not long since, and [gone] west."[10]

By July 24, 1834, more than two thousand armed and mounted Wichitas, Comanches, and Kiowas had gathered to parley with Dodge near the soldiers' camp, about a mile from Devil's Canyon on the opposite bank of the North Fork. When the dragoons broke camp the following day to return to Fort Gibson, representatives of those tribes, including a Spaniard who had long lived with the Comanches, accompanied them. A few of the notables among the dragoons of this expedition were Brigadier General Henry Leavenworth, who died in a sick camp, Lieutenant Colonel Stephen W. Kearney, First Lieutenants Jefferson Davis and Phillip St. George Cooke, and Captain Nathan Boone, the son of the famous frontiersman.

The stories old buffalo hunter J. C. Settles had heard about Devil's Canyon—accounts from both Mexicans and Indians—led him to the canyon ruins in the 1870's. Settles first entered Greer County in 1875 to hunt buffalo; when the buffalo were gone, he turned to wolfing.[11] He, too, testified in the Greer County case in 1892.

Once in the late 1870's Settles recalled, he and his hunters were camped on Buck Creek

when the Comanches came out on a big hunt. We had a Spaniard there who was telling us of his scraps with the Indians and white people, and he told us about a place in the mountains where there had been a big lot of Mexicans, and that they had had a big fight, in fact, two fights, and that the Mexicans whipped them, and then that they had another fight and the Indians whipped the Mexicans.

Settles said that he had once spoken to the Comanche chief White Eagle about the Mexican settlement and that the Chief had confirmed the Spaniard's story of the Indians' victory over the Mexicans.

Settles went on to say that the Spaniard

told me there was a place there they had been working for money or mineral, and that there was a place on the side of the mountain where they had dug down

through solid rock; had worked down through that, and that at the bottom of that place was all the money we wanted the way he told it, and that they had rolled a big rock on it and the Indians could not roll it off.

Settles said that he later found what he believed to be the old mine, about six miles upstream from Devil's Canyon and about two and a half miles west of the North Fork:

I failed to find the rock rolled over the hole, but we did find a rock rolled down in the hole and we had to blast it to get it out. Around the bottom we found a soft material that we never did get an assay out of. Below that we found something like coal; looked like coal. We also found part of the skeleton of a man in there; it seemed that one side had entirely decayed.

The buffalo hunter was sure that he had found the Mexican mine: "You can see beyond any doubt in the world that it has been worked, not with picks, but with something that looks like gads, and you can see chips all the way down, where it seems to have been worked with hammer and gad."

It was while Settles was seeking the mine and its reputed treasure that he found the ruins of the ancient settlement in Devil's Canyon known to early hunters as the "Spanish town." Settles believed that the settlement had covered about ten acres. Among the ruins he found "pieces of iron of different description," brass, old tools, copper, "and ashes in lots of places."

Near the ruins Settles found a cave, in which were what were "supposed to be old Spanish crucibles." They were "larger than a man's hat." They were shaped like basins and had withstood fire, he said. He believed that they had been used to melt metal. The cave contained a huge quantity of ashes, "no mistake about that; as much as eight or ten tons in it," he recalled. "We dug down fifteen feet and went down through the ashes for as much as ten feet." In the ash heap he found pieces of iron, whetstones, human skulls, arm bones, and a knife. Settles would not be the last to dig into the mysterious charcoal pit.

Surveyor William Kyle of Vernon, Texas, first visited the Wichita Mountains in 1850, forty-three years before he testified in the Greer County case in 1893. At that early date he was told of a Mexican silver mine near Navajoe Mountain, near the road to Santa Fe.[12] Kyle first crossed into present

Greer County on a scouting expedition with General Edward Burleson in 1849 or 1850, he said. Some time later he was a member of still another expedition of United States troops under the command of Captain Charles E. Travis, whose headquarters were at Fort Davis, Texas.

While they were on the Pecos River, Kyle recalled, the troops skirmished with a band of Indians, among whom was an old Mexican Comanchero trader, who changed sides when he saw the United States troops. After the engagement the company, commanded by a Major Simonson, traveled northeast to Red River, employing the Comanchero as a guide. As the troops arrived just south of the Navajoe Mountains—a small chain of granite buttes about ten miles south of Devil's Canyon—"the guide pointed to them and said there was a silver mine in the mountains there that had been worked by the Mexicans."

Mexicans were also searching the Wichitas for lost treasure at an early date. Just what they sought and where and what knowledge they possessed only legend has preserved. Many of their stories have been handed down and are still told around the treasure hunters' campfires when the moon is bright and the night still.

In 1893, fifty-seven-year-old José Martínez, who lived in Greer County, told what he knew about one of those early quests in which he had participated thirty-five years before.[13] In 1858 he joined a party of Mexicans at Camp Cooper, Texas, in a search for silver that had been buried in the Wichita Mountains. In the party were several who, years before, had mined in the mountains and had been guided there by three "Spaniards" who had lived in the mining settlement at Devil's Canyon.

Martínez distinctly remembered that the Mexicans who had been in the mountains earlier pointed out the Santa Fe Trail, which they struck shortly after crossing Red River (which they called Río Colorado de Natchitoches). "They called it the Santa Fe route," Martínez said. "They told me that there was a road coming in here—one from Natchitoches and a road from Nacogdoches. They told me that they were mining here in these mountains and the Mexicans from Natchitoches came up this way and the New Mexicans came down this way."

Traveling up what they called Red River—later

designated the North Fork—they encountered the ruts of the old road near Otter Creek, often dim and grassed over, in which occasionally they found good-sized trees and even mesquite. Four or five miles downstream from the Narrows on Otter Creek, the old road crossed to the west side, Martínez recalled, headed north through a gap in the mountains, and then turned northwest and crossed Tepee Creek near its mouth and led up the east side of the North Fork to the mouth of Devil's Canyon. From there it traveled upstream about eight miles and crossed over to the west side at Comanche Springs. Martínez believed that he had encountered the same trail farther northwestward at the head of the Washita River. His fellow travelers pointed out to Martínez the ruins in Devil's Canyon, where, they said, the Spaniards had once lived.

Martínez returned to the Wichitas later in 1858 as a member of Sul Ross's Texas Rangers and a short time afterward on an expedition under the command of Captain Dave Sublett. The Mexicans who had first accompanied him dispersed, taking their knowledge of former days—and of buried silver—with them.

Early in 1891, W. F. Cummins, the assistant state geologist of Texas, investigated reports of gold and silver in the Wichita Mountains, part of which lay in what was then Greer County, Texas (the North Fork served as the western border of the Comanche-Kiowa-Apache Reservation—land forbidden to the gold seeker).

While making his investigation, Cummins chanced upon J. C. Settles, a buffalo hunter who was living no more than a mile and a half from Devil's Canyon and its ruins of a long-forgotten city. It was only natural that Settles would show Cummins where Mexican miners had once lived—their town long weathered and crumbled so that only outlines showed where adobe houses had once stood. Two years later, in Austin, Texas, Cummins told the court what he had found.[14]

Cummins had examined two settlements in ruins, the site farthest west, which he believed to be the Mexican town, and the site a half-mile east, an Indian village, no doubt that of the Wichitas whom the dragoons had visited in 1834. Each site covered about twenty acres. Cummins hired several men to dig into the ruins. What remained of the Mexican settlement lay "between the mountains and a deep pond of water, the termination of a creek running out of the cañon [Devil's Canyon]," Cummins noted. "This pond extended along the entire south side of the old Mexican town."

The geologist observed that the ruins were twelve to eighteen feet long and about twelve feet wide and apparently had been constructed of sun-dried bricks. ". . . it was evident they were constructed of the clays of the immediate vicinity. The ashes, which I supposed to have been in the fireplaces, were always in one corner or end of the building. No excavation had been made for the walls of buildings, nor were there any excavations in the area inside of the buildings." He said that the "doors faced in no particular direction in the different buildings."

While excavating the mounds of debris among the ruins, Cummins found an array of articles: legs and ribs of buffaloes; bones of deer, antelope, dogs, raccoons, and turkeys; a foot of a small horse or donkey; scraps of copper, brass, silver, and iron; and beads, pipes, whetstones, gun flints, pottery, and buttons. He said:

A great number of fragments of iron and copper found in these houses would indicate that it was Mexican. Most of the iron found, however, was so badly decomposed that it was difficult, if not impossible, to tell what any of it had been. A butcher knife, piece of a chisel, and three-cornered file are about the only things we could identify. The fragments of copper were the remnants of thin sheet copper out of which the ornaments or other instruments had been cut. There were also some fragments of copper wire. The only thing we found that had been manufactured out of copper or brass was an ornament that had probably been fastened on some kind of leather. We found one gold button of American manufacture.

Cummins reported that the ruins in the Indian settlement a half mile east were "all round," and "had been constructed by placing cedar poles in the ground leaning towards the center, as many of the ends of the old poles were still remaining in the ground." All that remained "was a bank of earth, often two feet high." Always the fireplace or hearth was in the center of the circular mound and was filled with ashes eighteen inches to two feet deep. No artifacts were found among the Indian ruins except decayed bones.

Cummins was convinced that the Indian settlement was much later than the Mexican town because there were trees growing among the Mexican ruins that were eighteen inches in diameter, while those in the Indian village were much smaller. The cedar posts found in the Mexican ruins were "much more decayed than those found" among the Indian houses, and the mounds of debris at the former site showed more weathering and age. Another reason for his conclusion

is that at the place of the old Mexican town an Indian lodge that seemed to be of the same age as those in the old Indian town was constructed at the edge of one of the old houses in the Mexican town, and part of the material from the debris had been used in its construction.

Cummins added that the Mexicans always built their houses in a square or oblong shape, and those in the Mexican town followed that fashion. The timber in the Mexican town "had been cut with a heavy axe and from two sides only," Cummins noted, "while every piece that we found in the old Indian town had been cut around on every side."

The geologist pointed out that, while the mounds from the Indian lodges were usually twenty-five feet in diameter, the ruins in the Mexican site were "not more than ten or twelve feet wide and ten to eighteen feet long." He further observed that "in the construction of the Indian lodges the earth was dug out to the depth of about two feet and the dirt banked up on the outside," while all the houses in the Mexican settlement "were built on the level ground without any excavation."

Sad it is that trained archaeologists did not participate in this excavation of the 1890's. Perhaps far more might have been gleaned about those mysterious miners from Santa Fe who came with the seasons—and finally came no more.

One of the earliest prospectors in the Wichitas, A. J. Meers, a surveyor, civil engineer, and hotel manager in Mangum, settled in Greer County in April, 1885, when there were no more than ten or twenty settlers in all that vast stretch of land west of the North Fork. As early as 1886 he began filing on mining claims in the mountains and prospected intermittently for the next twenty years.[15]

Boundary lines did not mean much to him, for on several occasions he was bodily removed from the reservation by Indian police patrolling the reservation east of the North Fork. In 1889 and 1890 he served as county surveyor of Greer County and in 1891 visited geologist Cummins when the latter was partly excavating the ruins in Devil's Canyon—a scientific endeavor that has not resumed to this day.[16]

Meers examined the mysterious cave in a cliff near the ruins of the Wichita village where buffalo hunter Settles had found as much as "eight or ten tons" of ashes. Meers did not estimate the amount of ash and charcoal, but he did verify the cave's contents.

Meers must have been nearby in February, 1892, when a small silver rush occurred near Devil's Canyon, for about thirteen miles east of Mangum a miners' camp called Silverton sprang up. It was composed mostly of Colorado miners who worked for a few weeks and then disappeared.[17] One who took part in the search was C. F. Doan, who had established Doan's Store at the famous Red River crossing on the Great Western Trail. Doan had been in Devil's Canyon as early as 1879 and had found the ruins of three or four log cabins with rock chimneys—perhaps what remained of the ruins that Simon Cockrell had seen forty-six years before.[18]

About three years after Cummins dug into the low-lying ruins in Devil's Canyon, James Mooney, the renowned ethnologist of the United States Bureau of American Ethnology, also made an investigation. In October, 1893, former buffalo hunter and mustanger John M. Passmore, of Navajoe, guided Mooney to the ruins,[19] where he found a number of artifacts. Unlike Cummins, however, Mooney was not convinced that any were of Mexican or Spanish origin.[20] Passmore, who first visited Devil's Canyon as early as 1880, had found a Mexican iron quirt, a hammer, beads, arrow spikes, and human skull bones among the ashes in the cave nearby. Upon that first visit he observed the "foundations of four logs of an old log house about twelve feet square," but when he was in the canyon again some years later no signs remained of the cabin. Time and nature had erased all signs, and no record remained of the cabin's occupants.

Were it not for such eyewitnesses as Cockrell, who observed Mexican miners and their settlement in the Wichitas in the 1830's, perhaps nothing would have been known of those nameless miners from Santa Fe—many of whom, legends say, never returned whence they came.

Olin Talley, of Hobart, was another who found the ruins of the ancient habitation in Devil's Canyon and its mysterious cave of ashes. "Near the village were numerous springs of water," Talley recalled, "and up the side of the mountain there is a cave. I found several tons of ashes here. I know that cave was used as a smelter by the Spaniards many years ago when they extracted their gold."[21]

Legends handed down by old Kiowa Indians say that at some time immemorial they came upon a mine being worked by Spaniards. The Kiowas attacked and killed the miners after they had gathered fifty burro loads of gold, all of which was later hidden by the Indians. No one but the chiefs knew where it was hidden, and no member of the tribe was allowed to know except when he became chief. That is what the Kiowas told Talley, and he searched unsuccessfully the remainder of his days.

A story is told of a group of Mexicans who tried to retrieve part of the treasure their ancestors had buried. They knew that the gold had been hidden in the mountains, and they worked night and day digging for it. When they believed they were about to reach the gold, their leader sent two young boys to the trading post at a nearby river for supplies. When they were only a short distance away, the boys heard screams and turned back to see a large band of Indians attacking their camp. They knew that they could do nothing but ride on for help. When they returned to their camp, they found that all their people had been killed or taken prisoner. Such was the story revealed to G. W. Horne in 1893 by an aging Mexican who had been one of the two boys who escaped. A miner and later a prominent citizen of Lawton, Oklahoma, Horne himself had found knives, earthenware, and dugouts in Devil's Canyon, but its gold remained elusive.[22]

In 1901 a German named Mark Sauerberg opened a saloon at Lugert, several miles north-

Carved on elm trees at the mouth of Devil's Canyon are a turtle, left, and two sombreros, right, near the center and in the upper portion of the photograph. Tradition says that they were carved by Spanish miners.

west of Devil's Canyon. One day a Mexican about sixty-five years old appeared and remained about the area for two or three months. During that time he told Sauerberg a story, part of which the German later verified. The Mexican revealed that he had been with a group of hunters years before who had dug on the west side of King Mountain for a treasure that they knew to have been hidden by Mexican miners. The Mexican hunters were attacked by Indians and sought refuge on top of King Mountain. The old Mexican did not tell Sauerberg that he had now returned to find the treasure, but the German guessed as much. Sauerberg was just as sure that the Mexican had told the truth, for later he found a long-abandoned shaft on the west side of King Mountain, and at its summit lay the white bones of such an ill-fated party.[23] The treasure has never been found.

About the turn of the century an Indian woman who claimed to be 105 years old appeared at the Twin Mountains, seven miles southeast of Devil's Canyon. She was searching for three burro loads of Spanish gold which she and two warriors had buried seventy or eighty years before.[24] She told how her people had had a "big fight" with the

Spaniards and massacred the entire band while they were bringing a packtrain out of Devil's Canyon. She and two warriors captured three burros carrying gold and buried the packsaddles on the west side of the Twin Mountains. Later one warrior went to Texas and disappeared. The other died in the intervening years. The old woman looked over the ground for days, but finally she too left without finding the gold.

Perhaps the Twin Mountains hold something more than Spanish gold. Countless old rifle shells have been found around the twin buttes. And a cave somewhere on the mountains holds a room of "strange objects."

In the 1930's a young boy found the small cave, barely large enough to enter. He told his parents about his discovery, saying that he had glimpsed large chairs, tables, old weapons, and other "strange objects." The boy's parents did not believe him and dismissed his story as a wild imagination. But when the youngster grew older, he tried again to find the cave, never forgetting what he believed he had seen. In those searches his family also joined, but it had been too long since he had first crawled through the narrow passage

121

Early settlers who discovered these foundation stones in Devil's Canyon believed that they marked the remains of a Spanish mission built in 1611. Courtesy Western History Collections, University of Oklahoma Library.

Several primitive mine shafts discovered in the Wichita Mountains near the North Fork of Red River were said to be those of early Spanish miners living in Devil's Canyon. This mine is one of several found in the region. Courtesy Western History Collections, University of Oklahoma Library.

into the room. Had he found an outlaw's lair, a dwelling of prehistoric man, or a den for early explorers?

At the mouth of Devil's Canyon a number of mysterious carvings have been found on trees, among them a climbing turtle, two sombreros, arrows, and Spanish helmets.[25] Old settlers nearby tell of ancient Spanish writing found on the east side of looming Tepee Mountain. Numerous In-

dian petroglyphs appear on Soldier Spring Mountain, and other rock art resembling stair steps can be seen on the west side of Camel Back Mountain, seven miles east of Devil's Canyon.

Foundation stones discovered in Devil's Canyon by cattleman N. J. McElroy in 1868 were long rumored to be the ruins of an old Spanish mission. Lee Winters, who homesteaded in 1901 at the mouth of Devil's Canyon, discovered the same square-shaped arrangement of stones.[26]

While breaking virgin sod southeast of Cache, George Frampton unearthed this twenty-five-pound iron tether weight. Bearing the head of a Spanish knight, with helmet and plume, the weight may have been lost by early Spanish conquistadors who crossed this region. Courtesy Museum of the Great Plains.

Countless other relics have been discovered in southwestern Oklahoma. In 1893, I. E. Cowan was plowing on his farm southwest of Mangum when he unearthed a pair of Spanish ring bridle bits. Some time later Joe C. Thompson found a Spanish saddle horn on his land west of Mangum. L. H. Tittle found a pair of Spanish bridle bits on the west slope of Headquarters Mountain near Granite in 1935.[27] When George H. Frampton broke sod on his homestead in Comanche County, six miles south and three east of Cache (now the Art Runyan farm in the southeast corner of N.E.¼ of S.29, T.1N., R.13W.), he unearthed a relic of the Spanish conquistadors that no one yet has accurately dated, but many are convinced that the twenty-five-pound iron tether weight dates to

the sixteenth century. The bell-shaped weight— used to tether animals when stakes were few—is embossed with the head of a Spanish knight, complete with raised visor and flowing plume. Some believe that the ancient weight was lost by the Coronado expedition. It is the only relic of its kind known to have been found anywhere on the plains.[28]

In Devil's Canyon itself have been found Spanish swords, knives, and sheep bells; Indian arrow points, beads, and stone tools; and United States Cavalry spurs, bridle bits, buttons, bullet molds, and a .31-caliber, 1849 Pocket Model Colt.[29] All these were found after the country was opened to white settlement. The Winters family of Altus now has a large collection of relics that their

123

mother and father, the late Lee and Mamie Winters, found during the years they lived at the mouth of the canyon.[30] Some of the Winterses' army buttons and antiques were no doubt left by the First United States Dragoons, who visited the Wichita Indian village in 1834.

In August, 1901, the Wichita Mountains were crawling with gold seekers, and the stories of lost Spanish gold assured that Devil's Canyon was not overlooked. In April, 1902, the Mangum *Star* reported:

Great excitement has been caused at Lawton, by the unearthing by miners in the Wichita Mountains of an 85-pound nugget, 83 per cent pure gold. It was found in Devil's Canyon, the scene of one of the ancient mines of the Spaniards, where many crucibles have been recently unearthed.[31]

Such a disclosure doubtless drew a rush of its own.

One romantic story of those ancient mines appeared in the Wichita, Kansas, *Daily Eagle* of December 11, 1903:

Long ago, at a time remembered only by the traditions of the Indians here, a mine existed on Otter Creek in the Wichitas, rich with gold and copper. It was just east of the confines of the territory owned by Mexico, and her people visited it yearly. By an agreement with the Indians here, the Mexicans received only a share of the product of the mine. Their voyages with crude mining tools with which to perform the work, and burros with which to transport the ores, occurred every summer. The mine would be worked for a season, the entrance carefully concealed, and the visitors would then return to their native land.

Finally, while the visitors were here, winter came upon them unusually early, and they decided to remain and take home with them the products of two years' labor instead of one. While they were making preparations for their departure, the Indians, thinking this would be their last journey, fell upon them and exterminated all but three or four, who escaped. Maps and charts had been prepared showing the location of this mine in a crude manner, a copy brought with them and a copy left in Mexico. The mine was never again visited. In later years one or two of the survivors, with a small party, attempted to locate it, but they were driven away by the Indians. The chart of the country was preserved, and cowboys have almost yearly seen a party of Mexicans prospecting the vicinity of the "Lost Mine."

A few years ago, Mr. E. Bryan, whose address is Waco, Texas, was sheriff of Limestone county, Texas. While attending to some business at the penitentiary, he learned that an inmate, an aged Mexican, knew of

the charts locating this mine. The Mexican had been sentenced for life and had been imprisoned for twenty-five years.

He told Mr. Bryan that when a young man, he had hunted for this mine with one of the survivors of the massacre. He asserted that the chart showed the mine to be on the west side of Otter Creek, less than one-half mile from the south side of the mountains, near a series of oak trees marked by sawing limbs from the side nearest the mine. Mr. Bryan made a trip here and found the general description of the place to be as the Mexican had described it. No particular search was made for the place, but it has since been designated as the "Lost Mine," or the "Lost Mexican."

. . . Many rows of graves between a small lake on the west, and Otter Creek on the east, remain to tell the story of a conflict with the Indians and Mexicans. Some skulls whose forms prove them to be non-American have frequently been found on this spot by cattlemen. . . .

The mountains in this vicinity are known to be rich in ore. The "red iron," the miner's index for gold, can be found almost anywhere, and copper stains are common. Every foot of land subject to the pick and shovel between North Fork and Comanche County has a miner's monument upon it, and the location shafts are being sunk. Miners have come from California, Klondike and Cripple Creek, and all of them pronounce the outlook as most flattering.

. . . It has long been conceded no place in the Wichitas looks better to the prospector than the mountains west and northwest of Mountain Park. Prospectors no longer walk over this territory with the view of locating; everything has been taken. Claim holders weave the facts and traditions together, then go to their mines and expect results.

If the present prospectors are fools for spending their time and money here, they are not the first and only ones.

Still another search for a lost Spanish mine was made in August, 1907. These treasure hunters possessed maps given to them by Herman Lehmann, who had been a captive of the Indians for eight years. Lawton's *Daily News-Republican* carried the story:

Dr. F. R. Green and Forrest Edwards left this morning for Indiahoma, where they will secure an outfit of burros for an extended trip into the Wichita Mountains on a prospecting tour. Dr. Green has become deeply interested in the copper prospects of the Wichitas and has just returned from the East, where he interested capital in the project for an extensive mine out there.

He is now going into the mountains with his guide, Forrest Edwards, who for many years lived at Indiahoma. The chief point for which the expedition is headed is an old Spanish mine which Edwards located several years ago in company with the Indian captive, Herman Lehmann, who had charts of the mines which he had captured from a Mexican. This mine is known to have rich deposits of copper, and it is thought that if worked, ore can be taken in paying quantities.[32]

It is not known whether Dr. Green and Edwards reopened the mine, but Lehmann, who was known for his veracity, left a classic memoir of his eight-year captivity among the Indians.

Bert Cook was one who saw still another map of Lehmann's, a map not to a mine but to seventy-five thousand dollars in Mexican gold bullion. Cook remembers the incident well. In 1905 he helped his father build a smelter and worked in the Bonanza Mine at the head of Fawn Creek, near Elk Mountain. Early in 1907, Bert became one of the first forest rangers in what was then the Wichita Mountains Forest and Game Preserve, the present Wildlife Refuge.[33] Some time before, Cook had met Lehmann when the former captive lived just south of Indiahoma. They had known each other a year or two when Lehmann told Cook about his map and allowed him to examine it. It was the first time he had shown it to anyone, Cook believed.

Lehmann had been taken captive by the Apaches in 1870, when he was only eleven years old. Later he joined the Comanches until they surrendered in 1878, when Lehmann rejoined white society.[34] It was some time during that period that a band of Indians with whom Lehmann was riding attacked a party of Mexicans on the south side of the Wichita Mountains. Every member of that caravan was killed, or so the Indians believed, until Lehmann found one still alive but dying.

Lehmann, who spoke Spanish, talked with the Mexican, who divulged that his party had buried about 350 pounds of gold bullion, and gave Lehmann his map showing where it was hidden. Lehmann kept the map for thirty years before he attempted to find the treasure. A crude drawing, it showed little more than a large, oval boulder half buried in the ground just south of the mountains.

Cook remembers that when Lehmann showed him the map he readily identified the landmark, for he had traveled past such a boulder often between the Cook mining camp and Indiahoma.

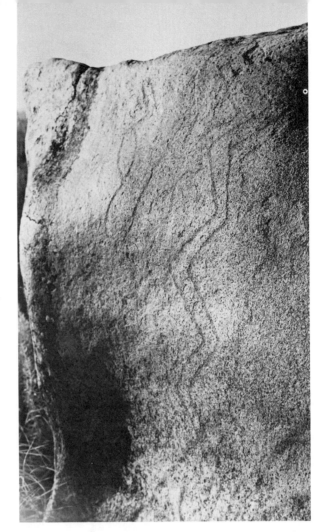

Mysterious Indian petroglyphs can be seen carved in granite on the west side of Camel Back Mountain, seven miles east of Devil's Canyon.

Lehmann agreed to share equally in any gold they might find and a short time later, met Cook at Elm Springs. From there they rode about half a mile northeast to the foot of the mountains, where Bert pointed out the lone, half-buried boulder that appeared on the map.

But someone else had learned about the Mexican gold, for not more than a few feet to the west was a hole in the ground about three feet deep. From the hole had been dug out a wide box. It had been broken up, and several of its boards were still lying near the hole.

Bert recalls that at the time they believed that all the gold had been found. But he wonders today whether the Mexicans did not bury several such boxes, which were of a size easily handled for transporting. The huge boulder remains today where it was when the Mexicans buried their gold.

A mysterious landmark found in Devil's Can-

Jay Winters, of Altus, displays some of the many Spanish, Indian, and military relics found by the Winters family when they lived at the mouth of Devil's Canyon, on the North Fork of Red River.

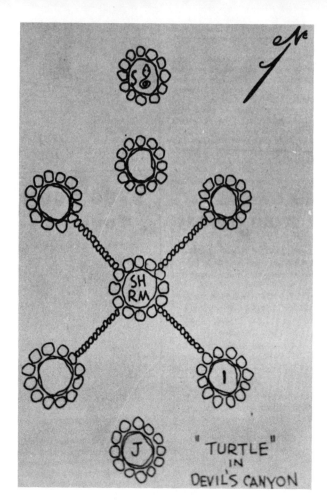

A drawing of a rock turtle, made of single stones and carved with cryptic symbols. It is one of many curiosities found in Devil's Canyon.

yon aroused much interest over the years. The curious marker was fashioned in the shape of a large turtle about twenty feet long. Eight large, flat rocks made up its head, shell, feet, and tail. Around each flat stone were twelve smaller cobblestones, each imbedded deep in the soil. Twelve more cobblestones led from each of the forefeet to the middle flat rock, composing the center of the body, while twelve more round stones led from each of the hind feet to the center stone. The head of the rock figure pointed northwest, the tail southeast. On the rock forming the head was carved an S and a coiled snake. Cut on the center rock were the letters SH and RM. On the east hind foot was inscribed an I. On the large rock composing the tail was carved a J. Some years ago a stock pond was built near the head of the canyon. It happened that the rock turtle was in the path of the pond spillway, and the landmark was bulldozed up. Its purpose or meaning remains a mystery.

Legend has it that a cave near the canyon holds the treasure from a small Spanish ship that was ferried up the North Fork to the canyon's mouth. Before the Spaniards could sail their craft, they were forced to remove the gold to the cave. The cavern was sealed, and the ship's anchor was left hanging outside to mark the burial site. The old rusty weight has been reported seen at various times.[35] But nature has managed to hold its secret.

Another story says that Spanish miners mounted a gold cross into the face of a tree, marking the burial of a gold-stuffed brass cannon.[36] Perhaps someday a heavy bulldozer that periodically invades the canyon will uncover the gold-filled cannon—or an equally valuable relic from centuries past.

At least part of the gold transported down the trail past Devil's Canyon was buried forty miles east of the gap. Tradition places the location on

Treasure seekers, among them Jack Brown, have long tried to decipher this crude drawing of a Spanish treasure map, which directs its owner to gold hidden in the Wichitas.

the west side of Mount Sheridan, not far from Meers, an old mining camp.

According to a surviving treasure map, a branch of the old Spanish trail passed just north of the tall, saddle-shaped mountain. As a packtrain slowly inched its way over the rugged trail, passing near the site of one of the Spanish mines, Indians poured down from the hills and attacked the caravan. The gold was hastily thrown into the shaft and partly concealed, but only a handful of miners survived to bury their comrades, and one of them made a map before they abandoned the gold forever. In the 1930's the father of Jack Brown, of Sunset, Texas, along with others, went into the Wichita Mountains with the map, acquired years before in Mexico from a Mexican who wanted to come with Brown but because of age and illness was forced to stay behind.

Old and yellowed with age, the treasure map led Brown and his partners to the summit of Mount Sheridan. Brown actually found many of the signs shown on the map but failed to locate the shaft. The Mexican had not told Brown how to read the secret code, or perhaps the Mexican himself had not known. But Brown believed that he could read the marks. He had found enough signs to believe that he was close.

The map bears the numbers 1677, perhaps a

date or a distance. On the chart appears a stream with two forks and four turtles within a circle, and two F's and an arrow can plainly be seen. A diamond figure with a line connecting it and the circle of turtles are shown, as are a ladder and a figure similar to a wagon wheel.

When I talked with Jack Brown in Sunset, he told me that he had been no more successful in his own search than his father.[37] He was only a boy when his father attempted to find the mine. He offered me the map and wished me better luck than he and his father had had.

Perhaps we will never know the whole story of Devil's Canyon or the forgotten Spanish road that meandered past it. Fortunately, eyewitness testimony has been left to us showing that the ancient trail was traveled as late as 1848 and that ruins of crude settlements were often found along its route.

Those many scattered ruins, the mysterious cave of ashes, the smelters, the countless relics—all lend credence to the many legends that Spaniards—or Mexicans—once mined in Devil's Canyon and its boulder-strewn environs. Some aged Indians say that the devil himself guards the Spanish gold, buried beneath skeletons dressed in heavy, shining armor. Perhaps they are right.

127

Wells Blevins holding a copy of a Jesse James treasure map. He has long pursued the trail to the hidden outlaw gold.

6. Jesse James's Two-Million-Dollar Treasure

No treasure has been sought in Oklahoma with the fervor, the dogged perseverance, or the intrigue inspired by the tales of Jesse James's hidden millions in the Wichita Mountains. Few treasures have been sought with such determination anywhere in the Southwest.[1]

Much like the Spaniards, wherever the James gang rode, they left their legends of buried treasure. One need but examine the newspaper files of every middle western state between Canada and Mexico—and a few on either side—for an inkling of the amount of hidden booty attributed to Jesse or his brother, Frank. If history had not recorded their daring deeds and the trails they rode, legends would show how far those trails stretched across the Middle West and into Mexico.

Obviously Jesse James could not have buried all the treasure attributed to him. But of all those reputed secret burials over a multistate area, the rugged range of hills in southwestern Oklahoma has drawn more attention and given rise to more stories than perhaps all the other potential sites put together.

I have woven the legend of Jesse James's treasure from many sources, both verbal and written. And although the source of the fabled gold and its final place of burial often vary, all stories lead to the Wichita Mountains and most often begin with the year 1876.

With hammer and chisel the most wanted outlaw of the West, Jesse Woodson James, painfully pounded the letters into the old brass kettle. "This, the 5th day of March, 1876, in the year of our Lord . . . ."[2]

It was the beginning of a strange contract that was to bind each member of an infamous outlaw band to secrecy about a golden treasure's hiding place. Jesse carefully chiseled the names of twelve deadly outlaws below the contract and then buried the brass bucket and its secret. The place was Tarbone Mountain, a roughhewn granite colossus easily approached from the north in the Wichita Mountains, in what was then Indian Territory. Jesse James had worked out a clever plan that no

other outlaw of his time had devised. It had all resulted from the winter before.

Somewhere in northern Chihuahua, Mexico, not far from the southwestern settlement of El Paso, Texas, Jesse and Frank with ten members of their gang surprised a detail of Mexican guardsmen driving eighteen burros transporting gold bullion. The brigands led the heavily laden packtrain across the Río Grande and over the plains of central Texas. Their destination was Indian Territory, a haven for wanted men and a region already familiar to both Jesse and Frank. When the outlaws entered the Wichitas, they were greeted by a severe winter blizzard. For three and a half days they traveled with little rest through snow almost a foot deep. His men were cold and weary, and Jesse knew that the gold had to be buried. And it was now obvious that their exhausted animals could travel little farther.

After almost three hours of slow, arduous travel east of Cache Creek, Jesse and Frank agreed to bury the golden cargo and burn the packsaddles to warm their chilled bodies. At the head of a small arroyo the band of men untied the packs from the burros and watched as the gold bars sank into the snow-covered ravine. After concealing the Mexican treasure with rocks and boulders and kicking the half-frozen earth off the side of the arroyo with their boot heels, the horsemen gathered round the packsaddles and set them afire. One lame burro was shot, while the others were set free to wander.

Jesse made two final but lasting signs to the gold. A burro shoe nailed into the bark of a tree served as one. Into a nearby cottonwood Jesse emptied both his six-shooters for a second mark. They would do until the day when the men could return to plant their gold in a much safer place.[3]

By March 5, 1876, Jesse had made up his mind about what to do with part of the two million dollars, plus other proceeds the gunmen had gathered while terrorizing banks and trains from Missouri to Mexico. As the ingenious Jesse now carved the contract into the brass kettle, he thought

Jesse James in 1875, the year before legend says that he and his outlaw band cached two million dollars in gold in the Wichita Mountains. Courtesy Western History Collections, University of Oklahoma Library.

Frank James in 1898, before he returned to his Oklahoma haunts to settle on a farm near Fletcher—and spend most of the remaining years of his life seeking outlaw gold in the Wichitas and the nearby Keechi Hills. Courtesy Western History Collections, University of Oklahoma Library.

to himself that neither he nor any of his cohorts would ever want for money—if and when they were taken by the law. But if anyone violated the brass-bucket pact, that fellow would personally answer to him. With that, Jesse James placed the brass bucket beneath a rock ledge on the side of Tarbone Mountain.

But the brass bucket with its secret treasure code was never to be retrieved by Jesse or any of his men, even though several would try years later. Only six months later almost to the day, the notorious James gang was shot up and dispersed while attempting to rob the Northfield, Minnesota, bank. Jesse and Frank were among the few to escape. Finally, on April 3, 1882, Jesse James met his death by the hand of a "coward" in St. Joseph, Missouri. Frank later stood trial and was acquitted of his past crimes. But he had not forgotten the hidden gold down in Indian Territory. He was waiting only for the opportune time to return as inconspicuously as possible.

Ironically, another former badman appeared in the Wichita Mountains country first—at least publicly. His name, too, appeared on the brass-bucket contract. Cole Younger had just completed a twenty-five-year sentence for his part in the Northfield, Minnesota, bank robbery. When released from prison, Cole made tracks for the Wichitas.

In December, 1903, Younger was in Lawton, Oklahoma, then a frontier boom town barely two years old. Cole was not particular about what he told the press. One paper reported in November that Cole was in Ardmore visiting a relative and planned to visit Dallas and the Texas Panhandle and then return home to Lee's Summit, Missouri, about December 1.[4]

Cole changed his mind, for on December 1 he was in Lawton. "Cole Younger was in the city Friday and Saturday with a view to locating. Reports have it that he will go into the newspaper business. He was given a reception by the citizens

Cole Younger as he appeared in 1876, the year his name was carved on the mysterious brass bucket buried in the Wichitas. He returned there briefly in 1903. Courtesy Western History Collections, University of Oklahoma Library.

and is pleased with the city," announced the paper.[5] Just how long Cole "visited" is not known, but apparently Frank was not convinced that he found much.

More than thirty years had passed since the border gold was hidden during the bitter winter of 1875, when Frank James made known his return to his old stomping grounds. In 1907 he and his wife, Ann, settled two miles north of Fletcher on a 160-acre farm between the Wichita Mountains and the Keechi Hills, the latter where Frank was later to dig up at least six thousand dollars of the outlaw loot.

Years before, Frank had hung up his guns for a final time. He was no longer the surly, though gentlemanly, outlaw whom so many had read about. Now sixty-four and balding, he remained soft-spoken and took no pleasure in recounting the past. His objectives he now kept mainly to himself. The news of Frank's purchase of the farm

spread fast when papers announced the story in November, 1907. Frank was then building his new home and planned to move in during the spring. He was also busy helping celebrate Oklahoma's statehood.[6]

My grandfather, C. E. Zorger, often recalled the time he first met Frank James. At the time C. E. was clerking in Blunt Baines's furniture store, at 512 D Street in Lawton. One day Frank was in town having a harness repaired. Baines and C. E. were looking outside when Baines pointed out Frank James. At the time C. E. was incredulous. "Ah, you're joking, aren't you?"

Baines smiled. "You'll see. When he comes back this way, I'll introduce you to him."

Some time later Frank returned up the street, and Baines called him into the store. "Frank James, I'd like you to meet C. E. Zorger." A young man in his twenties, my grandfather was satisfied that he was meeting the old outlaw himself, weather-beaten and wizened with long years of travel. Just how Frank and Baines had met C. E. was never sure. One thing he was sure about. Baines was interested in buried treasure, too, and even had several instruments made to aid him in that search.

On his sandy farm land Frank built a frame house, worked a plot of ground, and planted a grove of peach trees.[7] Just before his mother died, in February, 1911, she visited Frank and his wife at their farm. She died in Oklahoma City while en route back to Missouri.

Old-timers say that Frank James wore out six horses riding the trails, searching for landmarks to put him back on the road to the golden treasure. But the country had now been fenced and plowed. The Kiowa-Comanche-Apache Reservation had been opened to white settlement in August, 1901. Miners had swarmed into the Wichita Mountains to seek their own fortunes. Towns had grown up overnight, and new roads were now traveled. The old trails were not called by the names the outlaws had known them.[8]

Frank hoped that the old landmarks would help him recall his secluded haunts of thirty years before, the treasure code Jesse had laid down, and the brass bucket somewhere on Tarbone Mountain. It was one of Frank's day-after-day rides that attracted the eye of Dr. L. C. Knee, a

In 1907, Frank James built this house on his Oklahoma farm two miles north of Fletcher, between the Wichita Mountains and the Keechi Hills. It was later moved, and today it can be seen at Eagle Park, near Cache.

highly respected physician of early Lawton. While paying house calls near Apache, Dr. Knee observed every day for a week or more that Frank had ridden to the top of a hill about four miles east of Apache. There he sat astride his mount, facing south, staring as if in a kind of trance.

One day, out of curiosity, Dr. Knee drove his buggy up to the erstwhile bandit. After the usual comments about the weather Dr. Knee dismissed his manners. "I don't want to seem inquisitive, Frank, but why do you sit in that saddle up here for so long, just staring at the bald prairie? What is it you're looking for?"

It is not known what Frank replied, but it was not many weeks later that the doctor and two local men arrived with teams and fresno scrapers and dug out a portion of a small canyon. Their search

yielded the proper clues, for they had not dug long when they uncovered the skeleton of a burro, and not far away they found a burro shoe firmly embedded in a large tree. But it was their last clue, and after spending more than four thousand dollars, Dr. Knee gave up in disgust.

Frank had once explained that the eighteen burros had traveled so slowly after they forded Cache Creek in the winter of 1875 that it would take him only about a fifteen-minute ride on a good horse to cover the same distance to where they had unloaded the heavy golden cargo.

Dr. Knee may have known the old Fort Sill stage driver, Holsey Green Bennett, who one winter day early in 1876 spotted seventeen burros grazing at the base of Mount Scott. Bennett had thought it strange, for no military animals were allowed to

Following this pictographic treasure map, laden with coded symbols, Joe Hunter followed the Jesse James treasure trail into the Keechi Hills near Cement, where he unearthed part of the outlaw gold on Mrs. Belle Hedlund's farm.

roam that far from the fort, and the animals he saw carried no government brand.[9]

Former deputy sheriff Jim Wilkerson had been reared on stories of the James boys and their two-million-dollar treasure. He had worked with old deputies, who were aware that Frank was seeking part of the outlaw gold in the Wichitas. "None of them ever nosed in," Jim once told me. "Frank had an understanding with them."[10] Wilkerson also took a stab at finding the treasure and was not completely unsuccessful in his search. One telltale clue had been overlooked by Dr. Knee. Not far from the canyon in which the doctor had dug, Jim unearthed the rust-eaten buckles from eighteen burned packsaddles. "I was convinced more than ever that I was on the right track," Jim sighed. "But I never found anything more. And I don't think Frank did either."

One piece of property attracted Frank James perhaps more than any other he was known to have studied. Just east of Cement in the Keechi Hills, the farm was the property of a teacher, Mrs. Belle Hedlund. In 1907, not identifying himself, Frank inquired about an old spring and some symbols etched on a rock and asked Mrs. Hedlund whether he could look over her land.

The schoolteacher was curious and walked along with the stranger as he poked an iron rod into the ground in an inviting spot.[11] She showed him the only spring she knew about, at the foot of a lone knoll with a natural cave through one side, known as Buzzard Roost.

"If this is the right place, this is Jesse's kitchen," the stranger declared, pointing to a nearby rock as he bent down to reach under a stone. Soon he pulled out a rusted spoon.[12]

When Frank James revealed his identity to Mrs. Hedlund, she was momentarily frightened, she recalled later, but as he continued his visits to her farm over many months, she found him likable and always a gentleman.

As Frank continued his search, he confided in Mrs. Hedlund that he was seeking sixty-four thousand dollars that Jesse had taken during a robbery at Independence, Missouri. Jesse had carved a map and directions on a large rock and turned it upside down. That rock Frank believed was on Mrs. Hedlund's farm, near the spring, where the outlaws had camped on many an occasion. Frank

revealed that Jesse drew a similar map on his boot, later transferred it to paper, and gave it to his mother.[13]

Some time later Frank found some of the markings he was seeking. At the foot of Buzzard Roost he found the carving of a pair of crossed rifles cut deeply into a rock. The barrel of one pointed east to an aged tree, on which were etched the letters M. O. O. and, below, the letter Y. Beneath the carvings was a mule shoe nailed into a blaze.[14]

Not far from that tree Frank unearthed a copper kettle with a crock cover containing six thousand dollars—or so he said. One old settler who was sure that Frank's claim was true was Uncle Billy Royce, who owned the farm adjacent to Mrs. Hedlund's.[15] Billy Royce had met Frank James once before. He knew that the kettle of loot was not all that Frank was seeking. One day while Frank was in Cement buying supplies, Royce first spotted him. He took a double look and then hollered out, "Hello, Frank!"

The old outlaw wheeled around, staring, as if trying to remember where he had seen him before.

"I'm Billy Royce; we camped one night . . . ."

"'Nuff said," Frank interrupted with a twinkle in his eye. "Could I ever forget that supper you fed us?"[16]

The two men had met almost forty years before. Yet neither had forgotten that accidental run-in so many miles away up in Montana Territory. It was early in the 1870's, remembered Royce, that Frank, Jesse, and five others were making tracks between them and the law. After a long day's ride the brothers ran into a group of buffalo hunters. One long-haired sharpshooter recognized Frank and called out to him. Frank placed his hand close to his six-shooter and then almost instantly recognized the hunter as William F. "Buffalo Bill" Cody himself. That evening they camped together. Cody's cooks served a hot meal of venison and wild turkey. One of the cooks was Billy Royce, then only a tousled-haired youth of fourteen. Billy was the son of an Irishman who had served as a doorkeeper at the White House when Lincoln was president. The year before he met Frank James, Billy had gone to Denver and had later joined up with Cody.

Wide-eyed, Billy Royce listened intently that

night on the prairie as his employer and Jesse and Frank James talked and laughed, recalling earlier days. Royce never dreamed that he would ever see any of the outlaws again. He later scouted for the government and became a construction superintendent for a railroad. Finally he homesteaded in the Keechi Hills—coincidentally the very place where Frank and Jesse had hidden part of their booty and holed up on more occasions than Frank cared to recall.

As Frank and Billy Royce talked about the forty years that had elapsed since they had first met, Frank divulged what he was hunting in the Keechi Hills, part of which, in fact, he believed was on Royce's own farm. It was not long afterward that Frank unearthed the kettle of money. Royce was sure that Frank had not found it all, a fact that would later be proved.

Frank recovered at least six thousand dollars in the Keechi Hills; whether he actually recovered sixty-four thousand dollars no one knew for sure. One thing *was* sure. A cache Frank tirelessly searched for, time and again, he never found. And yet he must have walked over it a thousand times. The pot of gold—and pot it was—had been buried by Jesse. Frank had never known where. His mother had told him the vague details passed on to her by Jesse, but somehow they had got twisted around, and it was too late to double-check.

From the time Frank retrieved the cache of gold, Royce became a persistent treasure hunter of the Keechi Hills. In a newspaper article about him in 1932 the eighty-year-old settler reported that within only a few days a niece of Frank James and some male companions were due to arrive on a mysterious hunt.[17] What, if anything, they found has never been learned. But the story of Frank's niece turns up time and again in as many locations over the Wichita Mountains. What she was seeking, she—like her uncle—kept to herself. Plenty of people talked with her, but she divulged little.

There was at least one other cache that Frank removed successfully from its secret depository, and there are stories of still others. Everett Cook, a ranger for the Black Beaver Council Boy Scout Camp near Apache, remembers the story well:

It was one day in May, soon after Frank James had settled on his farm near Fletcher, that Harvey Yoder, my father-in-law, was sitting at the window of his home near Cache Creek. This was about seven miles northwest of Apache.

It was early morning and he was writing a letter on the windowsill. It was a warm day and the window was raised. As Harvey wrote, he heard someone walking across his yard. He looked up to see a covered wagon stopped in the road, and a man halfway to his door. He was a tall man, past middle age, and Harvey saw immediately that he was a man who had spent many long years in the outdoors. His face was weatherbeaten, and he walked with the bowlegged gait of a man used to having a horse under him. He wore cowboy clothing, including boots and spurs, even though he was riding in a wagon.

After the usual good mornings, he asked Harvey where the next crossing was down the creek. Harvey told him it was about a mile farther down. The stranger thought it over for a minute, then asked if there wasn't another crossing this side of there, near a big cottonwood tree. Harvey said yes, there was, but it hadn't been used since the country opened. The stranger thanked him and drove off.

Harvey finished his letter, saddled up his horse, and started toward the mailbox which was four or five miles away. When he got down the road a little piece, he saw that the man in the wagon had stopped and was unhitching his horses. As he rode abreast, the man said that the young horse he was driving had the colic, and that he was going to have to stop a while until the animal recovered. He also added that he was a prospector going to the Wichitas to look for gold. As far as looking for gold was concerned, he was telling the truth.

About this time, Harvey noticed that there was another man in the wagon, sitting in the spring seat. His back was turned, and he pretended to be busy with something on the floor of the wagon behind the seat. As he rode past, Harvey got a good look at his face. He positively recognized him as Frank James, who was well known in these parts by this time. Harvey rode on down the road, but couldn't help but wonder what Frank and the stranger were up to.

It was noon before Harvey returned from the mailbox. As he rode into the yard, his wife went to the door and told him that as soon as he had left, the two men had come back by the house and walked down to the creek carrying a shovel. A while later they came back on the opposite side of the creek carrying a kettle between them.

Harvey walked down to the big cottonwood tree and almost fell into a hole that had been dug in the middle of the trail, right even with the big cottonwood. He found the imprint where the big pot had sat. A few feet away from the hole, he found several handfuls of rifle shells of the old rimfire type. Apparently Frank had dumped them over the creek bank, thinking they would fall into the water. Neither Harvey Yoder nor his wife saw into the kettle, but the evidence was certainly all

The secret code on the map led Joe Hunter to Buzzard Roost, where, after many attempts, he unearthed a tea kettle containing a small fortune of Jesse James's booty, long sought, but missed, by Frank James.

there. What better place could you have hidden money than in the middle of a trail?[18]

Frank James confided in several friends that he was seeking outlaw treasure. His best friend in Fletcher, bank president E. W. Dilling, knew it, recalled L. A. Owen, of Fletcher, who as a young man saw Frank James on many occasions. Once Owen was talking with Dilling when someone rushed into his office, announcing that several men were digging for Frank's treasure. "Dilling left out in a hurry," Owen said, "apparently to check the story."[19] Even after Frank and his wife moved back to Missouri, she would return to Fletcher to visit the Dillings, often staying as much as a month at a time, and continued those visits after Frank died.

On another occasion, Owen remembered, Joe Cable once asked Frank about "a mule train of gold in Mexico." Frank thought about it for a moment and then, in his usual fashion of answering such questions in a half-serious, half-joking manner, replied that they "shot the mules and ran off the Mexicans."

There is no question that Frank James dug up two caches hidden near the Wichita Mountains. There are rumors that he recovered more, even as many as fourteen, each carefully guarded by landmarks known only to him or Jesse. Even though Frank recovered a portion of the outlaw loot, he did not retrieve it all, because he did not find the brass bucket with the outlaw contract carved into it. Nor did he find the iron teapot, which he must have walked over a thousand times in the Keechi Hills while searching Belle Hedlund's and Billy Royce's farms.

Even when Frank James finally left his Oklahoma farm about 1914 (only a year before he was to die), he must have thought often of the brass-bucket contract and the two million dollars in gold hidden during that bitter winter so many years before. Perhaps it was his niece who came back to find them, with Frank's final instructions. If so, she was no more successful than he, try hard though she did.

But the long treasure trail was not to end there. Actually it had only begun. A serious and determined treasure seeker named Joe Hunter made startling news when he unearthed the long-hidden brass bucket and many more of the treasure clues that Frank had missed. The long search began for Joe Hunter in 1932, the same year that Frank's niece made a final attempt to find her uncle's gold.

One day while Hunter was serving as a peace officer in Rush Springs, a gaunt, silver-haired oldster tottered into his office, asking for him. He told Hunter that his name was Cook and that he need not know more than that. He urged the peace officer to drive him outside town. Only there would he tell a story that he believed Hunter would be interested in.

Hunter had nothing better to do that day and, principally out of kindness, complied with the stranger's wishes. About three miles south of Rush Springs, alone with Hunter in his car, Cook unfolded a story so bizarre that Hunter at first found it difficult to believe. Cook revealed that because of his past friendship with Hunter's father he wanted him to have some treasure charts. If Hunter found the hidden money, the old man asked only for a rightful share.

Cook appeared to be about eighty-five years old and showed the signs of having lived a rugged past. He handed Hunter three maps, two made on cowhide and a third on goatskin, saying that his time was now too short to spend it hunting blood money.

"We buried it there about sixty-two years ago," said Cook in a tone barely above a whisper. "I hope you can find it. It'll be near a pile of rocks."[20]

Hunter and the old man then parted company. It was the first and last time Hunter ever saw him. The peace officer was skeptical of Cook's story, but Cook talked as if he must have been there. Hunter had no idea then that the treasure maps would haunt him for the remainder of his days, causing him to abandon job and family alike when he thought the trail was warm.

The first key to the hidden money was another map, inscribed on rock and buried in the rugged Wichitas. Cook described the place well to Hunter, and, as he later learned, it was only because of the old man's vivid description of the land that he uncovered the flat rock. By following the three maps, Hunter found a pile of rocks. Using the cairn and a distant landmark as two points of an equilateral triangle, he located what was supposed to be a third point—an old scrub oak.

Hunter soon chopped out the rock map from a hollow among the gnarled roots of the aged tree. He had no idea at that time that his search along the ancient trail of bloodstained treasure would last over a long period of years; otherwise, he

might have well quit long before he found the tantalizing clues—clues that goaded him on, always another day, another year.

His first discovery revealed that Cook had known what he was talking about. Soon Hunter discovered that Jesse and Frank James had established their own system of codes to lead them back to hidden caches, usually buried on the spur of the moment when time was precious and money only extra weight or when there was plenty of time and no place to spend the money. Many of the markings corresponded to symbols used by the Spaniards. Later Hunter came into possession of two more maps improvised by Jesse James, both of which were to prove valuable in his later searches. The charts had been left with an elderly man in eastern Oklahoma whose name Hunter never revealed. The old man was unaware that he possessed the maps until he had had them for five years. They had been hidden in the false bottom of a small chest. Soon after their discovery Hunter fell heir to them.

"I know now that I have the granddaddies of all the treasure maps," Hunter said in 1948, when he revealed much about his discoveries. "They have never been wrong. Jesse made one of these maps on a huge cowhide, the other on the tongue of his boot."[21]

Twenty-five years after Frank James's long quest in the Keechi Hills Mrs. Belle Hedlund found the strange rock he had so patiently sought. It happened one spring day, when Mrs. Hedlund was attracted to a large stone that appeared unnatural in its position. It reminded her of what Frank had told her years before. When she had it turned over, it was obviously the stone Frank had sought. Strange markings were etched on its underside. But there were no clear directions telling where to find the buried gold.

Joe Hunter read of Mrs. Hedlund's strange find. It was the moment he had been waiting for. Until then he had not known of Frank's early search on the Hedlund farm. The next day he got in touch with the aging schoolteacher. He studied the rock closely. With the information he had from his own maps he concluded that part of the treasure must be buried on the Hedlund farm, just as Frank himself had insisted.

For more than half a century this kettle guarded part of Jesse James's loot, including a large key-winder watch and a map etched on a sheet of copper.

Joe Hunter and Mrs. Belle Hedlund examine part of the James treasure find.

People had long ridiculed the idea of the James boys burying any of their ill-gotten gains. Even Hunter thought it was incredible, but if his maps were authentic, the treasure had to be there. Hunter was soon to learn the true worth of his maps. But even after his painstaking calculations it took him forty successive trips to the Keechi Hills before his searches yielded dividends. Only then did he unearth what Frank James must have wanted the most—the iron teapot. It was buried deep under the surface, just north of Buzzard Roost, the one knoll with a natural hole through it, a perfect landmark.

As Joe Hunter's spade struck the iron pot, he could not believe his eyes. His maps were genuine. The old man Cook had not steered him wrong.

Frantically Hunter brought the kettle to the surface, his hands trembling with excitement. Its lid was rusted shut, but soon Hunter had it pried open. The kettle was not overflowing with gold booty, but it held enough to make Hunter search the treasure trail for the rest of his days with a mania that only a treasure hunter can understand.

Inside the kettle was a small fortune in gold bullion, a quantity of jewels, several old coins, a large key-winder watch with a coin-silver case, and a rolled sheet of copper. One coin was an 1841 United States penny; another, a French five-franc piece dated 1811.[22]

Hunter turned over the gold to Mrs. Hedlund but retained the other articles. He placed a value of five thousand dollars on the watch because of its historical significance. Inscriptions on the watch indicated that it was number 3,400 manufactured by the New York Watch Company of Springfield, Massachusetts. The timepiece had probably been taken during a holdup by Jesse, for it had the name Theo E. Studley engraved in it. But the item of which Hunter was most proud was the sheet of copper, a treasure waybill in itself, exactly what Frank James had hunted so relentlessly. About two and a half feet long and eight or ten inches wide, the copper chart gave further details and code marks to a treasure trail that necessitated a full-fledged detective and code cipherer to unravel it.

This photograph, taken soon after the treasure was recovered, shows Jesse's tea kettle and some of its contents.

It was two years before Hunter uncovered his next clue. This time it was on an open prairie, and careful calculations led Hunter to it. Several feet into the earth his shovel struck an object that indicated he was on the right track. Nearby he dug another hole, which yielded an old pick head, its handle long decayed. When he dug still another such hole, again he found a rusted pick head. Its handle too was gone but bore the inscription Douglas Axe Mfg., Co. Hunt. The lettering on the other head had been hammered out. Still another hidden clue was a seventy-pound iron wedge. It told Hunter a story that only he knew how to interpret and told him in which direction to proceed.

The subsequent treasure key the cipher breaker unearthed proved to be the most interesting during his entire search and perhaps the most worthy in terms of historical value. That was the old brass bucket itself, with its contract chiseled deeply into its brass metal, binding each outlaw to secrecy. Hunter had indeed dug up a piece of the past, heretofore only an ingredient in a romantic legend.

The secret pact had been lost to history for seventy-two years, and most of the outlaws' names on the bucket were of men about whom little was known. In 1948, at the foot of looming Tarbone Mountain on the north edge of the cedar-clad Wichitas, Hunter unearthed what up to then had been mere legend.

"This the V day of March in the year of our Lord, 1876," read the contract, "we the under-signed do this day organize a bounty bank. We will go to the west side of the Keechi Hills which is about fifty yards from [here appears the symbol for crossed sabers]. Follow trail line coming through the mountains just east of lone hill where we buried Jack. His grave is east of a rock.

"This contract made and entered into this V day of March 1876. This gold shall belong to who signs below."[23]

Below the pact appeared the following names: Jesse James, Frank Miller, George Overton, Rub Busse, Charlie Jones, Cole Younger, Will Overton, Uncle George Payne, Frank James, Roy Baxter, Bud Dalton, and Zack Smith.

On the bottom of the bucket were inscribed the patent dates and the manufacturer. First patented on December 16, 1851, it was reinstated on March 24, 1870, and was extended in 1873 by E. Miller and Company.

Not far from where Hunter found the brass bucket under the rock ledge where Jesse had concealed it, he dug up a three-legged iron Dutch oven. Inside were the chain and fob that matched the watch he had uncovered in the Keechi Hills on the Hedlund farm, thirty miles northeast. Hunter now believed that he was nearing the end of the treasure trail.

Up to this time Hunter had had good luck. He had been successful in deciphering part of the outlaw code. But now his luck left him. Too many landmarks had changed. Too many clues had been destroyed. It had been more than three-quarters of a century since the outlaw gold had been hidden. Nature had played its role well in concealing it.

One of Hunter's waybills showed a grave, a horse and saddle, a cave, various symbols, and five caches of buried loot, with the descriptions: "$32,000 in gold, 136 paces north of cave; $28,000 in gold, 76 paces west of cave; $18,000 in gold, 72 paces north of cave; $38,000 in gold, 42 paces west of cave, and greenbacks and jewelry, 142 paces west and 11Hbg."[24] The long-sought

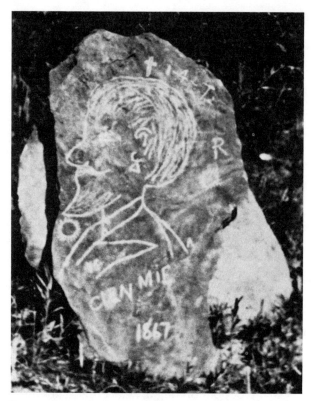

For years Frank James sought the coded symbols that he and Jesse had carved in the Keechi Hills. Mrs. Hedlund found this stone carving long after Frank had died. It later helped lead Joe Hunter to part of the outlaw loot at Buzzard Roost.

cave was known to Hunter as the Horse and Saddle Cave, used often by the outlaw band as a landmark. Hunter spent several weeks searching out the grave shown on the map and finally came upon the partly exposed bones of an extra-large man. The crumbled ruins of a cabin and a spring were nearby, close to Tarbone Mountain. But Hunter was never satisfied that he had found the cave the map called for.

During his long quest Joe Hunter took in a partner to help him. He was Slim Dillingham, of Lawton, a man who believes in the treasure so strongly that he has sought it for more than forty years. Slim accompanied Hunter on many of his discoveries and triumphs. I shall never forget the day I met Slim. As I walked into his hardware store, a buzzer made an awful racket, setting off a bell in the rear of the building. I walked to the back and found a tall, slender, near bald man working on a motor. "Is Slim Dillingham around?" I asked.

The old-timer looked up and frowned. "What do ya want with that old coot?"

"I was told that he could tell me about the James treasure."

About this time he took a spit from the wad of chewing tobacco he had in his mouth and missed the box. "Well, you're lookin' at that old coot. You say you're interested in the James treasure, huh?"

I nodded.

"Well, you know, finding a buried treasure is like finding a needle in a haystack. But it can be done. Yes, sir, it can be done," Slim drawled. He picked up a dusty pipe and commenced to pack tobacco into it.

"Son," he went on, "I could start this afternoon to tell you about the Jameses and their episodes in the Wichitas and talk until this time tomorrow afternoon and not repeat any one thing. But I'm just sittin' tight till I can get that treasure."

He puffed on his pipe. "The Jameses buried money all over those darn hills. But Frank got an awful lot of it, I know. Just what he did with it all, I don't know. But there must be an awful lot that he didn't get."

Slim readily admitted that he had never read anything about the James gang. The source of knowledge he constantly drew from was a long relationship with one who had known Frank James well enough to spend three years with him while he retraced his trail between the Wichitas and the Keechi Hills on the northeast. Slim always talked as though he had personally known both Frank and Jesse and always referred to the latter as simply Jess. Few unread people possessed the intimate knowledge of the outlaw brothers that Slim Dillingham did, who had heard all his stories from those in a position to know. Slim told me:

You see, Frank and Jess were planning on giving up their robbing and killing. They planned on having a ranch that stretched from the Wichita Mountains south to Red River. But they never saw those dreams come true. You know that, after Jess died, Frank left Missouri, came to Oklahoma, and bought a farm near Fletcher. Now you also know that he wouldn't have left his homeplace to come to this good-for-nothing country if he hadn't planned on digging up something pretty big. Yes, sir, Frank dug up a good amount of money on the very farm he bought. And he dug up more at other places.

You see, an old man named Jim Bevel used to hunt with me before he died. He told me a lot. Oh, how I've wished a thousand times I had had a tape recorder at my side over the years that we talked. Frank James

At the base of Tarbone Mountain, on the north side of the Wichitas, Joe Hunter unearthed the outlaws' brass bucket, on which Jesse James had carved a binding contract and the outlaws' names.

hired Jim for three years. Jim went with him whenever he was lookin' for something. Frank didn't tell him everything he knew by a long shot, but Jim watched and listened, and their relationship grew close during those years. Jim knew that Frank couldn't find one heck of a lot that he and Jess had hidden.

And there's one big thing that Frank would have given his eyeteeth to have had. That's why he didn't find all the money. That one thing is what Joe Hunter and I found—and that was the old teakettle with some of the loot in it, but more importantly a rolled up sheet of copper with a map drawn on it. But we couldn't figure out what all the code signs meant. God knows that Hunter and I came closer than any other living being, but even with old Jim's vast knowledge of Frank's searching all over those darn mountains, we lost the trail at a time when we thought the next day would surely bring success.

Since Joe Hunter's death in the 1950's, Slim Dillingham has done little searching for the remainder of the much-sought treasure. After Hunter's death many of the clues, along with the famous brass bucket, disappeared, and most of the treasure maps have scattered.

Even though Slim Dillingham has come to a virtual standstill in his forty-year search, there are others following the century-old trail of outlaw treasure. Each has his reason for believing the treasure is there—and each inherited his knowledge from those in a position to know.

Wells Blevins is one who could never be convinced otherwise. Living in the mountain settlement of Medicine Park, northwest of Lawton, he has turned up still other clues to the elusive James treasure—always one step ahead of its seeker. On the trail since 1926, Blevins has unearthed enough to satisfy even the most incredulous that he has been looking in the right places. What is more, Blevins inherited one of the James treasure maps from an original member of the outlaw band.[25] Blevins' searches have led him into the heart of the Wichitas, several miles north of the town of Cache and west to the mountains from Crater Lake. The outlaw plat bears the Spanish title Madrugada Estrella Mapa Oro, meaning "Early Morning Star Map to Gold." A clue to finding the treasure? Perhaps so. Appearing on the map are a stone foot or boot, a lone boulder, a large tree, and a trail. A tree stump shows a hole through it. A spring, an Indian encampment, a building with a flag, and another tree etched with a Spanish dagger are also shown. On either side of a small stream running west to east stand two men looking toward each other. One triangle is drawn over

141

THE LAWTON CONSTITUTION

ESTABLISHED AUGUST 6, 1901

Associated Press (UP) United Press   LAWTON, OKLA., SUNDAY, FEBRUARY 29, 1948   THIRTY-FOUR PAGES

Lawton Trio Believes End Of Trail Is Near In 16-Year Search For Fabulous Treasure In Expansive Wichitas

CLUES TO TREASURE.—Veteran Treasure Seeker Joe H. Hunter, upper left, is pictured as he spins a yarn of his 15-year-hunt for buried gold in the Wichitas. Immediately above is the picture of a watch and two coins which he dug up near Cement with a small amount of gold bullion. The watch, a keywinder, is cased in coin silver. The small coin is an 1841 U. S. penny, the other is a French five-franc piece. On it is a picture of Napoleon and engraved is "Dieu Protege La France, 1811." Upper right is the balance of the strange collection which has been unearthed from hiding places throughout the Wichitas. The left piece is a dutch oven, which the finders believe has significant markings on it; two pickheads lean against the center wedge, found in different places; the wedge upon which the pickheads are leaning is one of the most sought for clues in the hunt, but the brass bucket at the left is the most colorful. The bucket, unearthed near the dutch oven, has the names of Jesse James and his gang engraved upon its sides. They are Jesse James, Frank Miller, George Overton, Rub Busse, Charlie Jones, Cole Younger, Uncle George Payne, Frank James, Roy Baxter, Bud Dalton and Mack Smith. Above the names is a strange contract, disclosing where the treasure was hidden. (Constitution Staff Photo).

Kettle Bearing James Gang Names Displayed By Cityans

BY LINDSEY WHITTEN
Constitution Staff Writer

THERE'S a pot of gold at the end of a rainbow over the Wichita mountains. That's the opinion of three Lawton men, who believe they are near the end of a long trail which is leading to buried treasure in the Wichita mountains.

As evidence of their progress on the glittering trail, the trio displayed a strange looking brass bucket upon which is crudely engraved a contract, and the names of notorious outlaws whose forays are written in crimson on the pages of history. The contract speaks of treasure and where it is buried. The names are headed by that of Jesse James, the Missouri outlaw.

Many other strange objects make up the collection which these men believe are keys to immense wealth.

The story begins actually centuries ago. But for these three its beginning is less than a score of years old. Their pursuit of the fabulous gold has crisscrossed the nation several times and their leads often branched into foreign lands.

THE trio is headed by Joe H. Hunter, 55, of 304 Summit, who has come to love the hunt with a passion. He has lived and slept constantly with the thought of someday uncovering the riches; since the first clues were tossed unexpectedly into his lap at Rush Springs, Okla., in 1932. His partners, who were formed into a combine seven years later, are a Lawton father and son. They are Herbert Penick, pioneer of the Wichitas, and his son, Archie. The latter now is engaged in business in Lawton as owner of Penick's Myro-Flex agency, 522 C.

Probably no one knows for sure how much gold is buried in the Wichitas, if any, but these determined men are talking and thinking in terms of a fortune, two to three million dollars.

They believe it is the gold brought north by Spanish Catholic missionaries, later to fall in-

Cook. But to this day, Joe Hunter has never seen or heard of that old man again. And it was this old man who dumped the first clues of the strange quest into the bewildered hands of Joe Hunter.

Looking back over 15 years, during which most of his spare time has been devoted to breaking codes and digging up new leads, Joe Hunter remembers only a little of the old man. He wore a large white felt hat like typical men of the old west. His clothes were substantial, although not flashy and his eyes were piercing blue. The hair that showed at the edges of the hat was yellowish gray.

The maps relinquished by the old man were done so with the understanding he would share in any of the wealth discovered. But if the old man is alive today, he would be near the century mark. It's doubtful if he survives, Mr. Hunter believes.

IN THE seclusion of Hunter's

yield any word of the past.

It was the third trip before he found the pile of rocks which apparently had lain undisturbed for more than half a century.

HERE was his first puzzle. Although he dug and searched near the rocks, he could find nothing that resembled the map described by Cook.

Patiently he covered every foot of the ground. Finally, he hit upon an idea, fantastic though it sounds. Looking off into the near distance he readily sited a prominent high point. Using the pile of rocks and the distant landmark as two points of an equilateral triangle, he located approximately a third point. It was an old scrub oak tree.

Going to the old tree, Hunter began a search and finally he uncovered the object of his search. It was an innocent appearing rock, but inscribed with a series of unusual characters. It had rested for all those years in a hollow spot, down in the roots of the old gnarled tree.

The thrill of that first victory sent the blood of

James Loot Is Mystery In History

WHAT tales of adventure are beaten into the brass bucket that bears the name, Jesse James? Was the famous brigand in fact tached away from the eager eyes of the law in the recesses of the quiet Wichitas while Jesse and his band of 10 robbers pursued the mystery of missing Spanish gold?

History Unfolds

The battered treasure-bucket claimed by three Lawton adventurers conjures up pages of history alive with the James legend and

Bridges Says Congress To Adjourn By Mid-June, Maybe

WASHINGTON, Feb. 28.—(AP) —The senate appropriations committee is shooting at a mid-June adjournment date for congress.

Chairman Bridges (R-NH) said the committee decided Saturday to make "every endeavor" to finish up its work on the appropriations bill by that time. Action on appropriations normally is the final act of a congress.

Tulsan Is Found Guilty Of Murder As Insanity Plea Fails

TULSA, Okla., Feb. 28.—(AP) —A district court jury found Louis G. Moeller guilty of murder Saturday and fixed his punishment at life imprisonment.

Moeller, 32, was convicted of the Aug. 19 pistol slaying of his former sweetheart, 21-year-old Joan Cross. Moeller, for whom the defense had advanced an insanity plea, sat emotionless as the verdict was read.

In 1948, Joe Hunter broke his story of the fabled Jesse James treasure and documented for the world many of the treasure clues he had found in a search that had stretched over sixteen years. The Dutch oven, the pick heads, the iron wedge, the brass bucket carved with a contract and the outlaws' names, and, below, the key-winder watch and coins were clues that led Hunter on one of the greatest treasure hunts of the century.

Erstwhile outlaw J. Frank Dalton, left, and Joe Hunter discuss the famous brass bucket
and the secret pact carved on the kettle on March 5, 1876, and buried in the Wichitas.
Photograph by Robin Broun.

another, and along their sides appear such distances as 22 paces, 52 paces, 104 paces, 114 paces, and 164 paces, all leading from the "stone foot."

That Jesse and Frank buried money there is firmly believed by Blevins. Years ago a man who called himself John Von (or Vaughn) claimed that he had once ridden with Jesse's gang and was there when Jesse and Frank buried a "bean pot full of gold topped with a large diamond." Von

told Blevins that he had seen Jesse etch the map onto "half a copper kettle." Von remembered that Jesse walked around the side of a hill. "He had nothing to dig with but a bowie knife," Von recalled. There Jesse buried the "half of the copper kettle" on which he had carved the map. The other half he buried under the roots of a cedar tree.

"This half, mind you, I found with the help of Von," Blevins revealed, taking his eyes off his map

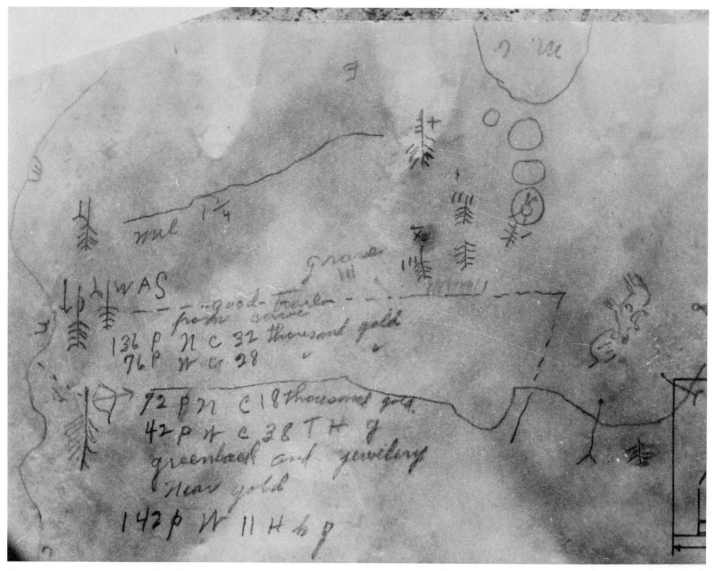

One of Jesse James's treasure maps, showing five caches of gold, greenbacks, and jewelry buried near the Horse and Saddle Cave. Though Joe Hunter succeeded in deciphering much of the code, he never found the treasure.

just long enough to look up at me as he told his story one summer afternoon in 1963. "But what we didn't find was the other half of the kettle with the map, and I don't believe Frank ever found it."

During their search Von guided Blevins to two graves near Crater Lake. "We dug into them both," Blevins said, "because I wanted to test Von's story. There was a bullet hole through one man's skull, right between his eyes. Von said there were three graves but we could find only two.

"In the second grave we found several gold bracelets which had been linked together. It was near there that we dug up half of the copper kettle

embedded in the roots of a large cedar tree. Not far away the bean pot must be buried. Von knew too much to be lying," Blevins stressed, "and he always proved himself right."

I did not interrupt Blevins while he told me a story about Von, one that I had heard before. His story differed little from the others, and this seems to be an appropriate place for it.

Blevins sipped black coffee and rubbed his eyes, thinking back about the former outlaw. "Von once told me how he had barely escaped the wrath of Jesse," Blevins began:

His duties during one particular robbery were to hold

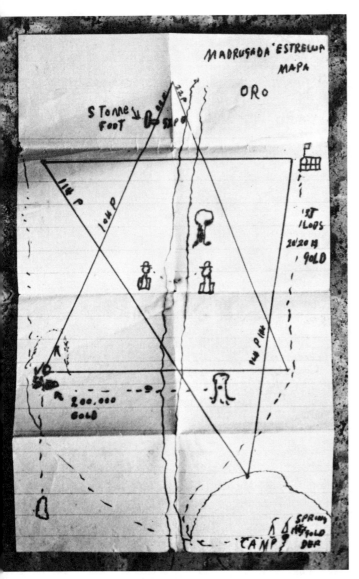

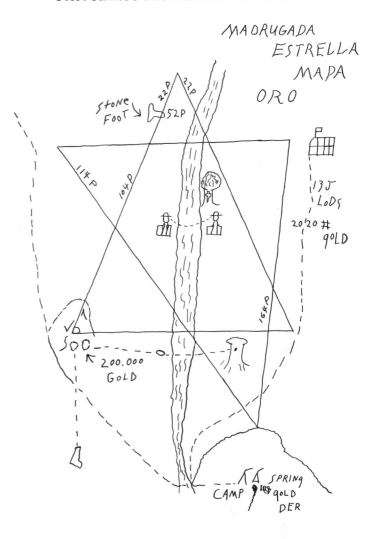

Wells Blevins inherited another of the treasure maps from a member of the outlaw band (inset and redrawn). Although many of the landmarks were discovered, the gold of the "Madrugada Estrella Mapa Oro" has never been found.

the horses. But instead Von got cold feet and fled. For some odd reason he had the nerve to meet Jesse and Frank at a later time. Jesse planned on killing Von and revealed his intentions to Frank. But one night Frank suggested to Von that he get out of camp before Jesse woke up. Von said he didn't even put his boots on for fear of waking him.

Frank told Von never to come back, because the next morning Jesse would kill him, and, if Jesse didn't, then he would. Von went to California, so he told me. When the country opened up, he returned to the Wichitas in hopes of taking up the bean pot full of gold. Somehow he seemed sure that Jesse had never recovered it. It was then that I happened to get acquainted with him. Von lived in Lawton many years until his death. I don't think he and Frank ever met again.[26]

Dean C. Salyer, of Lawton, first visited Oklahoma more than twenty-five years ago with the goal of finding the lost treasure. He has periodically sought $180,000 he believes to be secreted in the rocks not far from Cutthroat Gap, in the far northwest corner of Comanche County.[27]

Salyer, a tree surgeon, a former cowboy, a treasure hunter, and a downright good talker, is another who came into personal contact with an aging member of the outlaw band, but far away from the Wichita Mountains. At one o'clock one winter afternoon in 1958 I first stepped into Salyer's home.[28] I left sometime after six, having learned plenty about Salyer the man and Salyer

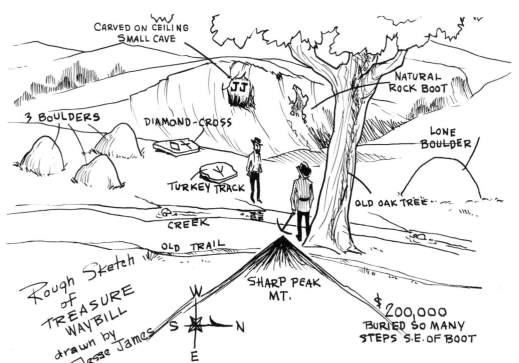

CARVED ON CEILING
SMALL CAVE

NATURAL
ROCK BOOT

3 BOULDERS

DIAMOND-CROSS

JJ

LONE
BOULDER

TURKEY TRACK

OLD OAK TREE

CREEK

OLD TRAIL

W

S

N

E

SHARP PEAK
MT.

$200,000
BURIED SO MANY
STEPS S.E. OF BOOT

Rough Sketch
of
TREASURE
WAYBILL
drawn by
Jesse James

Another version of the map, featuring the natural rock foot, or boot, shows treasure symbols found by hunters while they were searching for Jesse James's two-million-dollar hoard of gold. Drawing by Harvey Freeze.

the adventurer. Uneducated by today's standards, had he received training, his wit would have made him one of the country's cleverest lawyers.

His thumb and forefinger were stained yellow from countless rolling of Bull Durham cigarettes; he rolled them faster than any other man I ever saw. As his wife, a small, round little woman, brought him pitch-black coffee, he began his story, stroking his head of coal-black hair:

I haven't found anything, but I haven't given up looking, even though I've slowed down a mite. One thing I know. Jesse and Frank James buried one hundred and eighty thousand dollars in those hills. Make no mistake about that.

You might wonder how I came to know all this. It was all from an old outlaw in Brownwood, Texas— that's where I'm from originally—who was a good friend to Jesse and Frank. Even after Frank was acquitted of his crimes, he used to come down to Brownwood just to talk over old times with this man, whom I knew as Conley. I imagine they talked over buried treasure, too, although Conley never admitted as much.

During the Depression Salyer worked as a cook, carpenter, farmer, cowboy, or in any other job he could find. During that time he met the aged Conley. Conley and his family were hungry. Salyer asked no questions and slipped Conley a ten-

dollar bill. Over the months a great friendship developed. Salyer recalled with fond memories visiting Conley for hours at a time, listening to him tell of his strange past. He told me:

Conley spoke often of outlaws, but it was a long time before he said just who the outlaws were. He was more of a lookout man for Jesse as I gathered it. At first I didn't think too much of his story. But, you know, he talked like he must have been there. And, too, he had a cowhide map which he said was one of only three copies.

Salyer and Conley talked often of making a trip to the Wichita Mountains to reclaim the treasure that Conley knew had been buried—that is, if Frank hadn't recovered it himself, and Conley had his reasons for believing that he had not.

"Before the old man and I could make the trip, Conley died," Salyer went on. "But before he died, he gave me his directions and let me look at the map." The old outlaw told Salyer that the gold was hidden in a sealed cave. A natural stone corral known to the outlaws as Horse Thief Corral, a log cabin in Cutthroat Gap, and a Winchester rifle mounted in the fork of a tree were the signs leading to the hidden cave.

It was years before Salyer moved from Brownwood to Oklahoma, and it was several years more before he made his first trip to the Wichitas. Finally, in the 1950's, he enlisted the aid of J. B. "Burt" Holderbaum, an old prospector left over from the gold-rush days, and together they rediscovered the old stone corral in the shadow of Cutthroat Gap—a valley into the mountains from the north that had earned its title more than a century before (1833) when Osages massacred their Kiowa neighbors and placed their severed heads in brass buckets. Holderbaum was one of the few living persons who knew the location of the rock pen.

At first even Holderbaum had trouble locating the outlaw lair, but he knew that it was on level ground at the base of Mount Pinchot—the highest peak in the Wichitas, although it does not appear to be. An old trail ran past the corral, but the animals inside were hidden from view, Holderbaum remembered. In one corner of the corral stood the rotten stumps of two trees that had once served as gateposts. Holderbaum recalled having been shown the corral in 1901. At that time a rock fortress said to have been used by outlaws was still visible about two miles north.[29] Its breastwork was constructed from boulders stacked in a large circle on top of a lone hill, which in 1901 had but one lone cedar growing on it. It had been some time before that Holderbaum found a rust-eaten rifle hanging in an oak tree just west of the makeshift fortress.

"The cabin in Cutthroat Gap was a clue that I could never forget," Salyer said, as he rolled and licked a cigarette. "A bandit queen once lived in the cabin. She apparently purchased the food and supplies for the outlaw bunch. Old Conley often mentioned her, always with a smile."

At the summit of Mount Pinchot a long, black streak plunges twenty feet down a bluff. Salyer declared:

The black streak is a sign, too. The gold is between the streak and the hanging rifle, if Conley didn't err in his directions. My partners and I searched continuously for six weeks during one spell. We looked every day except Sundays but had no luck in finding anything more than the corral, fortress, and ruins of the cabin. The hundred and eighty thousand dollars was part of a payroll robbery at Dodge City as I remember.

Ever since early boyhood in Brownwood, Texas, Salyer had heard tales of a prominent banker there who was believed to be the real Jesse James but who went under the name Colonel Henry Ford. But there is no record that Ford ever admitted such or even pretended to be James. However, even today, old residents of Brownwood will swear that Ford was indeed Jesse, for he had no other reason to keep a mysterious trunk in his house under lock and key. Too, many residents believed the legend because both Frank James and Cole Younger made trips to Brownwood to see Ford, and Frank's sister, Susan, and brother-in-law, Allan Parmer, lived nearby, just outside El Dorado.

Ford first appeared at Brownwood in the 1870's, later served as its mayor and then as president of the Coggin Brothers and Ford Bank.[30] It is possible that Ford was a member of Quantrill's guerrillas or even one of the original outlaws who rode with Jesse. Whoever he was, Frank and Cole had a lot to talk over with him after the turn of the century.

Salyer regrets that he and Conley never made their trip to the Wichitas before Conley died. But at that time it seemed impossible. Occasionally Salyer still pokes around in the shadow of Cutthroat Gap.

Frank James recovered some of the loot. Joe Hunter unearthed some of the treasure that Frank had failed to find. The clues have been too many to dismiss as legend: the brass bucket with the outlaw contract, the silver watch, the graves, the gold bracelets, the copper sheet with its secret code, and, of course, the maps—too old and perhaps too cryptic for anyone to read now. Yet treasure seekers still dig in lonely canyons, scan out-of-the-way pinnacles, and explore musty-smelling caves in quest of Jesse James's two-million-dollar treasure, secreted in the Wichita Mountains at a time when those hills harbored some of the deadliest outlaws of the West.

Frank himself is said to have once revealed that the treasure was buried alongside the old Chisholm Trail between Fort Sill and the Keechi Hills. It must still await some lucky finder, one who can break its secret code and follow the long trail that Frank James rode hard enough to wear out six horses.

Silas Lee Ison, the last of the old prospectors, stands at his homemade test smelter in the Wichita Mountains Wildlife Refuge.

7. The Last of the Old Prospectors

On the eve of the last great land opening in the West, gold seekers from virtually every mining district descended on the Wichita Mountains, soon no longer to be part of the vast Kiowa-Comanche-Apache Reservation carved out for those tribes at the Treaty of Medicine Lodge in 1867.

In August, 1901, miners' camps mushroomed across the craggy, humpbacked hills from Fort Sill on the east to Granite, a settlement sixty miles on the west. It was the birth of the last great gold rush east of the Rockies. Bearded sourdoughs from the Black Hills, Cripple Creek, Nevada, California, Arizona, and even Alaska, Mexico, and Australia poured in with high hopes of making a rich strike in a storied mountain range that theretofore had been forbidden land.

Virtually untouched by the prospector's pick and shovel, the Wichitas, with their tales of lost Spanish mines, abundant in wild game, timber, and mountain streams, were a gold seeker's paradise, an oasis on the Plains.[1]

Wrote reporter W. R. Draper in a lengthy story for the *New York Times*, which was picked up by the *Scientific American Supplement* of November, 1901:

> The rush to the gold fields of the Wichita Mountains has commenced in earnest. The trails are all covered with a rushing mass of humanity. Everyone seems confident that the future will bring forth rich strikes. Fully 20,000 persons have been into the mountains since the opening. Six thousand claims are staked. The Wichita Mountains have begun to draw like the Klondike.

The mining camps Wildman, Oreana, Doris, Golden Pass, Poverty Gulch, Craterville, Lightning Gulch, and Meers teemed with gold seekers, each wistfully hoping for his own bonanza in the new land.

Two, three, perhaps five thousand prospectors staked their claims, sunk their mines, and eagerly waited for the reports of their assays. The names they christened their mines were often the names of bonanzas they had known in western mining camps. Rich claims sold for five to ten thousand dollars in cash—one report said twenty-five thousand dollars—as ore wagons rumbled over the mountain trails hauling precious rock to one of a half-dozen mills belching smoke from their high smelter stacks.

Meers, a mining camp nestled at the base of Mount Sheridan, rising eight hundred feet above the prairie floor, straddled an ancient Indian trail leading into the rugged granite mountains from the north. Later the miners replanted their bustling city one mile beyond Mount Sheridan, on the first rise just north of Medicine Creek, where it would grow to a population of three hundred miners and their families.

Twenty miles or so westward at the foot of Nest Egg Mountain, five miles south of Roosevelt, was Wildman, established illegally early in the summer of 1901, before the reservation was opened to settlement. The year before, Fort Sill soldiers had destroyed the miners' smelter and burned their shacks. Later the miners and homesteaders often contested each others' rights to land, and one heated debate ended in a gunfight in Cutthroat Gap. The concrete ruins of the huge cyanide ore mill Wildman's miners built near the gaping Gold Bell Mine are still impressive to view.

Rich gold pockets assayed up to three thousand dollars to the ton—on one occasion twenty thousand dollars. Silver, platinum, lead, and copper followed suit. Expectations ran high, as clearly shown in Meers's weekly *Mount Sheridan Miner*, Wildman's *Otter Creek Miner*, Lawton's *Mineral Kingdom*, and in columns devoted to mining in newspapers over the state. But the real bonanza always chose to remain a will-o'-the-wisp. The smelted bars of silver and copper were few, and the gold little more than buttons. By 1907 the bustling gold camps had dwindled away until only the crumbling smelter ruins, ore-crushing arrastras, and water-filled shafts with their barren mine dumps remained to tell the dramatic tale of Oklahoma's gold rush.

Silas Lee Ison, a centenarian prospector, hard-rock miner, and treasure hunter, was the last

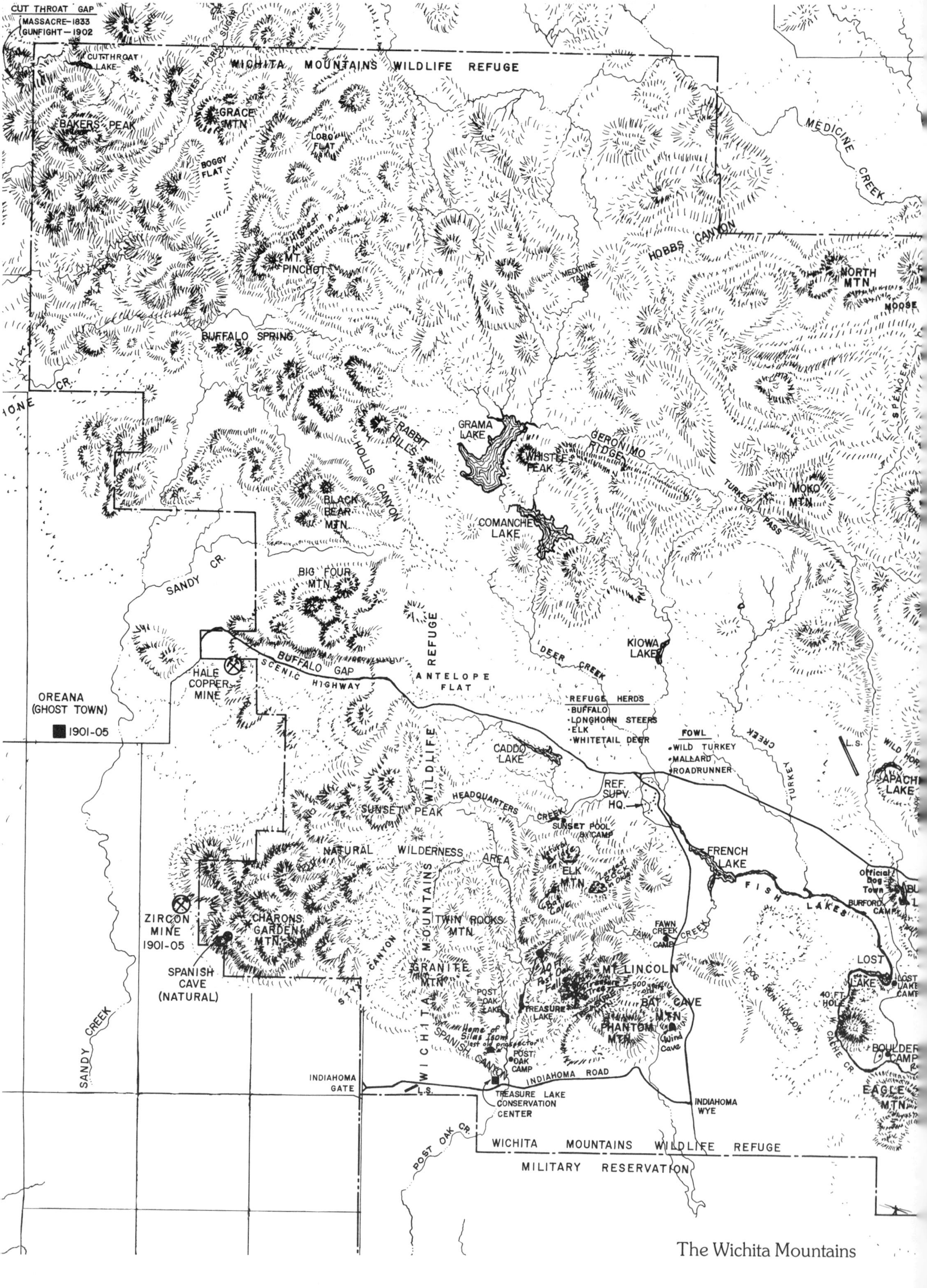
CUT THROAT GAP
MASSACRE-1833
GUNFIGHT-1902
CUT THROAT LAKE
WICHITA MOUNTAINS WILDLIFE REFUGE
WEST FORK SUGAR
GRACE MTN
BAKERS PEAK
LOBO FLAT
BOGGY FLAT
MEDICINE CREEK
"Highest Mountain in the Wichitas"
MT. PINCHOT
HOBBS CANYON
MEDICINE TANK
NORTH MTN
MOOSE
BUFFALO SPRING
CR.
GRAMA LAKE
RABBIT HILLS
HOLLIS CANYON
WHISTLE PEAK
GERONIMO RIDGE
SPENCER
TURKEY PASS
MOKO MTN
BLACK BEAR MTN
COMANCHE LAKE
SANDY CR.
BIG FOUR MTN
REFUGE
BUFFALO GAP
SCENIC HIGHWAY
HALE COPPER MINE
ANTELOPE FLAT
DEER CREEK
KIOWA LAKE
OREANA
(GHOST TOWN)
1901-05
REFUGE HERDS
·BUFFALO
·LONGHORN STEERS
·ELK
·WHITETAIL DEER
FOWL
·WILD TURKEY
·MALLARD
·ROADRUNNER
CADDO LAKE
WILDLIFE
CREEK
TURKEY
L.S.
APACHE LAKE
REF. SUPV. HQ.
HEADQUARTERS CREEK
SUNSET PEAK
SUNSET POOL
NATURAL WILDERNESS AREA
ELK MTN
Bat Cave
FRENCH LAKE
FISH LAKES
Official Dog Town
BURFORD CAMP
ZIRCON MINE
1901-05
CHARONS GARDEN MTN
TWIN ROCKS MTN
WICHITA MOUNTAINS
FAWN CREEK CAMP
FAWN CREEK
SPANISH CAVE
(NATURAL)
GRANITE MTN
MT LINCOLN
Treasure Tree
BAT CAVE MTN
DOG RUN HOLLOW
LOST LAKE
LOST LAKE CAMP
40 FT. HOLE
POST OAK LAKE
TREASURE LAKE
PHANTOM MTN
Wind Cave
Home of Silas Lcom "last old prospector"
POST OAK CAMP
SPANISH CANYON
CACHE CR.
BOULDER CAMP
SANDY CREEK
INDIAHOMA GATE
L.S.
INDIAHOMA ROAD
TREASURE LAKE CONSERVATION CENTER
INDIAHOMA WYE
EAGLE MTN
POST OAK CR.
WICHITA MOUNTAINS WILDLIFE REFUGE
MILITARY RESERVATION

The Wichita Mountains

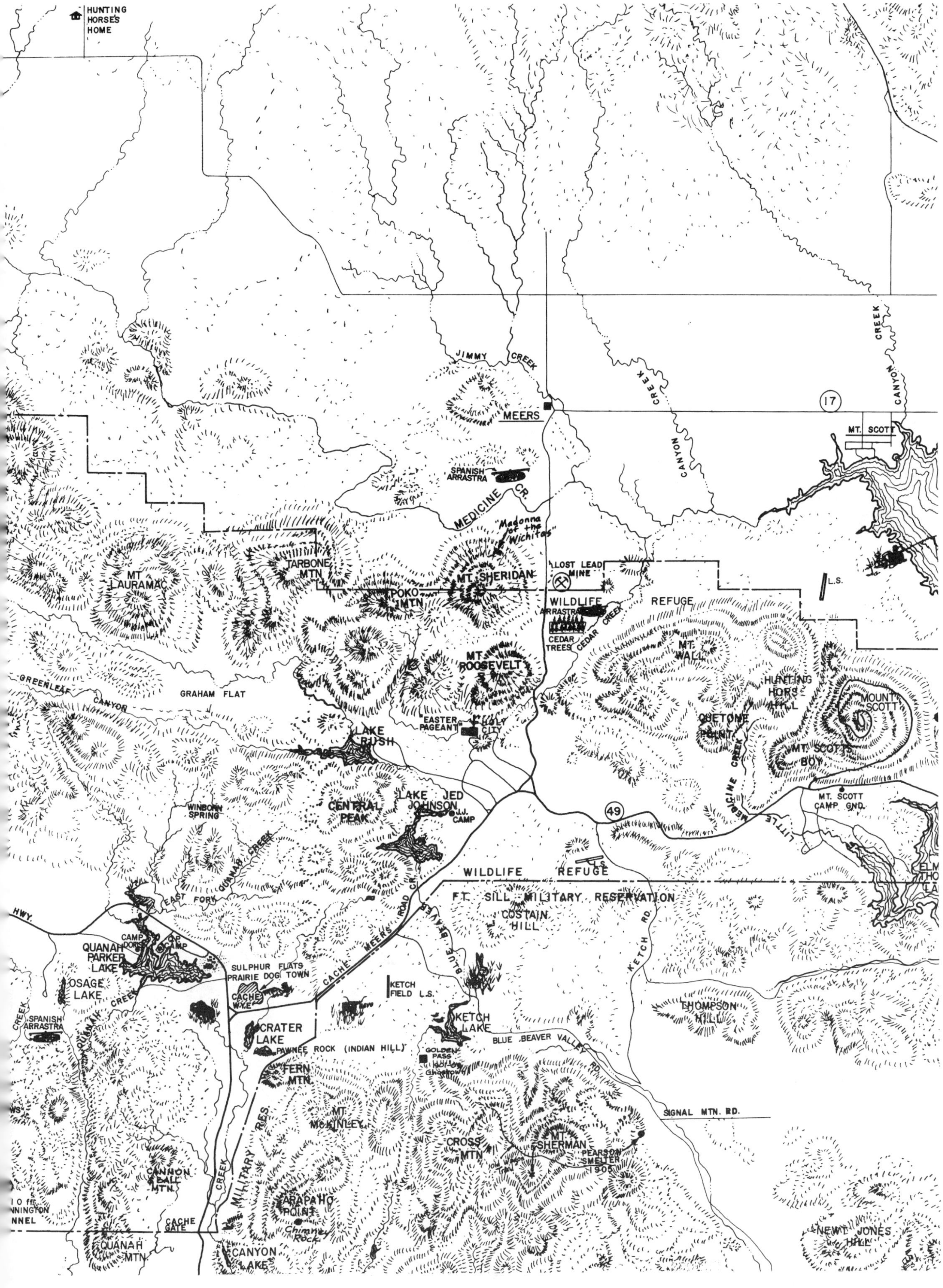

HUNTING HORSE'S HOME
JIMMY CREEK
MEERS
CANYON CREEK
17
MT. SCOTT
SPANISH ARRASTRA
MEDICINE CR.
Madonna of the Wichitas
TARBONE MTN
MT LAURAMAC
MT. SHERIDAN
LOST LEAD MINE
POKO MTN
WILDLIFE ARRASTRA
REFUGE
L.S.
CEDAR TREES
CEDAR CREEK
MT. WALL
MT ROOSEVELT
GREENLEAF CANYON
GRAHAM FLAT
HUNTING HORS HILL
MOUNT SCOTT
QUETONE POINT
EASTER PAGEANT
HOLY CITY
LAKE RUSH
MT. SCOTTS BOY
MT. SCOTT CAMP GND.
LAKE JED JOHNSON
J.J. CAMP
CENTRAL PEAK
WINBORN SPRING
49
LITTLE MEDICINE CREEK
WILDLIFE REFUGE
QUANAH CREEK
EAST FORK
FT. SILL MILITARY RESERVATION
COSTAIN HILL
HWY.
QUANAH PARKER LAKE
SULPHUR FLATS PRAIRIE DOG TOWN
CACHE MEERS ROAD CR.
BLUE BEAVER CR.
KETCH RD.
OSAGE LAKE
CACHE W.Y.E.
KETCH FIELD L.S.
THOMPSON HILL
SPANISH ARRASTRA
QUANAH CREEK
KETCH LAKE
CRATER LAKE
BLUE BEAVER VALLEY RD.
PAWNEE ROCK (INDIAN HILL)
GOLDEN PASS
FERN MTN
SIGNAL MTN. RD.
MT. McKINLEY
MILITARY RES.
CROSS MTN
MT. SHERMAN
PEARSON SMELTER 1905
CANNON BALL MTN.
ARAPAHO POINT
Chimney Rock
CACHE GATE
CREEK
NEWT JONES HILL
QUANAH MTN
CANYON LAKE

In 1903, Dr. S. J. Hardin, of the Shawnee Mining Company, erected this eight-thousand-dollar smelting plant at his Lost Lead Mine, a mile east of Mount Sheridan, near Meers. The mine, left, reached a depth of 108 feet, and was cased with square-sawed timbers. From Joe B. Baker, *Souvenir of Lawton, Oklahoma*, 1907.

Between 1903 and 1909, Hardin spent more than $19,500 at his Lost Lead Mine. A steam-engine-powered windlass lowered miner and ore bucket more than one hundred feet into the solid-granite shaft. Courtesy Western History Collections, University of Oklahoma Library.

Mount Sheridan looms above the seven-foot-square shaft of the Lost Lead Mine. Today nothing remains but a gaping hole and a mound of tailings—testimony to the gold seekers who lived and worked there during the Wichita gold rush.

In 1905, after nine months and thirty-five hundred dollars, John Pearson completed this twenty-five-ton firebrick smelter at Camp Homestead, at the foot of Mount Sherman, near Golden Pass. From his mine came enough ore to yield several bars of copper and silver. From *Mineral Kingdom*, October 12, 1905.

News of the Wichita gold camps drew front-page coverage over Oklahoma Territory. Excitement ran high when the Pearson smelter yielded bricks of bullion.

THE CACHE REGISTER.

VOLUME 1.   CACHE, OKLAHOMA, THURSDAY, OCTOBER 5, 1905.   NUMBER 8.

PEARSON SMELTER MAKES RUN.

Two Bricks of Bullion Run Off Last Evening. Bullion Is Mostly Silver.

Carl Reid, G. W. Harrell and Arch Isle came in from the Pearson Smelter today and reported that everything is highly satisfactory from the recent run and two bricks were drawn off last night and Profs. Tucker and Gullett and all the members of the Homestead Mining and Milling Company are highly elated over the returns. The bricks are said to contain about $22. worth of mineral principally gold and silver. The capacity of the smelter is about 25 tons but in this run the smelter was not tested to it full capacity as the engine which was used was not thought to be of sufficient power to run the blower at its full.

A. J. Lawrence returned last night from the smelter and reports that everything was working entirely satisfactory. Mr. Pearson assured him it was no experiment as far as the values of the ore was concerned and of course it was only a question of the smelter's being a success.

The assays which Profs. Tucker and Gullet have obtained from this ore result in the neighborhood of about $45 per ton. The results obtained from tests of the bullion run off last evening are identically the same in values as those made from the ore, thus proving beyond any doubt the existance of the minerals and the valuable quantities of it in this ore. It also proves the Pearson Smelter and the smelting process for this ore no longer a thing of experiment but an absolute success proven by established facts.

The two bricks run off weighed together 176 lbs. The amount of ore smelted was about 1000 lbs or ½ ton. Tests of the bullion gave results of $257.76 with $18 gold and $239.76 silver per ton bullion, making the value of the mineral in the two bricks of 176 lbs. at about $22.68.

Prof. Tucker was especially highly pleased with these results saying it was very rich. He was also much pleased with the success of the smelter. He will leave for Wildman tomorrow but may return to superintend another run in the near future.

A number of Cache citizens have been watching this test run with intense interest. They have interests in the Wichitas and know too that it means a boom for Cache.

Crowds of expectant miners and visitors have been watching the results of this run, the roads leading to and from the smelter being kept hot by passing vehicles. Now that the results are known and have been made public it is expected that in a very short time great crowds of miners and capitalists will be flocking from the mining districts of the neighboring states and of the world into this wonderfully rich field.

TEACHERS MEET

Association's First Program.

District No. 2 of the Comanche County Teachers Association will meet October 14, at 1.30 p. m. in Banks Hall, at Cache and render the following program.

Song - - - - - - - - Association.
Prayer - - - - - - - Rev. Rushing.
Welcome Address - C. E. Hank, Pres. Board of Education.
Song - - - - - - - - Cache School.
Benefits to be Derived from Study of History - - - Supt. E. B. Nelson.
Vocal Solo - - - - Hazel Tomlinson.
Primary Number Work - Rachel Cook.
Recitation - - Pupil of Cache School.
Primary Language Work - Ethel Collins.
Cornet Solo - - - - - J. F. Piercy.
Busy Work for Primary Pupils Mae Smith.
Vocal Solo - - - - Vernon Brooks.
Home Help for Pupils: Its Nature, Uses and Dangers - - - Mr. Beaver.
Song - - - - - - - Joy Colvin.
Two Minute Talks on: To What Extent Should the Teacher Enforce the Study of Technical Grammar,

Visiting teachers will be provided with dinner at the Harrell Hotel.

The interested public are invited to attend this meeting.

DEAD LETTERS.

Cache, Okla., Aug. 1st, 1905.

The following is the list of letters remaining uncalled for in the Post Office for the month ending August 1st, 1905:

Broker, Fred   Hunt, David B.
Reeves, Miss Loly   Sang, Alice
Steele, Tom A.   Schlereth, Jno.
Thomas, I. M.

If not called for in thirty days these letters will be sent to the Dead Letter Office.

Please say advertised when called for. One cent will be charged for advertising.

F. P. Runnels, P. M.

STANDARD OIL WILL CONTROL.

Reduces Price of Refined Oil and Raises Price of Crude Oil.

It is reported that the Standard has already commenced war on the independent refineries of Kansas. The price of refined oil and gasolene has been lowered in Kansas territory 2 and 3 cents per gallon and still there is more to follow.

It is rumored also that agents for the Standard are now going about among the oil producers offering to contract for oil at 80 cents per barrell provided the producer will sign a five year contract. This will of course look pleasant to the producer who has been forced to take 25 cents per barrell or let his oil stay in the tanks, but just how the Standard can afford to reduce the price of refined oil and gasoline 20 per cent and at the same time raise the price of crude oil 200 per cent will not be apparent to the ordinary plug citizen unless the Standard is willing to admit that it has been robbing both producer and consumer during the past. The fact is the Standard will try to grind the independant refinery beneath the upper and nether millstone. What is more the grinding is likely to be a success. It certainly will unless the independent refiners have enough territory of of their own to supply their refineries.

The maximum rate laws and the anti-discrimination laws passed last winter will make it harder for the Standard to squeeze the life out of the independents but then it can afford to let down the price below living rates all over Kansas in order to kill off the opposition.

Right here we think a state refinery might have proven to be a great help. It could not have been killed off by the Standard. The price of crude oil might be raised on the one hand and the price of refined lowered on the other until the state refinery would have been an unprofitable venture so far as the books of the institution would show, but the people of Kansas would have been getting more benefit on the one hand than the loss at the state refinery would amount to on the other. It may be said that the people of the state are being saved money by the present cut in prices, which is true, but if the Standard can crush out opposition it is safe to gamble that prices of refined oil will not continue to stay down or the price of crude oil to stay up.

The independent refiners must not flatter themselves, either, that producers and consumers will stand by them in this war with the standard. They will not. They never have in the past, and they won't now. If they can sell their oil for 5 cents per barrel more to the Standard than the Independent refiner will pay, the Standard will get their oil. If the consumer can buy oil and gasoline for a cent less per gallon from the Standard than from the Independent refiners, the Standard will get their trade. John D. and his adjutants understand these traits in human nature and that is the reason the Standard Oil Company comes so near having a monopoly of oil business of the world.

GAME LAWS IN OKLAHOMA.

When to kill Turkey, Deer, Mosquitos, Chiggers &c etc etc &c.

It shall be unlawful for any person to wound, kill, snare or entrap in any manner within this territory any deer, antelope prairie chicken, quail, wild turkey or pursue the same with such intent or to have the same in their possession, except that it shall be lawful to shoot prarie chickens and wild turkeys between the first day of September and the first day of January following, and that it shall be lawful to shoot quail between the 15th of October and the 1st of February following and it shall be lawful to shoot plover and dove between the 1st of August and the 31st day of December following. Persons desiring to hunt on any premises other than their own must get the consent of the owner or occupant or stand liable to prosecution.

Any person having lawfully taken any of the game mentioned in this act, or any person lawfully having any of said game in his possession may sell the same to persons living in the territory for consumption therein.

This summary of the "rules made provided" is promulgated by the El Reno American;

According to the game laws of the territory chiggers and mosquitoes may be killed with impunity, or with anything else from kerosene to chloroform, or by hand, at any time between April 1st and March 31st. House flies may be killed out in the yard, front or back, and blue bottle flies may be killed with small bottle. excepting Sundays, when Iron Brew must be used. Large game, such as Eagles and Elks killed any season. Deer must not be killed at any time and Bovalapus cannot be hunted in Canadian county except in leap year. Other games such as draw and stud poker, two-bit limit, almost extinct. Two victims in the county jail.

WEDDING BELL.

A very pretty wedding took place at the residence of Mr. and Mrs. C. M. Clingan the bride's parents last evening at 9 o'clock when Mamie Colvin aged 27 and R. E. Banks aged 28 were united in marriage by Rev. Rushing, Clay Clingan acting as brideman and Miss Mina Claypole as bridemaid. A large crowd of guests numbering about 40 from Cache and vicinity were present and many very beautiful gifts were presented the young couple. After the ceremony an elegant supper was served. The remainder of the evening was passed in singing, playing games and dancing. Miss Laura Leininger of Lawton was a visiting guest. Among those from town were: Messrs. Walter Clark, A. G. Norris, G. W. Harrell A. C. Goetting, S. W. Banks, F. P. Runnels, Capt. Bury and their families. Also Mesdames Tarder and Morrissey, Misses Winter Trader and Mina Claypole, Messrs Guy Webb, John Sneed, Claude Bury and P. M. Teter.

Today only ruins remain of the once-massive smelter Pearson built near his mine at Camp Homestead, which was later to be included in the Fort Sill Military Reservation.

MINERAL KINGDOM.

Devoted to the Mineral Interests of the Wichita Mountains

VOL. 2. No. 47.   LAWTON, OKLAHOMA, THURSDAY, SEPTEMBER 28, 1905. $1 PER YEAR.

PEARSON SMELTER

PREPARATIONS BEING MADE TO FEED ORE NEXT WEEK

The smelter of the Homestead Mining & Milling Company is expected to be in readiness for active operation by the first of next week. On Monday of this week the fire was started in the smelter, a small amount of fluxing material and lead were added, this to test to a certain extent the reducing powers, when a damper which had been placed in the smoke-stack gave way, falling into the furnace and entirely stopping the draft from the blower.

It was seen by Assayers Gullett and Tucker who were in charge that something must be done at once, and accordingly the air was shut off and the damper removed from the furnace, which required about thirty minutes time. While this was being done, on account of the smelter not having been blown in a sufficient length of time to be thoroughly heated up, it became chilled and it was necessary to let the fire cool down for the purpose of cleaning out the slag which had collected in a ring just above the tuyere irons.

This will not prove serious in any way, with the exception of delaying the time of the actual blowing in until the first of the coming week.

This smelter is located on homestead land, which is owned and claimed by the company under the United States mining laws, and has been built wholly by the capital of the company, is of 25 to 30 tons capacity, and is a model of neatness and substantiability.

We are told that Professor Tucker is well pleased with the construction of this plant, and while he has returned to Wildman to look after business matters during the time the cleaning of the interior of the smelter is going on, he will return in ample time to assist in the blowing in.

Assayer Gullett has been on the ground from the first and thoroughly understands the situation, both as to the character of the ore and the values contained therein. He as well as Professor Tucker have no fears but that the same will be successful when actually blown in.

This is the first smelter in the Wichitas that has been constructed in a substantial manner, and the outcome of its initial run is being watched with much interest.

There is still doubt existing in the minds of some Lawton citizens as to whether pay values exist in these mountains, but a successful run of this smelter will eradicate all this nonbelief.

The builders of this plant are to be congratulated on their untiring efforts, and it is to be hoped that they will have success as their reward.

MOST FAVORABLE SURFACE INDICATIONS

"There is no mineral district in the United States that shows better surface indications than in the Wichita Mountains," said a prominent prospector the other day, and one who has visited nearly every mining camp in this country.

This is the idea of every mining man who has ever visited the hills, and had there never been an assay made, would be sufficient cause for development of the numerous well-defined fissure veins to be found in the Wichitas. And in addition to this many assays have been made by reputable, well-known assayers, the results of which have proven beyond the question of a doubt that pay mineral does exist and in quantity sufficient to warrant development.

Since the time of the opening of this new country to settlement, and the extension of the United States mineral laws over it, prospectors have been constantly at work, seeking to furnish absolute proof of commercial values. At this time they are well nigh unto success. This success will bring with it much satisfaction as well as a decided increase in the size of the wallet, and the prospector who has lived the past four years amid privations and hardships, will welcome the day when he can view his mining properties and say they are valuable, without fear of contradiction by the skeptic.

The Wichita Mountains have never experienced anything like a boom but have marched steadily to the front amid much adversity, until at this time many outside people with capital are turning their attention this way, and ere any great length of time has passed by, the Wichitas will be known as a busy mining camp.

DR. ROWELL WILL CONTINUE WORK NEXT WEEK

"I shall continue work on the San Domingo next week and will then continue until the 100-foot mark is reached," said Dr. J. F. Rowell, "and I know I have values in this property, as I have practically assayed it myself."

Thursday of this week Mosher Bros., near Meers, made several tests on the above property, and in each case recovered a nice button. While they are not professional assayers, they have obtained a knowledge of the treatment of the Wichita ores, and the laboratory of Dr. Hardin is at their disposal, made the tests for Dr. Rowell, he assisting in the work.

This property certainly has a promising future and it is the belief of the owner that when a depth of 200 to 300 feet is reached very rich ore will be shown up. The assaying that has been done heretofore has been by eastern assayers in New York and Philadelphia, and the returns from these parties have been sufficient to continue development work.

WILL DEVELOP IF SATISFACTORY

"If we find conditions and values to justify, we shall commence development on the Hardin property within 30 days," said C. R. Woodruff, of St. Jo, Mo., while waiting at the Keegan hotel for a team to go the mountains last Thursday morning.

Mr. Woodruff is one of the parties who was here about two weeks ago, looking over the same property and made a conditional contract with Dr. Hardin.

There seems to be no question as to their being able to finance the deal within themselves, and after they have thoroughly satisfied themselves as to the values contained in the ore, if satisfactory, will at once begin operations. Mr. Woodruff will take with him to Kansas City an ample amount of the ore for testing.

SERIOUS ACCIDENT AT TEXAHOMA CAMP

Jake Stammer was seriously injured last Wednesnay while working in a shaft near the Texahoma camp, north of Mt. Scott.

It would seem that he was alone in the shaft, using a ladder to climb out, and feeling faint, started to ascend the ladder. When well up the ladder, he does not know how far, he fell to the bottom, where he was found by his companions, with a broken leg, a broken hip, and numerous gashes cut about the head. It is thought that he will recover.

RUMOR OF MILITARY RESERVE TO BE ENLARGED

There is a rumor afloat that the military reserve is to be enlarged, and when done that it will take in Mt. Scott and the area intervening. It will also include the present site of the Pearson smelter. This is only a rumor and could not be done except by act of Congress.

Gold and silver rushes once enlivened virtually every county in Oklahoma, but only in the Wichita Mountains did the miners have their own newspaper, spreading tidings of the last great gold rush east of the Rockies. First called the *Mt. Sheridan Miner*, the paper was later named *Mineral Kingdom*.

Craterville, just north of Cache, at the entrance to the Wichita Mountains, was one of several gold camps established when the Comanche-Kiowa-Apache Reservation was opened to settlement in 1901.

LAWTON NEWS=REPUBLICAN.

VOLUME II. LAWTON, OKLAHOMA, THURSDAY, SEPTEMBER 24, 1903. NUMBER 42

BOOM IS NOW ON

Eighteen Tons of Ore Shipped to Colorado Smelters by Lawton People Sells For $11.60 Per Ton.

PEOPLE ARE EXCITED

Hundreds of Assays are Being Made That Outclass the Ore Shipped.

SWARM TO MOUNTAINS

The Gold Fever Has Struck the People and Hundreds of Prospectors Have Joined the Already Large Number of "Pioneer" Miners---Gold is There.

The Big Four Mine pans out. Returns from the car load of ore show conclusively that Lawton lies at the foot of a rich mining district.

Mr. Benbow and Mr. Spence returned from Denver last Monday morning and since then groups of people may be seen congregated all about town discussing the news.

The company expresses itself as a little bit disappointed at the results, but it should not be as $11.60 per ton can be worked at a profit of something like $9.00. Below we give the estimate based on a knowledge of the ore as shown in the car load lot, made by Mr. Beam one of the leading assayists of Denver.

It is Mr. Beam's intention to establish a branch office at this place at once. His report and the accompanying letter reads as follows:

Denver, Colo., Sept. 18, 1903.
J. S. Spence, Big Four Mining Company, Lawton, O. T.

Dear Sir:---We have handled several traders and merchants are influenced by competition, by an over-stocked market, by vibrations in the price of raw materials and by conditions of the financial centers. Farming depends largely on the weather and even when every thing conspires to produce good crops, market and trust conditions are frequently such as to subject the farmer to loose his entire season's work.

The product of the mines is always the same. The mines are the treasure vaults established by nature; are not affected by runs, have a market that is always certain, with a demand that is constantly increasing and a wealth of resource, the limit of which is co-extensive with the world.

But there is one thing that people who start in to mine must never forget, that mines are made not found, and a paying mine is not made in a day.

When any other business is built up investors do not look for a divided untill a market is created and the supply suf-ficient to meet the demand.

Many good prospects and mines have been ruined by the haste of stockholders in demanding dividends before the mine is put in condition to pay, and more by the refusal to recognize the necessity for a large out lay to make dividends certain.

Also by the too often system of installing some relative perfectly ignorant in the requirements and experience necessary to success.

This is so in all lines of business, a man is generally chosen for his fitness from his experience, by absolute contact with the work in hand.

It takes years and knocks and misfortunes hunger and exposure, to make a man a capable mine manager.

Can it be wise to educate a new man at the risk of a fortune, from inexperience, if experience is a needed quality in other lines of business it is doubly so in this.

There are many failures, to be sure in the mining field, but three-fourths of them can be traced to new managers with scarcely any experience to set out with, but when a proposition is carried on a business system the same as in other branches, there is no chance for a failure.

With a proposition where you have an abundance of ore of an even grade with a known system for recovery, with every convenience at hand, with ordinary business management, there can be no place to find failure.

Gentlemen, I believe you will make a great mining country where you are at, the first to get the right start will be the first to get the money that makes mining attractive.

Thanking you respectfully submitted,
A. MILLS BEAM, M. E.
"BIG FOUR MINING CO."

Cost to mill 100 tons per day:
Cost to mine, 50 cts. per ton _____ $ 50.00
Cost to mill $1.25 per ton _____ 125.00
90 per cent recovery, 10 per cent ___ 58.00
Interest on $40.000 _____ 6.00

Total expense _____ $ 239.00
100 tons ore $11.60, per ton _____ $1160.00
Expense _____ 239.00

Total net per day _____ $ 921.00

DID THEMSELVES PROUD.

The Concert Given Last Tuesday Evening Was a Splendid Success.

The Lawton Conservatory of Music and Dramatic Art gave a delightful concert at Odd Fellows hall last Tuesday evening. The attendance was so great that something like a hundred were turned away for want of room.

The stage was nicely arranged and decorated. The program was certainly every thing that the most sanguine could have anticipated or desired. Every number was more than creditable. That Lawton has exceptionally fine local talent was demonstrated beyond question.

The ladies in charge of the conservatory of music and dramatic art are certainly to be congratulated on this their first concert.

Call For Farmers.

The most important meeting yet held under the auspices of the Comanche County Farmers' Institute will be held on Saturday, October 3rd one mile east of Lawton in the "Lost Bridge" grove.

Several prominent agriculturalists, including President John Fields of the Stillwater Territorial Agricultural college, and Secretary Thoburn of the Territorial Board of Agriculture, will be present and address the farmers.

It is also requested that farmers having products of a creditable character bring them for display and comparison at this meeting, and funds have been provided for suitable prizes for samples of merit.

Amusements have been arranged for the entertainment of the visitors, and it is desired to have an all-day meeting, with a basket dinner at noon. This is the opening meeting for the winter campaign of the Comanche County Farmers' Institute, and all members as well as all progressive farmers should attend, as great benefit cannot fail to result from the visit of John Fields and Secretary Thoburn. These picnics will be an annual feature of the Institute and will be held in various parts of the county each year.

WALLACE H. HORNADY, Sec.

All Interested.

H. J. McGill, representing the Daily Oklahoman of Oklahoma City, was in town yesterday-investigating the mining situation.

"The Wichita mines" said Mr. McGill "are the topic of greatest interest in one part of Oklahoma just now. There are thousands of people visiting Oklahoma from the north on the excursions and the first question asked as a rule is, what is their in the mineral stories from the Wichita mountains."

Mr. McGill is gathering all the data he can. He is interviewing those most largely interested in the mines and will go to the mountains with a photographer and make a personal investigation of the situation. He says if the reports that are being given out prove true

---

After the Lumber Trusts

Judge Gilbert is after the Lumber Trust. At Hobart recently the lumbermen were subpoenaed before the grand jury to testify regarding the alleged combination, which has existed for years in all the leading towns of Oklahoma. The statutes of the territory provides a remedy, but the law has not been enforced. But there is danger of a new deal. Two lumber dealers, who refused to testify before the grand jury, were fined $50 for contempt and committed to jail for refusing to answer question which they alleged might incriminate themselves. These judgments were remitted upon the agreement of the defendants to testify. The judge's opinion in the contempt cases was as follows:

"The first question is in reference to his knowledge touching the action of the different lumber companies in Ho-bart in entering into a pool for the purpose of controlling the prices of building material. The second question is as to his knowledge as to whether or not these corporations have employed one Sutton to check up the business of the several lumber yards and prorate their profits upon each day's or week's sale. The fifth question was as to whether or not the defendants had received any instructions from the president, manager or auditor, or the general agent of these companies, authorizing the witness to recognize any pool or agreement to regulate or control the prices of lumber or other building material in the city of Hobart, and the sixth question is if the different lumber companies of Hobart, including the William Cameron Lumber company, keep a blank book in which the witnesses are required to enter each day a list of their sales and profits."

SIMPSON'S BIG STORE.

See His Big Ad on Another Page—Many Inducements.

M. S. Simpson has a page ad elsewhere in this issue. This concern is now ensconced in its beautiful new building on Fourth and C and is one of the model establishments of Lawton. A large stock of fall and winter goods have and are arriving daily and a full corps of efficient salespeople are in attendance. Simpson's Bargain Store is one of the pioneer business institutions of the city and is constantly seeking new business and offering inducements to that end. Read the big ad.

From Walter.

Col. Reaves returned from Walter yesterday, where he was attending to business matters. He reports prosperous conditions out there. The merchants are feeling good and say they are enjoying a larger business than they anticipated. A large amount of produce, much larger than was looked for, is being marketed. The gin is doing a good business and the farmers are putting their fields in first-class shape for wheat and many of them are already drilling wheat.

Failed to Score.

A fellow holding a check signed by W. J. O'Connor for $88.80 on a Geary bank tried to cash same in Lawton. He was a stranger. The bank was advised that it might wire the Geary bank to see that it was all right. But the banks here didn't bite and a little later it was discovered through a message from Geary that the man who was supposed to have signed the check was in Geary and the man with the check should be arrested, but he was not present and probably will make his presence mighty

COUNCIL WRANGLES.

All Parties Agree That Very Little Was Accomplished.

Last Monday night the city council was in session and spent a long session without accomplishing anything of importance.

A large number of bills were allowed, some of which were strenuously objected to by members of the council.

Some time ago Policeman Davis was discharged. He wore a suit of uniform gray that belonged to the city. On the other hand the city owed him for services. He sold his bill to Mr. McClennan and wore the suit away. After considerable wrangling the council passed the bill for the full amount and Davis is ahead his suit.

An effort was made to cut the bill of the Democrat down some thirty dollars but the majority was with the paper and the bill was allowed for the full amount claimed. The law fixes the price to be paid for legal publications, but does not regulate the price of stationary, etc.

The council is still keeping the franchise bill in cold storage and the probability is that it will freeze to death. As a proposition it got a decidedly cold reception and has never been good and warm.

Mrs. Blair was employed by the council to collect the street sprinkling tax.

The committee on sidewalks was instructed to get estimates on the cost of stone crossings for the business part of town. This is certainly a good move. The present crossings are almost as expensive and are constantly needing repairs. Stone crossings are much more economical.

Hereafter telegraph and telephone poles must be set in the alleys instead of

---

"The Boom Is Now On," announced the *Lawton News-Republican* on September 24, 1903.

WONDERFUL "WICHITA" MOUNTAINS

Rich Enough in Gold and Other Minerals to Become World Famous.

ORE ASSAYS FROM $10 TO $60 PER TON

Claims Are Practically All Taken Up and Developments Are Being Rushed as Fast as Facilities Will Permit—The Chance of a Lifetime for Profitable Investment.

Although the general public is not familiar with the mineral richness of the Wichita mountains in Oklahoma, yet a gold field is being rapidly developed there which promises to become one of the greatest producers of the yellow metal in the world. The general topography of the country shows a strong volcanic action and true fissure veins are in evidence in many places throughout the mountains.

attitude of the Indians inhabiting these lands. A few years ago a number of the prospectors who sought to develop these mountains were killed by the Indians and the government took steps to prevent prospectors going in until such time as it could be done with safety. Since the opening of the mineral lands great changes have taken place, and from a wild, mountainous district, overrun by Indians, busy mining camps are springing up.

THE WICHITA MOUNTAINS, SHOWING MT. SHERIDAN

The outcroppings in various places on these mountains are richer than the veins of many mining camps and careful prospecting has shown enough ore to keep a large number of mills busy for years.

Here are found well defined leads from the surface which assay from $10 to $60 per ton gold, and as the shafts increase in depth the assays show an increase in value.

Some wonderful deposits of platinum, sil-

There are now 2,000 organized miners in these mountains, developing five distinct mineral districts.

Fidelity Mining and Milling Company's Claims.

The gold producing territory, so far as known at present, has been thoroughly prospected over and all claims showing any value have been rapidy taken up. The Fidelity Milling and Mining Company owns

property is within investigating distance no one can afford to shut his eyes on such an opportunity. The Fidelity Company's properties are located in the Chandler district, at the foot of Mount Sheridan, and extend about two miles north of the mountain. They are twenty-five miles from Lawton, with good wagon road. A railroad is projected, and the townsite of the city of Canaan will be formally opened the first of the coming year. Although considerable development work has been done in the immediate vicinity, the developments are further advanced about fifteen miles west, where a small smelter is now in successful operation.

An Expert's Report.

Mr. J. E. Hall, with offices at 335 N. Y. Life building, Kansas City, Mo., together with a party of three others, made an investigation of the district September 2, 1902. The entire district was gone over thoroughly and the report was extremely favorable. In mentioning the "Hill Top" claim of the Fidelity Company, Mr. Hall says:

"The lead rises about 150 feet from the surface and can be distinctly traced the whole distance. The hill is one solid ore body, varying in richness, average surface assays $10 per ton."

On the "Ada" claim, another of the Fidelity Company's properties, he reports as follows:

"The 'Ada' claim adjoins the 'Hill Top' claim, and has a vein the full length of the claim 40 feet in width and assaying $17 gold and 48 ounces silver per ton. The ore in this vein crops out at various places along the lead as it winds and turns to the 'Myrtle Lode.'"

Of the Valley claims, Nos. 1 and 2, Mr. Hall reports both as carrying well defined leads highly mineralized, but no assays were made on either of them.

A Government Expert's Observations.

Mr. B. F. Whitney, government supervisor of the Wichita mountain forest reserve, with headquarters on Cache creek, near Oreana P. O., Comanche county, O. T., in conversation at our office in this city, said: "I have read your report of our mining district in the Wichita mountains and I do not feel that you have told it one-half as good as it is." I replied that I was aware of that fact, but that it was my intention to write a conservative statement.

"Well, you have," he replied, "given to the public a very fair idea of what you saw in the Chandler district. But when you broaden out over the whole mining field your report fails to describe the marvelous resources of the mineral belt in that country.

"My former residence was at Keystone, South Dakota, where I was engaged in mining for eighteen years until I received appointment from the government giving me the entire supervision of the forest reserve of the Black Hills mining country, where I remained until last June ...

ed the developments where shafts were being sunk, and conversed with many miners during the past three months. I find that the vein matter is invariably separated from the wall by a narrow vein or gouge showing a contact.

"I have also seen reports of assays made by such reliable and competent assayers as

STERLING PRICE ILES.
President Fidelity Milling and Mining Co.

Mr. Burlingame of Denver, Colo., the Kansas City Smelting company, the Michigan School of Mines and others, all giving good showings of rich values. The outcroppings run in a northeasterly and southwesterly direction, being heavily mineralized, and carrying lead, copper and iron pyrites. One assay made from a sample of ore weighing about four pounds, [illegible]

JOHN A. BUCKNER,
Secretary and Treasurer Fidelity Milling and Mining Co.

tained results that are as astonishing as they are true.

"The sample was taken from a lead about nine miles southwest of Mount Sheridan.

"This ore yielded readily to treatment, giving over $1,500 per ton; gold predominating—over $1,200 of the value was in gold, or about 75% of the values.

"I therefore confidently predict that the time is close at hand when the forest reserve of the Wichita mountains will step forward into the front ranks of her now leading contemporaries, and her products will surprise and convince the most skeptical.

"Allow me to add that if Stewart's oxidizer will successfully treat the ores in the reserve, the success of that mining region is assured beyond any question of doubt.

"(Signed) B. F. WHITNEY.
"Witness: J. E. Hall, 335 N. Y. Life Bldg., Kansas City, Mo."

How the Claims Were Located.

The veins of the old Spanish smelters, operated before the Louisiana purchase in 1803, can be located in this district, and some rich mines will probably be discovered in their vicinity. Mr. Sterling Price Iles, president of the Fidelity company, whose portrait appears in this article, gained his information as to the value and extent of the vast mineral deposits of the Wichita mountains from his father, who was an early California miner and prospector of large experience. Mr. Iles' father visited this district in 1872. Mr. Iles has had rich experience in the Black Hills and Colorado mining district, and during the past six years has spent most of his time in the Wichita mountains. It was through his efforts that the Fidelity claims were located.

Our Milling Proposition.

The Fidelity Milling and Mining company has contracts from mine owners in this district to furnish our mills with from 500 to 1,000 tons of ore per day as fast as we are able to handle it. The first mill to be built will have a capacity of 70 tons of ore per day, and new mills will be built as fast as practical. It has been estimated that new mills of the same capacity can be built out of the profits of the first mill at the rate of one every 60 days. It is the intention to provide a milling capacity of 1,000 tons as soon as possible. The Fidelity company has a bond for the full price of the mill that it will do the work and get 85% of all metals out of ores.

The cost of milling the ores of this district at the present price of coal, which can be delivered to the mill at $5 per ton, is $2 per ton. This is a very conservative estimate, and the cost will, if anything, be reduced rather than increased. The contracts with the mine owners are $4 per ton for milling, leaving a profit of $2 per ton on all ores milled.

First in the Field.

The Fidelity Milling and Mining company is organizing along practical lines with practical mining men in control. The men who now offer you a chance to come in with them and join in making this company the foremost in the new gold fields show their confidence in the enterprise by advancing all the capital that has been needed to ...

THIS IS YOUR GOLDEN OPPORTUNITY

Stock Is Now Offered at 50 Cents Per Share for a Limited Time.

OFFER MAY BE RECALLED AT ANY TIME

Personnel of the Company and the Basis of Organization Will Satisfy the Most Careful Investor—Small Capitalization and No Salaried Officers.

With four valable claims (80 acres), and five more likely to be added, a capitalization of $500,000 is not only justifiable but extremely conservative. One successful claim would pay dividends on this amount and the prospects for large profits are more flattering than offered by any other form of investment. The properties alone are worth double the capitalization and time will prove that this statement is not idly made.

The Fidelity Milling and Mining Com-

Officers.

Officers—The following is a list of the officers and directors: Sterling Price Iles, president; James E. Penick, vice president; H. H. Uitermarkt, second vice president; John A. Buckner, secretary and treasurer; Francis C. Prest, auditor.

DIRECTORS.

Sterling Price Iles, miner and prospector, Rosedale, Kas.

James E. Penick, stockman and real estate, Weatherford, O. T.

A TRUE FISSURE VEIN ON MT. SHERIDAN.

pany is incorporated under the laws of Oklahoma. Its capital stock is $500,000, divided into 500,000 shares, par value $1 each, and full paid and non-assessable. A limited amount of the treasury stock is now being offered for the purpose of building a 70-ton mill. Just as soon as this amount has been raised, the stock will be taken off the market as further developments can be made out of the profits when opera-

H. H. Uitermarkt, formerly shoe merchant, Kalamazoo, Mich.

John A. Buckner, late salesman for Nelson, Baker & Co., manufacturing chemists, Kansas City, Mo., Detroit and New York.

Francis C. Prest, assistant secretary North American Trust company, New York city.

Frank C. Davis, druggist, Kansas City, Kas.

Broadsides heralded the Wichita gold fields and urged investors to seize their "golden opportunity." Promoter Sterling Price Iles sank twenty-three mines in the Meers region.

THE MT. SHERIDAN MINER.

VOL. I — SATURDAY. — MEERS, COMANCHE COUNTY, OKLA., OCTOBER 24, 1903. — SATURDAY — NO. 1.

Best bargains in LAND and MONEY see LATHAM & HOIG, Broadway.

Dr. Hardin's Faith in the Wichita Mountain Gold Shown by His Work.

When Marconi announced to the world that he had discovered a method by which he could transmit a message without the aid of wires, it was doubted. When the great scientist, Dr. Roentgen, discovered the ex-Ray and announced it, people again doubted. When we read of Prof. Chas. E. Tripler's wonderful experiment with liquid air, we are again inclined to doubt its real-

When Dr. Hardin of Mt. Sheridan first announced to the people of Oklahoma that he had discovered gold in the Wichita Mountains, it was doubted, doubted by many, in fact, but few compartively speaking believed the story. As the story goes, "Truth will prevail," and with Dr. Harden the desire for gold-[illegible] itself does not exceed his desire to demonstrate and prove to the people the truth of his assertion that there is gold in the Wichita Mountains.

The world recognizes no greater incentive to the accomplishment of a work or purpose, than the demonstration of the truth of a theory

the compay will ship their ore to Denver or El Paso. They expect to begin shipping in a very few days.

What these people are doing others can do. The people here extend an invitation to all who wish a profitable investment. We invite capital to come and investigate. Don't take our word but come and see for yourself. We confidently believe that many millions in gold and silver will be taken out of the Wichita hills within the next few years.

Yours truly,
A MINER.

The Wichita Mountains.

With this, the initial number of the Miner, it will not be amiss to briefly review the history of the Wichita Mountains, the coming El-Dorado of the world.

For nearly three hundred years the fact that gold could be found in large quantities here has been known to the white man although for a long interval after the Spanish ceded their possessions on the American continent to the United States, this knowledge was of no value from the fact that the country was in possession of the Indians who bitterly resisted all efforts to devel-

values and the reports handed in at Washington to the effect that there was no gold here worth digging for, were repeated with such persistancy that the government at Washington apparently became convinced that such was the case, and thus was brought about a great injustice to the country and to those sturdy prospectors who refused to become discouraged in the face of adverse decisions, and even arrest by the soldiers as sooners and tresspassers, and it is to these men of strong faith and determination that the country will ever owe a debt of gratitude for their constant "pressing forward toward the mark," and their determination to bring the matter before the government that justice might be done and victory perch upon their banner.

That there are gold and silver in large quantities in the mountains can no longer be doubted and those who haven't the requisite knowledge to see and know the indications are readily convinced when they behold the assayer with his fluxings and his fire, extract the yellow metal from the rock that they themselves may have selected. Many are they who have believed the mines salted until they have person-

the same [illegible]itions, that point beyond Behring straits to Asia, as the land from which their forefathers came in pa[illegible]ges. They owned this vast contin[illegible]t and posessed it for ages. So much for their origin. After the [illegible]ty of Dancing Rabbit creek the Choctaws and Chickasaws came to the country from Mississippi (from 18[illegible] to 1845). Most of them settled at Doaksville and Boggy Depot."

[illegible] is Stopped.

Mu[illegible] [illegible] Chairman [illegible] Commission recei[illegible] a telegram [illegible] from the Interior Department instructing him to cl[illegible] the allotting division of the Ch[illegible] Land Office at Tahlequah. [illegible] departments of work there will [illegible]tinue.

No cause assigned by the Interior Department for closing the allotment [illegible] at Tahlequah, but it is supp[illegible] to result from a suit brought by the Delawares against the Goverment for $1,000,000 damages becau[illegible] of loss of a case involving 15[illegible]00 acres of land segregated to th[illegible]

C. R. B[illegible]kenridge, member of the Dawes Commission, who has charge of [illegible] work at Tahlequah,

Destiny.

A friend said to me one day,
That it seemed a cruel fate,
That we were "chained to the wheel,"
And whether 'twas early or late
That destiny overtakes us,
That then we needs must go,
Whether to scenes of gladness,
Or down to eternal woe.

But Burleigh says 'tis Time
That drives the shuttle [illegible]
[illegible]
So whether for good or ill,
We are not chained to the wheel,
But are "free agents" still.

There are many broken places
In the web of every life,
And as you're weaving day by day,
It may seem a weary strife.
But don't call your trials fate,
For it seems a braver plan
To meet the trials squarely,
And face life like a man.

You only are responsible,
For all your own mistakes,
And talks of kismet, destiny
And chance are equal fakes
So handle each thread carefully,

The Meers gold camp issued the first edition of its own newspaper on October 24, 1903.

MINERAL KINGDOM.

FORMERLY THE MOUNT SHERIDAN MINER.

Devoted to the Mines and Mining in the Wichita Mountains, and the Mineral Interests of Oklahoma and Indian Territory

VOLUME 2.   LAWTON, OKLAHOMA, THURSDAY, JANUARY 26, 1905.   NUMBER 15.

A Warning to Wichita Miners

In a personal letter, a Mexican mining operator relates the situation as follows: "The trust, the American Smelting & Refining Company, has got its grip upon us, and it is a d—d hard one. They have practically knocked the spots out of this particular district (Parral)."

It might be some consolation and also might serve as a warning to the mine operators of this district to know that the smelter trust is a gigantic concern, cares not for the small fish, that they always try to freeze out the small operator, in which they are generally successful. In the Wichita Mountains we have all the combinations of ores for the successful operation of smelters, our advantages in other directions are very far ahead of Mexico, but yet if we are not on the alert, the trusts will have us going down the incline, and will reap the benefit of our discoveries and labor.

There is now no question in our minds but this smelter trust has proven no small factor in the attitude of the Government officials have taken toward us as a mining district, and that this trust are not yet ready for this district to be opened up for active operations, and that they are using their influence to our detriment.

The miners of the Wichitas have demonstrated over all opposition that they have the values, have been willing to deny themselves the almost neccessities of life to do this, and now that they are nearing the goal of success we wish to admonish them to use caution, allow no man to swindle them out of their property, and they will soon reap their just reward.

Smelter Assured

The smelter proposed to be built at Meers on the property of the Shawnee Mining Com-

MINERS' TRIALS

These are the leads that carry the gold,
Found by miners courageous and bold,
Found in the Wichita Mountains old,
Of which the half has never been told.

This is the expert, false and cute,
Who said it was proved beyond dispute,
There was not enough gold in a yard of rock,
To pay for a patch on a poor man's sock.

This is the poor man, innocent fool,
Who never had gone to a lying school,
Who give up his chance in the ancient hills,
And swallowed the dose of expert pills.

This is the grave the poor man fills,
Caused by taking fever and chills,
After he had left the hills,
Leaving his family to pay his bills.

H—l is where Bane and DeBarr will go,
For fooling the innocent miners so,
Robbing him of his hard-earned dough,

Important Decision

In a recent decision handed down by the general land office, the decision of the local land office at this place is affirmed, and the Welsch homestead, located near Mt. Sheridan, is declared as being more valuable for mineral than for agriculture.

The case referred to above is that of the Shawnee Mining Company vs. Elisha B. Welsch, wherein the mining company sought to prevent the final proof Mr. Welsh on his homestead entry, and declaring the same very valuable for the mineral contained therein.

The trial before the local land office was long drawn out and very strongly fought by the mining company, they proving the general character of the land by numerous witnesses, and the character and values of the veins by several witnesses who were qualified to testify on that point. Photographs were taken showing the true fissure veins and were shown as evidence. It was shown that the mining company had installed valuable machinery with which to develop the property.

After due consideration the officials of the local land office rendered their decision recommending that the tract of land in question be classed as mineral land and not subject to homestead entry. An appeal was taken by the entryman to the general land office, with the result as above stated.

This decision is a very important one and reveals the fact that one tract of land in the Wichitas has been declared mineral in character by the Government and more valuable for mining than for farming purposes.

This is but a forerunner of that which is to follow and it may be expected that in the near future the miner of the Wichitas will be recog-

---

MINERAL KINGDOM.

Devoted to the Mineral Interests of the Wichita Mountains

VOL. 2. No. 32.   LAWTON, OKLAHOMA. THURSDAY, JUNE 15, 1905. $1 PER YEAR.

Camp Meers

Meers, the mining camp of which we herewith present a birds eye view, is located almost within the shadow of Mt. Sheridan, on the north side. This camp was established in the forest reserve at the time of the opening of the country, but the residents were ordered to move during the next year, and the entire town was moved and established on school land one mile north of the first location, where it stands today, and where this illustration was taken.

To say this rag town has had its ups and downs with principally the latter is putting it mild, and many times it seemed that the little city would be entirely deserted, but she would again revive, so that she has about held her own amid the difficulties she was obliged to encounter.

This camp is the base of operations for practically all the eastern end of the mountains, having a postoffice supplied with daily mail service, the same being carried from Ft. Sill. She now has a store in which are kept all the necessaries of life. There are school and church facilities, both being held in a

locality of the district, but they do claim and know that they have valuable mineral that when developed and worked on a moderate scale will make them world famous.

For health there is probably no locality in the United States that is more healthful, there having been but 3 deaths in this camp since its establishment, and these from natural causes with which the climate and general conditions had nothing whatever to do. and the services of a physician is rarely ever needed.

This mining town is located almost in the pass between the mountains, and this being the only like place for miles, it is thought that when railroads are built that one road at least will secure right of way through this natural roadway, and in this event Meers will lie directly in the

CAMP MEERS, AT THE FOOT OF MT. SHERIDAN

Miners vs. Townsite

Quite a warmly contested legal battle was pulled of in Judge Perkins' court in which Phillip Myers, member of the Wheeling Townsite Company, sought to restrain I. F. Thompson et al from working mining property located on this townsite.

It seems that a man named Green owned the homestead prior to Mr.

the person who will develop the property, as no matter how rich the mineral may be, if allowed to lie buried in the earth there is no benefit to be derived by anyone.

Good Way of Advertising

This office printed and distributed to the members of the National Editoral Association last Saturday morning 600 extra copies of a spe-

---

Mineral Kingdom served the dual purpose of informing the gold seekers of the region and promoting the boom.

Mt Sheridan Daily Miner

VOL. 1.   MEERS, OKLAHOMA, THURSDAY, AUGUST 25, 1904.   No. 3.

AN EXPERT IN NAME ONLY.

A Political "Pull" and Big Salary His Only Qualification.

We clip the following "roast" from the columns of the Sterling Star. The editor of that enterprising paper seems to recognize a fraud when he sees it:

"At this particular time there is much comment, both in the press and out of it, relative to the official report of one J. F. Bain as to the mineral bearing of the Wichita Mountains. As is well known, this man Bain is the Government expert (?) geologist who was sent to the mountains for the purpose of making investigations and report- delved in the bowels of the earth as a business and knows nothing else, having followed it as his life's work, knowing the soils, rocks, stratas, etc., by actual and continued observation and experience, is the man that should be recognized as the one who knows what he is talking about—the very man who obtained his information and knowledge with a pick, hammer and drill, at his side; while the so-called expert obtained his knowledge by reading what some other fellow has written, while smoking a ten-cent cigar, and the smallest portion of his anatomy projecting above a three-inch linnen collar, and the largest portion adorned with a pair of patent-leather shoes their experience and knowledge, are the men whose judgement is to be relied upon, in nearly every case; and when this great army, augmented by the number of assayers who corroberate their opinion, agree that there is mineral beneath the jagged ridges of our mountains, then we believe the report, it matters not what may be said to the contrary by our fashionable high-collared "expert" from Washington. We are not from Missouri, but we know enough to be from that grand old state, and that being the case, the Missouri rule inversely applies in our case, that is if there is no mineral in the Wichitas we will insist on being shown that fact, for we have seen too much already to

For a time, Meers even boasted a daily, published by twenty-one-year-old Frank C. Davis (also the town druggist, an assayer, a charter member of Aurum Mining Company, and president of the Chandler Mining District and Protective Association).

In 1904, Sam Remer built his massive smelter southwest of Mount Sheridan on Blue Beaver Creek to refine ore from his nearby Snake Mine. From *Mineral Kingdom*, January 12, 1905.

Of all the Wichita gold camps only this lone store at Meers survives. From its back rooms once rolled the weekly *Mt. Sheridan Miner.*

Begun in 1904, this fifty-ton cyanide processing plant one mile south of Wildman was erected by Wildman's founder, E. A. Williams, at a cost of seventeen thousand dollars. The tramway led from the ore mill to the Gold Bell Mine, a quarter of a mile away. Courtesy Hugh Corwin.

Relics of Oklahoma's forgotten gold days still lie scattered about the state. This huge ore bucket once dangled from the shaft house of the Gold Bell Mine near Wildman.

In Wildman, a mining camp established illegally before southwestern Oklahoma was opened to settlement, miners built this fifty-ton water-jacket smelter next to the Lyon Lode, five miles south of Roosevelt. Courtesy Mrs. Frank R. Wildman.

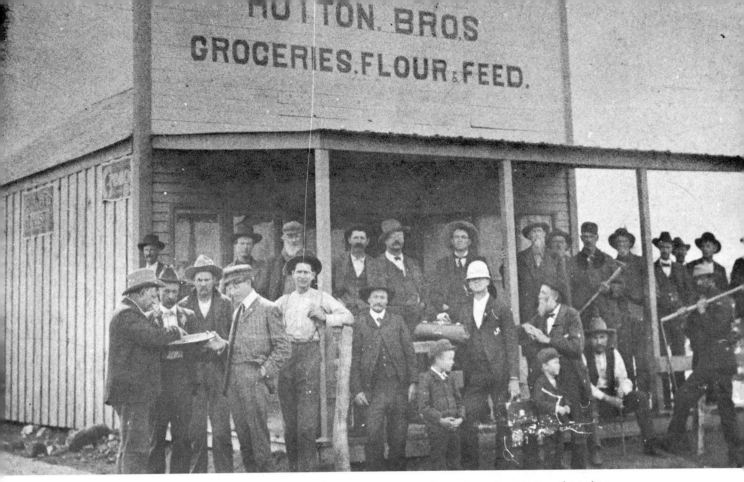

The miners of Wildman, hailing from mining camps throughout the West, gathered at Jim Hutton's grocery in early-day Roosevelt to discuss their diggings—and the bonanza they were sure would come. Courtesy Guy H. Parker.

Bearded miners of the Wichitas, who were often in conflict with homesteaders of the region, posed for this early picture on the outskirts of Wildman. Courtesy Mrs. Frank R. Wildman.

The miners of Wildman founded the first post office on the Comanche-Kiowa-Apache Reservation several months before the land was opened to white settlement. The town's founder, E. A. Williams, stands at the right of the door. Courtesy Mrs. Frank R. Wildman.

The Lyon Lode was sunk within the townsite of Wildman. While digging the shaft, the miners discovered still older diggings from previous gold seekers. Williams stands in front of the boiler in the background. Courtesy Mrs. Frank R. Wildman.

Mounds of mine tailings and a deep shaft remain of Wildman's Gold Bell Mine, abandoned in 1910.

Nest Egg Mountain looms behind the foundation ruins of Wildman, a once-bustling gold camp boasting a two-story hotel and saloon and a population of about three hundred.

Today only massive concrete steps and a deep circular trough remain of Wildman's cyanide mill.

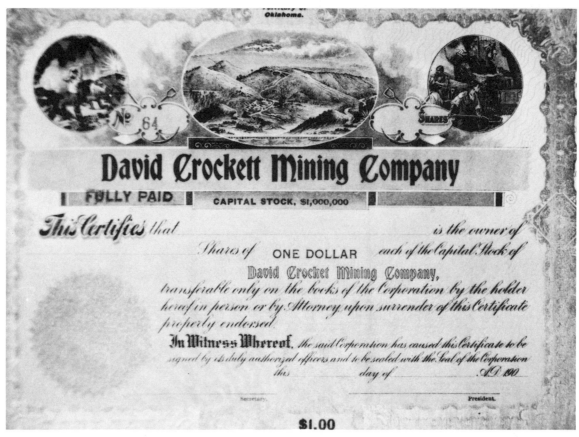

Mining companies selling shares of stock were plentiful throughout the Wichita Mountains even though gold was scarce. Pages 168, 169, 171.

INCORPORATED UNDER THE LAWS OF THE TERRITORY OF OKLAHOMA.

№ 26   Shares

LONE STAR MINING & REDUCTION COMPANY.

FULLY PAID.   CAPITAL STOCK, $1,000,000.00.   NON-ASSESSABLE.

This Certifies that A. H. Stewart is the owner of
Ten thousand Shares of ONE DOLLAR each of the Capital Stock of
LONE STAR MINING AND REDUCTION COMPANY,

transferable only on the books of the Corporation by the holder
hereof in person or by Attorney, upon surrender of this Certificate
properly endorsed.

In Witness Whereof, the said Corporation has caused this Certificate to be
signed by its duly authorized officers and to be sealed with the Seal of the Corporation
at Lawton, Okla. this 7 day of Nov A.D. 190 3

_____   _____
SECRETARY.   PRESIDENT.

SHARES $1.00 EACH

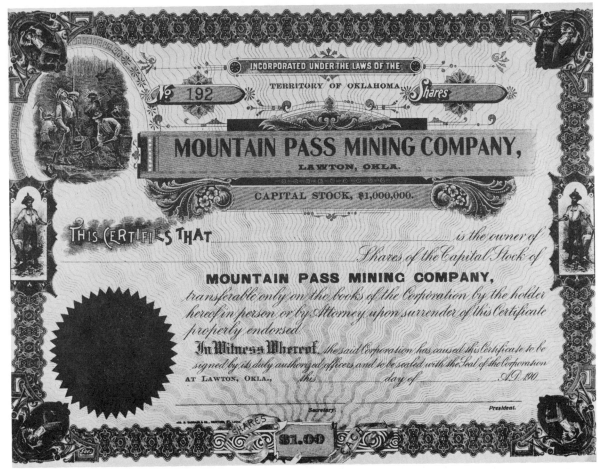

INCORPORATED UNDER THE LAWS OF THE
TERRITORY OF OKLAHOMA   Shares

№ 192

MOUNTAIN PASS MINING COMPANY,
LAWTON, OKLA.

CAPITAL STOCK, $1,000,000.

THIS CERTIFIES THAT _____ is the owner of
_____ Shares of the Capital Stock of

MOUNTAIN PASS MINING COMPANY,

transferable only on the books of the Corporation by the holder
hereof in person or by Attorney upon surrender of this Certificate
properly endorsed.

In Witness Whereof, the said Corporation has caused this Certificate to be
signed by its duly authorized officers and to be sealed with the Seal of the Corporation
at LAWTON, OKLA., this day of A.D. 190

_____   _____
Secretary.   President.

SHARES $1.00

CONSTITUTION OF

CHANDLER MINING DISTRICT

ARTICLE 1. The officers of Chandler Mining District shall constitute a President, Treasurer and Recorder, to be elected annually in last meeting in December of each year to hold their offices one year and until their successors are elected and take their offices.

ART. 2. The duty of the President shall be to preside over each meeting, and to call meetings on his own motion or on the motion of any member, for good cause shown in writing. In the absence of the President, a President pro tem shall be chosen from the members.

ART. 3. The duty of the Recorder shall be to act as Secretary at all meetings and to record and keep all applications for locations and other instruments in a book published by and belonging to the miners of the district, and issue a certificate for such instruments or location, for which he shall receive in advance, seventy-five cents.

ART. 4. The duty of the Treasurer shall be to receive and keep a correct record of all money received by him from the District and to pay the same out only on warrant of the Recorder signed by the President and to report the financial standing quarterly to the District.

ART. 5. At least fifteen days notice shall be given by posting a written notice in some conspicuous place at some central point and a two-third vote shall be necessary to change any article of the constitution or by-laws.

ART. 6. The mets and bounds of Chandler District shall be Township 4 and 5 North and Range 12, 13 and 14 West, including six townships.

Local Laws.

ARTICLE 1. The discovery of a mineral vein or deposit shall immediately post at the point of discovery a plain notice or board and build a monument giving full description of the claim the date of location and name of locator and number of feet claimed and shall within twenty days from date cut the ground four foot by six foot and six inches deep and shall then have sixty days thereafter in which to distinctly mark his surface boundary by placing a stake at the four angles of his claim at least two feet high and record his claim with the District Recorder.

ART. 2. The width and size of a mineral claim shall be or may be 600 feet wide and 1,500 feet in length.

ART. 3. No person company or corporation allowed to file on lead or cross leads inside of boundry lines of any other claim.

ART. 4. All locations must be sworn to, to be correct and not conflict with any other claim.

ART. 5. Notice of location on claim at point of discovery as shaft and corner must be cut in wood or painted to take effect January 1, 1903.

By Laws of Chandler Mining District.

ARTICLE 1. When a miner of Chandler Mining District shall have complied wit the federal law and district regulation it shall be the duty of the miners of said District to protect by protest and truthful evidence in court said member in his just right.

ART. 2. Should written charge be preferred against any officer for failing to perform the duties of his office it shall be the duty of the president to call a meeting of the miners of the District and a committee of three be appointed to investigate charges, report the finding to the body which may be a two-third vote of members present, relieve him from office and regularly elect his successor.

ART. 3. Roll fees shall be twenty five (25) cents.

ART. 4. Five members shall constitute a quorum.

Mining districts throughout the Wichitas drew up their own constitutions. The Chandler district, including the Meers region, abided by the regulations.

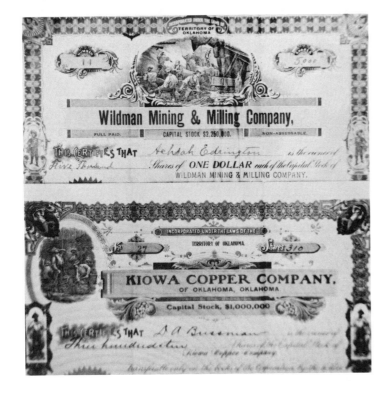

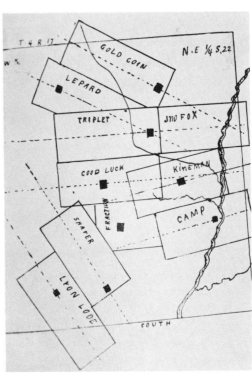

Just east of the townsite of Wildman and west of Middle Otter Creek, five miles south of present Roosevelt, mining claims with colorful names dotted the landscape, as this old plat reveals.

The Consolidated Mineral Company.

(INCORPORATED)

BRANCH OFFICES:
PHOENIX, ARIZONA.
WILDMAN, OKLAHOMA.
MOUNTAIN HOME, ARKANSAS.

GENERAL OFFICES:
209-210 LYCEUM BUILDING,
KANSAS CITY, MO.

MINES AND PROSPECTS:
ARKANSAS,
OKLAHOMA.

WILDMAN, OKLA., _Sept 26_ 190_

Received of S E Andrus for R W Kayel $15
fifteen Dollars being payment in full for one
surveyors instrument   E. L. Geary

REGISTRY RECEIPT.

Post Office at _Wildman Okla_

Registered Letter Parcel No. _10_ Rec'd _Jan 23_, 1903

of _S E Andrus_

addressed to _The President_

Roldine Patent #

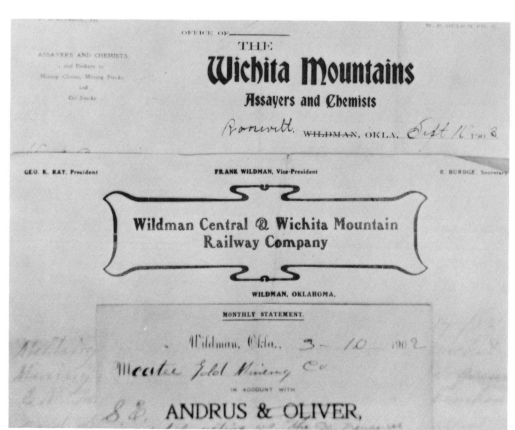

OFFICE OF ——— THE

Wichita Mountains
Assayers and Chemists

Roosevelt, WILDMAN, OKLA. _Sept 12 1903_

GEO. R. RAY, President   FRANK WILDMAN, Vice-President   R. BURDGE, Secretary

Wildman Central & Wichita Mountain Railway Company

WILDMAN, OKLAHOMA.

MONTHLY STATEMENT.

Wildman, Okla., _3 — 10_ 1902

Meatee Gold Mining Co

IN ACCOUNT WITH

S. E. ANDRUS & OLIVER,

Stationery and prospectuses of assayers, chemists, railroads, and mining companies were once commonplace in the Wichitas.

The last smelter erected in the Wichita Mountains was built at the head of Fawn Creek Canyon, near Elk Mountain, in 1906. Miners T. E. Cook and his son, Bert, recovered a slug of gold the size of a .38-caliber bullet from the ore of the Bonanza Mine at the head of the tramway. Courtesy Bert Cook.

Virtually every mining camp in the Wichitas had its own furnace for smelting ore. In 1906, Olive Wells completed this four-ton, nine-foot-high test smelter at Golden Pass, north of Cache. Courtesy Bert Cook.

Between 1901 and 1907 more than twenty-five hundred shafts were sunk in the Wichita Mountains. Most were crowned with horse-powered hoists and shaft houses, such as this one near Snyder. Courtesy Western History Collections, University of Oklahoma Library.

The Gold Blossom, or Campbell, Mine at the north base of Mount Scott in the Wichitas was sunk sixty-five feet deep with a thirty-foot tunnel. Courtesy Oklahoma Historical Society.

The Mount Scott Post Office, just north of the mountain, did a brisk business during the gold-rush activity in the Wichitas. Courtesy Museum of the Great Plains.

As late as 1917 placer gold was dredged from the streams south of Snyder, in Kiowa and Tillman counties, where grains of yellow metal could be panned or trapped in sluice boxes. Courtesy Western History Collections, University of Oklahoma Library.

Keith Walker examines the ruins of a miner's log cabin near Treasure Lake in the Wichita Mountains.

Relics of Oklahoma's gold-rush days are still found scattered among the rocks where prospectors once grubbed for precious metals. These picks, pans, crucibles, bottles, stove parts, and firebricks are among the artifacts picked up in the Wichitas.

The 110-foot-long Pennington tunnel in West Cache Creek Canyon, on the south side of the Wichitas, sold for five thousand dollars a half interest in 1903. The tunnel was dug into solid granite.

The entrance to Pennington tunnel, which remains an attraction for visitors to the Wichitas. Left to right: Linda Wilson, Ellen Jahnke, Lillian Ewing, and Ken Jahnke.

In 1901, William Larve, known as "Dutch Bill," who mined thirty years in the West and Mexico, built this Spanish-type arrastra just east of Mount Sheridan on Cedar Creek. It is typical of many crude ore grinders found over the state. The rock was crushed by drag stones pulled round and round by burros.

Above: The author examines the remains of a Spanish-type arrastra built by gold seekers on Panther Creek in 1905. Below: Another view of the arrastra. Burros harnessed to a cedar crossbeam pulled a drag stone around the trough, crushing ore in preparation for separating gold and silver with mercury. Photographs by Ruth Gartland.

Miner Sam Remer constructed his crude arrastra on the north bank of Medicine Creek west of Meers. Little remains today except these circles of stone, which once served as the trough for the ore crusher.

survivor of those gold seekers. When I first met him, in 1958, he was living just where he lived in 1901, when he camped his family in a tent on a claim his father had staked almost thirty-five years earlier, in 1867.[2] At the foot of the granite peaks in the southwest corner of the Wichita Mountains Wildlife Refuge, Silas lived alone in his cobble-stone cabin shaded by the far-reaching branches of an ancient oak. A dim trail led from the refuge highway to his secluded cabin, nestled in the moss-backed rocks.

Silas Ison's optimism never flagged. Wizened with hard years, Silas remained always hopeful, always believing that the day would come when he would yet strike his golden bonanza. On my first

visit, more than fifteen years ago, I was surprised to find a gentle yet firm old gentleman who knew just what he wanted out of life and was determined not to let anyone rob him of his peace or liberty, as some tried to do.[3]

I drove down the sod trail to his cobblestone cabin, partly hidden among large post oaks, crossed a small stream, and opened the gate of the barbed-wire fence enclosing several acres of his land. Big Texas longhorns and a small herd of buffaloes grazed nearby.

Old Silas, built short to the ground, was standing behind the screen door of his cabin. A big grin spread across his unshaved face as he greeted me. He was wearing a red-, white-, and black-checked

While living on the mining claim his father staked in 1866, Silas Ison never gave up his mines in the Wichitas, first sunk in 1901.

shirt, baggy brown pants supported by suspenders, scuffed, untied shoes, and an uncreased broad-brimmed hat. He opened the door and invited me in. I ducked my head and walked onto the cement floor of his cozy cabin.

While the old hard-rocker stuffed some Granger tobacco into a corncob pipe, I eyed an artist's conception of Christ hanging on a wall, a yellowed, dusty plat of Silas' mines on another, and a sorted collection of rocks and minerals cluttering a nearby table. By now the aroma of his pipe had saturated the room. Sitting on his bed, his shoes not quite touching the hard, cold floor, Silas began his story.

A Virginian by birth, he was obviously proud of his southern heritage. He was born on February 6, 1872, near Esterville. When he was still a boy, the Ison family headed westward. Finally, in the 1890's, they settled at Duncan, Indian Territory, at that time the nearest railroad terminal thirty miles east of the rugged Wichitas and the hopping-off point for what one day soon would be Lawton.

In 1896, Silas took for his bride the beautiful Dove Murray, a sister of William H. "Alfalfa Bill" Murray, later to become the ninth governor of Oklahoma. After the Kiowa-Comanche-Apache country opened, Silas brought his wife to the mining claim, where his father had already settled, and in the years that followed the couple reared five boys and four girls.

In the beginning Silas and his war-hardened father, George W. Ison, a former Confederate soldier, opened four mines: first the Atlas and then the Old Maid, the Mennonite, and the Half Moon. All told, they sank thirteen shafts on their land, each sunk into solid granite, studded with shiny quartz and sprinkled with small quantities of gold, silver, copper, tin, and molybdenum.

As he talked, Ison puffed his pipe at a faster pace:

I only had three or four years of schooling, but, by golly, I studied a lot at home on my own. Why, you ought to hear me when I get in court. I'm as good a lawyer as any and have beat every case I've been up against. I know every mining law there is, and if anybody wants to know anything about mining laws, they can just come to me.

On several occasions he went to court to defend his claims on the government refuge. "If there's one thousand people in the United States," he declared with a determined look, "I make up one-thousandth of our government. I ain't beat, and I never will be beat."

After the gold rush had died out, the government expelled the prospectors who remained on the wildlife refuge, which was at that time a national forest and game preserve. Silas and his father, used to fighting for what they believed in, would not leave, claiming that they had a right to the eighty acres on which their mining claims were located, legally filed, and worked according to law. George Ison had staked his first claim there in 1866 and periodically returned to the Wichitas to look after his prospective gold mine.[4] He was not about to give it all up, after years of working it and protecting it from would-be claim jumpers. Silas was just as firm. Finally, during the last court action in 1942, the government decided to grant Silas the right to remain on his land.

I could elaborate far more on Silas' mining experiences and endless legal battles, but this is his story about buried treasure, a subject that Silas knew well and was always eager to tell.[5] Many of these stories, including those of the James boys, Silas inherited from his father, who met both Jesse and Frank on more than one occasion in the Wichitas and who in later years was often visited by Frank.[6]

George Ison enlisted in the Confederate Army at sixteen and served in the Sixteenth Regiment, Company A, of the Tennessee Cavalry. Because of his age his name did not appear on the muster rolls. He served throughout the war, and for a time rode with Colonel John Morgan's Raiders. Like many of his contemporaries, young, vigorous, and sickened by civil war and its aftermath, Ison headed west to the beckoning gold camps. He sought his fortune first in the rowdy boom camps of New Mexico and later in Colorado. Interested in becoming a chemist, he soon took up assaying. He staked several claims for himself and later sold them for handsome profits. When he left the West a year later, he took his fortune of thirty-two thousand dollars with him.[7]

While homeward bound across the Plains, George heard stories of hidden wealth in the raw, unsettled Wichita Mountains, little explored since the days of the Spaniards. He learned that some prospectors were in the mountains, seeking lost treasure buried by the Spaniards more than a century before. The temptation was more than the adventuresome Ison could withstand. He turned his horse and headed the pack animals carrying his gold in the direction of the Wichitas. After he had made that choice, he was forced to pursue it, for he detected a pack of Indians following him. If he could reach the hills now emerging higher from the Plains, he knew that he could find a craggy lair in which to hide or, if necessary, to fight.

Ison sighted an inviting mountain and raced toward it. When he had hidden himself and his animals behind some large boulders, he sighted his rifle and waited. The Indians rode past into a nearby valley. Ison stalked through the underbrush to spy on his pursuers. In the distance he could see a miner hacking away with an ax. Suddenly several Indians swooped down on the miner. Ison had no choice but to watch. He decided that day that he would rather take the hardships of the gold camps than risk a knife in the back from hostile Indians.

But if these mountains were rich in gold, as he had been told, he was not leaving without first staking his claim. When he prepared to leave a few days later, he had found the piece of ground he fancied, at the foot of the Charons Gardens Wilderness, the same piece of earth on which his son, Silas, lived more than one hundred years later.

George returned to Virginia, but after a year the

Wichitas beckoned again. Home was never the same. His family could not change his mind. On his return trip to Indian Territory in 1867, Ison first visited a camp of soldiers nestled in the foothills of the Wichitas before going to his claim. Later that camp would become known as Fort Sill. Ison was warned to stay out of the mountains, for gold seekers were considered poachers. The commanding officer took a personal interest in Ison. One day Ison was summoned to the general's quarters. "Look here, young man, what do you mean to do? Don't you know the Indians will get you in the mountains?"

Ison thought a minute. "Well, sir, if they do, I'll get plenty of them first."

The general eyed the young man's pistol strapped on his waist. "Have you enough ammunition?"

"Nearly two hundred pounds," Ison grinned. "Now don't you worry, General. I know Indians, and I know how to protect myself. You won't have to send an ambulance squad after me."

The general frowned on Ison's intentions but did not stop him from going on his way. It was *his* scalp. A day or so later Ison found the claim he had staked the year before at the foot of Charons Gardens Mountain. There he set up camp and began sifting the earth for precious metal. Indians were camped all about him, but most seemed peaceful enough. Many strange things occurred in the storied hills. A soldier or prospector found alone might be killed and scalped, and in later years the telltale bones of such victims were discovered. But the Indians seemed to like the young prospector and visited his camp often, trading various ornaments for some interesting object he possessed.

Then there were the outlaws who harbored in the hills. Ison did not look for them. Their signs were obvious enough. One day while he squatted at the edge of a stream, a large gold pan in hand, several men rode swiftly down from a nearby ridge. Before Ison could grab his rifle, he was surrounded. Each man was heavily armed and looked as if he had not seen civilization in months.

The bearded horsemen looked the prospector over thoroughly. Finally they introduced themselves. Two were Jesse and Frank James; a third was Cole Younger. Ison knew the James boys, for

their exploits had already begun to appear in the newspapers. Too he knew of them from the war while he was a member of Morgan's Raiders. They asked Ison what he was doing in Indian country. He could have asked them the same question but merely replied that he was prospecting for gold.

"Prospecting for gold!" they laughed. "Why, that's what we're doing!" George Ison did not look surprised. He knew that their gold had a different texture from his. Ison and his self-invited company talked long that evening. Naturally their talk turned to memories of the war, when they had ridden with William Quantrill's guerrillas, and of course, how they hated Yankees and how it might have been if the Confederate cause had not been lost. Each man was seeking his own fortune in one form or another.

During their talk Jesse handed his fellow former Confederate twelve hundred dollars and thanked him for the use of his mining claim as a safe depository for their gold. Ison took the money, knowing full well he was in no position to refuse it. And why should he, he thought. If they wanted to hide money on his claim, who was he to object?

Early the next morning Ison's visitors were gone. Just where the loot was hidden Ison did not care to know. But that it did not remain long he was sure. Some weeks later Jesse and Frank rode swiftly into his camp, unearthed the gold, and were again on their way, saying little more than, "Howdy," and, "Thanks," for watching their gold so carefully. Jesse James and his gang rode off to become the most feared and deadliest outlaws known in the annals of the West. Ison never crossed their paths again, until Frank returned after the turn of the century, and often visited Ison at his log cabin—poring over maps on which appeared cryptic symbols. What stories could those log walls tell?

Ison continued panning the creek beds for color. His assays convinced him that the mother lode would be found but that it would take a lot of machinery and capital. It would be years before he could legally transport machinery of any kind into the mountains. His mine would have to wait. It would be more than twenty years before Ison would again sink his pick into the hard granite rock of the Wichitas.

When he returned to Virginia, Ison married

Margaret Clark, and he later moved his family to the Middle West. In 1891 he settled in Duncan, Oklahoma, near the forbidden Wichitas. Between that year and 1901 he made frequent trips to his mining claim—even though the country was still off limits to prospectors. Although soldiers and even United States Marshal Heck Thomas jumped Ison about entering the reservation, he succeeded in guarding his interests. Finally, in 1901, the day came that the land was officially opened.

George and his son, Silas, moved their families onto the claim, first staked thirty-five years before. There they built the first smelter to refine their ore, only to have it later tied up in litigation—another legal battle.

George believed the stories he had heard about lost Spanish gold secretly buried by miners from Mexico. He had discovered what he thought was evidence of the ancient mines in the hills and had found the ruins of a smelter that Mexicans had built near Red River. Many legends told of the seventeen burro loads of gold bullion hidden in the mountains.

Then there were the rampant legends of the James treasure. George Ison was not convinced that any of it had actually been lost until one day Frank James knocked at his door. Neither had seen the other since Jesse and Frank rode out of Ison's camp that day in 1867. Frank visited the Ison camp on many occasions, always seeking information about this or that landmark, an old trail, a certain tree, a strange rock. Ison helped whenever he could, but he knew that there were many things Frank was unable to find, and he finally left, frustrated by his lack of memory.

Once a nephew of the old miner, Bob Ison, visited his uncle. One night the elder Ison recalled the stories of hidden treasures he had heard over the years. Young Bob stayed up half the night, prodding for more details. The look on his face showed his belief. Several nights later Bob Ison stormed into his uncle's half-dugout and threw a piece of metal onto the table, urging that it be put on the fire for a test. George Ison seized the metal. He did not need to perform a test. He could tell outright that it was a piece of almost solid gold. The old miner questioned his nephew about the find. Bob claimed that he had stumbled onto it in

the mountains but refused to say anything more. Both George and Silas were worried about the boy's boasts of his discovery, but no one could talk sense to him. His mind was crazed with gold.

One night as Bob was returning home he was fired upon from both sides of the road. Several masked men leaped from behind rocks and dragged him into the woods, while another placed a rope around his neck and bound his arms to his sides. The rope was thrown over a huge limb and then pulled until the boy hung just off the ground. As he screamed for help, writhing to stretch the lariat, his attackers panicked and fled. Barely able to touch the ground, Bob struggled all night before freeing himself. The next morning he staggered into his uncle's house to tell of his ordeal. Later that day a stranger dropped into the Ison camp, relaying to Bob that some people wanted to see him in Indiahoma. Believing that they were his friends, Bob followed the stranger into town. A day passed, and the Isons began to worry about the boy. When still another day went by and he had not returned, a search was begun. He was found in town. He had been severely beaten, and townspeople were caring for him. He had been horse-whipped when he refused to tell where he had found the gold.

No one ever learned how Bob Ison had come by his gold. Whether or not he had actually found it could only be conjectured, for he told no one. Later he left the Ison camp for the West.

George Ison was always prepared to guard his claim from poachers. He was convinced that his property held precious ore, and he kept his gun well oiled to defend that belief. His son, Silas, always shared his father's faith in the Wichitas.

In 1933, at the age of eighty-nine, George Ison died. He was a soldier, an indomitable gold seeker, a plainsman, one of the first to sink a pick into the Wichitas in quest of gold. His life ended an era of romance and adventure. But his son, Silas, a rugged pioneer himself, a prospector of the old school, kept alive the adventure of the great Wichita gold rush.

As he talked to me, Silas Ison lay back on his bed and crossed his feet. Then, without turning around, he took a long kitchen match and struck it on the wall behind him to relight his pipe, and

In his cobblestone cabin, Silas Ison shows a bar of metal smelted from his mines and a zircon crystal found in the adjacent hills.

INCORPORATED UNDER THE LAWS OF
OKLAHOMA.

NUMBER
48

SHARES
1000-

The Central Mining Company.

CAPITAL STOCK $1,000,000.

THIS CERTIFIES THAT *R. B. Stuart* is the owner of *One Thousand* Shares of **One Dollar** each of the Capital Stock of THE CENTRAL MINING COMPANY, transferable only on the books of the Corporation by the holder hereof in person or by Attorney upon surrender of this Certificate properly endorsed.

In Witness Whereof, the said Corporation has caused this Certificate to be signed by its duly authorized officers and to be sealed with the Seal of the Corporation.

Lawton, Okla., this _____ day of *September* A.D. 190_

SECRETARY.

PRESIDENT.

SHARES
$1.00
EACH

George W. Ison and his son, Silas, organized the Central Mining Company and sold stock to work their thirteen mines in the Wichitas.

continued his story. About 1907, Silas said, he drove his wife, Dove, and his father to Red River on a fishing trip. A few miles north of the river Silas caught a glimpse of a tin horn lying across the roadbed. Three feet long or more, the round tube had been flattened as if a wagon wheel had rolled over it.

"Wait, hold up the wagon!" Silas shouted, as he jumped out to investigate. He put the flattened tube in the wagon. When the Isons reached their fishing hole, Silas' father took a wagon rod and straightened the tin tube. It was obviously old; none of them had seen anything like it before.

As George peered into the tube, his heart began to pound with eagerness. It was a once-in-a-lifetime discovery. Gently he pulled out a tarnished parchment, on which was scrawled Spanish script and symbols. No one could make heads or tails of it, Silas remembered. But it seemed to show where something was buried. It could be nothing less than a Spanish treasure map.

The old prospector's eyes gleamed as he recalled the discovery. "Yes, sir, that map showed two treasures, we later learned. A hidden cave with a cache of gold was one of 'em. The other was four jack loads of gold bullion buried in deerskins not over a mile and a half west of here. It's buried twenty feet deep. I know this because I

186

stuck a metal rod clear down to it. The gold is there, all right.

"Those bars are buried on another man's land though," Silas said. "Oh, I offered him one-fourth of the discovery, but, no, sir, he wanted at least three-fourths. I said, no doing. I'd just wait. Maybe he'll move away or sell out. Right now, I'm still waiting."

According to Silas, the chart was extremely difficult to read, but with the help of Dove, who could read some Spanish, they finally translated the mysterious parchment. One peculiarity about the map was a row of small letters that appeared across it. Silas said, "The map was stolen several years later, when no-good thieves burned our house and fled for their lives with it. I think that map has changed hands at least three times, and I don't guess I'll ever see it again."

The old hard-rocker paused a minute, pulling on his mustache, and then laughed aloud. He continued:

You know, I haven't found any buried gold, but I know for a fact where some was buried, and I know that I came mighty close to gettin' it—mind you, real close. I went after our cows one evening. They had wandered over to Elm Springs, just south of here. I was walking past an old oak tree and noticed an auger-like hole about three feet up the trunk. Three feet higher was another auger hole. Both those holes had wooden plugs in 'em. That seemed mighty peculiar to me.

Well, I thought there must be a reason for it. I backed up to that tree and stepped out about six feet. I'll be a monkey's uncle if I didn't fall into a shallow hole. It was almost dark, so I figured I had better go on after the cows. When I got back home, I told Pa and Sis about it and wanted to go back and dig right then, but they said it would wait until morning. So I waited.

Early the next morning I was back at the big oak, and I'll be dad blasted if someone hadn't beat me to it! Yes, sir, an old iron kettle with its side busted out was lying on top of a big pile of dirt. The imprints of those silver dollars showed all over that darn pot! Just all over it!

As the sun sank beyond the horizon, Ison rose and lighted a coal-oil lamp. I noticed his old-style telephone, which he'd had for ages. In a few days, he said, the company was putting him in a new "fancy dial telephone." I thought to myself that it would be a shame to clutter his rustic cabin with such a foreign apparatus. But he seemed tickled by the prospect.

As I walked from Ison's stone cabin, the aroma of the burning coal oil hung in the night air. Only a dim light showed from his cabin window as the silence was broken by a howling coyote.

The old hard-rocker had played a leading role in the history of the ancient blue Wichitas. Perhaps that was always his real treasure. His father had been among the very first to seek his fortune in the Wichitas. Silas was the last of that historic breed of men.[8]

Bat Cave, where A. S. Keown may have found a ledge of platinum. At top left an iron boiler remains from a past attempt to pump water from the cave. At bottom right a wire fence hangs down in the cavern.

8. Skeletons, Jewels, and Platinum

Old Jim Wilkerson sat back in his chair and stroked his graying hair, staring at me for a good minute. "I guess it won't hurt to tell you the whole truth about this," he said somewhat nervously.

I had found Wilkerson in his cobblestone cabin snuggled against the hillside in Medicine Park, a mountain settlement nestled in the Wichitas.[1] I knew that Wilkerson had once served as a deputy sheriff and because of that fact was somewhat reluctant to tell all he knew about Dick Estes. He made it clear that he had known Estes a long time before he became a deputy and then went on to fill in the missing parts of his story of the little-known outlaw Estes—and his forgotten gold.

In 1902, Dick Estes pulled a robbery in Denver, making a sizable haul of forty thousand dollars in jewels and watches and another $20,000 in gold coins. Estes lost no time seeking refuge in Oklahoma Territory, where he had previously eluded the law. "He was a tough bird, and knew this country well," Jim said. Estes had a mountain hideout up Panther Creek toward the north side of the Wichitas. The dugout evidently was a lair for many of his kind. Estes once boasted that on the roster of visitors was the notorious Oklahoma badman Bill Doolin.

While holed up at his mountain lair, Estes cached his haul of jewels, watches, and gold, keeping out only enough so as not to appear conspicuous.[2] For his treasure he chose a bank of dirt at the base of a cedar tree ten paces west from the dugout. Then he rode into Lawton and sought out Jim Wilkerson, whose family he had known for years. "As a kid I used to cook for a lot of those characters," old Jim smiled.

Estes had a knack for losing what he had. It was not long before he discovered that his trail was too warm to remain any longer in Lawton. Finding himself in dire need of a fresh horse, he offered Wilkerson a trade no reasonable man would pass up. In exchange for a horse and saddle he gave Jim the directions to the sixty-thousand dollar cache and invited him to help himself to a fair share. Estes was convinced that he would be back to retrieve the remainder in due time.

But Jim was sure that that time never came for Estes. He was soon apprehended, lodged in the Lawton jail only to escape soon after, and remained at large for about two years in New Mexico. There he was recaptured, returned to Lawton, and jailed again. Soon afterward Jim lost touch with him.

Some time passed before Wilkerson made an attempt to find the outlaw hideaway and the treasure at the base of the cedar tree. By then prospectors were all over the mountains and digging at any place other than a mine might arouse suspicion. When he finally found the old haunt, the key to finding the earthen bank had disappeared. Many of the cedars in the area had been cut for fuel, no doubt by miners. Jim found what he believed was the stump of such a tree, but his shovel yielded nothing around its base.

Jim Wilkerson never got to tap Dick Estes' cache, which is still hidden somewhere up Panther Creek in the heart of the rugged, boulder-strewn Wichitas. He had been confined to a wheelchair for years when I last talked with him. But old Jim never flagged in his belief that the sixty thousand dollars still remains just where Estes buried it— near the old outlaw dugout.

The Wichita Mountains have long been considered a paradise for outlaws' gold by those in a position to know. Many of those tales have been overshadowed by the stories of Jesse and Frank James and their two million dollars hidden in the hills. But one only has to examine turn-of-the-century newspaper accounts to get an inkling of outlaw lairs discovered when the Kiowa-Comanche-Apache country was opened to white settlement.

The Indian reservation—virtually all of southwest Oklahoma—had become forbidden land to white intruders at the Treaty of Medicine Lodge in 1867. The government feared a repetition of the Black Hills gold rush and massacres. Fort Sill soldiers and Indian police alike patrolled the reservation, frequently arresting interlopers, but prospectors still came with pick and shovel, as did men wanted by the law, seeking refuge in caves and twisting canyons where few white men were seen.

Their telltale bones often revealed a grim story. In November, 1895, a party from El Reno discovered the charred skeleton of a prospector in a deep canyon between Mount Scott and Mount Sheridan "who had evidently been killed by the Comanche Indians." Near the remains were found mining tools, a crucible, and a claim marker that showed it had been staked the February before.[3] It was not the first nor last such discovery.

Lost Wagon Train Gold

In 1847 or 1848 a long wagon train composed of forty-five families slowly rumbled out of Clarksville, in north Texas, heading west up Red River for California. Made up of emigrants and merchants who had lived near the settlement, the train was led by two men remembered only as Ryan and Alexander, who were driving along a large herd of cattle.

At first the wagon train tried to follow the Prairie Dog Fork of Red River but upon finding it far too rugged for travel turned back and steered north up North Fork, at that time the eastern border of west Texas. But the train had gone no farther than fifty to seventy miles upriver when hostile Indians attacked. Many of the emigrants were killed and their stock driven off. A few who escaped wandered on the Plains for almost a year before making it back to Clarksville.

Years later, in 1859, James Pollard, who told the story long afterward, joined a party from Fannin County to search for remains of the ill-fated train.[4] Pollard knew that some of the party had returned, for he had seen them. But the only remains they found was the skeleton of a man named Gilbert who had died at the base of a tree on what later became known as Gilbert Creek, in present Clay County, Texas. His bones were returned to Bonham, Texas, for burial, where Gilbert had lived and had built the first mill in that settlement.

In 1899 a woman about sixty years old appeared at the home of J. M. Goff, two miles south of Carter, Oklahoma.[5] She told Goff that when she was about ten years old she was with an emigrant train traveling up the North Fork. She remembered that the wagons were attacked near the river at the mouth of a canyon. She was taken captive by the Indians and lived with them until she escaped several years later.

Some time after the turn of the century a farmer named Lee Castillo discovered the grisly remains of what may have been that wagon train on his river farm about four miles south and four west of Carter (in S.18, T.8N., R.22W.). He found more than a dozen bleached skulls and bones scattered over the prairie. Bones of the Texas emigrants? Local tradition has long had it that near a rock crossing on Elm Creek a wagon train of emigrants hid their gold and valuables just before an attack by Indians.[6] The treasure has never been reported found.

Dead Men Tell No Tales

White men crossed the Kiowa-Comanche-Apache Reservation at their own risk. One day in April, 1900, Henry Wicker was prospecting on Otter Creek when he happened upon the skeletons of a man, a woman, and two children. Wicker estimated that they had been dead about six months. Their camp outfit, saddles, and an empty Winchester gave no clues to the tragedy.[7]

The opening of the Indian country brought still more gruesome discoveries but few answers to the mysteries. On Christmas Day, 1902, the Lawton *Weekly News* told of another strange find in the mountains about three miles northeast of Cache.[8] A party of hunters had found the skeletons of a soldier and an Indian who years before had killed each other in a deadly duel. The brass buttons of the uniform had begun to rust, and the wooden grips of an empty-chambered pistol had decayed. The soldier's skull had been crushed as if struck with a blunt instrument. It was surmised that the Indian had leaped on the soldier with his tomahawk, while the soldier emptied his pistol at his assailant.

The valley just east of Mount Sheridan is a natural route into the Wichitas from the north. It was an ancient Indian trail when white intruders began using it to slip into the mountains to prospect for gold or to lie low from the law. It was in this area that the charred bones of a prospector were found in 1895. In early April, 1903, another human skeleton was found in a ravine near Mount Scott by the children of Sam Remer, who was mining nearby.[9] The victim's fate was easily determined, for a bullet hole had penetrated the back of the skull and exited just below the left eye.

A month later Ed Caine, the bartender at John Gillespie's Saloon in Lawton, was exploring in the same area when he stumbled across a badly rusted gun barrel.[10] The barrel was about .44 caliber; its stock, hammer, and triggers had disappeared.

In December of the same year A. M. Saule was hiking through the mountains about six miles northwest of the Comanche Chief Quanah Parker's home, Star House, originally built by cattle barons just north of what became the town of Cache. Saule came across the mouth of a cave and decided to explore it. Part way into the hole he spied a saddle half-buried in the rocky floor. It was a strange place for a saddle, Saule knew, and explored farther.

Though there was barely enough light left to see, Saule found a human skeleton lying on a crude bed.[11] Scattered about were a pair of boots, gloves, a tie, and other clothing. Saule was convinced that he had stumbled upon an outlaw's lair. Later he showed the lower jawbone to the authorities. All the teeth were present and were well preserved. Might the cave's occupant have died from lead poisoning? No one was ever sure. But the discovery of two skeletons south of the mountains a few years later might well be the clues to some missing outlaw gold.

A Dying Man's Story

Lying in a hospital bed in Dallas, Texas, the outlaw knew that his chances of recovering from his gunshot wounds were slim. The nurse had been good to him, and, even if he did not recover, he wanted to make it up to her.

He motioned the young nurse to his bedside and painfully whispered in her ear. His story was short. There was not time enough for details. The dying man revealed that there had originally been three of them, all partners in a bank robbery in Kansas. They had escaped to Indian Territory and had holed up in the Wichita Mountains bordering old Greer County, Texas, on the east. After leaving the hills, they were attacked by Indians shortly before they reached Red River. Two of them were killed. Badly wounded himself, the outlaw buried the money and somehow escaped being killed. Several days later he found himself in the Dallas hospital, and now he was near death. The outlaw tried to direct the nurse to the hidden gold as best he could. Two days later he was dead.

Several years afterward the nurse organized a search party to help her find the outlaws' gold.[12] At first her search was without reward. But after Indian Territory opened to settlement, she continued to examine the country, a little at a time. She believed that she had found the place where the three bandits had been overtaken by Indians, and she centered her search around an area about four miles west and two miles south of the present community of Geronimo, Oklahoma.

The nurse had already given up her search when what might have been a clue to the cache was discovered in the fall of 1907. Lawton's *Daily News-Republican* reported the find:

While removing stone from a Big Pasture quarry near Emerson, T. C. and B. F. Moore found a human skeleton and numerous articles that may lift the veil that shroud some mystery of days gone by. The men were first attracted by the muzzle of a gun that was partly unearthed, and once having their curiosity aroused, they followed the cue which led to the discovery.

After digging a short distance, to their surprise they found a human skeleton, saddle, two guns—one an old-style buffalo rifle, the other a Winchester saddle gun—together with bullets and a number of empty shells. One of the guns was in a good state of preservation, while the other was so badly rusted it could not be opened.

Lettering upon the saddle could be read and disclosed the fact that the saddle was made by Fred Ripps, Wichita Falls, Texas, and upon the skirts of the saddle the name of A. E. Kelley was stamped.[13]

The story went on to speculate that the person had no doubt been killed by Indians. Others believed that he had shielded himself behind a bank of earth and that the soil had given way, burying him. A number of solid-silver Indian trinkets were found with two pocketbooks. One contained a nickle and a ten-cent piece, while the other held a large roll of bills, so badly decayed that the value could not be determined.

Three years later, still another important clue

came to light. In 1910 a second human skeleton was found exposed on a creek bank six miles south and three miles west of Geronimo, or about four miles south of where the nurse had concentrated her search for the hidden gold—and just north of the skeletal remains found near Emerson. Could this have been the second outlaw killed by Indians? Not long afterward several Texans appeared with a map to the hidden cache of gold. They were convinced that the remains were those of one of the outlaws. But they were no luckier than the nurse. To date no Kansas bank money has been found, but many are sure that it lies buried not far from where the two skeletons were found in later years.

The Keechi Hills Mystery

The evidence is clear that Frank James unearthed part of his legendary treasure near Buzzard Roost in the Keechi Hills. Few still-living old-timers can remember when Emmett Dalton, the sole survivor of the Coffeyville fiasco, posted a ten-thousand-dollar reward in Lawton for anyone who could direct him to a certain cave in southwest Oklahoma. Many believed that the cave was in the Keechi Hills and that it held seventy-five thousand dollars. No one ever collected Dalton's reward, and many believe that the treasure itself was never found.

There was nothing uncertain about a strange discovery made in later years in the Keechis. In March, 1908, one James Kinder was breaking prairie sod on the farm of George Lucas near Cement when the plow he was walking behind struck a large chest.[14] Kinder hurried back to the house for a shovel and returned to unearth a large wooden trunk. The lid was tightly sealed, but Kinder managed to pry it open, to find a human skeleton lying among an assortment of clothing, tinware, and other articles. In no time onlookers were digging in similar sunken plots of earth. Nine more human graves were found, as well as partly decayed saddles, shoes, shawls, silk handkerchiefs, and even a bottle of camphor. No one had ever known of a wagon-train massacre there, but many speculated that an overland supply train to Fort Sill had been attacked by Indians and that soldiers who set out to find survivors found only

bodies and buried them on the spot. Of course no one knew for certain.

The Skeleton and His Gold

Bill Argo knows that in a lonely canyon on the south side of the Wichitas, almost in the shadow of Mount Scott, are hidden two saddlebags stuffed with $39,500 in gold coin.[15] He has no doubts that the stolen bank loot is still there, for a small portion of it has been found, as have the bones of one outlaw who helped steal it.

One summer day I found Argo outside his cabin south of Cache. I had gone to see Bill about the story of seven jack loads of Mexican gold on Pecan Creek, near the old schoolhouse by that name, eight or ten miles south of the mountains. But I became less interested in the Mexican gold when Bill told the story of a Wichita, Kansas, bank robbery.

"I heard the story from my uncle," Bill explained, "who heard it from a member of the posse who chased the outlaws into the Wichitas and later hunted the forty thousand dollars in gold they hid in the rocks."

Three men robbed the bank, Bill went on. Two were white; the third, a black man. But the holdup did not go according to plans, and in the getaway one of the whites was shot. The three fled south to the territory and holed up in a canyon southwest of Mount Scott. There the wounded man died and was given a quick burial in a shallow grave. In the meantime Indians stole their horses, presenting still more problems.

Their saddles were now worthless, and the four saddlebags of gold were far too heavy to carry out of the mountains. Not far from the grave of their dead accomplice they hid the three saddles among some boulders and then cached the four saddlebags of gold in an equally secure place.

Sometime later, perhaps near Fort Sill, the two robbers commandeered horses and rode east toward the Indian nations. They had not gone far when the white man shot the black man and left him in an arroyo. But making himself sole claimant to the bank money did him no good. Outside Marlow he was overtaken by a hard-riding posse and shot down in a deadly barrage of fire. His final words were muddled, and no one could make sense from what seemed to be directions. But enough of his trail had been picked up to cause the posse to believe the bank gold was discarded somewhere southwest of Mount Scott. Argo continued the story:

I believe it was in 1935 when my uncle began grazing cattle on rangeland a few miles south of Mount Scott. One day he was riding through a canyon when he was attracted to pieces of decayed leather that appeared as if some varmit had dug them out of the rocks. He was too busy pushing steers to investigate right then and just put it in the back of his mind for the time being.

When he did go back some days later, a cousin and I went along. We found the decayed leather without any trouble. It was old and twisted from years of exposure to the weather. Some small animal had dug it out all right because under a pile of moss-backed rocks we found what was left of three rotted saddles.

It wasn't much distance away that we found what we thought might be a grave. We didn't have to dig far when we exposed the skeleton. No doubt the outlaw had carried twelve silver rings in a pocket because we found them next to a leg bone. We found nothing more that day even though we combed the canyon fairly well.

Argo stopped his story and stood up to stretch. He looked toward the distant, blue-hued Mount Scott. They found part of the gold, he went on. Months later his uncle and cousin returned to the canyon on the south flank of the Wichitas and searched farther down. Bill said:

They turned stones all day, I guess, because hidden back among some granite boulders they found one saddle pocket. It held five hundred dollars in gold, although I didn't know this at the time, but found it out some time later. We all hunted at various times after that for the other three saddle pockets. I've always believed they were hidden in a cave or beneath an overhanging rock ledge that caved off years before we found the saddles and grave.

At such a place Bill had poked a steel rod into the ground ten or twelve feet and had struck a rock. He had followed that procedure several times, extending out a few feet with each probe. When he stopped hitting what appeared to be the same rock, he had worked over an area twenty feet in length. Several large oak trees that forked at the surface enforced his belief all the more. It was reason enough to believe there had been an overhanging ledge under which three saddlebags might have been placed.

"Someday I'm going to try again," Bill said. "I should have long ago but always kept putting it off. I'm not real worried, though. You could be twenty feet away from that place and never recognize it if you hadn't seen it before. It's not likely it'll soon be found."

Keown's Lost Ledge of Platinum

A. S. Keown was a grizzled prospector who showed up in the Wichita Mountains almost a decade after the last great gold rush on the Plains. But where others of his breed had failed to find gold, Keown claimed to have found metal even more precious.

No one knew just what he had found, and Keown kept his secret for sixteen years before it became public. Even then it was not until the prospector was found shot in the head that the mysterious metal that he had discovered and guarded so well was reported in the papers.

However hard the close-mouthed prospector tried to keep his discovery secret, he knew that he was watched, which made his actions all the more mysterious. Little is known about him, except that his home was Baltimore, Maryland, and that he made his headquarters in Fort Cobb, some miles north of where he had uncovered a rich ledge of platinum.

It is known, too, that the fifty-four-year-old prospector built a small cabin on the George Thomas Ranch, about fifteen miles northwest of Meers. From that mountain home Keown would walk almost daily to the north into the sprawling limestone buttes known as the Slick Hills.[16] There he would disappear as though the ground had swallowed him up. It was believed that Keown found his ledge of platinum in the bowels of Bat Cave. The cave, a natural cavern in southern Caddo County that sinks into the earth almost ninety feet to its first level, was named for the dark cloud of bats that rose from its mouth at dusk.

The chasm, a gaping hole almost thirty feet in diameter amid a grassed-over limestone plateau, narrows as it descends. Today the only entrance into the cave is by way of a wire fence that hangs in the deep pit for most of its depth. Below the cavern floor are still other rooms, but they are filled with water supplied by an abundant underground source. A water pipe extending down from a windmill at the entrance leads through the cave and at the floor slants downward still another twenty feet into one of several water holes in the cavern. Keown is believed to have dived into the water and found still another chamber above the water level which held the precious platinum, far more valuable than gold.

Early in 1924, Keown began to take action to obtain legal title to the land. He employed an attorney named Blum from Baltimore to assist him. Both Keown's wife and Blum had been living in Fort Cobb while he prepared to gain possession of the land that held his still-secret discovery.

In June of that year, when Keown's long dream of gaining legal claim to his rich discovery seemed to be materializing, he left Fort Cobb and drove to Oklahoma City in his Model-T Ford. It was not his first trip to the capital city. He had made other such trips, almost every time to sell a small portion of platinum to a trusted Oklahoma City jeweler. But this time Keown was apparently carrying papers perhaps finalizing a legal claim to his mine that revealed its location.

Whatever papers Keown carried on him, someone had planned to get them, for the prospector was later found in his car on the road between Anadarko and Fort Cobb on his way home from Oklahoma City with a bullet hole through his head. "His pockets had been searched and all his papers were missing," reported the *Daily Oklahoman*.[17]

Because Keown had disappeared into Bat Cave on many occasions, reports soon began circulating that he had discovered a hidden room in the cavern that guarded the fabulous platinum. Rancher Frank Ketch was sure that it was a rich discovery. He talked with the Oklahoma City jeweler, who revealed that Keown had sold him scrapings of platinum. From Keown's visits the jeweler had learned that Keown had mined about sixty pounds of the precious metal and would later sell it. Where he kept it the jeweler did not know.[18]

Ketch, owner of the sprawling Circle K Ranch, was convinced that Bat Cave held the secret to Keown's platinum mine. In 1927 he hauled a boiler and a pump to the cave. He hoped to pump out the twenty-foot water hole beneath the cavern floor and then search for the secret room that Keown was believed to have visited periodically somewhere in the inner depths.

Harvey Freeze examines the cave on top of Long Horn Mountain in Kiowa County. The cave is said to have once served as an outlaw lair.

Ketch pumped water for eight days but lowered the level a mere two inches. If Keown had discovered a secret treasure chamber, he had found a way to it that no one else knew or had sealed it so well that no one could find it. Ketch gave up his search more than forty years ago. Today a massive iron boiler lies at the cave's opening, mute testimony to the search for Keown's lost platinum mine.

Keown's killers were never apprehended. To this day, his rich ledge of platinum remains undiscovered. But many are still convinced that a secret subterranean room in the bowels of Bat Cave holds the secret that Keown kept for sixteen years before falling victim to his discovery.

Cave of Jewels

Not many miles northwest of Keown's reputed platinum discovery lies Long Horn Mountain, on the western end of the sprawling Slick Hills, about two miles north and five miles east of Cooperton, in Kiowa County. On top of the limestone butte and near its center is a distinguishable dip. There lies another legendary treasure cave.

Barely large enough to climb into, the entrance drops about fifteen feet into a small room, which opens into a large chamber. In years past sections of the ceiling caved off, causing large blocks of limestone and calcite to seal the opening to still two other rooms in the cavern. Long Horn Cave is the largest cavern in the Wichita Mountains area.

By one account a prospector is credited with finding the cave. While he was poking around the summit of the butte, he came upon a curious-looking flat rock. When he pulled the stone aside, he found the opening to the cavern. It is said that outlaw money was once found there.

Still another story has it that one day a boy was hunting alongside a mountain resembling a haystack when he spotted a rabbit run under a flat rock. The boy ran to the rock, intending to bag his game, but when he raised the rock, he saw that the rabbit had fallen into a deep hole. When he observed closer, he could not believe his own eyes. The cavern floor gleamed with jewels and watches and gold and silver coins. The boy replaced the stone and ran home. On the way he was bitten by a rattlesnake. When he neared the house, he called for his father who ran out and took the boy in his arms. The youngster revealed what he had found, but it was too late to save him. Later a search was made for the mysterious cavern, but with no success.

Once in 1893 a Mexican visited this country hunting such a cave sealed by a flat rock. He told Jim Wilkerson that the cave held more gold than either of them would ever need in a lifetime, but all attempts to find it failed.

Lost Cave of Guns

There are three known caves in the limestone country five miles north and six west of Porter Hill, in Comanche County. One cave in the area holds the skeletons and firearms of several victims, so swears Lloyd Stone, of Meers.[19] Forty years ago, Stone told me, he and several boys found the cave. One youth was lowered into the narrow opening by a rope, but he remained just long enough to yell to be pulled up, and scrambled out so fast that he cut his head on the rock walls. He was trembling so much that no one could make sense of his story, Stone recalled.

Because the opening was too small for the older boys, a younger one was persuaded to go back into the cave. Six or eight feet down he lost his flashlight. When he was dropped another, one look was all he needed. A half-dozen or so skeletons lay on the floor, some with their skulls lying between their legs. Rifles were propped up against the walls. "We made several attempts to find that cave again," Stone said. "But the opening was just barely large enough for a small boy to slip into. I expect that over the years rocks and brush completely concealed the hole, hiding the skeletons and rifles and whatever else it contained."

Cave of Lost Saddles

On the far western spur of the Wichitas looms Tepee Mountain, conspicuously higher than any of the granite peaks around it. Ever since the region was opened to settlement the story has been told that somewhere on Tepee Mountain is a cave large enough to ride a horse into and that hidden inside is a cache of sixty saddles and a sizable sum in gold and silver. The story was revealed by an elderly woman who lived at Granite during its early years. She was known to have been a member of an outlaw gang that had preyed on cattlemen as they herded their cattle through Greer County on the Great Western Trail, which led north through Vernon, Texas, crossed Red River near Doan's Store and led through a pass in the Wichitas skirting Soldier Spring and Tepee mountains on its route to Dodge City. It was an important trail. More than three hundred thousand head of cattle crossed Red River in 1881 alone, and all told an estimated seven million cattle and four million horses traveled up the trail.[20]

In the 1890's, revealed the elderly woman, she and four men, all wanted by the law, had accumulated sixty saddles and a large amount of gold and silver, which had been concealed in a cave on Tepee Mountain. Because of narrow escapes with the law, the outlaws agreed to make a map to the cave, go their separate directions until a designated time, and then rendezvous at Tepee Mountain. Each of the four took an equal part of the map.

The plan might have worked, but three were later killed in gunfights, and the fourth remained in hiding in eastern Oklahoma. The woman revealed this story years later when she had become blind and was no longer able to look for the cave herself. Apparently it has never again been found.

Mystery of Jester's Cave

Nothing is lost about Jester's Cave in the gypsum hills of western Greer County, although it may hold or have held part of the James gang's loot. The tunnel-shaped cave travels underground as much as fifteen miles before emptying into a beautiful gypsum canyon about ten miles north of Reed, where even today ancient arrowheads and lead balls are picked up.

Jester's Cave could have been a paradise for outlaws on the run. Cool running springs flow out of the cave the year round, and in the heat of the summer no cooler place is to be found for miles around.

In the 1940's a treasure hunter camped at the cave for most of the winter and part of the spring in a laborious search for outlaw loot. At the right of the main entrance is seen a narrow tunnel, which winds through the gypsum to a small chamber. At this juncture the seeker hand-dug a tunnel barely large enough to crawl through for a distance of thirty feet or more to still another chamber, carting the rock out on a small narrow-gauge track. There his digging suddenly ceased. What the stranger found he kept to himself. But there were those who glimpsed several old rifles among his belongings. The narrow steel tracks reaching far into the tunnel can still be seen, just as the stranger suddenly left them.

Treasure of Cutthroat Gap

Cutthroat Gap, a valley leading into the Wichita Mountains from the northwest, was appropriately named for a tragic event that occurred there in the spring of 1833, the year the "stars fell," as noted by Kiowa Indians on their pictographic calendar. A spectacular meteoric shower turned the night as bright as day throughout North America. It was a notable event for the Plains tribes.

The treasure that was buried in Cutthroat Gap was also noted on the Kiowa calendar. The first part of the story occurred early in 1833, not in the Wichita Mountains but on the Canadian River in the Texas Panhandle.[21] A party of a dozen Missouri traders returning home that winter from Santa Fe with ten thousand dollars in silver specie packed on their mules were attacked by a Kiowa war party. The traders made a bulwark of their packs and dead animals and for thirty-six hours held off the Indians. Two of the traders were killed, another was wounded, and all the animals were killed or lamed. The men decided to carry what silver they could and bury the rest in the sand. During the night they made a dash for freedom and escaped the war party. After days of wandering in the wilderness, the traders split into two parties. Five of the men eventually reached friendly Creek settlements on the Arkansas, but only two of the second party survived.

The Kiowas, who had lost only one man, found a few scattered silver coins on the ground and gathered them to beat into ornamental disks. Some time later they met Comanches, who told them of the shiny metal's value. The Kiowas returned to the river, sifted through the sand where the traders had barricaded themselves, and uncovered the bags of silver.

That spring the Kiowas moved to the headwaters of Otter Creek, and one band camped in what was later to be named Cutthroat Gap in the Wichita Mountains. Early one morning when the Kiowa warriors were away, a band of Osages struck the camp. They beheaded their victims, and the grisly trophies were each placed in brass buckets and scattered over the battlefield. Hence the names Cutthroat Gap and Cut-Off-Head Mountain, the latter just east of the massacre site.

Among the dead was a Kiowa chief who had attacked the Missouri traders the winter before. He was buried along with his share of the silver coins somewhere near the gap, in the present

Cutthroat Gap, in far northwest Comanche County, was the scene of an Indian massacre in 1833 and a gunfight between miners and homesteaders in 1902.

extreme northwest corner of Comanche County. The silver dollars were never found, but as mining progressed in the Wichitas in 1901, prospectors kept picks and shovels handy while traveling through the gap, for coins would occasionally appear after a storm.

Camp Radziminski's Payroll

Otter Creek has an important place in the lore of the Wichitas. A tributary of the North Fork of Red River that once harbored the animals for which it is named, it branches several miles west of what is today Snyder, one stream heading north through granite peaks, the other northeast to Cutthroat Gap on the north side of the mountains. It served as the base of operations for the first punitive expedition sent into the region by the United States government.

In September, 1858, four companies of the celebrated Second Cavalry and one company of the Fifth Infantry commanded by Brevet-Major Earl Van Dorn, and a force of 135 Wichitas, Caddoes, and Tonkawas led by Lawrence "Sul" Ross were sent north of the Red River from Fort Belknap, Texas, to war on the Comanches who were raiding the Texas settlements.[22]

Three camps were established on Otter Creek, each named Camp Radziminski in honor of a former officer of the regiment, Lieutenant Charles

Radziminski. From their first camp on the east bank of Otter Creek near present Tipton, Oklahoma, Van Dorn led his troops on a thirty-six-hour ride to engage Chief Buffalo Hump's Comanches, encamped near the Wichita village not far from present Rush Springs. Van Dorn's cavalry and Indian allies killed seventy of Big Hump's warriors and scattered the remainder.

Two months later Van Dorn moved his troops upstream several miles, where they wintered, and in March, 1859, he chose a third camp farther upstream, on the west bank of Otter Creek. The camp was protected on the north and west by granite peaks, about two miles north and two miles west of present-day Mountain Park, in southwestern Kiowa County. Mule and wagon trains from Fort Belknap kept the soldiers supplied. A well was dug, but facilities were few. The officers lived in small picket, mud-chinked huts with stone chimneys, and the enlisted men camped in the new conical Sibley tents.

In late April, Van Dorn led his troops four hundred miles northward into southern Kansas and again defeated the Comanches near present Dodge City. The cavalrymen returned to Camp Radziminski at the end of May. Five soldiers who died at the camp were buried a half-mile away (the bodies were moved to the National Cemetery at Fort Gibson in 1933).

197

Tradition has long held that outlaws cached forty thousand dollars in the granite rocks somewhere about old Camp Radziminski, where only scattered foundation ruins now remain.

On December 6, 1859, after ten months of occupation, Camp Radziminski was abandoned when the Second Cavalry was recalled to duty in Texas. Shortly afterward a regiment of Texas Rangers occupied the post while patrolling the region against the Kiowas and Comanches.

Camp Radziminski also has its tale of buried treasure. The tale has drawn hunters armed with evidence that a government payroll of forty thousand dollars was shipped by wagon to the camp to pay the soldiers for several months' back salary. Some distance from the camp a band of raiders seized the gold. Van Dorn's marksmen lost little time in overtaking the robbers and shot them all. But when their bodies were examined, no gold was found. Local tradition says that somewhere about the environs of Otter Creek near the old military camp the payroll is still hidden.

As late as 1927 the blackened chimney of the cook oven was still visible, but today only a few scattered foundation ruins remain of the camp. Many glass-blown wine bottles have been found at the site, along with hammer-made chisels, brass ornaments, army buttons, poker chips, square-headed nails, an 1854 Canadian dime, and an 1852 United States gold dollar. Residents are sure the gold will be found one day.

Bob Herring's Lost Loot

No one knew about the thirty-one thousand dollars that Bob Herring cached on rugged Flat Top Mountain one day in 1894. He kept the secret for more than thirty-five years before telling his cousin, Josh M. Drake, and Drake's son, who ranched in the shadow of the Wichita Mountains.[23]

Inside the prison walls of Huntsville the aging outlaw handed Josh Drake a sketch to the buried gold, carefully watching that he was not being observed. "Josh, I've got T.B., and I'm dying," he whispered. "You're the only kin of mine that has come to see me since I came here. I've got five more years to serve, and I can't make it. I'm going to tell you where you can find my gold."

Born in Eastland County, Texas, in 1870, Bob Herring stole his first horse when he was fifteen and fled to Indian Territory. Some years later he joined Joe Baker and two other fugitives from justice known only as Buck and Six Toes. One day in 1894 the four robbed a group of cattlemen near Vernon, Texas, taking more than thirty-five thousand dollars in gold. Their tracks ran north. A newcomer to the gang, Herring did the camp chores. One afternoon Baker sent him off to shoot some game for supper. Herring had an inkling that the men might be plotting to cheat him of his share of the gold. He slipped back to camp undetected. His suspicion turned out to be right when he overheard his three partners plotting to do away with him. Baker said that he wanted to shoot Herring as soon as he returned, but Buck and Six Toes were in favor of killing him after he had gone to sleep that night. Herring had heard all he needed to know. He slipped back into the brush and shot a couple of rabbits. When he rode back into camp, he tossed the rabbits beside the campfire and began rubbing down his horse.

It was a warm evening, and the three had stripped to their waists, but Baker still had a .45 tucked in his belt. Herring walked between the men and their guns and then whipped out his own pistol. Holding it on the three men, he told them to lie on their stomachs with their arms outstretched. Then he removed the .45 from Baker's belt. He took their firearms, loaded the gold, tied their horses behind his own, and raced northward.

He rode all night, stopping the next morning to choose the best two mounts and turn the others loose. With the gold on one mount he traveled the rest of the day and that night bedded down in the Wichitas. While there he chose a bank under a handy rock somewhere on Flat Top Mountain to

198

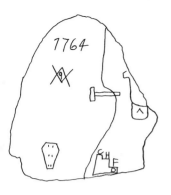

Neither cryptic drawings nor legends of Spanish and French gold are in short supply in Oklahoma. But if this sketch of a stone carving found near Erick is ever deciphered, it may reveal that Englishmen, too, were in western Oklahoma in 1764. On the opposite side of the stone is: "In captive by Indians. J. VanCloor, London, Eng."

hide his gold, keeping out four thousand dollars.

He traveled north to Kansas, then into Montana, and later back to Texas. In the meantime the Baker gang split up, but Herring knew that the three men were looking for him—and for the gold he had taken from them. Baker was killed tracking Herring in Montana while trying to steal a horse. Texas Rangers caught up with Six Toes a year later and sentenced him to the Texas State Prison at Huntsville for shooting a man in Austin. He died in 1899 trying to escape.

Herring heard nothing of Buck for several years. Authorities had a good description of him but had no identification of Herring, who was living in Dallas, where no one suspected him. By coincidence, Herring met Buck one day in a Dallas gambling house. Herring promptly hurried back to his hotel room for a gun, knowing well that Buck would follow. As Buck walked into the dimly lighted hallway, Herring opened fire. Buck was killed instantly, as were two bystanders. In 1900 Herring went to Huntsville for thirty-five years.

In that same year young Josh Drake went to Oklahoma Territory with his father, who filed on a quarter section of land. Josh had never seen his notorious cousin, though his adventures had become a family legend. In 1920 he bought a ranch in Greer County, and every year he made a trip into Texas to buy cattle. Once when he was near Huntsville, he decided to visit his notorious cousin. Every year after that when he went south for cattle he visited Herring. On his last trip he took Josh, Jr., and it was at that time that the old outlaw related the foregoing story of the stolen gold.

"The prison doors had kept cousin Bob away from his treasure for thirty years," Josh, Jr., told me in his Mangum home. "He wasn't the fierce-looking man that I knew from old family photos. He was old, bent, and sick. He shook my father's hand and cried as we were introduced. They had

brought him from the infirmary to the visiting room."

Five months after their visit, Josh said, word was received from prison officials that the old outlaw had died. He was buried in the prison cemetery as he had requested. Some time later the Drakes brought out the sketch their cousin had given them inside the prison. They had no trouble locating the mountain on which the treasure was buried as the rough waybill directed.

"But we could never locate the rock that resembled the one cousin Bob had sketched and said his gold was buried under," Josh admitted.[24] "We dug for a week, I guess, and never found the money. I still go out to Flat Top Mountain in Kiowa County looking for that one rock, but to date I haven't found it. Maybe I will someday. It must be there, somewhere."

A Cryptic Message

J. C. Stratton and his brother were building a new fence in the hills of western Oklahoma one day in 1905 when they found a small stone bearing a strange message.[25] They were working along a smooth slope about ten miles south of Erick, northwest of Buehge Springs, when they discovered the stone, which was about five inches wide and one-half inch thick and was facing southeast toward Haystack Mountain. On one side appeared the cryptic carvings of a trail; the date 1764; the letters C, H, F, and D, each placed on a stairstep; drawings resembling a hammer, a coffin, and a saddlebag; and two X's drawn together with a 9 between them. On the opposite side was carved: "In captive by Indians. J. VanCloor, London, Eng."

Stratton, now of El Paso, Texas, recalled that about a year later contractors excavating for a paved highway unearthed the skeletons of two white men three miles west of Erick. Whether there was any connection between the two discoveries was never determined. The Strattons carried on a long search to trace the name J. VanCloor, with no results.[26]

The meaning of the strange message is anyone's guess. Was J. VanCloor an early English trader who ventured too far into hostile Indian country and carved this last-minute message, hoping that someone would decipher its meaning? What the figures meant may never be known.

199

A group of three old time stage coaches, that did noble service in the sixties, and seventies. Photo made by Enright, Perry, Oklahoma.

Stagecoaches played an important role in Oklahoma's history—and contributed heavily to its treasure lore. These three styles of coaches were prominent in the 1860's and 1870's. Courtesy Western History Collections, University of Oklahoma Library.

9. Gold the Stagecoaches Never Delivered

It was a cold December day in 1936 when Master Sergeant Morris Swett heard tapping on his office window. As historian and librarian of the Fort Sill Field Artillery School, Swett was used to friends stopping by for some fact of information. He looked up to see a stranger, gray-haired, bent, and obviously used to living outdoors. Speaking softly, he asked Swett to close his door. He had something to say that he did not want others to overhear. Swett complied.

The oldster identified himself as G. W. Cottrell and said that he worked a farm just outside Levelland, Texas.[1] He was seventy-two years old and had fallen heir to a story that he needed help with, and he had no one else to turn to. He had not been to Fort Sill for years, he said, but remembered well the days back in the 1880's and 1890's when he herded cattle through the Kiowa-Comanche country to link up with the Chisholm Trail on the east.

He had stopped often at the old Post Trader's Store to buy supplies and at the well nearby to water his horses. It was at that same well that Cottrell now wanted to dig for one hundred thousand dollars in gold and silver. "Six saddlebags of it," he nodded. "Four of gold and two of silver."

It had been buried in 1892, the old cattleman told Swett. Three men held up a stage north of Red River carrying the money in gold and silver specie. Things did not go according to plan, and two of the bandits were shot and killed. The third, named Allen, retrieved the six bags but before he managed to escape with his heavy load, he was severely wounded.

Allen's route of escape probably would have been different if he had not been wounded. As it was, all the gold and silver in the world could not save his life if he did not soon receive medical attention. The nearest outpost was Fort Sill. Allen headed his mount and treasure-laden pack animals in that direction.

He rode in late one night and tied his horses to the hitching post at the well near the Post Trader's Store. Allen knew there was always a lot of traffic around the well. What better place could he hide his treasure than at such an obvious landmark? He walked a few feet from the well and in the dark dug a hole barely deep enough to conceal the six saddlebags. Then he led his animals back and forth over the fresh earth, trampling it so that it appeared no different from the sod around it.

Weak with loss of blood, Allen sought aid from the post doctor, still hoping he would go undetected. He had no such luck. Weeks later, when he was able to ride, he was sent to the Huntsville prison, steadfastly refusing to reveal where he had buried the stagecoach treasure.

The federal government showed no mercy with Allen. He remained behind Huntsville prison walls for thirty-three long years. When the gates opened for him one day in 1925, he was no longer the reckless outlaw of 1892. Five feet ten inches tall, slender, and pale, he weighed only about 140 pounds. He settled on a farm outside Levelland, close to G. W. Cottrell.

Allen thought often of the treasure he had hidden near the well when Fort Sill was only a frontier outpost. He paid a visit to the fort to find the well and its hidden gold only to find that his luck had not changed over the years. He had barely gotten near the well—or what remained of it—when, as he later scorned, "I was driven off by the damn pickets." Allen returned to his farm, still hopeful that he might retrieve the hidden money—one hundred thousand dollars as he remembered, although he admitted it might have been less.

Over the years Cottrell, his closest neighbor, became his closest friend. Allen confided his secret to Cottrell, asking him to find the money, knowing that he would never have a chance at it and that at his age it would do him no good anyway.

Allen died before Cottrell was able to take time from his farming responsibilities. Cottrell's luck was little better than the old outlaw's. He was told that he would first have to have permission to make a search. He had now come to Sergeant Swett, hoping to receive that help.

The Post Trader's Store at Fort Sill about 1878. The well, a short distance southwest (left of photograph), was used as a marker by an outlaw named Allen to stash six saddlebags of gold and silver. Courtesy Fort Sill Museum.

The old stone corral at Fort Sill was built by United States soldiers in 1870. Here it appears in 1925 before restoration. Courtesy Fort Sill Museum.

This aerial view shows the stone corral at Fort Sill as it appeared in 1928. The Wichita Mountains can be seen in the background. Courtesy Fort Sill Museum.

The Post Trader's Store at Fort Sill in 1897. Courtesy Fort Sill Museum.

Cottrell asked Swett to see the post commandant and put the matter through the necessary channels. Naturally Cottrell wondered whether he could legally claim the treasure or any part of it. Cottrell believed that there was no construction on the site and that it should require only about an hour to locate, if Allen's memory was correct. Swett was interested in Cottrell's story and said that he would do what he could. Cottrell returned to Levelland to await the necessary permission.

A few weeks later Cottrell was granted his wish. On January 27, 1937, he returned to the post with the papers giving him permission to dig. As a military escort watched, Cottrell found the well not far southwest of the old trading post (long since removed from the intersection of McBride and Cureton avenues a few blocks north of the historic stone guardhouse and museum). He dug a four-foot hole ten feet south of the well, which years before had been bulldozed in. The only visible trace of it was some limestone rock protruding in the gravel floor of post garage 631. One corner of the building sat almost over the center of the well. Apparently Cottrell was unsure in which direction the gold had been buried from the well, for he dug similar holes six feet north of the well. None showed any sign of the buckskin bags.

Cottrell may not have been aware that four to six feet of dirt had been hauled into the area to build up the hillside at the same time the well was filled in. In any case, he swore he would make another try. He left Fort Sill, saying that he would

return in six weeks with the equipment needed to find the treasure. His search, however, was not resumed for more than three years. Sickness and family obligations forced him to postpone his search, as he revealed in a series of letters to Sergeant Swett during those years.

In 1940, Cottrell, who was still ailing, decided to send a substitute to carry on his search. He penned Swett this letter on September 23:

Dear Sir: Am writing you concerning the well proposition there and am recommending Mr. Van Webb to you. I have lost my health and am unable to travel. He will finish my job there. I will appreciate anything you can do in regard to this. He has proper instruments to work with.

When Van Webb arrived at Fort Sill, however, he was told that he would not be allowed to dig because he had no identification. The post commandant insisted that only Cottrell had permission to dig, subject now to some added provisions: the digging would have to be performed under the supervision of the post provost marshal; any treasure found would be turned over to the commandant for safekeeping until the War Department and the Department of Justice released it to Cottrell, after holding the money one year to allow bona fide claimants the opportunity to prove ownership.

Finally, in October, 1940, Cottrell, who had recovered, returned to Fort Sill with his wife, Webb, and a diviner, Mrs. Edna Crowder, to make a final try for the stolen money, hidden almost half a

Morris Swett points to the site of the well of the old Post Trader's Store at Fort Sill.

century before. The search "equipment" they brought with them proved rather unusual. Shown where the treasure was believed buried, Webb used a divining rod, and Mrs. Crowder consulted an earth mirror and a crystal ball.

After a few moments of effort both seemed satisfied that the stagecoach treasure was no longer there. Webb demonstrated the accuracy of his rod by placing a gold watch on the ground and then a silver coin below it, which attracted the rod downward. Mrs. Crowder claimed that her mirror and crystal ball could penetrate the earth and that she would "see" the treasure. She claimed that the mirror and crystal ball had been mined, ground, and polished in India and that both she and Webb had but recently unearthed some Spanish gold on the Washita River between Tishomingo and Madill,

Oklahoma, by applying their unconventional methods.

Cottrell left Fort Sill, never to return to the historic grounds in which Allen said that he had buried his treasure. Once Cottrell had told Morris Swett that, because of his cooperation, "if I find that treasure, you and I are going to be rich." He would have kept his promise had he been successful, Swett was sure.

No one sought the outlaw treasure after Cottrell, until April, 1964, when the United States Army decided to try to find it. For some time others had asked for the opportunity but had always received steadfast no's. The *Lawton Constitution* and the *Daily Oklahoman* quickly seized up the story, the latter reporting "Army to Dig for Treasure If Any's Done."[2] Colonel Stanley J. Cherubin, staff judge advocate, had dug out a 1961 regulation that forbids private searching for buried treasure on military posts.

On April 1, Fort Sill officials decided to make the search. The headline in the *Constitution* told the story: "Army Starts Digging for Sill's Treasure."[3] Of course, no one could deny that Uncle Sam needed some treasure. At 8:30 in the morning army engineers began digging with a large earth auger. By noon they had dug fifteen holes ten feet deep just south of garage 631 under the clothesline of Mrs. Alfred N. Champion, of 630 Lower South Lauman.

On April 2 the headlines announced their findings: "Sorry, Folks, There Isn't Any Treasure."[4] The story urged treasure hunters to stop writing for permission to dig. There was no treasure, because the auger had not hit any.

The tales told about the old Post Trader's Store in the heart of the United States Army Field Artillery Center are many. The tale of the six saddlebags of gold and silver will not soon die.

Forgotten Stage Trails

A stage clattering around a twist in the road or on an uphill grade was easy prey for masked highwaymen hiding in waiting. No stagecoach making its scheduled run over the wind-swept Plains was safe from ruffians. Many stage trails crossed the Indian Territory. The coaches that traveled them played an important role in Oklahoma's history and contributed heavily to its treasure lore.

204

The Southern Stage Company established a route between Caldwell, Kansas, and Fort Sill in 1874. This photograph, taken in 1887, shows the Concord stage ready to leave Fort Reno on its 120-mile journey to Caldwell. Courtesy Western History Collections, University of Oklahoma Library.

In the fall of 1868, R. S. Dorchester helped establish the first stage route into Fort Sill, whose site in the Kiowa-Comanche country would be chosen the following January. Employed by the El Paso Stage Company, Dorchester distributed the necessary stock for stage stations every twenty-five to thirty miles between Boggy Depot, on the Clear Boggy River in the Choctaw Nation in present Atoka County, and Fort Sill, about 150 miles west.[5]

Stage stands were set up at Negro Squire Wolf's home (later called Cheadle Crossing) on the Blue River; Mill Creek; Fort Arbuckle, which had been abandoned to the Confederates during the Civil War and was reoccupied by federal troops in 1865; Wild Horse Creek; and upper Cow Creek near present Duncan, the last stand before Fort Sill, thirty miles west.

As the Missouri, Kansas & Texas Railroad stretched across eastern Oklahoma in 1871, the freighting of supplies and mail to Fort Sill was transferred from Boggy Depot to Caddo, several miles southeast. The new Caddo–Fort Sill road ran by way of Nail's Crossing on the Blue River, Post Oak (Emet), Tishomingo, Mill Creek, Sulphur Springs (Sulphur), Cherokee Town, Pauls Valley, White Bead Hill, Beef Creek (Maysville), Erin Springs, Rush Springs, and then thirty miles southwest to Fort Sill. The fare for the almost two-hundred-mile journey was twenty dollars, and

baggage was limited to one hundred pounds for each passenger. The eight-passenger stage made the dusty journey in four days, while the freight wagons took twice that time.

Another early stage line into Fort Sill was opened in 1874 by the Southern Stage Company, and operated between that military post and Caldwell, Kansas, some two hundred miles northeast.[6] When the Fort Worth & Denver Railroad reached Henrietta, Texas—about seventy-five miles south of Fort Sill—in 1885, the Caddo–Fort Sill line was abandoned, and the stage and freight route was opened to Fort Sill from the Texas railhead.

Early in 1892 the Chicago, Rock Island & Pacific Railroad extended its line through Rush Springs, and shortly afterward the freight and passenger line was reopened from that settlement to Fort Sill and remained in operation until the road was abandoned forever in September, 1901, when the Rock Island blew its whistle through the new tent city of Lawton.

The most noted stage route through the Indian Nations was the Butterfield Overland Mail, which ran from St. Louis, Missouri, through Indian Territory, and across Texas, New Mexico, and Arizona to San Francisco, California—a distance of twenty-eight hundred miles. About two hundred stage stations were established over the route, most of them about twenty miles apart. It operated until

205

the Civil War. The route went through the most dangerous land in the Southwest, threatened by hostile Indians and outlaws alike.

The fare from St. Louis to San Francisco was $150 or to points in between at ten cents a mile. Each passenger was allowed forty pounds of baggage, and both passengers and luggage were shifted into a fresh coach about every three hundred miles.

"Remember, boys," John Butterfield instructed his drivers, "nothing on God's earth must stop the U.S. Mail!"[7] The first coach left St. Louis on September 16, 1858, and arrived in San Francisco at 7:30 A.M. on October 10, twenty-three days and twenty-three hours later—one day and one hour less than contract time. In Oklahoma the stage made twelve stops between Skullyville (or Poteau, depending on high water) and Colbert's Ferry, on Red River, southwest of Durant.

Many other stage lines crisscrossed Indian Territory. One led from Tahlequah to Fort Gibson and Muskogee. This stage was seldom safe from lurking highwaymen. One robbery occurred in June, 1894, another just two months later, and a third in July, 1896.[8]

In May, 1894, the stage between Hennessey and Watonga was rifled of its contents. In August, 1896, the Doolin gang robbed a stage between Okeene and Lacey. During the same month the Grey Horse Stage was held up in Osage County. A month later four bandits swooped down on the stage near Cheyenne. Three rode away with eight hundred dollars; one remained behind, dead.[9]

In the 1890's other stage routes were opened between Perry and Pawnee, Cleveland and Tulsa, and Mangum and Oakdale.[10] In June, 1894, a line was established from Edmond to Arcadia, Ingram, Chandler, and the Sac and Fox Agency south of Stroud. As late as March, 1901, another line was opened from Kiowa, Kansas, to Burlington, Driftwood, Cherokee, Yewed, Augusta, and Cleo, Oklahoma.[11] Desperados had no trouble choosing coaches to prey upon, and tales of their ill-gotten loot remain a colorful part of Oklahoma's frontier lore.

Panther Creek's Lost Well

One story has it that once somewhere on Panther Creek in the Wichita Mountains a lone bandit on horseback stopped just long enough at an abandoned well to drop a heavy chest into it while dodging a posse. No one has ever found the well, but one who looked for a chest of gold there was Ray B. Dean of Horton, Missouri.

In October, 1947, he won permission to dig for two large express boxes taken from a stagecoach and hidden in the Wichitas—he believed in the Wildlife Refuge.[12] Dean was told by the government that he could keep anything he might find. Apparently he found nothing. Today 60 per cent of any treasure trove uncovered in the Wildlife Refuge goes to Uncle Sam.

Fort Sill's Lost Payroll

One of the oldest tales told about the Wichitas concerns the stage and freight route established in 1885 between Henrietta, Texas, and Fort Sill. The stage made periodic trips to the fort, carrying soldiers, dignitaries and their wives, Indian agents, mail, and, occasionally, the government payroll. In good weather the trip took one day.[13]

Soon after the route opened, the stage company is said to have contracted to transport ninety-six thousand dollars in gold specie to be paid to the soldiers. On this occasion no soldiers were dispatched to trail the stage, believing that they would only arouse suspicion. As the stage rumbled out of the Henrietta station at daybreak, everything appeared safe enough to the driver and the armed guard, both of whom were new to the route.

Everything went well until they neared Red River, where they were to get a fresh set of teams at the Charley Crossing relay station. Several miles outside that stage depot, seven masked outlaws rode out from behind their cover and surrounded the coach, ordering the guard to throw down the bags of gold. Once he had done so, the driver was motioned to move on.

When the coach was well on its way, the outlaws headed for the Wichita Mountains, where any number of places could be found to lie low. The stage raced on to Charley Crossing, and from there a rider was dispatched back to Henrietta to telegraph Fort Sill about the robbery. Once the message was received, a patrol of soldiers began searching the hills, having been told that the outlaws were last seen heading in that direction. The troops traced the main trails into the mountains, hoping to find fresh tracks of the seven horses. They found the tracks, and all led to Cutthroat Gap. To the surprise of the soldiers and the outlaws, the two groups met in the gap. Outbursts of gunfire echoed off the canyon walls as the troops snubbed the reins of their mounts and scurried for cover. The battle raged on for what seemed like hours. As the troopers closed in, the outnumbered fugitives knew that they were doomed unless they made a break. But before that objective was realized, five had been killed and another badly wounded. Only one remained unhurt.

When the two outlaws saw their chance to break out, they tied the bags of gold onto two animals and spurred their mounts to a fast trot, staying behind the cover of huge boulders. When no one returned their fire, the soldiers stopped shooting. The soldiers buried the dead outlaws in unmarked graves.

For the moment the two outlaws had escaped their hunters. They rode west to a creek crossing, believed to be about four miles south of present Cold Springs on the Lower Narrows of Otter Creek. The injured bandit had suffered a severe loss of blood. He dismounted from his horse and lay down on a blanket to rest, while his partner carried the sacks of gold to the creek. On the west side he buried the money, knowing that they would have to travel light and fast. He was confident that the soldiers would not be far behind.

Afterwards he checked his partner. The gold would do him no good now. The lone survivor of the seven gave his partner a decent burial—mountain style—by piling stones on top of the body. Finally he unsaddled his horses and turned them loose. He hoped that the soldiers would

follow their tracks, believing the ruse was his only chance to escape to Texas. He followed the creek downstream, where he could seek cover if he suddenly needed it.

The soldiers found the grave of the sixth dead man, and they followed the horses' tracks, eventually catching up with them. But the horses carried neither the rider nor the gold.

As the years passed, the payroll robbery became a legend. Everyone had his own version of what had happened to the gold. In 1925 four strangers from Texas appeared in the little community of Cold Springs, asking about an old creek crossing. Perhaps one man might know of such a crossing, they were told.

The four went to Arthur Henderson, who owned the town's only grocery store.[14] They told him the story of the robbery and said that they had a map to the buried payroll but needed the location of a certain creek crossing to find it. Henderson knew of only one ford that resembled the one they were seeking. It lay about four miles south on the Lower Narrows.

The strangers left, saying that they would not forget Henderson's help if they were successful. Even though Henderson never heard from them again, he later saw the holes that someone had dug on Otter Creek. Whether one of them had held the buried sacks of gold no one knew.

The old road across Otter Creek had been known as the Navajoe Trail, Henderson told me. It was used while traffic flourished between Fort Sill and Fort Elliott in the Texas Panhandle. Henderson should know; he wrote a lengthy manuscript about local history that was destroyed in a tornado that scattered it to the four winds. He believes that Fort Sill's lost payroll still lies not far from the old crossing on Otter Creek, near the grave of a nameless outlaw who gave his life for it.

The Wichita Mountains were forbidden land to the gold seeker's pick and shovel until 1901. The bones of those who defied the Indian treaties were often found concealed in some remote canyon or cave in the rugged mountains.

10. Lost Cave with the Iron Door

Deep in the ruggedest part of the boulder-jumbled Wichitas men have sought a fabulous lost mine and its treasure for the better part of three-quarters of a century. Second in popularity only to the two-million-dollar Jesse James treasure, the legendary Lost Cave with the Iron Door has drawn treasure seekers from both far and near.

The cave is reputed to hold eleven million dollars in Spanish gold. The treasure consists of gold ingots stacked like cordwood and baskets filled with gold doubloons—all guarded by a heavy door of iron, a massive chain, and a huge lock—not to mention the skeletons of seventeen Indians who watch over the golden treasure. The rust-eaten iron door was closed more than two hundred years ago, and no one has opened it since—except perhaps one party who glimpsed its contents for a brief moment.

That is only one version of this strange story, for some say that it contains two hundred thousand dollars of the Jesse James loot, while others believe that the cave holds five hundred thousand dollars of Belle Starr's booty. And then there is the story of a seventy-year-old woman named Holt who came to the Wichitas from Missouri in 1908. She brought with her a large iron key and a map to the cave and claimed that a dying outlaw had revealed to her its whereabouts.

Still another tradition says that the Cave with the Iron Door was not only a storage vault for gold but also a prison for Indian slaves working Spanish mines in these mountains during the eighteenth century. When Indians drove the Spaniards from the hills, they closed their mines, and pounded an iron spike into an oak tree nearby to mark their return route if that day came.

To support this story, there are those who will point out that some years ago such an iron spike was found deeply embedded in an ancient oak that had been cut down near Treasure Lake in the Wichita Mountains Wildlife Refuge, the very area in which the Iron Door has most often been seen, for on more than one occasion it has been found. Even though conflicting stories are told about the mysterious cave, they only stir the enthusiasm to find it.

One treasure hunter who believes the legend of Spanish gold—and that it will be found in an underground, concretelike vault is Dave Hungerford, of Faxon, southwest of Lawton.[1] One summer afternoon Hungerford told me about a Mexican who had inherited a curious map showing more than one hidden Spanish cache in the Wichitas, deposited for safekeeping during the days of the Spaniards' mining operations. The map, made of fine silk, was about five feet long and two feet wide. Each of the treasure sites appeared in its own beautiful design and color. The Mexican always wore the prized cloth around his waist, inside his clothes, knowing no one would ever take his guarded possession unless that person killed him first.

The Mexican had once tried to find the huge underground gold storage. He failed, although he claimed to have found some of the smaller caches. Finally one day he permitted a friend to copy the silk map on paper but warned him that he would only be wasting his time to look for the hidden vault, for all attempts to find it had failed.

The names of those involved in this story have long been lost. But that an expedition was led into the Wichita Mountains some time in the 1850's is a story believed as fact by Hungerford, for he heard the story from one who had seen the copied map and knew its history. Despite the Mexican's warning the seekers actually found the cave. After much difficulty they found the ground under which the ancient vault was mapped to lie, hidden several feet below the surface. The leader instructed his men to dig. Several feet into the earth one workman struck the side of a rock wall. Frantically he swung his pick against the stone barrier, eventually working a small passage into the dark, musty tomb.

He lit a torch. What he witnessed was unreal—treasure beyond his wildest dreams. More of the men climbed down into the dark pit to cast their eyes on the unbelievable discovery. Gold bars were stacked against the walls like cordwood. Baskets on the floor overflowed with gold coins glittering in the light of the torch. In one corner of the dark room sprawled human skeletons. The intruders were not given time enough to count the grisly creatures.

Before they had had a chance to examine their new-found wealth, a sentinel on top yelled "Indians, Indians!" The cloud of dust rising from their tracks revealed that they were many in number. In terror the men clambered out of the hole, jumped on their horses, and galloped for shelter.

Most of the day passed before the fortune hunters crept back to the treasure hole, only to find to their dismay that it had been entirely filled in. So the Indians knew about it, too. They could not risk the excavation again. The next time they might not be so lucky. The bones they had seen in the treasure vault were sufficient. After marking the place well, the adventurers rode south. Added troubles and the Civil War prevented a further attempt to retrieve the treasure, but their story lives on vividly in the mind of Dave Hungerford, who has spent many a day seeking the lost treasure vault.

Others have happened upon the ancient iron door when least expecting to. Some time in the early 1900's an old man and his son were riding their horses from the Wildlife Refuge headquarters to Indiahoma, a small settlement south of the mountains.[2] It was already late in the afternoon, and in order to reach the home of friends before dark, they took a short cut through the hills near Elk Mountain instead of riding the long road around.

While traveling through a remote canyon, a rust-worn door set into the face of a cliff caught their attention. Perhaps it was the right time of day, the right reflection, that attracted their eyes to the metal door. Or perhaps it was only a mirage. But it was strange. Because they wanted to reach their destination before nightfall, they rode on. But for the rest of their journey they discussed the discovery found so far from the nearest road.

When they arrived at the home of their friends, the father told about seeing the mysterious door and asked if anything was known about it. Their host reacted excitedly. Yes, he said, he had heard

of such a cave that had been sought for many years. As their lanterns burned long into the night, they made plans to return to the cave the next day.

The search party got underway early the next morning. The old man and his son were positive that they would have no trouble retracing their tracks to the canyon where they had seen the door. But once they were in the maze of canyons, carpeted with scrub oak and cedar, father and son disagreed on the route they had taken. One canyon now looked like another.

After talking it over, the men rode up a familiar trail and then another. Nothing was found. They returned to a junction and took still another trail through the mountains. Again the route proved unfruitful. Unable to find the lost canyon, the party spread out, spending the remainder of the day combing the rugged mountain terrain.

That night the father and son returned home, still trying to recall through which of the maze of canyons they had ridden. The following morning they started their search anew from the refuge headquarters. But again the trail revealed nothing. It was almost as if the canyon had been swallowed up, taking the legendary door with it. Afterward the old man and his son camped in the mountains, spending weeks at a time combing the mountain wilderness. But always their painstaking attempts were futile. They never forgot what their eyes had seen. Whatever it was, they were sure that it was no mirage.

The father and son were not the last to stumble onto the disappearing portal. About 1910 a boy named Prince happened to be at the right place at the right time. Accompanying him were a girl and another couple who all plainly saw the door and its large, rusted padlock. Prince knew nothing about the cave then, but the picture of that massive metal door remained vividly in his mind. Years afterward he heard stories about the cave and hunted it many times with his brother, who today lives in Indiahoma. They, too, failed to refind it, and Prince believed that only a landslide could have concealed it. He recalled that he had come upon the iron door while walking in a canyon somewhere north of Treasure Lake—the same area in which the old man and his son had glimpsed the strange door.

The grand old prospector of the Wichitas remembered still other seekers of the hidden cave. Silas Lee Ison hunted the door for more than seventy years, and was sure that someone would someday find it.[3]

"I've worn out a good many pairs of shoes lookin' for that darn door!" said Silas emphatically, as I sat in his rustic cobblestone cabin at the foot of rugged granite peaks. "About 1908," he went on, dumping the ashes from his pipe, "a woman named Holt showed up at our camp. She was seventy years old I guess, and told us she had come from Missouri."

The woman, who had brought with her a crude map, asked for help in finding certain landmarks in the mountains, Silas said. Later she admitted that she was seeking the iron door. For almost a month, while a guest at the Ison home, she combed the country for clues, assisted by Silas' father, who had met Jesse and Frank James there in 1867. Mrs. Holt had also brought a large iron key with her, which, for reasons known only to herself, she was sure would fit the huge lock to the iron door. But even her map led her no closer to the treasure. All attempts at finding the mysterious door ended as always before.

When Mrs. Holt finally left the country, she took the map and the strange-looking key with her. What she knew she managed to keep a secret, divulging nothing more than was absolutely necessary.

With a twinkle in his eye (and a yen to take another look himself) Silas recalled another occasion on which he believed the lost door was found. About thirty years ago—perhaps more—some men were hunting raccoons one evening on the western side of the mountains. When their dogs treed one of the animals, a hunter was attracted to something in the distance that seemed to reflect the sun sinking behind the mountains. He climbed around a huge boulder to have a better look.

The eye-catching object turned out to be a massive hunk of iron set into the face of a cliff. It was dusk, and the hunters had no time to investigate. When they returned at their earliest opportunity some days later in hopes of discovering the cave's wealth, they could not find the door.

Another version of this tale claims that the notorious outlaw Belle Starr and her associates waylaid a train from which they took half a million dollars in United States government gold and silver.[4] The gang had already picked a cavern for the loot but needed a cover for the hideout. The door of the baggage car seemed fitting. Both the money and the steel-bound door were hauled to the cavern in the Wichitas, where Belle had been storing supplies and accumulated spoils.

The door was set in place so that it could be swung open and closed and locked. Brush, trees, and stones were placed so that the door was impossible to detect unless one was directly in front of it. Some time later the members of Belle's gang were killed. On February 2, 1889, the bandit queen was murdered in eastern Oklahoma by a killer whose identity has never been established for certain.

Others have found the lost door. A man named Stephens reported that he found it while hiking in the mountains. He tried to break it down and then climbed to the top of the mountain on which the door was fixed and there piled stones to serve as a marker. When he returned to the mountains with his brothers, he failed to find the mountain or his cairn.

In the late 1920's three boys were traveling on foot from Cooperton, northwest of the Wichitas, to Indiahoma. One of those boys was John French, of Lawton.[5] When nightfall was near, the boys cut across country to save time. French told me that before they entered Cutthroat Gap they found an old rock pen that looked as though it had not been occupied for years. From it they traveled south and soon afterward found an oak tree from which hung an old rifle, which they cut down and took with them.

When they neared Mount Pinchot, their path took them past a rusty door that appeared to have been mounted over a cave or mine. The iron-bound door was fastened with hinges and a large padlock and was so thoroughly secured that they made no attempt to open it.

An old Indian later told French that behind the iron door was a great treasure and that the spirits of dead ones inside guarded it. The aged warrior believed that he knew the location of the cave but

The Lost Cave with the Iron Door still beckons seekers bent on finding its legendary riches, somewhere in the rugged Charons Gardens wilderness in the Wichita Mountains.

said that tribal laws forbade him to show it to any white man. The Indian died keeping his tribal secret.

John French has never forgotten the strange door he chanced upon fifty years ago, but all his searches for it ended as before. Nearly all who have found the door have placed it in the mountainous terrain north of Treasure Lake, near Elk Mountain. French and his party, however, believed that they found it several miles farther north, near Mount Pinchot.

One summer during the depression of the 1930's a farm worker decided to hike to Lawton from his home in Hobart. After traveling all day, he set up camp at dusk. The next day his route took him through the mountains past Elk Mountain. As he walked, he saw the rust-stained door, barely exposed on the face of the mountainside.

He had heard the iron-door legend, and he was determined not to leave without a look inside. For most of the day he tried to open the door, banging and prying at it with rocks and tree limbs. But it had been sealed far too long. The corroded metal would take modern tools to pry it from its hinges. He walked on to Indiahoma to solicit help in opening the cave.

In town two men furnished picks, hammers, and dynamite. The trio hurried back to the hills and hiked to Elk Mountain, determined to find the riches or prove the legend a hoax once and for all.

The worker and his partners climbed Elk Mountain. They spent much of the day scanning the nearby peaks from the top of the mountain, but nowhere was the door to be seen. The laborer had been positive that he could walk directly to it again. For days the men combed the boulder-strewn hills—some of the most rugged parts of the Wichitas—but, like all the others who had discovered the door, they were unable to find it again.

As late as June, 1967, I received a telephone call from an Oklahoma City resident who claimed to have glimpsed the iron door while riding horseback not far north of Treasure Lake. When he returned on foot, no door was to be seen.

How long will the door, rusting among the red-granite rocks, hide from those who would dare to reveal its secrets? When again will it reveal itself, always to the ill-prepared traveler who least expects to stumble across it?

Rancher Cy Strong points to one leg of large V symbol formed from single stones, one of the cryptic markers believed made by Frenchmen in 1804 to guide them back to six cartloads of gold ingots.

11. The Frenchmen's Gold at Sugar Loaf Peak

As early as 1844 frontiersmen were seeking the Frenchmen's gold—all six cartloads of it. But perhaps none knew that it might be buried within a stone's throw of Sugar Loaf Peak in the barren country of what was once known as No Man's Land. Today this parched land is the Oklahoma Panhandle, and the rock-strewn Sugar Loaf can be found some fifteen miles northwest of Boise City, in Cimarron County.

But not all the clues were known in 1844. Old trappers and ranchers knew about the three Roman numerals made of stone that ranged for almost a quarter of a mile over the surface of the land. They knew, too, that those stone markers were six miles apart and that the center of that triangle was Flag Spring, a water hole on the Santa Fe Trail. What they did not know was that there was still a fourth cryptic marker but nine miles away and that it was not shaped like the other three.

Rancher Cy Strong, the owner of a nineteen-thousand-acre spread in Cimarron County, found the fourth marker several years ago.[1] From then on the Frenchmen's treasure was believed buried not at Flag Spring but instead between Sugar Loaf Peak and the Cimarron River a short distance away. But that is only conjecture, for no one has yet deciphered the meaning of the massive Roman numerals carefully placed in the ground more than 150 years ago.

When Cy Strong's grandfather established a trading post in eastern New Mexico in 1844, he became familiar with the lost treasure, known then as the *tres piedras* ("three markers") gold. But there was more to go on than just a legend. A diary was kept in the back of an old Spanish Bible. The strange story that diary revealed is this:

In the late summer of 1804 seven Frenchmen, their Spanish guide, and fifteen Indian servants were traveling from Santa Fe into the Black Mesa country in what is now the Oklahoma Panhandle but was then a part of Spanish Mexico. They were leading six large, heavily laden oxcarts. Concealed in the carts beneath layers of furs were five hundred ingots of gold weighing seven and a quarter pounds apiece.

As night veiled the lonely prairie, they rolled up to a water hole known later as Flag Spring. Perhaps they chose the spring because of the company it offered. Indians had used it since time immemorial, for many arrowheads have been found there. But on this occasion it was occupied by four mountain men, probably French traders, who were cooking their evening meal.

The seven Frenchmen lost no time telling the strangers that they were hauling their furs to New Orleans, where they would receive a better price, since the Spaniards frowned on Frenchmen in their territory.

The four traders had just come from the Louisiana Territory and their news was a hard blow to the Frenchmen: Louisiana had been sold to the United States. It no longer belonged to France. The Frenchmen acted as though that would make no difference in their plans, but that night they slept little.

Once the four traders had broken camp the next morning, the Frenchmen discussed the probability that the Americans would never allow them to ship their gold to France but instead confiscate it on the spot. The Spanish guide, a metal worker named José Lopat, who had been hired to mold the gold bars and then guide the Frenchmen to New Orleans, suggested that they send two of their men ahead to determine whether the strangers' story was true. If it was, they could arrange to have a boat pick up the gold somewhere along the coast.

Lopat's idea seemed the only sound one. Two of the hardiest Creoles were chosen to continue to Louisiana to see whether the gold could be safely taken to France. It was estimated that the round trip would take three and a half months. In the meantime the others would set up a temporary camp.

When four months passed and no word had

come from their compatriots, the Frenchmen elected to bury their gold. When they were assured of safe passage to France, they would return for it. Before they did so, however, they would have to send the Spaniard Lopat, as well as the Indian servants, back to Santa Fe. Lopat owned no part of the gold. He had been employed only to mold the ingots and guide the party to New Orleans. Now there was no longer a need to keep him.

Lopat and the Indians were escorted for the first one hundred miles back to Santa Fe, far enough to satisfy the Frenchmen that they were the only ones who knew where the gold would be buried. Lopat had observed his employers well, however, and what he knew he would later detail over the years until finally it filled more than fifty pages carefully recorded in the back of his most prized possession, the family Bible. It is because of Lopat's vivid memory that this story can be told with far greater accuracy today.

Lopat had learned enough about the Frenchmen's shady past to put a hangman's noose around each of them. In the beginning there had been thirteen of them, and they had gone to Mexico from New Orleans shortly before 1800. While in Chihuahua they had attacked a group of Spanish muleteers guarding a small packtrain of gold and silver and killed all but two guards. Fleeing with more than one hundred pounds in gold, the Frenchmen were pursued into present-day New Mexico before Spanish officials gave up the chase.

Later the Frenchmen turned up in Taos. About 1801 they began prospecting for gold and made a meager living panning the mountain streams. When a small gold strike was made in the Marino Valley, the Frenchmen were once again conniving about how to increase their profits. In the following months they murdered about twenty miners, as Lopat had learned while working for them. But their unsavory ways put six of them in their graves, leaving the remaining seven with all the more profits to share.[2]

Although the gold strike was of small scale, historical records tell of placer mining east of Santa Fe in the early 1800's. By the time of the Mexican War about three million dollars in gold had been wrested from the streams by Mexican miners.[3] The Frenchmen had done well in their raids—so well that they hired Lopat to melt the gold into ingots so that it could be easily handled and transported over the long journey to New Orleans.

Lopat was known for his knowledge of metallurgy, having worked with metals in Mexico City. In three months he molded five hundred of the bars. He said that the weight of the ingots never varied. These details were assembled in later years by Lopat's son, Emanuel, who pasted the pages, one after another, in the back of the Bible.

Lopat was convinced that the gold bullion was buried somewhere far out on the Plains, probably near Flag Spring, for not too many months after he returned to Santa Fe one of the seven Frenchmen was seen there. He was Pierre LaFarge, an excommunicated priest who had once served a prison term for killing a nun. Though defrocked, he still went under the guise of a padre.

LaFarge was the only one of the seven to return to Santa Fe. LaFarge told Lopat that all his other companions had been killed either by Indians on the Plains or in knife fights in New Orleans. LaFarge was now the sole survivor and considered himself the owner of the five hundred ingots and that only he knew where they were buried. But soon it became apparent that not even LaFarge would claim the bloodstained gold. Tuberculosis was slowly killing him. He worsened until he was bedridden. Moreover, his presence in Santa Fe had been detected.

It was known that LaFarge had been among the Frenchmen during a raid at the placer diggings in which two miners were murdered. Two sons of one of the miners were now freighters in Santa Fe. When they learned of his arrival, they organized a lynch mob. LaFarge barely managed to escape by concealing himself in a cart loaded with straw. Lopat never saw LaFarge again, but was satisfied that he died just two weeks later, for one of the two men who had buried him later told Lopat.

With LaFarge's death went the secret of six cartloads of gold buried far out on the Plains in a vast wilderness of few landmarks. He left one clue. More than once LaFarge spoke of the "gold buried near the spring." Lopat knew that spring could only be the Flag Spring of today. He made but one attempt to find the gold. Upon his arrival at the spring no obvious signs remained of the burial site and he knew absolutely nothing of the four mas-

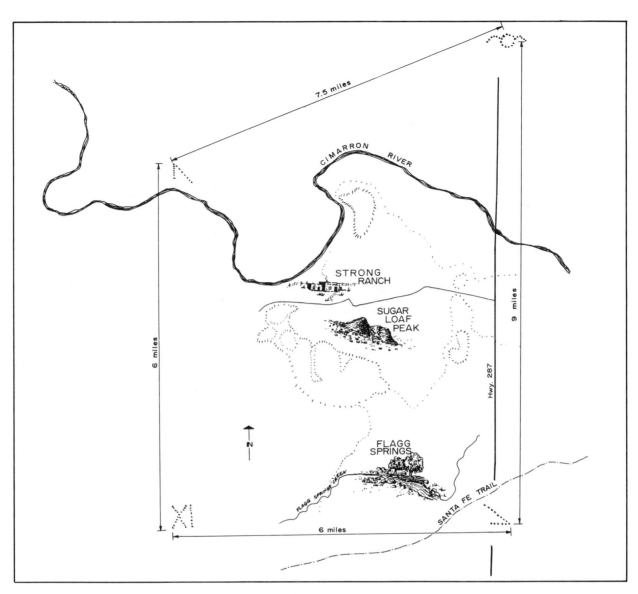

Landmarks for the Frenchmen's gold in Cimarron County. Note the symbols in the four corners. The northeastern symbol was discovered in recent years.

sive markers the Frenchmen must have devised so that they could retrace their steps to the gold.

Though the treasure had become legendary by 1844, twenty years after the Santa Fe Trail was blazed through that country, the stone markers were not discovered until the 1870's, and even then only three of the four man-made landmarks were known. Although each marker apparently had an intended meaning, only one, with the Roman numerals XI, has any obvious explanation, and even it may be a code.

From this stone marker, forming the southwest corner, two others resembling V's are found six miles east and six miles north. Nine miles north of

the southeast symbol is yet a fourth marker, entirely different from the others. It appears to form a large circle with a wing on either side, very similar to the Greek letter omega. All four symbols are made from single stones, some large and some small. Each symbol forms a corner of land encompassing an area of more than thirty-six square miles, the center of which appears to be just northwest of Sugar Loaf Peak.

Today Sugar Loaf Peak is on Cy Strong's ranch fifteen miles northwest of Boise City. When I talked with Strong one summer day in the shade of a large elm, I learned very quickly his feelings about the old legend.

This historical marker north of Boise City marks the route of the Santa Fe Trail southwestward across the Oklahoma Panhandle.

Sugar Loaf Peak, where many believe that the Frenchmen concealed their cargo of five hundred gold bars. It is the only landmark for miles around and is near the center of the four man-made symbols.

Above and page 220: The Black Mesa country, first looked upon by white men when Coronado and his horsemen and foot soldiers passed there in 1541. It is still a forbidding land, holding mysteries both old and modern. Photographs by Fred W. Marvel, Oklahoma Tourism and Recreation Department.

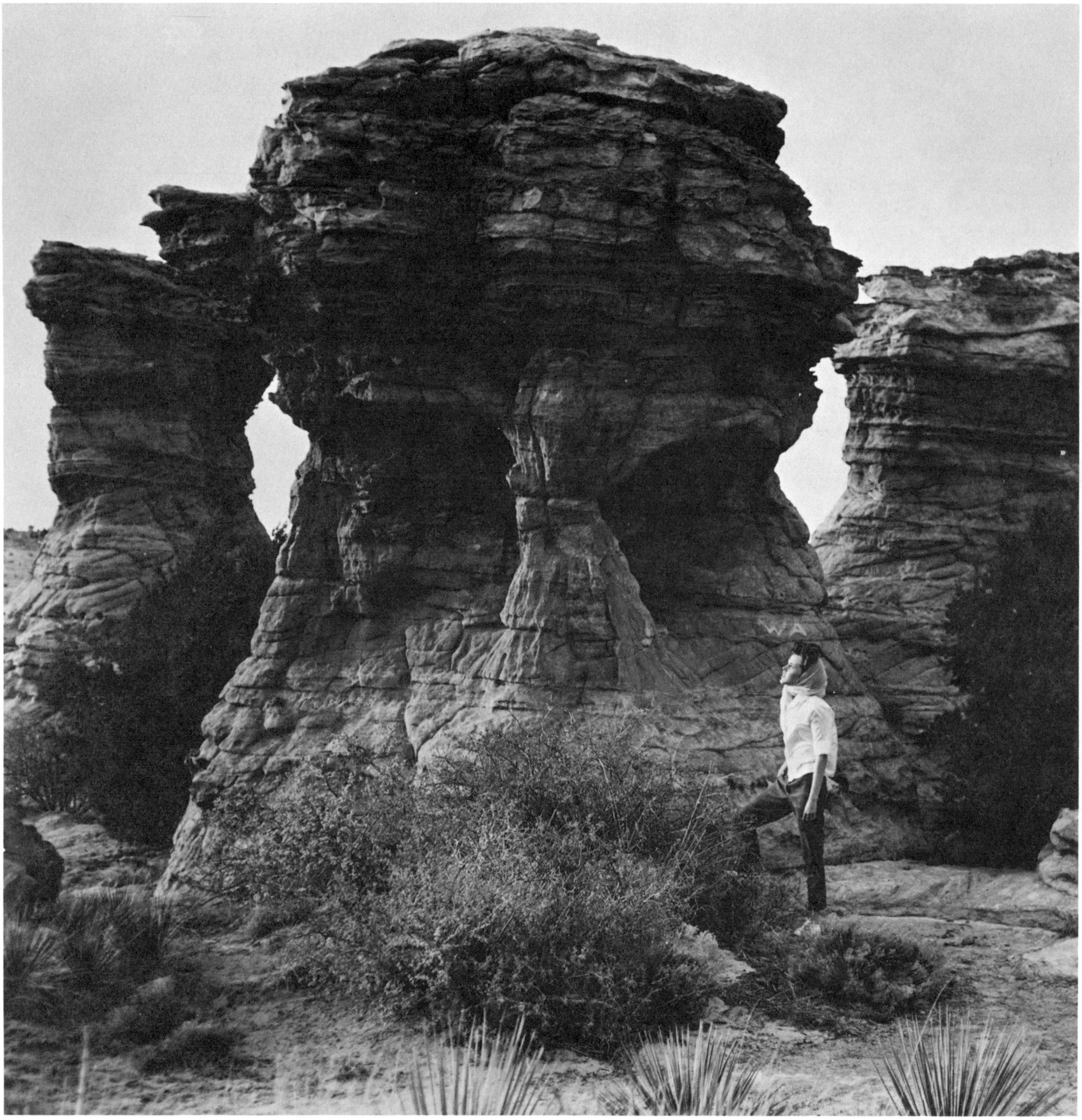

Occupants of the Black Mesa country centuries past recorded their passage in petroglyphs on canyon walls. Photograph by Fred W. Marvel, Oklahoma Tourism and Recreation Department.

Flag Spring, near the Santa Fe Trail, was one of two water holes found in the Oklahoma Panhandle.

The deep ruts of the Santa Fe Trail are still visible (at top of photograph) where the trail crossed the Panhandle south of the Cimarron River.

The story of the *tres piedras* gold, sought as early as 1844, is one of Oklahoma's oldest treasure legends.

"Listen," he whispered, wiping the sweat from his brow, "I know the treasure has got to be here. I've seen and found too much evidence for it not to be." Strong has good reason to believe as he does. Once the official surveyor of Cimarron County, he surveyed the stone markers and discovered the fourth some years ago.

"When the Frenchmen laid out those four markers," he insisted, "they used a compass all right. There's no doubt about that, because the county township line runs almost parallel to the south two markers. But they used magnetic north instead of true north. The southeast marker, only about half a mile east of Highway 287, is off about twelve degrees and located half a mile farther south of the township line."

Probably the first person to dig for the treasure was Strong's great-uncle, Michael Ryan, who knew nothing of José Lopat and the notes in his family Bible but by a mere coincidence became involved in the search. Ryan had lived most of his life in the West and had learned to speak Spanish while playing with Mexican children. For years he had heard about the treasure from the Mexicans, who always referred to it as the *tres piedras* gold.[4]

According to tradition the trail to the treasure was marked by many huge stones, which were spaced irregularly apart in the ground but which formed the gigantic letter V. Chiseled on the underface of the stone at the point of the letter was the symbol V indicating the direction in which the next marker would be found. These stone symbols were scattered from five to ten miles apart all the way from Santa Fe eastward to Las Vegas, New Mexico. From there the trail had been lost.

Ryan knew that several priests had hired guides and made an intensive search for the remainder of the stone markers. They picked up the trail and followed it to within thirty miles of Clayton, New Mexico, but there the trail was lost again, and the search was abandoned.

In all probability Ryan would never have stuck a shovel into the ground after the elusive treasure had it not been for an incident that occurred about 1900 and caused him to pursue the trail of the *tres piedras*. It happened when Ryan was traveling in eastern New Mexico. His horses strayed from camp one night, and he was left afoot to

search for them. Ryan had chased the animals for several hours when he happened onto his first clue—a clue that would captivate him in a treasure quest for the remaining days of his life.

As he sat down on a stone to rest, he noticed that the rock formation around him appeared unnatural. It was obviously the work of man, for it formed the distinct letter V. It brought to mind the *tres piedras* legend. On the bottom of the stone that formed the point, Ryan found the symbol V deeply chiseled. He knew that the site was much beyond the point abandoned by the priests. He carefully marked the spot and some time later returned to renew his search for other markers.

During the next two years he searched for the trail, at times finding it only to lose it again. Ryan continued his quest until the stone markers led him into the Black Mesa country. The end of the trail finally came in Cimarron County, where he found the three markers, until then never associated with the long-sought treasure.

Ryan ran a triangulation that convinced him that Flag Spring was the treasure site. He dug there intermittently for years, finding nothing except what he believed were adobe bricks. He never knew of the fourth stone symbol, miles north of the site.

Strong is sure the gold is buried nowhere close to Flag Spring (which was named at least twenty years after the Frenchmen camped there) but is instead somewhere just south of the Cimarron River and northwest of Sugar Loaf Peak. For not far from what should be the center of the four cryptic stone markers Strong found the ruins of an ancient dugout that he has always believed predated the Santa Fe Trail. Just west of those ruins, in the side of a rugged hill, he discovered what he believed to be the winter headquarters the Frenchmen used while they waited for their two companions to return from New Orleans. There, Strong thinks, they set up camp in a small cave and constructed the outside wall of adobe bricks. Pieces of decayed cartwheels found nearby reinforced his conviction.

As Strong and I drove over his ranch in his panel truck, the cattleman pointed out Sugar Loaf Peak, which can be seen from all four stone markers. We traveled about three miles south to Flag Spring. Later we crossed the old trail to Santa Fe; in places its deep ruts still plain to see. Finally we came to the southeast marker. Formed of single stones, it was similar to the northwest symbol and made the distinct letter V, with one side longer than the other. At the point of the huge marker was an even larger stone, much too heavy for one man to carry.

The Lopat family Bible records that José Lopat was born in Madrid, Spain, on October 17, 1769, and that he died in Santa Fe on June 4, 1856, at eighty-seven years of age. His son, Emanuel, who wrote his father's story in the back of the Bible, was born in Santa Fe on June 5, 1819, and died in Denver, Colorado, August 3, 1906, also at age eighty-seven. Emanuel's daughter, Angelina Lopat, had for years listened to her grandfather tell of the Frenchmen's gold and knew the story in every detail. When she died in 1925, also at eighty-seven, her niece, Mrs. Frank Boyles, of Denver, inherited the Lopat Bible.

Of all the notations recorded in the Lopat Bible, all written in Spanish, three summarize the story:

In ninety days I poured 500 gold ingots into a mold I made myself, and each weighed seven and one-quarter pounds according to the scales we had.

Raymond [unidentified in the notes] told me he himself murdered five miners and all the others had blood on their hands.

Father LaFarge was not happy to see me, and told me with great reluctance of the deaths of the others in the party.[5]

In the past half century, Strong has seen many treasure hunters come and go, some traveling from as far as Canada and Mexico. But to date no one has had any luck in solving the mystery of the tres piedras.

"I think the place to dig is in the center of the four markers," Strong offered. "But you have to realize that the center today probably wouldn't be the same place the Frenchmen picked. There's bound to be some deviation, and that difference could mean a lot of digging."

The seven Frenchmen employed a shrewd method of assuring themselves they could return to the hidden gold when the time was right. For them that day never came. Their secret was clever enough that the six cartloads of gold—today worth more than two million dollars—has eluded recovery for more than a century and a half. Someday, Strong is sure, someone will find it.

E. A. Williams and his wife, Emma, at their Arizona mining camp in 1916. In the 1890's, Williams surveyed much of west Texas; platted the ruins of Cascorillo, found in Washita County in 1895; and founded Wildman, in the Wichita Mountains, before the Indian country was opened to settlement. Courtesy Mrs. Frank R. Wildman.

12. The Mystery of Cascorillo – A Lost City

No one knows who first struck gold in the red sandstone hills of present-day Washita County, in western Oklahoma Territory, that hot summer day in 1895. Perhaps no one cared, for the gold fever swept the plains. Sodbusters-turned-miners deserted their fields, and soon it appeared that there were thirty-five hundred gold seekers in the hills.[1]

The stores of Cloud Chief were almost emptied of their goods, and fifty wagons loaded with lumber left for the gold diggings in the northern part of the county. Arapaho (then spelled Arapahoe), a settlement in what is now Custer County, was nearly deserted; the merchants were moving their stock to the mines, fourteen miles southwest. Every day passenger hacks left the Arapaho hotels at 7:00 A.M. and 11:00 P.M. bound for the mines.

From Golden, a bustling camp, one reporter penned these words for a "Special Gold Edition" of the *Cloud Chief Herald-Sentinel*: "Town alive with excitement! Shovels worth $5 each! Picks can't be had! Gold assays $500 to the ton!"[2] The reporter declared that the country was staked with mining claims for ten miles square. The date was June 14, 1895, and miners' camps were swarming: Williams' camp, at the head of Boggy Creek; Warren's camp, three quarters of a mile northeast; and Monument camp, on Turkey Creek, where a strange grave had been found.

The assays on Boggy and Turkey creeks were reaching three hundred to five hundred dollars to the ton in gold, and the newspapers reported that a big Colorado mining company had already shipped its entire outfit, including several carloads of machinery and 150 men, to work the new gold fields. Old-timers were saying that "the palmy days of forty-nine were out done and that the Black Hills and Cripple Creek were now in the Washita County gold fields," which only three years before had been part of the Cheyenne-Arapaho Indian Reservation.

It was during this frenzied rush that some miners discovered a grave with four human skeletons on Turkey Creek. It soon became evident that other gold seekers had discovered the field, for nearby were found old Spanish inscriptions on a large sandstone rock. When interpreted, the etchings read: "Gold discovered here in 1676"—or perhaps the date was 1876; no one seemed sure. But below was carved "IV Best" and two or three other names that time had made illegible.[3] The rock had obviously been used for a gravestone. The place was afterward dubbed Monument Camp. Later were found two old crucible ladles, the kind the Mexicans had used in smelting gold, the miners were sure.

Soon other papers reported similar discoveries. One week after the gold discovery broke, the *Arapahoe Argus* released this story:

That there is gold in paying quantities in the western portion of G [Custer] County, there is no doubt, and that these mines were worked in ante-bellum times there is also no doubt.

The richest discovery was made by Messrs. Cramer, Burns, and Porter, all old Colorado miners. They traced the placer leads from Boggy Creek over into G County, where they found the bed rocks, some ten miles west from Arapahoe. Close to these mines they found where an old wagon had rotted down and some badly rust-eaten tools. Arapahoe has been crowded with prospectors for the last week, and the hotels are unable to accommodate them all.[4]

Still more telltale artifacts were uncovered as shown the following week by the *Arapahoe Bee*:

While prospecting for gold in the western part of this county last week, T. J. Osburn and companion found the skull and a number of bones of a man, an old-style Mexican bridle bit, the blade of a Mexican sword, a pair of apothecary's balances, a hoe blade, part of the iron trappings of a saddle, and eleven Mexican silver dollars of the mintage of 1846 and 1848.[5]

Little more was thought about the strange discoveries until a few weeks later, when another prospector discovered a rusty old rifle near a human skull and six Mexican silver dollars, all dated 1849. It was reported that the miner was forming a company to dig further.[6]

Little by little evidence was accumulating about

The Herald-Sentinel.

HERALD Established July, 1892. SENTINEL Established August, 1892. DEMOCRAT Established October, 1892. Consolidation, April, 1893.

VOL. 4, No. 39. CLOUD CHIEF, OKLAHOMA TERRITORY, AUG. 30 1895. By F. T. Cook.

EDITORIAL.

The Marlow Magnet runs a free column.

Medford is to have some horse racing on the 31st.

The Rock Island, like the Santa Fe, will haul seed wheat free.

The ElReno baseball nine seems to be entitled to the championship.

Chickasha now has three papers: The Express, Gazette and Record.

The deputies who killed Willets near Kingfisher, have been arrested.

The Choctaw road will soon be completed through to South McAlister.

The Yukon weekly contains the best territorial news of any of our exchanges.

Grading is again to commence "within thirty days," on the Oklahoma Central.

ElReno did herself proud by the hospitality shown the editors. Success to ElReno.

The Guthrie Leader gives the Press meeting the most complete writeup of any of our exchanges.

Elsie Thralls, formerly sheriff of this county, now sheriff of Garfield county, has charge of Zipp Wyatt at Enid.

We are in receipt of a complimentary ticket to the Oklahoma State Fair to be held at Guthrie, October 8, 9, 10, 11, and 13.

It is authoritatively reported that parties are now in the west part of the county contracting for corn at 35 cents per bushel.

Louis N. Hornbeck of Minco and D. F. Smith of Chickasha are preparing a map showing the individual holdings in the Chickasaw nation.

CASCORILLO.

The ruins of the ancient Mexican town discovered in the Gold diggings of Washita County.

It has long been supposed that a town had existed in this country long before title to the land had been acquired by the United States. An old Mexican known as Pedro Jaungonzales tells a story that sounds like a romance, and if not corroborated so thoroughly by recent discovery, would in all probabilities be taken for pure fiction. Old Pedro Jaungonzales is between

CASCORILLO.

Don't go Bare-headed

When you can select you a hat that will fit, at a reasonable price. My stock of hats are especially complete, call and examine them.

It's Too Hot to go bare footed!

I have a large stock of well selected foot wear, which will be on sale in a few days. If you are needing anything in this line remember I can fit you. Prices satisfactory.

C. E. Sumner,
Successor to JOHN BINGHAM.

H. A. LAMBERSON
Attorney at Law,
CLOUD CHIEF, OKLA.

Bush & Grigsby,
Attorneys At Law.

Above: News of the discovery of the ancient town of Cascorillo had front-page coverage in the *Cloud Chief Herald-Sentinel* of August 30, 1895. A plat of the ruins was furnished by the Washita County surveyor, E. A. Williams.

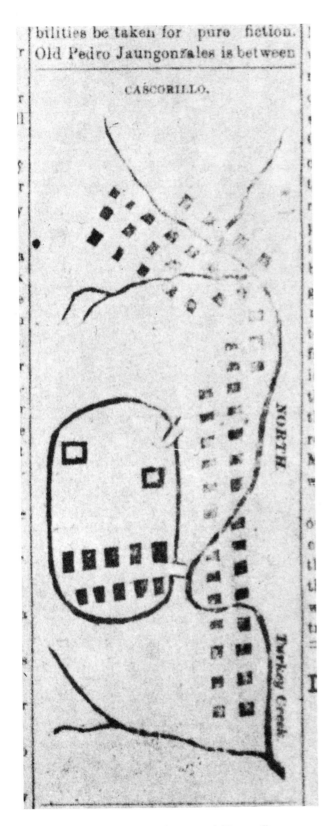

CASCORILLO.

NORTH

Turkey Creek

Detail of Williams' map of Cascorillo.

a story of a much earlier quest for gold—and untimely deaths for its seekers. Less than a week later two other prospectors, named George Fleener and Joseph Patterson, rushed into Cloud Chief with human bones, brass trinkets, several old implements, and thirty-two Mexican dollars they had found in a ravine near their diggings. They believed that there was more such treasure and were hiring men to help them dig.[7]

In little over a month's time seven human skeletons and forty-nine Mexican coins had been reported found. By that time it had become obvious that the Spaniards had discovered the area long before and had mined it for years. That conclusion was borne out by the discovery of several mines and the ruins of crude furnaces used to smelt the ore, farther west, in Roger Mills County.

E. A. Williams, a transplanted Texan and county surveyor of Washita County, began searching for more gold deposits on the west. Williams helped settle much of west Texas and platted Amarillo. His integrity was unquestioned. He wrote this letter to the Cloud Chief paper telling of his discoveries:

I have just returned from a trip further out west, G. W. Ohampett, H. J. Easterwood, J. E. Ranball and myself, prospecting and surveying out claims. We made a new discovery in Mills County. We found gold and silver in lumps as large as grains of corn, and on a creek called by the Spaniards, "Kaskarado," we found ancient mines which had been worked by the Spaniards before the Mexican War.

The old furnaces which were used by them for smelting are plain to be seen yet and signs of a village of about 1,000 inhabitants were found at this place. We have located rich mines. I learned yesterday that the old Spanish town on Turkey Creek had been found.[8]

Williams' reference to the Turkey Creek discovery made front-page headlines on August 30, 1895. The *Cloud Chief Herald-Sentinel* released the story after an exclusive interview with an old Mexican who had lived there many years before, while Williams furnished a sketch showing an outline of the ruins as they were found:

CASCORILLO
The ruins of the ancient Mexican town
discovered in the Gold diggings of
Washita County

It has long been supposed that a town had existed

in this country long before title to the land had been acquired by the United States. An old Mexican known as Pedro Juangonzales tells a story that sounds like a romance, and if not corroborated so thoroughly by recent discovery, would in all probabilities be taken for pure fiction. Old Pedro Juangonzales is between seventy-five and eighty years old, and says that when he was a boy he was captured by the Indians and brought to this country and afterwards made his escape, and in his wanderings found a fort garrisoned by Mexican soldiers, and he remained with them about a year when Mexico got into war with Texas, the troops were all called home. There was quite a population of citizens that lived in a little town surrounding the fort, who occupied their time by digging and smelting out gold and silver. This story caused people to begin to search for the old town, which was located on Turkey Creek, township 11, range 19. The mines [ruins] had probably been passed over hundreds of times and would never be noticed [as] more than slight rises in the ground, all covered with grass and a growth of shinery. On examining it was found that these raised places appeared at regular intervals and in rows, also each about the same size, about 12 x 14 feet square. Numerous streets were found, and at the edge was plainly discerned the remains of the old fort, which is about 200 feet wide by about 400 feet long, inside of which was two large buildings probably 30 x 40 feet, and at the other end were two rows of smaller buildings about 20 x 24 feet.

The fort had two openings, on the north side and next to the creek. E. A. Williams, county surveyor of this county kindly furnished us a correct plat of the town as discovered, from which we get our sketch. Numerous old articles were found which goes to prove the story of the Mexican. A part of an old crucible is now in the possession of Judge [H. A.] Lamberson of this city, which was found there. Mr. Williams has also furnished us with the plans [plat] of another town or mining camp further west in Mills County, which we will illustrate as soon as we get full particulars. Old Pedro Juangonzales says they called the town "Casco-rillo," and that mineral was mined and carried to Nacogdoches, Texas, on pack mules. The houses were evidently made of adobe, and have by lack of care and heavy rains, gradually crumbled down until now there remains only low ridges to mark the walls of the once famous town. These ridges vary in height, which would indicate that some buildings were higher than others. The streets are narrow, which is characteristic of Mexican villages, and are laid out without regard to the compass.

According to the plat Williams made, the ruins of Cascorillo would have been located two or three miles southeast of present Canute, perhaps near the head of Turkey Creek. The discovery of Cascorillo will not be found in Oklahoma history books. In fact, it is likely that few historians have even heard of such a find, for apparently little attention was given to the tantalizing discovery.

Since 1895 no one has dug into its ancient ruins, and no one is alive today to point to the place where Cascorillo was found. Seldom has such a historic discovery been made and then all but lost from the pages of history. But in the days after the opening of the Cheyenne-Arapaho country few settlers had time to concern themselves about history. Careful investigation today, however, might uncover the site, or at least relics from it.

Yet how can it be that history failed to record this Mexican fortress far out on the plains? We know from testimony recorded in *The United States* v. *The State of Texas* concerning Greer County that the old Spanish trail from Santa Fe once led through this area (see Chapter 4) and that a Mexican village was established for some time in Devil's Canyon not many miles south of Cascorillo. Might Cascorillo too have been an outpost, a traders' rendezvous, or a lair for Comancheros on that early road?[9]

Nothing more about the Mexican town that surveyor Williams found in Mills County appeared in the Cloud Chief paper. If anything more was found there, it went unreported. However, in 1909 this strange find was made near Butler, about twenty miles north of the Washita County discoveries:

A nugget of gold that was evidently left many years ago by a band of Mexicans who traveled through this part of the state has made a rich man of Edward Mershom of Butler. He found the nugget several weeks ago while digging around a tree on his farm four miles north of town, and shortly afterward left for the West.

One day last week it was learned that from the proceeds of a sale of the nugget, he purchased an irrigated farm, valued at several thousand dollars, in Arizona. Prior to the discovery, Mershom was a poor farmer. He slipped away quietly and it was not known generally what had become of him until now.[10]

About ten years earlier, in 1900, more evidence of Spanish travelers had been discovered west of Vici, in eastern Ellis County. A large number of human bones were found exposed in a long, narrow canyon partly covered by sand dunes.

Legend has it that Spaniards crossed there with a large caravan of burros laden with gold and that Indians annihilated them in the canyon. Perhaps the legend is true, for in 1912 several Spanish coins were discovered in the region after a hard rain.[11]

Perhaps someday Cascorillo will be rediscovered, or perhaps more human bones or relics or even coins will turn up from beneath a farmer's plow, shedding more light on this lost city. If so, another chapter of Oklahoma's history will be written, for sun-bleached bones and rust-eaten tools tell no lies.

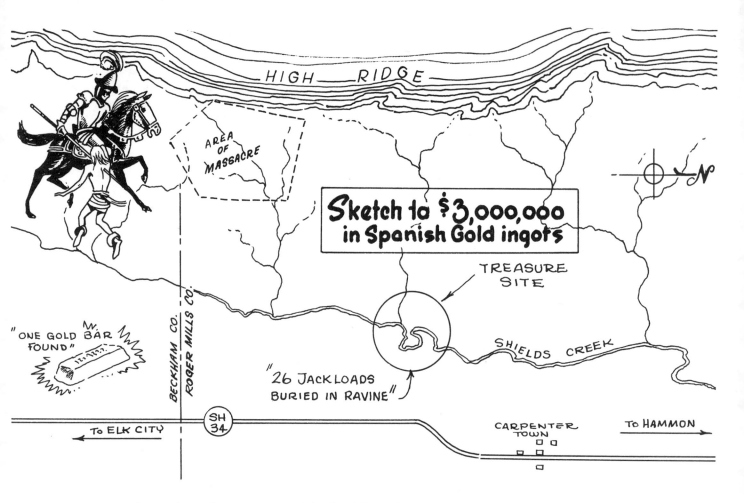

Legend says that twenty-six jack loads of Spanish gold lie hidden in Shields Creek in Roger Mills County. From a sketch provided by H. O. Stockwell. Drawing by Harvey Freeze.

13. Cartloads, Jack Loads, and an Aztec Sun God

More than a century ago Mexican traders crossed the Great Plains with long burro- and ox-drawn cart trains, heavily laden with golden cargo. Their journeys to St. Louis and New Orleans are a well-recorded part of history. Not as well recorded are the tales of the treasures buried along those trails. Even though historical records often fail to record such things, treasure hunters have more than once found evidence that the tales may be true.

Some years ago the renowned meteorite hunter H. O. Stockwell, of Hutchinson, Kansas, furnished me with a sketch describing what he believed to be the approximate location of twenty-six jack loads of gold bullion hidden in what is now western Oklahoma. Legend says that the Mexicans were taking the pack animals over the hilly country of present Roger Mills County. The year was 1849, and the packtrain was traveling from Santa Fe to St. Louis to market the gold, as was often done during that period.

While crossing a high ridge, the packtrain was ambushed by an Indian war party, and the Mexicans were forced to flee down a ravine. But they were no match for the savages, and Indians say that not one gold freighter remained alive.

About 1890 an Indian appeared at the Cheyenne-Arapaho Agency with a solid gold bar and reported having found it somewhere on White Shields Creek near Hammon. He then said that his grandfathers had been members of the party that destroyed the caravan. When questioned further, the Indian refused to say anything more, and although several searchers tried to follow him, he always succeeded in losing them.

"If the Mexicans made it to the island in Shields Creek," Stockwell believed, "they would have had water and perfect protection between the creek banks. The creek makes almost a complete circle here." Stockwell had learned that a flat rock found near the top of the ridge had served as a marker to the gold. Under the stone was found an arrowhead pointing east down the ravine.

"I may go back again this fall with my metal detector," Stockwell wrote. "Am sending information and sketch as I remember the country. I'm afraid I've got the hunting fever again." I hope he goes back . . . .

Lost Aztec Sun God

The sun-baked plains of the Texas Panhandle are well known for their many historic sites and for the Spanish expeditions that crossed them in the seventeenth and eighteenth centuries. Not as well known is the story of the lost Aztec sun god.

One summer day in July, 1910, a secretive character named Sisney, from Tucumcari, New Mexico, appeared on the George Griffs ranch about ten miles south of Higgins, close to the Texas-Oklahoma border in Lipscomb County.[1] He claimed that the United States government had offered him twenty thousand dollars for the graven image of an ancient Aztec sun god that he knew was buried in the region, along with forty thousand dollars in Mexican gold.

Sisney had come by maps to the treasure and had found what he believed to be the right engraved markings on gnarled trees. He had even found several old Mexican gold coins near a spring on the Griffs ranch that convinced him he was on the right trail. Sisney told how, in 1859, the Mexicans carrying the forty thousand dollars in gold coin were being escorted across the plains by a small band of Kiowa Indians. When they neared what is now Higgins, a party of Sioux attacked them.

Fearing that they would lose their gold and the priceless Aztec idol they had procured in Mexico, the Mexicans separated from the Kiowas and buried the treasure in loose sand at the edge of a water hole. They marked the site and then escaped before the Sioux missed them.

Years later several expeditions were made to the springs of the Griffs ranch. Many believed that part of the treasure had been removed, but no one could verify the fact. Sisney was luckier than most. He found several coins that had apparently been spilled near the burial site. With his delicate magnetic needles he attempted to find the rest of the gold and also the Aztec idol. But if Sisney found anything more, no one knew it.

Northwestern Oklahoma

Gold in the Antelopes

Still another story of Spanish treasure near Oklahoma's western border centers just northwest of Crawford at the Antelope Hills, in Roger Mills County. Sometime in the late 1850's a party of Mexicans traveling from Spanish Peaks in Colorado veered southeast.[2] When they neared the Antelope Hills, they encountered a roving band of Cheyennes and Comanches.

The Mexicans had mined a large quantity of gold in Colorado and were transporting nuggets and gold dust home on pack animals. Before the Indians attacked them, they hid the gold in a cave on the slope of one of the hills and then quickly formed a makeshift fortress from nearby rocks. The Mexicans held their ground for several hours, but after using up what shot they carried, they tried to escape. Only two, brothers-in-law, succeeded.

Old residents in the Antelope Hill country will tell you that in 1905 a Mexican appeared there who claimed to be the son-in-law of one of the survivors of the ill-fated party. He possessed a crude chart and in his attempt to follow it dug in the hills for several months, but no treasure did he find. The erosion of fifty years had completely concealed the lost cave. The Mexican's story is but one more of the tales told about the rolling Antelopes.

Forty Jack Loads of Gold

Enough gold bullion to require forty pack animals is believed to be buried not more than five miles south of Oklahoma City on an eastern branch of Lost Creek, a short distance west of Western Avenue. "Ever since this country opened in 1889," an old settler told me, "we heard the story of forty jack loads of Spanish gold bricks dumped in an old spring or gully wash here on Lost Creek."[3]

During those early days when settlers first plowed the prairie sod, many human bones were found in the vicinity that seemed to corroborate the story of a battle. It was always believed that the packtrain was transporting the gold from Santa Fe to St. Louis, where the freighters could market their gold at a much higher price.

When the Mexicans reached what is now called Lost Creek, the guards were attacked by Indians. At an old spring along the trail the guards dumped the gold bullion into the deep pool of water. Old Indians say that the creek bottom was littered with the dead bodies of Mexicans and their pack animals. Even today pioneers point out the bleached bones of an animal still to be seen protruding from the creek bank, perhaps remains from that massacre.

Once several hunters sank a shaft on the east branch of Lost Creek beside an old spring. They installed a boiler and a pump to hold back the water as they dug. But after spending a large amount of money on the treasure hole, they abandoned the pit.

Old settlers are firm in their belief that the forty jack loads of gold are yet buried on Lost Creek, somewhere near the bleached bones of those who transported it across the hostile plains.

Many Spanish relics have been discovered in the Oklahoma City area. On display at the Oklahoma Historical Society are a Spanish sword found near El Reno and a spur unearthed near Yukon.[4] Near Union City a piece of Spanish armor was found embedded in an aged tree. The armor had been placed there untold years before; the tree had grown around it. A shallow grave nearby yielded the remains of a human skeleton and an ax, while a partly buried headstone bore an undecipherable Spanish inscription.[5] Perhaps the burial site of a fallen conquistador?

Still other Spanish treasure was sought in central Oklahoma. As early as 1895 a company formed at Norman "to hunt for a large quantity of gold that is supposed to have been buried east of that city by some Mexicans a number of years ago."[6]

A year later an even more dramatic search was made:

Mayor D. L. Larsh, vice-president of the Citizens national bank; J. C. Clark, capitalist, and W. N. Elledge, merchant, are searching for a valuable treasure on the farm of John Savage, ten miles east of Norman.

Mayor Larsh, a year ago, discovered an old Mexican history, printed in Spanish, which told of the adventures of a party of Mexicans who were on their way from Mexico to St. Louis with gold bullion in the amount of $500,000.

The history minutely describes the course taken by the party, and states that when in the vicinity of the place where the Savage farm now is, all of the party, with the exception of two Mexicans, were massacred by Indians. The two escaped men dumped the bullion in a spring and returned to Mexico.[7]

If Mayor Larsh and his party found the gold, no mention was made of it. But what became of the old Spanish book?

The Brass Twins in the South Canadian

More than thirty years ago Claude E. Hensley, of Oklahoma City, had business in Fort Sill. As he was driving through Anadarko, he picked up a cowman named Bunt Lindsey. While recounting his ranching experiences, Lindsey told of roping two brass cannons that he and other cowhands had seen at an ancient trail crossing on the South Canadian River on his father's ranch near Taloga.

The cannons were brass, no mistake about that, Lindsey said, and were embedded in quicksand eight or ten feet deep but apparently rested on a rock ledge. Almost every time the river rose, the brass tubes were exposed. Then, as the waters receded, they were recovered with sand. Lindsey was firm in his belief that the cannons were of Spanish origin. Once the cowboys lassoed the tubes, attempting to pull them from their river tomb, but they were much too heavy for their horses.

While at Fort Sill, Claude Hensley contacted Captain Harry C. Larter, Jr., of the post museum, and they agreed to meet in Taloga the following weekend. That area of the South Canadian is rugged with canyons. Living in one they found a one-armed former railroader named Fred Lance.

Lance had his reasons, too, for believing that the buried cannons were Spanish. He invited Hensley, Captain Larter, and two accompanying officers into his cabin, where he showed them a metallic brick—the color of tarnished gold—about eight inches long and four inches wide that he had found nearby between two flat rocks. On the face of the metal ingot appeared the sign of the compass and other peculiar markings.[8]

Lance later left the canyons of the South Canadian. Other attempts were made to recover the buried brass cannons, but river sands have a way of hiding such objects, and the chance offered the cowboys that one afternoon has not occurred since.

Museum officials at Fort Sill have sought two

lost cannons of their own, pre–Civil War iron siege howitzers taken there from Fort Arbuckle and elsewhere during the 1870's. Several cannons lay scattered over the old post for years. In 1934, while museum personnel were busy gathering the abandoned tubes, a contractor widening Cureton Avenue came across them and bulldozed them into a deep ditch. A few years ago, Museum Director Gillett Griswold led an unsuccessful search for the fieldpieces, buried somewhere on the north side of Cureton Avenue between Lauman and McBride.

Nine Cartloads

About 1905 a stranger from Kansas came into the newly opened Comanche Indian country with a map to nine cartloads of Spanish gold and silver buried at a group of "seven springs" somewhere between Cache and Big Beaver creeks. Finally the stranger decided that the springs were located on the farm of Charley Thomas, about seven miles east and two miles south of Lawton. The Kansan dug around for some time, but failed to turn up anything.[9]

Several years later another hunter appeared but did not make it known that he was looking for gold. Known only as "Dad," he once boasted of having dug up a one-hundred-thousand dollar cache near Perry on Black Bear Creek. He might have done so, for he always had plenty of funds, Jock Thomas once told me, recounting his memory of meeting Dad when Jock was a youngster.[10]

Dad rented a plot of land from Charley Thomas to raise a truck garden and remained for three or four seasons. Every so often Charley or one of his boys would catch him prodding a steel rod into the ground. It was evident that old Dad was looking for something, though he gave out no details. One spring when his garden was ready to harvest, the old man disappeared as quickly as he had come, leaving his crop, wagon, everything in his shack, and even a team of horses. He was never heard from again.

Jock Thomas is sure that Dad retrieved at least part of the gold, for a large cottonwood standing near the springs bore a huge cross hacked into it. Dad seemed to know what the sign meant. The tree long ago rotted away. Where Dad went—and what he took with him—was anybody's guess.

236

Search at Mud Creek

Comanche, in Stephens County, has been the scene of many intriguing treasure hunts, some of which have been by candle or moonlight in the dead of night. Old settlers remember that about 1905 two Mexicans appeared in Comanche searching for fourteen jack loads of Spanish gold hidden near Mud Creek.[11]

At that time many strange markings on area trees and rocks were still plain to see. Among them were a half moon and rattlesnake carved on a flat rock pointing toward another such sign hacked into a tree limb, on which also appeared an etched turtle. Nothing was found then, but later, in Lost Canyon, a settler discovered a solid silver statuette which came to be known as the "Silver Doll" to many of the early farmers around Comanche.

The silver figurine was discovered in a washout about three miles east of modern Comanche Lake. Still later several small silver bells were unearthed, adding even more credence to the Mexicans' story. About a mile southeast of the lake several "lead wedges" were found, and even more interesting was a small box of Spanish money plowed up when the land was first broken, not far from a grave unidentified by any of the earliest settlers.

Today on the southeast side of Comanche may be found eight rocks that bear etched letters and signs, many of which have weathered away. Those that remain are MINA, VWC, a cross, and EMA. Still other markings are hewed-out grooves in four large, flat rocks, each groove about two and a half feet long, four inches wide, and four inches deep.

Old Indians say that the Spaniards had a large settlement near Comanche and that soldiers periodically left the village with large caravans of empty wagons but always returned heavily loaded—the Indians knew by the deep ruts the wagons left. The legend says that the miners built a smelter there to melt the native gold into ingots. To support that belief, one treasure hunter found what appeared to be an old Spanish arrastra (a crude ore-grinding mechanism constructed like a circular rock trough) about five miles south and east of Comanche.

The Spanish treasure in southern Stephens County has lured many seekers, and many more are just as sure that there will be others hunting around Comanche.

Treasure of Chouteau's Fort

In 1835 Colonel Auguste Pierre Chouteau, of Missouri fur-trading fame, built a stockade fort and trading post atop a small hill on a creek that today bears his name, about five miles northeast of Purcell in Cleveland County. Although the post remained only three years, it has been called "the first important trading post west of the Cross Timbers."[12]

On top of another hill about one-half mile north a military post known as Camp Holmes was established at about the same time. Although both posts lasted but a few years, they later became stations on the forty-niners' trail, the last stop for supplies before crossing the Plains.

After they were abandoned in 1838, several noted expeditions visited the sites. The first was Josiah Gregg's party, which stopped there in 1839 while hauling merchandise to Santa Fe. In 1843, Captain Nathan Boone, youngest son of the famous Daniel, and one hundred soldiers camped there while on a mission to protect traders on the Santa Fe Trail. Two years later Lieutenants James Abert and William Peck on their expedition down the Canadian examined the ruins of the posts.

After the California gold strike the famous frontiersman Jesse Chisholm reopened the old Chouteau post, maintaining a considerable trade with the Indians and overland travelers until his death in 1868. Later the post was occupied by whisky peddlers, cowboys, and outlaws. It was last used as an Indian payment station and trading post. The ruins of the post and of Camp Holmes remained standing until the opening of the Unassigned Lands in 1889.

Many relics have been found over the years at both sites. At least one story of buried treasure centers around them. The pattern of the story is a familiar one. In the late 1840's or early 1850's several Mexican traders were passing that way carrying a large quantity of gold when they were attacked by Indians.[13] Only one Mexican escaped. He buried one companion on the bank of Chouteau Creek beside a large walnut tree and at its base planted the treasure.

Nothing was known of the gold until 1900, when an elderly Mexican appeared at the homes of several settlers seeking landmarks. He possessed a map describing the location of the hidden money and dug on the creek for several weeks but, as far as anyone knew, found nothing of value.

Years later the channel of Chouteau Creek was diverted into the Canadian River about two miles north of Lexington (previously it had flowed into the Canadian south of town). The new stream eroded large portions of soil from the banks, and in 1920 a farmer discovered a human skeleton washed out on the creek's edge near the stump of an old walnut tree.

Nothing more was found until some time later, when a farmer plowed up a large iron pot about a mile north of Chouteau's Fort near an old spring. Its contents were few: only a small kettle in which remained a small amount of gold dust. Had the Indians or other traders found the Mexican treasure and then discarded the pot and its kettle alongside the water hole?

Tulsa's Lost Gold

In 1933, Bill Foresman, a resident of Tulsa, recalled his search for a fortune in Spanish gold doubloons supposedly buried in what later was to become the city of Tulsa.[14] In 1904 he had become acquainted with a man named Fraley, who owned a yellowed map about eighteen inches square on which were given the directions to the buried Spanish gold. At the time Tulsa was only a hamlet with a few wooden buildings. Fraley worked at anything he could find to grubstake himself. He interested Foresman in the treasure, and the two proceeded to search together.

Fraley admitted that he knew very little about the map—only that his father had happened upon it and had later given it to him. He implied that he had traveled long distances to get to Tulsa but never divulged just where he had come from. Foresman remembered that the map depicted a creek that emptied into the Arkansas River near present Twenty-first Street. A small black dot stood for a huge cottonwood tree, and the tree was marked with cryptic symbols. A ring nearby represented a large spring.

In 1904 the spring was about nine feet in diameter and three feet deep and overflowed into the river. The map showed a ford across the river just north of the spring. The men found the ford, the creek, the tree, and the still-flowing spring of fresh water, but by then the bark had grown over the etchings on the tree. Even though Fraley managed to peel away the bark and find the symbols, they proved useless to the hunters, for neither man could understand their meaning.

But the chart had proved accurate. The gold, too, must be there, they reasoned, buried in or near the spring just south of the huge cottonwood. They continued to prod the spring and all around it with long iron rods, striking nothing. Finally Fraley applied his divining rod, a crude magnetic needle that would detect buried iron, hoping that the gold might be buried in an iron container.

Fraley held his needle tightly in his hands as he walked around the spring. Suddenly it plunged downward. Frantically, he called for Foresman to witness his discovery. They dug a ditch to drain the reservoir, placed planking across the basin, and on their hands and knees dipped out the muck and water with buckets. Finally they stood in the mud to shovel it out, believing that at any minute the golden treasure would be revealed.

After they had scooped out about two feet of the black ooze, their shovels struck a metallic object. On hands and knees, they unearthed the metal. But, instead of gold, it was only a decayed shovel of an early design with rotten wood in its handle socket. But it was a good sign, Fraley believed, and the men continued digging.

Fraley tried the needle another time. Again it repeated its downward swirl and dipped at the same location. More frantic digging followed, until mud and water violently spewed into the hole, filling it. The two worked still harder, standing in water almost up to their shoulders. It was then that they found the second metallic object; it, too, only another similar rust-eaten shovel.

Again they tried the needle. This time it remained motionless as the spring filled with water. More work would require pumps, and the instrument detected nothing more.

Today the cottonwood is gone, and the spring has been filled, as has the creek nearby. The spring was just south of present U.S. Highway 66 on the east side of Riverside Drive. Foresman always believed that one important fact might have been overlooked: if the gold had been buried in any-thing other than an iron container, the magnetic needle would not have detected it. Perhaps they had just not gone deep enough, Foresman thought.

Fort Arbuckle.

14. The Treasures the Arbuckles Guard

The peaceful, gently rolling Arbuckle Mountains of southern Oklahoma, formed of limestone eons ago, have provided the setting for tales of lost Spanish gold, outlaws and their secret lairs, and even a small gold rush at the turn of the century.

A Spanish Mine Found

Several old mines said to have been worked by the Spaniards have been discovered in the area. The one that aroused the most excitement was found in 1912 near Bromide, in Johnston County.[1] Prospectors had been searching for the lost mine for more than a quarter of a century without success, until one day in September, 1912.

A company composed of Missouri, Oklahoma & Gulf Railroad employees was formed to hunt the lost mine after engineer, Dan Beltchamber, learned its location from an aged Indian. The shaft was found just where the Indian said it would be, about fifteen miles from Bromide. A lease on a twenty-acre tract of land was quickly secured by the men, who incorporated as the Mystery Mining & Milling Company.

The stockholders in the company secured ore samples from the ancient diggings that assayed two hundred ounces of silver to the ton and about 63 per cent lead. The old mine had long since caved in and the massive timbers inside had rotted away, attesting to its age. The miners hauled in equipment and reopened the mine but apparently failed to find ore in substantial quantities.

Gold, Silver, Lead, and Brass

In 1896 a search was made for thirteen jack loads—thirty-nine hundred pounds—of Spanish gold hidden in a cave about seven miles west of Davis and five miles south, on the edge of the Arbuckles.[2] One legend has it that the Spaniards had opened a rich mine there when they penetrated into a cavern leading to a labyrinth of tunnels.

The venture began in 1892, when an old Mexican who lived on the west Texas plains told a friend about the hidden cave in the Arbuckles. The man found the cave and four years later began opening the clogged tunnel with a six- or eight-man crew. Once during the search, when the workers reached a depth of twelve feet, they unearthed old cooking utensils, a decayed pair of buckskin gloves, and other relics. But if they found more, they never revealed it, although, according to a later tale, a cryptic map was discovered etched on copper, laden with enough Spanish signs and symbols to confuse even the most ardent treasure seekers.[3]

The tale is still told of Spanish traders who dumped twenty mule loads of silver bullion into what is popularly known as Bullion Hole, near Eight Mile Creek. Several other strange discoveries have contributed to the Spanish lore of the Arbuckles. A number of old shafts, hewn into the hillsides in the fashion of ancient mining, have been found. Gnarled trees with carvings of a tortoise (said to reveal a mineral outcropping) and a frog jumping in the direction the lead runs are other such finds. In two separate places were found large, flat stones with hollowed-out gutters once used to channel molten metal into receptacles.[4]

And then there are stories of lost lead mines. E. B. Johnson (son of Montford Johnson, the noted "Chickasaw rancher") told of an almost pure lead deposit in the hills that the Chickasaws had mined for their bullets for years. While stationed at Fort Arbuckle, about eight miles west of Davis, just north of present State Highway 7, United States soldiers are also reported to have mined lead for their bullets. It is said that the commandant once notified the government that the soldiers needed no lead, for they were able to make their own bullets from the lead deposits in the hills.[5]

T. D. Moore, a Cherokee, remembered that when he was a child an old man used to bring his father large chunks of lead found near their farm, four miles west of Fort Washita, some miles southeast of the Arbuckles. No one ever found the lead

Gold, silver, and lead were mined in the Arbuckle Mountains. In the early 1900's the Ragnett and McQuire Lead and Zinc Mine was sunk eight miles southwest of Davis in Murray County. Courtesy Western History Collections, University of Oklahoma Library.

Another of the several lead and zinc operations near Davis was the Hope and Sober Mine. In 1896 treasure hunters opened a cave nearby in hopes of finding a hoard of Spanish gold. Courtesy Western History Collections, University of Oklahoma Library.

deposit, the Cherokee believed, just as no one ever retrieved an old cannon dropped into the fort's well before the Civil War.[6]

O. J. Testerman, of Springer, knows the Arbuckles well, having explored virtually every natural cavern in the hills. In his possession is a mysterious brass brick weighing twenty-eight pounds, measuring eight inches long by four inches wide, and narrowing at its base. In 1943, Testerman's father-in-law plowed up the brass ingot in his cotton field, five miles north and two miles west of Marietta. Testerman told me:

The brass bar was uncovered at plow depth about three steps south of an old stump. On it are marks revealing who molded it, but we can't make them all out. We thought we had found a gold bar when it was

O. J. Testerman, of Springer, displays a twenty-eight-pound brass ingot plowed from a field south of the Arbuckle Mountains.

first plowed up. Who molded the metal and where it came from we don't know. But I expect the Spaniards or early traders hauled it through here and, for some unknown reason, buried it three steps south of the old tree.[7]

Lost Brass Cannon of Hickory Creek

When Earl Abner Brown settled his farm up Hickory Creek several miles south of Ardmore, almost in the shadow of the Arbuckles, he knew nothing of the Spanish brass cannon stuffed with two bars of gold and four of silver.[8] But over the months, as he broke his land in Carter County (in the south half of S.25, T.5S., R.1E.), a strange story began piecing itself together. First, the trees along Hickory Creek that he cut for firewood were riddled with Minié balls. Then, on the side of a wooded hill, Brown found a crude fortification of stone and a shallow trench where a small party of men must have defended themselves. It was after Brown had made these discoveries that a stranger began searching his property alongside Hickory Creek and filled in the missing parts of the mystery.

There had been a battle, said the stranger, as

the lead balls found in the trees clearly indicated. A party of Spaniards pulling two brass cannons and transporting a small amount of gold and silver were attacked by Indians. They retreated to the hillside and there held off the Indians, using one of their small brass cannons. The other cannon, in which the stranger was now interested, would not fire and so considered dead weight. The Spaniards stuffed their two bars of gold and four of silver into its muzzle and sank it in Hickory Creek. A silver plate buried near the creek pointed to the broken cannon and its contents.[9]

The stranger was convinced that the artillery piece had never been retrieved because the silver plate remained unfound, but he had no luck finding it. Over the years early-day settlers have periodically sought the silver plate that would guide them to the lost cannon, probably not far from the hillside battle site.

Even though Spaniards or Mexicans figure in almost all the treasure tales, there is another version to the foregoing story. In this account the men were not Spaniards but Confederate soldiers stationed at Spanish Fort, Texas, and were returning from Devil's Den, near Tishomingo. When they made camp on Hickory Creek, they were attacked by Comanches. During the confusion they lost their brass cannon in the creek but managed to throw up a breastwork of stones and earth and held out against the Indians. They buried no gold but had no luck retrieving their cannon.[10]

The Mexican Mine

One of the earliest searches for lost mines in the region north of the Arbuckles occurred in 1891, when a very old, sick Mexican appeared in Ada.[11] He revealed that as a boy he had accompanied his father and others on an expedition into the region and for a time had worked a rich mine. Plains Indians attacked their party, and his father and all but one of the other miners were killed. He and the other survivor managed to escape.

A rancher who had found evidence of old diggings south of the Canadian River learned about the Mexican in Ada and offered his assistance in rediscovering the mine. Finally the Mexican agreed, and together in team and buckboard they traveled the country for days. One day the Mexican nodded,

In 1903 impressive ruins still remained of Fort Washita, built in 1842, near present-day Madill, in northwestern Bryan County. Legend says that a cannon was dropped into the fort's well during the Civil War. Courtesy Western History Collections, University of Oklahoma Library.

"Yes, this is our mine. The graves of my father and friends should be not far away." As he believed, the graves were found.

The Mexican did not live to reopen his mine, for shortly after returning to Ada, his health worsened, and soon he was dead. No further attempt at opening the mine was made, although in late 1899 a newspaper reported that "copper mines are being prospected in Pottawatomie county, which were worked by Spaniards seventy years ago."[12]

Frank's Sixty Thousand Dollars

In late 1907, A. J. Nichols, of Shawnee, reported that he believed he could recover sixty thousand dollars that had been hidden in the Arbuckle Mountains by Jesse James in the 1870's. Two reputable citizens who had heard Frank James speak at the Dallas fair two years before, in 1905, said that the former outlaw had offered a reward of twenty thousand dollars "to anyone who would locate a certain mark on a rock in the Arbuckles in the Chickasaw Nation, and that he would do the rest."[13]

The sign that Nichols had found met the description that Frank James had given in Dallas,

and Nichols was planning to get in touch with Frank, who was then living on his farm near Fletcher, in the shadow of the Wichita Mountains. But if Nichols was ever given the reward, no publicity was given to it.

Fort Arbuckle's Lost Payroll

Early one morning in 1869 a heavily guarded caravan of wagons rumbled out of Fort Leavenworth, Kansas, bound for Fort Arbuckle. The iron-rimmed wheels of one wagon left broad, deep ruts in the dirt. It carried a United States government gold payroll.[14]

The caravan safely journeyed through the Indian country and was approaching the designated outpost. A few miles more and the journey would be completed. But as the wagons rounded a bend in the trail near Mill Creek, a barrage of shots from a dozen or more rifles caught the soldiers by surprise. The military detail promptly returned a volley, instantly killing five outlaws who had dared show themselves. All the soldiers were killed in the ambush.

The outlaws removed the gold from the wagon, fearing that more troops would be dispatched from the nearby fort when the caravan failed to

Fort Washita was abandoned by United States troops in 1861 and was occupied by Confederate soldiers. Here it appears partly restored by the Oklahoma Historical Society. Photograph by Fred W. Marvel, Oklahoma Tourism and Recreation Department.

arrive on schedule. Then they placed the wagons together and set them afire, making it appear that Indians had raided the train. The outlaws knew that they had to travel fast and therefore had to hide the gold. Farther downstream they buried the payroll, picking three separate locations, each just deep enough to hold that part of the cache. Then the raiders split up. Soon afterward one of them was captured. It was believed that the others were killed, except for one Mexican, who made good his escape.

The story of Fort Arbuckle's lost payroll was all but forgotten until one day in the late 1890's, when a penniless former convict stumbled into a livery stable in St. Joseph, Missouri. The stranger was ill and begged for a handout. The liveryman gave the sick man what accommodations he could. Even when the old outlaw continued to fail in health, the stable owner continued to take care of him. The old man seemed to realize that he was dying, probably from consumption contracted in prison.

Finally one day he called his host to his cot and told him that he wanted to repay him for his kindness. The outlaw revealed that he had only recently been released from the federal prison at Leavenworth and that he had been sentenced for his part in the killing of a group of soldiers and robbing a payroll shipment near Fort Arbuckle. He unfolded the story that has been related here and then drew a crude map showing as best he could the location of the three caches of buried money. A few days later he was dead.

The story had convinced the stable owner. The old man had been too familiar with the details of the story to have made it up. The liveryman had no idea how much gold had been hidden but knew that it had taken a wagon to haul it. In a few weeks he had settled his affairs in St. Joseph and was on his way to Davis, Oklahoma, the closest town to the long-since abandoned fort.

At first he tried to follow the treasure map the dying outlaw had sketched. And although it was closely related to the rugged terrain of the country, the site of the buried gold was indicated only vaguely. Weeks turned into months. The hunter combed every nook, trail, and hill around Mill Creek. He dug holes when he thought he might have the right spot, but his spade never struck gold.

Still the Missourian refused to give up. He believed too strongly in the outlaw's story and was convinced that a dying man does not lie. The gold had to be there. He finally built a small cabin in the hills so that he could live near the region of his search. Later he married an Indian woman, and she kept house while he searched daily for the elusive payroll.

The years passed, and the "Arbuckle Mountains treasure hunter," as he had come to be known, grew old and weak. He had long since used up his money and now lived off the land. His wife refused to care for him any longer, sometimes leaving him at the cabin without food for days at a time. It was at this time that Samuel H. Davis entered the picture. He was a successful mer-

Only chimneys remain of what was once Fort Arbuckle, west of Davis.

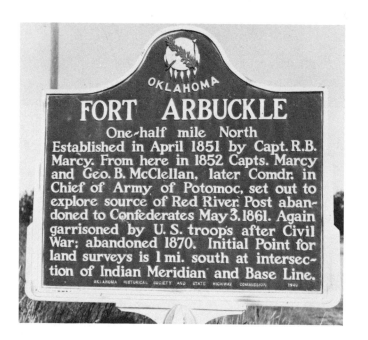

This historical marker, seven miles west of Davis, tells about Fort Arbuckle's past.

chant of the region, and the town had been named for him. He had met the Missourian shortly after he arrived from St. Joseph. The two had become good friends, and the old man divulged much of his story to Davis.

In the last years of the old man's life Davis made many trips to his cabin to take him food and supplies. For a while he grubstaked the old treasure hunter for a share of the find. After the Missourian became too weak to search any longer, he gave Davis the crumpled, torn map the dying outlaw had drawn years before. As late as the 1930's Davis himself was spending his weekends searching for the soldiers' gold, always believing that it was hidden somewhere on the meandering Mill Creek.

One morning Davis stopped to talk with a rancher whose land included a portion of Mill Creek. A surprise lay in store, for he learned that at least part of the treasure had been unearthed.

The rancher told Davis that in the past years many people had gone to the creek looking for the gold. He said:

Only last month a group of Mexicans came by and asked if they could camp and fish down on the creek for a few days. I said it'd be all right, so they set up camp. It didn't actually look like they were doing much fishing though. I went down there once and found where they had been digging a lot of holes.

"Robber's roost" caves like this one in Seminole County, Oklahoma, served as lairs for outlaws and their gold. Photo by William Mahan.

None were very deep. I asked them about this, and they explained they were digging for worms, which seemed logical enough at the time. A few days later I noticed they had gone. Some time afterward I was down to the creek and noticed a deep hole they had failed to fill. In its bottom sat a rusted iron pot. They got the treasure all right. I could plainly see the imprints those coins made on the kettle.

Davis believed that the Mexicans had been directed by the one outlaw who had escaped after the ambush back in 1869. No one else could have given them the information they needed. Davis knew that the third cache of gold was the largest. The money had been placed in empty coffee cans and buried in the floor of a cave. Davis dug into the floor of practically every cave he came across in the Arbuckles, but none yielded the gold.

The caverns are many in the Arbuckles. Any one of them might be the treasure cave. One maze of underground rooms is known as Dead Man's Cave; another, Wild Woman Cave. Then there are Crystal Cave and three bearing the name Jesse James, supposedly named for the occupant. Still more caves are unnamed.

Part of the United States government payroll may yet molder in some dark, musty cavern near Mill Creek, not far from the deserted ruins that were once Fort Arbuckle. Perhaps someday rodents will expose the gold-filled coffee cans. If so, some lucky spelunker will have chosen the right cave to explore.

One of the symbols in Seminole County said to lead to Spanish treasure. Photo by William Mahan.

15. Tales of the Indian Nations

Tales of mines and treasures lost by the Spaniards in what is now Oklahoma are indeed many. If their recorded history in this part of the Southwest is sparse, the same claim cannot be made for their legends. Perhaps it was the Spaniards' way of telling us something the chroniclers failed to record.

Many of the stories relate to the streams and hills of the eastern half of the state, once known as the Indian Nations. There are some records of mines in the region, as well as evidence that at least some of them have been found.

The Bonanza Patrick McNaughton Found

Perhaps the first mine to be rediscovered was the one found in 1877 by John Patrick McNaughton. When he started his quest one hundred years ago for lost Spanish mines in the Indian Nations, he had no idea that his trail would lead him not only to lost mines but to a hidden bonanza that would one day yield millions in lead and zinc. The son of Scotch-Irish parents, McNaughton was thirteen years old at the end of the Civil War. The war had not been kind to the McNaughton family: it had taken the life of an older brother, a captain in Confederate gray, and had left the father incapacitated at the Battle of Shiloh.[1]

Young Patrick McNaughton left his home and schooling in Petersburg, Tennessee, and migrated to Fort Smith, Arkansas, where he worked as a laborer. In 1867 he took a job as a teamster hauling cotton to Springfield, Missouri. The years that followed were spent in the Indian Territory, Fort Worth, and Salt Lake City, where he worked as a bullwhacker; in Arizona, as a mule skinner; and in Sherman, Texas, as a freighter. During those years McNaughton picked up a familiarity with minerals and a smattering of Indian languages—both of which were to prove useful in years to come.

In September, 1877, McNaughton had business in Kansas City. On the trail he met an elderly Shawnee Indian who was trying to return to his people. McNaughton detected the Indian's plight and invited him along, paying his transportation to Vinita and seeing that he had food.

As the two traveled together, McNaughton had no idea that the remainder of his life would soon be changed by the story the Indian was about to tell. Before they reached their destination, the Shawnee revealed a story that was to lead McNaughton to one of the greatest and richest ore beds in the Southwest. The Indian said nothing about lead or zinc. His story concerned lost Spanish mines, to which miners from the south had journeyed with caravans in many years past and from which they had led pack animals heavily laden with shiny rock.

At first McNaughton placed little confidence in the Indian's tale, for he had heard similar stories. But as he listened, something about the Shawnee's story rang true. Business in Kansas City could wait. He parted company with the Indian at Vinita and rode to Seneca, Missouri, a border settlement, where he hired a team and buckboard and bought supplies. Then he headed west for the unsettled region along Spring River—the land of the Peoria Indians in the extreme northeastern corner of the Indian Nations.

In a few hours the frontiersman halted his horses. He found the primitive mines with little difficulty. Crude shafts and tunnels were scattered over an area of at least forty acres. It appeared that extensive digging had been done there over a long period of time. McNaughton estimated that between five hundred and one thousand men must have participated. Some shafts were three hundred feet deep, all round in customary Spanish fashion. In none of the mines did he find any gold or silver and discovered only a small amount of lead. The old Shawnee had known what he was talking about, for in his search McNaughton noticed literally acres of white flint chips scattered about the excavations "like the floor of a china shop." The site was indeed old.

McNaughton believed that the Spanish miners had not exhausted the lode, and he decided to

Above: John Patrick McNaughton, upper right, and family in 1900. While seeking lost Spanish mines in 1877, McNaughton discovered what later became a bonanza in lead and zinc.

prospect the country further. First he asked the Peoria Indian agent, Hiram Jones, for permission, saying nothing about having already located the mines, but Jones would not hear of it and forbade him to enter the region. McNaughton was aware of the law prohibiting prospecting in Indian country, but it did not deter from continuing his search.

He returned to Sherman, Texas, where he interested others in his undertaking and managed a grubstake from George W. Newcombe, a wealthy resident. Together they decided to take the matter directly to the Department of the Interior. McNaughton went to Washington and persuaded Secretary of the Interior Carl Schurz to grant him a special permit to prospect for mineral on the Peorias' land—but that was all. He was still prohibited from mining or selling ore. Even so, he could now carry on his search.

In 1878, McNaughton obtained leases from the Peorias and began prospecting west of the Spanish mines near what later became the settlement of Peoria. There he found not gold but lead and zinc. For more than a decade it seemed that he would never be permitted to exploit his bonanza.

The Department of the Interior held firm to its original prospecting-only restriction.

In 1889 McNaughton's dream began to come true. He hauled in mining equipment from Texas, organized the Peoria Mining Company, and sank a shaft to pay dirt. By 1891 about fifteen hundred whites were in what was later to become Ottawa County, more than half of them miners or associated with mining.[2] Peoria soon boasted a hotel, a blacksmith shop, a post office, and a schoolhouse surrounded by an array of miners' huts and shacks. Peoria's population swelled to eight hundred, and in the middle of it all was Patrick McNaughton.

But Peoria's boom was not to last long. The longevity of any mining camp depends upon its ore reserve. One company after another moved out, and by 1896 Peoria's population had dropped to 205. Although McNaughton had rediscovered the Spanish mines and went on to find what became a bonanza in lead and zinc, he never realized the wealth that others were to wrest from the underground treasure. In 1897, while digging a shallow well four miles north of Miami, a farmer

Willis McNaughton, Patrick's son, examines one of the mine shafts discovered by his father near Spring River in the 1870's. Courtesy Revis Ann Grubb.

ported finding lead on Cowskin (Elk) River in northeastern Oklahoma in 1850. Twenty years later the Indians were working the deposits for shot, according to H. A. Andrews, the Indian agent of the Quapaws at Miami. By 1873 several lead deposits were being worked on the Missouri border four miles south of Seneca.[5]

By 1950 the lead and zinc mines of southwestern Missouri, southeastern Kansas, and northeastern Oklahoma were to produce more than one billion dollars in ore, and for some time outproduced all other states in zinc, furnishing one-half the nation's entire output.

McNaughton was not the only one to rediscover early mines believed to have been worked by the Spaniards. East of Spring River, near Peoria, W. S. Peabody, of the United States Geological Survey found an eighty-foot shaft. From its dumps large trees were growing. Peabody found several ladders made from saplings on which had been left short stumps of limbs. Hacked into the sides of the shaft were notches in a zigzag fashion, used by miners to climb in and out of the shaft. Other relics were a crude spike and a decayed pack that had perhaps been used to carry out the ore.[6]

In December, 1908, it was reported that old Mexican mines "consisting of eight or ten shafts ranging from twenty to fifty feet deep were discovered near Afton recently by a member of the state geological survey." The mine was believed to have been deserted about 1840, when Creek Indians drove off the miners. Other mines were found five miles north of Seneca, along the old Seneca–Peoria road in Ottawa County—all abandoned long before.[7]

Joe Payne's Silver Mine

The Spaniards were not the only ones to "lose" mines in the Indian Nations. Joe Payne was no prospector, but he knew silver when he found it. At least that was what he dubbed a vein three feet wide and more than four feet deep when he gave up drilling. It happened while Payne was serving as a deputy United States marshal around 1881. While he was following some lawbreakers into the hills just south of Tahlequah, he lost their trail. Instead of riding home emptyhanded, he decided to do some deer hunting.

struck a vein of rich lead ore, and within months Lincolnville had arisen.[3] After the turn of the century other strikes brought still more mining camps. Tar River, Hattonville (later Commerce), Couthat, St. Louis, Hockerville, Cardin, Quapaw, Sunnyside, Century, and finally Picher sprang up almost as fast as Peoria had before them.

Years before Patrick McNaughton pioneered the strikes, others had discovered lead deposits, and in times of need had worked the surface veins. As early as 1818, Henry Schoolcraft, a Missouri geologist, reported finding in southwest Missouri "lead ore throughout the region from the grass roots down." He also found traces of earlier miners, for their shallow workings and crude log smelters were evident.[4]

In 1838, John R. Holibaugh told how trappers and traders melted the lead ore and molded it into shot. G. W. Moseley, a Missouri miner, re-

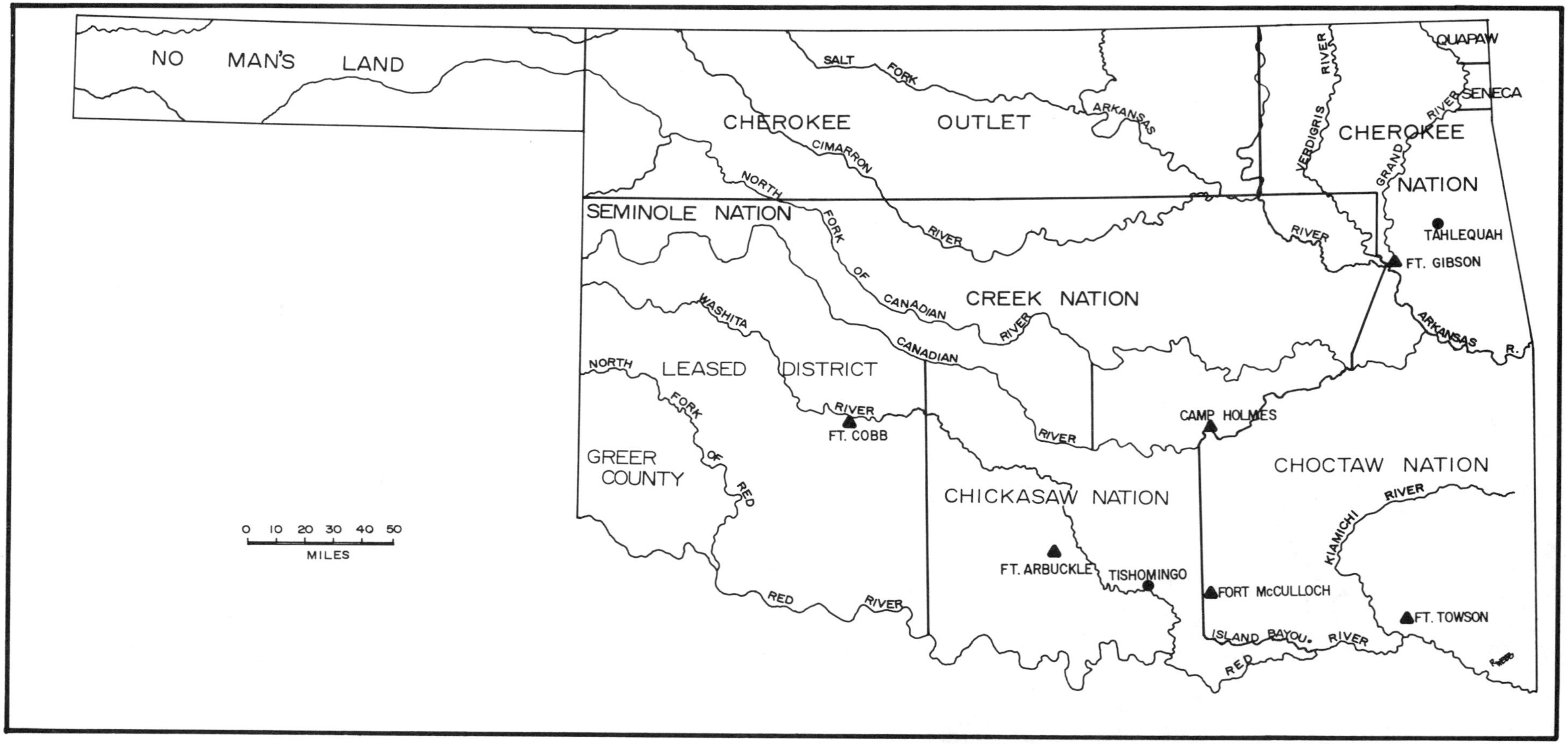
NO MAN'S LAND
CHEROKEE OUTLET
SALT FORK
ARKANSAS
CIMARRON
NORTH FORK OF CANADIAN RIVER
QUAPAW
SENECA
VERDIGRIS RIVER
GRAND RIVER
CHEROKEE NATION
TAHLEQUAH
FT. GIBSON
SEMINOLE NATION
CREEK NATION
ARKANSAS R.
WASHITA RIVER
CANADIAN RIVER
LEASED DISTRICT
NORTH FORK OF RED
GREER COUNTY
FT. COBB
CAMP HOLMES
CHOCTAW NATION
CHICKASAW NATION
KIAMICHI RIVER
FT. ARBUCKLE
TISHOMINGO
FORT McCULLOCH
FT. TOWSON
ISLAND BAYOU
RED RIVER
0 10 20 30 40 50
MILES

Indian Territory, 1855–66

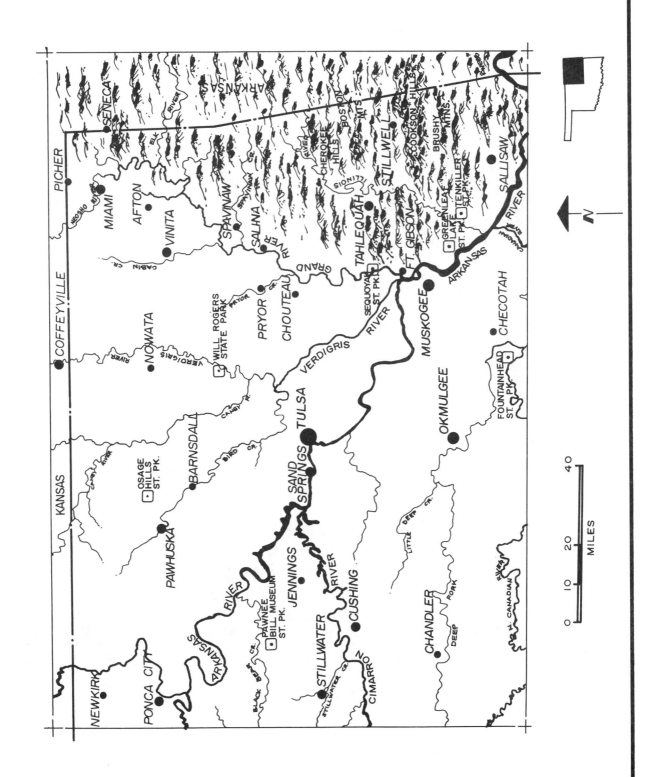

Northeastern Oklahoma

Primitive horse-powered mine hoists like this one were typical of those used in early lead and zinc mining in northeastern Oklahoma, where legends of lost Spanish mines led Patrick McNaughton in 1877. Courtesy Western History Collections, University of Oklahoma Library.

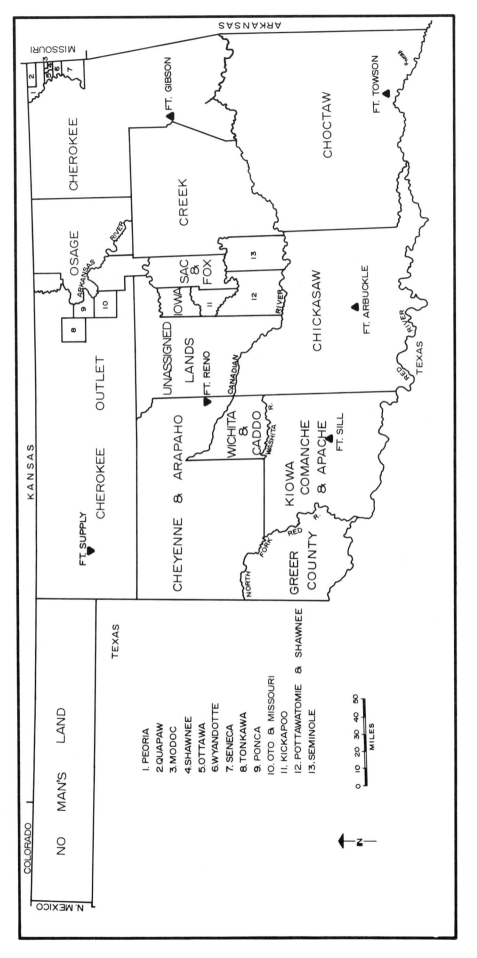

Indian Territory, 1866–89

COLORADO

N. MEXICO

KANSAS

MISSOURI

ARKANSAS

NO MAN'S LAND

TEXAS

CHEROKEE OUTLET

FT. SUPPLY

CHEYENNE & ARAPAHO

GREER COUNTY

NORTH FORK RED R.

WICHITA & CADDO

FT. RENO

CANADIAN

UNASSIGNED LANDS

OSAGE

ARKANSAS RIVER

CREEK

CHEROKEE

FT. GIBSON

IOWA

SAC & FOX

13

12

11

CHICKASAW

FT. ARBUCKLE

RED RIVER

TEXAS

CHOCTAW

FT. TOWSON

KIOWA COMANCHE & APACHE

FT. SILL

WASHITA R.

8

9

10

1. PEORIA
2. QUAPAW
3. MODOC
4. SHAWNEE
5. OTTAWA
6. WYANDOTTE
7. SENECA
8. TONKAWA
9. PONCA
10. OTO & MISSOURI
11. KICKAPOO
12. POTTAWATOMIE & SHAWNEE
13. SEMINOLE

N

0 10 20 30 40 50
MILES

The Netta Mine, a lead and zinc mine at Picher, Oklahoma. Courtesy Western History Collections, University of Oklahoma Library.

Inside the Netta Mine, three hundred feet below ground. Courtesy Western History Collections, University of Oklahoma Library.

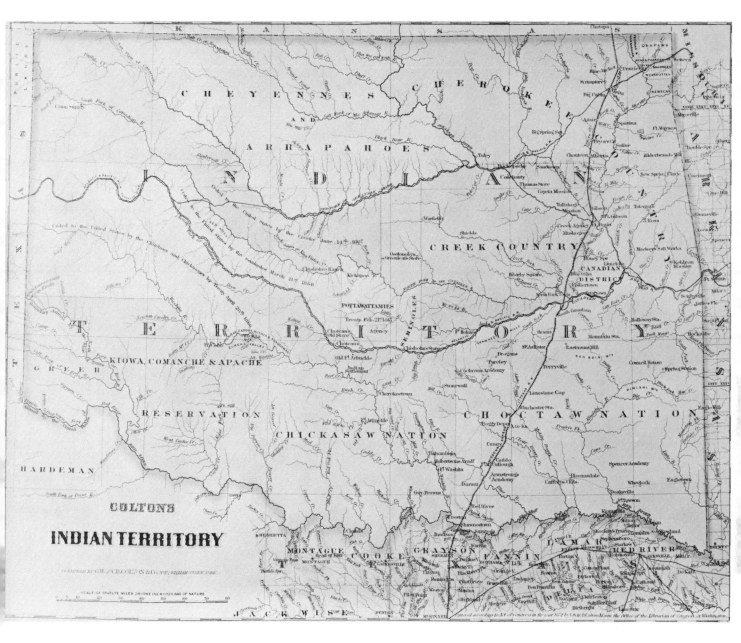

G. W. and C. B. Colton's map of Indian Territory, 1873. Courtesy Gilcrease Institute
of American History and Art.

He had been walking for some time when he sat down on a creek bank to remove a small stone from his shoe. The stream ran clear, and as Payne glanced down, something glistened in the sunlight. He turned his head back to take a closer look. The gleam appeared to be a vein of pure silver at least three feet wide and stretched across the entire creek bed. Payne was well aware of the no-mining laws of the Nations. But that did not stop him from investigating.

Several days later he returned to the silver vein with a hand auger to test its depth. After working for several hours, he had learned all he needed to know: he had penetrated the vein more than four feet, enough to show that several tons of rich ore awaited him. Although he could not legally mine his discovery, there would be a day when he could, and he wanted the silver vein to be available when that day came.

The only way he could conceal the silver without filling in the creek was to cut down several large trees growing near the vein. Once this was accom-

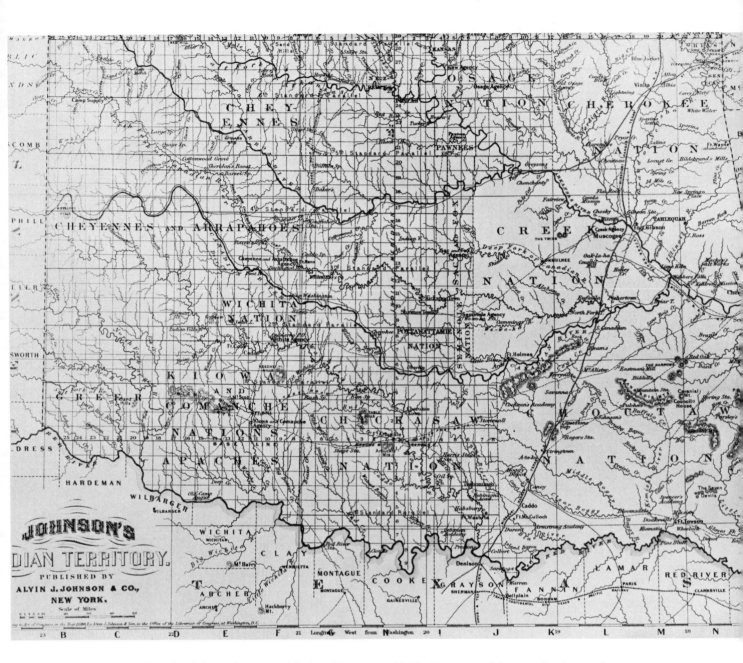

Alvin B. Johnson's map of Indian Territory, 1883. Courtesy Gilcrease Institute of American History and Art.

plished, the shining silver was concealed. Soon the huge trees would collect debris and perhaps even channel out a new path. No one would find the lode as long as it was covered, Payne was sure.

Months became years, and in 1904, before Payne had an opportunity to file on his discovery, fate took his life. Before his death he had passed a waybill to a friend, hoping that he might file a claim. But the piece of paper did its new owner no good. The cryptic drawing made no sense except

to Joe Payne, who had found and then hidden his own silver bonanza.[8]

Lost Mines of the Kiamichis

The dense-timbered hills of southeastern Oklahoma have been the scene of many a treasure search. One range of hills in particular has been explored for countless years. More often than not the quests were for lost French mines instead of Spanish ones. In recent years the search has turned to the lost mines of the Choctaw Indians—all in the Kiamichi Mountains.

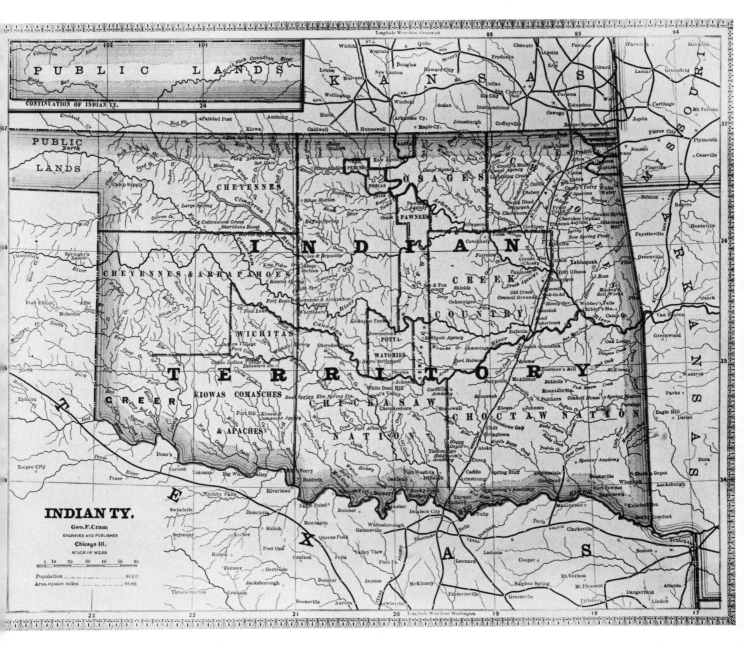

George F. Cram's map of Indian Territory, 1883. Courtesy Gilcrease Institute of American History and Art.

The French were well aware of silver mines in the region, as early reports verify. United States Indian Agent John Sibley gave an account of what he had heard concerning the mines on the Kiamichi River. The Indians called the river Kiomitchie, he wrote in 1805, but the French knew it as La Rivière la Mine, or Mine River, which they reported contained clear water and was "boatable about sixty miles to the silver mine, which is on the bank of the river, and the ore appears in large quantities, but the richness of it is not known."[9]

Sibley's report seems to place the silver mine near present Clayton, in Pushmataha County. He wrote that "the Indians inform of their discovering another, about a year ago, on a creek that empties into the Kiomitchie, about three miles from its mouth, the ore of which, they say, resembles the other. . . . About the mine the current of the river is too strong for boats to ascend it, the country being hilly."

Sibley was writing about the same region through which the French explorer Bénard de la

259

Harpe had journeyed in the summer of 1719 and reported finding various minerals of interest. Near the Kiamichi River a few miles southeast of present Clayton, he noted in his journal that the mountains there exhibited "some metallic mines judging from the different colors of the earth, the marcasites [iron pyrites] that were found there, and the assurances that were given to us by the savages."[10]

A few days later, traveling northwest, perhaps a few miles from present-day Hartshorne, La Harpe wrote that his party camped "at the foot of several mountains" and added: "I found in this place several black marcasites, lined within by several grains resembling gold, and some flint lined with a white metal. I picked some up, and I do not doubt by any means, that if they do not find metal in these stones, that they will not fail to denote metallic mines."

Several miles above the mouth of the Deep Fork of the Canadian, La Harpe found "a pearl of a very beautiful luster" in "a brook full of large shells" and northward a day later near Coal Creek observed large deposits of coal. A few miles northeast of what is now Haskell, the Frenchmen were told by an Indian chief that "six days' journey" away was a small hill "where there was yellow metal" that the Spaniards coveted. Such reports no doubt led other Frenchmen into the region and to the eventual naming of the Kiamichi as Mine River.

Fifty-five years after La Harpe's travels, a French trader named J. Gaignard journeyed up Red River from Natchitoches, Louisiana. In his diary of October, 1773, he told of hearing about two silver mines from Caddo Indians. While in their camp on Red River, about 165 miles north of present Shreveport where Gaignard remained eighty-four days, he heard of both silver mines. One, the Indians said, lay only about 36 miles northeast, probably in Arkansas. The other was located on the Kiamichi River 150 miles northwest, perhaps near present Clayton.[11]

Who the miners were and how much silver they ferried down the Kiamichi before abandoning the mines the records do not tell us. But the remains of many of these ancient diggings have been discovered in recent years. Numerous deep pits were found along the Kiamichi River southeast of

Kosoma. Early residents believed that one of them was an old Spanish silver mine—or might it have been French?[12]

Early chroniclers record that there are at least two gold mines in the Kiamichi Mountains that have not been rediscovered by white men—or at least not by more than one. The mines were worked by a missionary and twelve Choctaw Indians as late as 1884. The story was not revealed until in the early 1920's by the Reverend W. J. B. Lloyd, who was then in his seventies. While Lloyd was a missionary in the mountains of northern McCurtain County, some Choctaws told him they had found gold. Lloyd said that he was shown "a vein of pure gold filling a fissure or crevice in a ledge of outcropping rock, located at the head of a small canyon."[13] Later another vein was found about fifty miles away.

To keep lustful white men from swarming into the area, the missionary and twelve tribesmen formed a secret pact not to reveal the location of the vein. In the years that followed, they chipped away only enough gold to fulfill their meager needs and to purchase tools and supplies for the tribe. Finally they had hacked away the gold so that it could no longer be reached without blasting the rock loose, and since mining was then illegal in the Nations, the missionary ruled it out.

A Choctaw named Simeon Cusher, assisted by other Indians of the secret clan, filled the crevice with stones and boulders. When they abandoned the mine, they began working the golden pockets of the other vein some fifty miles distant. This vein led down into the mountain, and the only way to dig it out was to follow the vein. They were forced to sink a shaft—not a large one, but one big enough to allow a man to chop away the vein as it led underground. They could easily dig without blasting, for the vein was rich and easily penetrated.

After several months of working in this manner, reports of the missionary's operations reached the Department of the Interior. The secretary ordered that the mining cease at once. Reverend Lloyd ordered the mine filled and carefully concealed. Both of the mines remained hidden, and in later years the men took the secret of their locations to their graves. The pledge remained unbroken.

In 1957, Everett Bush, of Muskogee, found these silver ornaments under a small bluff in the mountains near Enterprise, in Haskell County. They are of French origin, probably dating from the late 1700's. Top to bottom: two arm bands, a headband with lions and a wreath in the center, and two disks. The headband has the letters SALS, probably the silversmith's identification. Bush also found among the debris a brass curb chain, a piece of bridle bit, a stirrup, several buckles, and the remains of a saddle. Courtesy Museum of the Great Plains.

The Mormons' Lost Mine

From the Spavinaw Hills of Mayes County comes an incredible tale of a lost gold mine worked by early Mormons. From this rich lode they are said to have obtained a portion of the wealth they acquired to build their temple in Salt Lake City. Those who believe the tale point out the ruins of an old stamp mill on Spavinaw Creek which they claim the Mormons built decades ago and the huge granite grinding stones once used in the mill now lying below Spavinaw Lake dam.[14]

The founder of the Pryor orphan's home, W. T.

Whittaker, came closest to finding the lost Mormon mine. One morning in the early 1920's Whittaker received a letter from Ohio. The writer told Whittaker that he had once lived in the Spavinaw country and had since learned the secret location of what could still be a valuable gold mine worked by the Mormons. He possessed maps showing its location and proposed that if Whittaker would help him he would travel to Pryor to reveal the mine.

Whittaker was willing for the Ohioan to show him the mine, told friends about the stranger's

Dayne Chastain, left, and his brother, Jet, of Seminole, search the ruins of an old cabin for coins and caches. Photo by William Mahan.

wish to come to Oklahoma, and asked them to join in the search. Every man was eager, and Whittaker agreed to write to the Ohioan and ask him to come at once. But before he completed the letter, Whittaker suffered a heart attack and died soon afterward.

While going through his papers, his family failed to find the letter from Ohio. It was long hoped that the Ohioan would write again, but, probably feeling that his offer was rebuffed, he never attempted to write again.

Some years later Tulsa bought the land on which Spavinaw was situated. The town was

moved a few miles away, and the creek bed was cleared for Lake Spavinaw. Many believe that the mine was covered when the lake filled, covering the old townsite, landmarks, and ruins of the stamp mill. Yet others are just as sure that the Spavinaw Hills still hide the lost Mormon mine and its legendary riches.

The Little Caches

In 1931 a Spavinaw resident swore that he knew where three separate caches were buried and could find them if only he had some means of detecting the buried money. Eighty-year-old "Un-

The trail of Seminole County ciphers begins with twin snakes cut deeply into stone.
This series of photos by William Mahan.

cle" Johnny West, a Cherokee, had been born and reared in Spavinaw and with his wife had lived for more than fifty-two years in the house his father had built.

"It was back in Civil War times," reminisced Uncle Johnny.[15] "All our money in this country was in gold and silver then, and we Cherokees wanted to be careful of what we had. With so much fighting going on, the soldiers might come in and rob people any time, so Wooster McCoy buried $250 in gold and silver on the bluff back of his house."

McCoy later contracted pneumonia and died. No one knew exactly where his money was buried.

After the war McCoy's sister told Johnny about the money. He looked for it often with a mineral rod, but when McCoy concealed his savings, he did a thorough job of it. No doubt it is still there—just where McCoy stashed it.

Then there was old Tom Hicks, who buried six hundred dollars where the Kansas, Oklahoma & Gulf crossed Grand River near his farm. But before he could reclaim it, some Confederates learned that he was a Union sympathizer and shot him. His money still rests where Hicks planted it.

A third cache was the five hundred dollars that an old man named Perdue buried. Perdue lived behind Johnny West. He buried his money near

Another of the many snake ciphers.

The ace of spades points up the hill to the next sign.

A carved horse appears on the trail.

A Spanish boot and spur point the follower onward.

A snake's head directs the seeker along the trail.

an unusual old hickory tree. One long root of the tree that grew out of the ground pointed straight to the hidden gold. Like Hicks, Perdue was later killed by Confederates.

"I've tried to find all these treasures," said Johnny West. "It's all there. We all know it's there. But we just can't find 'em."

Seminole County's Silver Ingots

Old Indian legends say that Spanish explorers carved a secret message in the sand rocks ten miles northeast of Seminole. The strange symbols of snakes, horses, stars—even a Spanish boot and spur—greeted white settlers when they arrived in Seminole County, appearing as ancient weathered marks even then. Stretched out for more than three-quarters of a mile, the carvings appear in a crescent-shaped area. No one knows who chiseled

them, or when, nor has the cryptic message been deciphered. But less than two miles away Dayne Chastain, of Seminole, who has recorded 150 buried treasure sites in Seminole County alone, also unearthed a cache of thirty-five silver ingots, each bearing the date 1714 and a cross. Each bar weighed eight ounces and was 3 inches long, by 1¼ inches wide, and ½ inch deep. Each one assayed 40 per cent silver, the remainder being copper and other alloys. Other nearby markings carved deep in stone led Chastain to the silver bullion.

The Man Who Scoffed Only Once

Andy Moore scoffed at such things as buried treasure. He may or may not have been from Missouri, but he was a man who had to be shown. One day in the early 1890's a stranger approached

A trail seeker examines a twenty-two-foot snake, the largest carving found.

Moore and obtained his permission to search for treasure on his farm fifteen miles northeast of Pryor. Moore laughed and said, "Sure, look all you want."[16] The stranger prowled around a week or two and then one day, without a word, was gone. At first Moore believed that he had become discouraged and quit. He went on:

It was then that I happened to see a mound of upturned sod in one corner of my field. When I went to investigate, I found a hole and an overturned rock with corrosion on it where an iron kettle had sat against it. I knew then that the fellow had found his treasure and lit out. What really made me the maddest was that I had plowed over that very spot only two weeks before while sowing radishes, and never knew there was a pot of money a couple of feet below my plow.

That was the first and only lesson Andy Moore needed in hunting buried treasure. From that day there was no more persistent seeker of hidden wealth than Moore. By 1931 he had devoted forty years to the quest, and in that time, probably no other man knew more about such things than he did.

When he was asked which of the hidden caches he would like most to find, he pondered a moment, scratching his head. "Well, I'd never thought of it like that before," he said. "It's always the one you're lookin' for that seems best at the time." Moore's answer was apropos, for it was not so much the gold itself that he wanted as it was finding the gold.

Another snake appears on the side of a stone.

Moore looked for all the treasures. He said:

Not long ago I was hunting the money Belle Starr's niece told me was buried in the hollow north of Spring Creek on the Grand River. I would sure like to have found that money. I don't know what the amount was, but they say it took sixteen trips up the mountain with the best horses they had to carry it. I'm told Belle's gang had robbed a large payroll shipment.

When I went to look for the booty, there were plenty of markings around and it didn't look like the money would be hard to locate. There are horse shoes cut on the rock, and Belle Starr's name, and the figures 7 and 11, as well as a woman's hand. A finger points right to the ground. I worked hard on that deposit. The money, so I was told, was buried thirty-six feet deep under a large rock. I went down twenty-six feet and struck water. That finished the hunt for us.

Then there was Meadows and his gang, who staged a robbery at Pryor Creek that netted them $135,000 in gold and silver coins. Old man Meadows himself told me years ago that they had buried the money near the water tank at Pryor in the days when there wasn't much more there than the water tank. The last member of the Meadows gang died three years ago, and the old man himself served eighteen years in the penitentiary at Lansing, Michigan, his confederates having all turned state's evidence against him.

I've looked for that money, too, and so did Meadows. But it has sunk. And there's no telling how deep. People hunt for it every once in a while, but there's a lot of earth around the Pryor water tank, and the chances of anyone's ever finding the bit of earth that cuddles the $135,000 is mighty slim.

Everyone knew about Andy Moore's interests, and everyone tried to help. Whenever a friend or neighbor came to Andy with a story, he would pack his truck with provisions and equipment and

In this carving the snake's head crosses the body. The rattles lead in a new direction.

be off to the diggings. If he ever passed up a potential site, it was not because of lack of interest.

Moore once heard about a highwayman who robbed and killed a Texas cattleman just after he had sold his holdings and was traveling east with his family. The robbery occurred halfway between the Mayes County line and Claremore. Soon the bandit found that the money was too heavy to carry very far on his saddle, and to spend it at any town nearby would arouse suspicion.

While the rancher's wife raced to the nearest settlement for help, the outlaw carried the money down to the creek bank where the trail turned and buried it. Although he was never caught, he later died in a gunfight. He attempted to tell a friend where to find the money, but his directions did the friend no good. Moore said that he had been no more successful, but he was sure that the money had never been found.

In 1894, Moore recalled, he witnessed a robbery by an Oklahoma desperado:

I was at Saline courthouse the day the Strip payments were being made to the Cherokees by the government, when Henry Starr came riding into town at the head of his gang and robbed a jewelry salesman of his entire stock of diamonds, watches, and rings valued at $100,000.

Then he took the loot, or so I have been told, a mile west of Rose in Mayes County and cached it on a farm now owned by a man who knows the jewelry is somewhere on his land, but can't locate it. And he won't let anyone else try either. I guess it's pretty aggravating knowing you have $100,000 worth of diamond stickpins in your backyard, only you can't find 'em.

Once Moore hunted Spanish gold secreted in the crevices of Bald Mountain only six miles from his farm. Somewhere on the hill's rugged side are two underground rock vaults, Moore believed, each chamber holding 320 gold bars. A tall, lone

The horse's head misguides the follower. The broken lead rope points in the next direction.

tree grew beside each vault, but to this day no one has found the 640 bars of pure gold. But Moore was not giving up hope.

Another Spanish cache he sought had been placed in a cave on the side of a bluff near Morgan's Inn on Grand River. Moore and his partners found a bluff that fitted the description. It was almost perpendicular and towered high above the river. On the side of the cliff they found three caves, but getting to them proved to be a problem.

It required three weeks to rig up the necessary pulleys to lower platforms to each opening. Andy's mineral rod indicated that something big was in one of the caves, but their efforts were fruitless.

Andy Moore's stories and adventures remain a part of Oklahoma's hill-country lore. So far as anyone knew, he never found the pot of gold that he had once come so close to, only inches deeper than his radish plants, but he never stopped trying—or believing.

The Indian points in the correct direction.

The bottom tip of the star leads to the next marker.

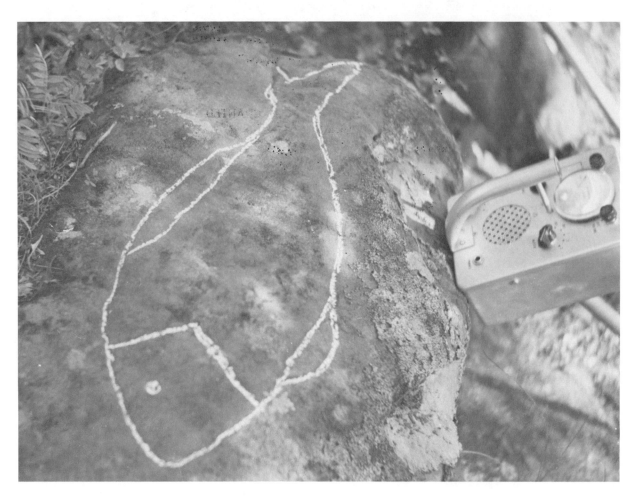

A carved fish appears on the trail.

Devil's Promenade in 1890. Courtesy Western History Collections, University of Oklahoma Library.

The German's Cache

In 1867 the Piankashaw Indians moved from their lands in Kansas to Indian Territory. They settled on Spring River, a few miles northeast of what is now Miami. Not long after they moved to the region, an old German shoemaker squatted nearby. It was common knowledge that the man was a miser, hoarding every bit of wealth he could put his hands on. It was also believed by some that he had come from a wealthy family in the old country.

The old man constantly worried that someone would steal his gold, though he kept it safely tucked away in a large tin box that turned black over the years. The Reconstruction period was a dangerous time in the Nations, and the shoemaker began to worry more and more about his gold. He once told an Indian friend that he could not sleep at night for fear his treasure would be stolen from his cabin. He had visions of ruthless men killing him in the night. Finally he decided to bury his money away from his cabin.

In a high sandstone bluff known as Devil's Promenade, where Rock Creek empties into Spring River, the old shoemaker planted his gold. In the dead of night, with his tin box clutched in his arms, the shoemaker clambered up the bluff to a narrow cave in the side. He disappeared into the crevice for a few moments and then returned to his cabin empty-handed.

The next day he told his Piankashaw friends that he had concealed his money and that for the first time in many nights had slept like a baby. Several months passed, and his Indian neighbors noticed that the old German seemed to be growing tired and weary. One day they looked in on him and found him dying.

He summoned one of his Indian friends to his side and whispered in a weak voice where he had hidden his gold. Inside the great bluff, he muttered, was a hollow room. On a shelf along the wall he had concealed his tin box. The German asked the Indian to find the money and use it for his tribe. Soon the old shoemaker was dead. The Indians buried him near his cabin.

The Piankashaws later searched for the German's tin box of gold, but either they found the wrong cave or their friend had hidden it so well that not even they could find it. The old German's gold became a legend among the Piankashaws. The tin box must still be there, somewhere in Devil's Promenade.[17]

The Lost Payroll

In Pawnee County, just west of Jennings, rise two knolls known as the Twin Hills. Once a patrol of soldiers escorting a government paymaster to Fort Sill made night camp between the two hills. Indians had been raiding the country for some time, and if the soldiers were attacked, they did not want to be caught on the open prairie.

In the late afternoon, just as the soldiers began to settle down, Indians encircled their camp, sending the soldiers scurrying behind cover. When they tried to send out a messenger to bring help, he had no more than saddled his horse when he was picked off by an arrow. The soldiers knew that their only chance was to bury the payroll and try to break through the Indians.

The paymaster concealed eleven thousand dollars in gold and the troopers made a dash for freedom, but only a few broke through the encirclement. When they returned with help, the Indians had long scattered. The paymaster, the only one who had known where the gold was buried, lay among the dead. The soldiers made a thorough search, but the paymaster had concealed the money well. Finally the search was called off. It is believed that the payroll still lies where the army paymaster planted it.[18]

Captain Goldie's Lost Gold

In 1862 one Captain Goldie led a wagon train of settlers into Indian Territory from the gold fields of California. The safety of the caravan was not challenged until the wagons approached the Osage Hills, near present Pawhuska. There a band of Pawnees charged down from the hills.

The men quickly drove the wagons into a circle and prepared to fight. Several of the settlers had hit it rich in California, and, all told, the train was carrying about one hundred thousand dollars in gold. The Indians far outnumbered Goldie's men, and the captain realized that there was no way for the families to escape.

The wagon master rounded up all the gold,

packed it on horses, and told the owners that he was taking it to the edge of the timber to bury for safekeeping. Everyone agreed that it was the best thing to do. But Goldie in fact had different intentions for the money. He succeeded in his escape with the gold, watching from a nearby hill as a final sally was launched against the helpless wagon train.

It was later learned that the Indians had known about the gold on the wagons and had trailed the caravan from Wichita, Kansas, into the Osage Nation. One scout who had seen the gold was offended when the "white captain with the big nose" would not trade some of the coins for a pair of ponies. The Pawnees searched each wagon but found no gold. Then they turned their wrath on the scout and threatened to burn him at the stake unless he could produce it.

The scout carefully searched each wagon, but he was no more successful. Then he remembered the captain with the big nose. A search was made of the dead. The captain had disappeared. Early the next morning the Indians began tracking Goldie. As dusk neared, they saw the lone survivor in the distance. Goldie realized that he was being followed and was forced to bury the gold so that he could travel faster.

By then he had reached a dense forest near the Caney River. He chose two large trees growing from the same trunk, and between them and Artillery Mound to the north, Goldie concealed the gold. As an added marker he placed a musket in a hollow tree between the old California Trail and the banks of the Caney River. Then he turned his horses loose, hoping that the Indians would follow them. By the time the Indians had detected Goldie's ruse, the animals had led them far astray.

Captain Goldie reached his home in Missouri. Not long afterward Goldie became seriously ill. He confided in his wife what he had done and drew her a map showing where he had hidden the wagon train's gold. A few weeks later Goldie died.

Goldie's wife knew of no one whom she could trust with the map, and her only child, a boy six years old, was too young to make the journey with her for the gold. She decided to wait until they could make the trip together. That wait was to last for twenty years.

In 1882 young Goldie appeared at the farm of Joe Boulanger, an Osage Indian who lived near the Caney River. Young Goldie had no trouble finding Artillery Mound, but south of it was no dense forest as his father had said. The land was now cleared and planted in grain.

Young Goldie asked Boulanger about the forest and learned that Boulanger himself had cleared the land. When Goldie asked about the two large trees that grew from the same trunk and an old musket placed in another, Boulanger remembered he had found such a musket and believed that he could walk within fifty feet of where the trees had grown.

Goldie then revealed his story and asked the Indian's permission to dig for the gold. Boulanger consented and gave him what directions he could. Goldie probed and dug for days, but each hole yielded nothing. When finally he decided it was no use, he left Boulanger a copy of the map his father had made and asked that if the gold was ever found to see that a portion of it was sent to his mother. Boulanger agreed to do so.

The farmer never attempted to dig further for the gold, since young Goldie had checked all possible sites in his search. But apparently Goldie later told someone else about the treasure, for one morning in 1901 the landowner found a deep hole in the center of his cornfield. Busy with chores, he did not bother to fill the hole that day.

The following morning he went to the field to cover the hole and found that it had been dug still deeper during the night. Boulanger decided to stay awake that night to catch the intruder, but no one appeared. But the following night, when Boulanger was not expecting his visitor to return, someone again deepened the hole and dug still others nearby.

Finally Boulanger reported the occurrences to the Indian agent. Several Indian police were sent to guard the field, but no one appeared.

Goldie's family long ago gave up the search. But if the captain's memory was accurate, one hundred thousand dollars in gold lies near the banks of the Caney River, somewhere just south of Artillery Mound.[19]

Billy Stinnett's Cache

Three miles south of Tahlequah lies Park Hill.

In the extreme southeast corner of the old town stands a lone and ghostly sentinel, a blackened chimney of brown sandstone. When it was built, and by whom, no one seems to know. But many believe that treasure lies hidden within sight of the ancient smokestack.

The hillfolk will tell you that the hidden money was once part of the great fortune of "Uncle" Billy Stinnett, who settled there in 1828 and established a trading post near the Illinois River. On the hillside just across a small stream from the chimney lies the grassed-over grave of Billy Stinnett. When the old trader died, it was well known that he had saved a large amount of gold, for the trading post had always done a good business, and Stinnett and his wife lived meagerly.

Although advanced in years and crippled by rheumatism, Mrs. Stinnett kept the post going. One day a young fortune hunter introduced himself. He continued the friendly visits, and one day he asked Mrs. Stinnett to marry him. She accepted, and soon they were wed. But her happiness was short-lived. Several months later she died, and the young husband disappeared.

As far as anyone knew, Mrs. Stinnett died a natural death. But the Park Hill residents were sure that neither she nor her second husband had found Uncle Billy's gold. Somewhere near the old Stinnett place and within sight of the vine-covered stone chimney lies the hidden treasure, the hillfolk say. In later years a mysterious light was seen on winter nights just west of the stone chimney. Whoever was seeking Billy Stinnett's gold chose the darkest of nights to make his search.[20]

"Grandpap" Melton's Find

Another story involves the old stone chimney at Park Hill. In 1844 an oldster known as "Grandpap" Melton lived nearby the ruin. One October afternoon he took his dog for a stroll through the neighboring woods. Some distance away Melton's dog spied a rabbit and chased it into a cove in the side of a bluff.

Melton followed and entered the small cave, poking and feeling his way with his cane. He could see that the cave led back into the mountainside for a considerable distance, but he had no light to investigate. While poking his cane into the rocks, he found an obstruction and raked it out. It

was neither the rabbit nor an ordinary rock, but a chunk of almost pure silver the size of a coconut.

In 1844 the laws forbade gold or silver prospecting in the Nations, but in later years old pioneers remembered Melton's discovery. But by then Grandpap Melton was no longer around to tell where he had made his strange find.[21]

Buffalo Head's Gold

It must have been in 1828 or shortly afterward that bushy-haired William Y. Williams built his cabin a mile north of Park Hill and set up his blacksmith shop. It was said that he had once served as a gallant soldier, although Williams never boasted of his past. One thing of which he was proud he did not try to hide—the most abundant and curly head of hair in the region. Because of that abundance he was given the sobriquet "Buffalo Head" Williams.

Buffalo Head was a skilled artisan and once was employed by the government to forge works of art for the Indians. Not only was he a successful blacksmith, but he was a good farmer and fruit grower and believed in saving his hard-earned dollars.

One day about the time of the outbreak of the Civil War, Buffalo Head rose early in the morning to fire his forge. He kept it hot most of the day and with bellows and hammer made a large steel chest. Into the box he placed his savings. Like many of his contemporaries, he wanted to be sure that he still had his gold after the war's end.

Williams buried his money chest somewhere on his property, away from the house. Wherever he secreted it, he was confident that it would not be found by freebooters. But the old soldier did not live to see the end of the war or to spend his well-hidden earnings—buried so carefully in the large steel chest.[22]

Robin Bobb's Cache

Near the entrance to Baumgarner Hollow, a few miles east of Tahlequah, once lived old Jim Bobb and his son, Robin. Bobb had gone to California in the 1850's and had left the gold fields one of the lucky ones. When he returned to the Cherokee Nation, he brought back a pack mule laden with gold coins that he had traded for dust and nuggets.

Jim Bobb and his son were men of simple tastes. They had a good herd of cattle and farmed a large acreage, which brought in more than enough for their needs. When Jim Bobb died, his son inherited his property—and the gold coins.

To the already large pile of coins Robin Bobb added still more as he profited from the land. By 1861 the treasure had grown until it was no longer safe to keep it in the house. Robin transplanted the coins into a large iron cooking pot and put it into a heavy bag. He mounted his horse, Old Fizzle, and rode off into the hills about ten miles east of Tahlequah across the Illinois River. He disappeared for some time. When he returned home, Old Fizzle was wet to the shoulders.

Several hillfolk saw Robin return from his hunting trip. To conceal his purpose, he had taken along his double-barreled shotgun, and he brought back a wild turkey. There was no need for Robin to call upon his gold. He had plenty with all his cattle and land, and, too, the war had just begun. The gold was best kept buried.

Sometime later Robin Bobb suddenly fell ill and died without revealing where the gold was hidden. Time and again his family searched without success for the large cooking pot. His gold lies buried somewhere east of the Illinois.[23]

Chimney Rock's Lost Treasure

In the wooded hills near the Illinois River about five miles southeast of Tahlequah a natural stone formation known as Chimney Rock rises sixty feet from the base of a limestone bluff. Hidden near the Rock was enough gold to require two large pack animals to carry it, say old settlers familiar with the story.

It seems that six drifters raided a settlement in Louisiana and fled northwest into the Cherokee Nation. A band of determined townsmen pursued them hell-bent on retrieving the stolen goods. Day and night the Louisianans followed the robbers' trail.

Finally, between Wauhillau and the Illinois River, the pursuers came within shooting range and triggered off several shots. Two robbers dropped from their horses, while the remaining four spurred their animals still faster. From their tracks the Louisianans could tell that they had forded the Illinois at the mouth of the Barren Fork River, about two miles southeast of Chimney Rock. Again the pursuers came within range of their quarry, and a third tumbled mortally wounded from his mount.

The remaining three headed their horses into dense timber, and somewhere near Chimney Rock stashed their heavy cargo into crevices, and dashed away. Eventually all three were caught and slain between Tahlequah and Fourteen Mile Creek. The Louisianans were convinced that the gold had been hidden somewhere near the bluff that supported the natural stone chimney, but all their searching failed to yield a single piece of booty.

"Great Scot, man, I can't tell you what it's all worth," said one old fellow who had hunted for it over the years.[24] "If its weight was too much for two big horses to pack, you oughter be able to sort of calc'late what it'd all come to in dollars!"

Fort Gibson after restoration. Photo by Fred W. Marvel.

Belle Starr and Blue Duck. The lost treasure of the female desperado is still sought in the hills of eastern Oklahoma. Courtesy Glenn Shirley.

16. Gold the Outlaws Never Spent

One dark night in September, 1932, H. Kohlmeyer, a farmer who lived near Barnsdall, in Osage County, was awakened by the loud barking of his dogs. Wiping the sleep from his eyes, he peered out his window to see a light flashing in the distance. It was not an ordinary light; it seemed to be bobbing up and down and at times completely disappeared.

It was not the first time that sort of thing had happened. In fact it had been occurring for the past few nights—at all hours. If Kohlmeyer was right again, he would find another deep hole in his pasture the next morning. But this time he was determined to catch the culprits.

Kohlmeyer called his farmhand to get his gun and hold the men while he called the police. The hired hand found six men armed with shovels. As he approached, all but one scattered. The laborer held him at gunpoint. He confessed the names of the others, and later that evening they were arrested. Two of them had pistols and were charged with carrying concealed weapons. Each man was fined twenty-five dollars.

The men said that they had been digging for outlaw gold amounting to eighty thousand dollars long believed to be buried on the Kohlmeyer farm. For more than a year different parties had hunted the booty, but only one group had obtained permission from Kohlmeyer and offered him a five-thousand-dollar share. Since that time other parties had come in without obtaining permission. Kohlmeyer announced that he had no objections to the digging but that the next party had better get his permission and dig when his sleep would not be interrupted. His request was a reasonable one.[1]

Cole Younger's Treasure

Tales of the James, Younger, and Dalton gangs predominate in the hills of Oklahoma, especially in the rugged terrain around Sand Springs and Pryor, in the northeastern part of what was once Indian Territory. More than once hidden caches have been unearthed in these areas, and there are those who believe that more booty will be found in the future—more like the $37,200 found near Oglesby in 1913.

Robber's Canyon lies five miles west of Pryor. It was here that the James-Younger gang supposedly buried $110,000 in gold. Cole Younger verified the story in later years, say old settlers who knew him personally. In his autobiography, *The Story of Cole Younger*, the old outlaw gave no hint about hidden loot. But old residents of Pryor say that Cole revisited Robber's Canyon about 1910 to recover the long hidden plunder. But ill luck still haunted the old desperado.

Cole told several Pryor friends that in the 1870's the gang made several daring raids in southern Kansas and Indian Territory, collecting more than $110,000. They often holed up in Robber's Canyon because of its superb vantage. They dug a deep pit, placed the gold specie in a large iron cooking pot, and lowered it to the bottom of the hole. When their horses had trampled the earth, Jesse James—who usually marked the burial sites—took a heavy pocketknife and carved a rattlesnake around a nearby stone. Jesse fashioned the snake so that it coiled around the rock, its head pointing up the canyon. When they returned for the loot, the sign would be all they would need.

The money would wait for a rainy day—but that day never came. Cole Younger and his brothers rode north to Minnesota. A bank robbery got them twenty-five years in prison. A few years later Jesse met his end. Frank James knew about the gold, but whether he ever attempted to retrieve it no one knew (apparently he spent his time seeking two million dollars in gold bullion down in the Wichita Mountains).

One account has it that Cole had tried much earlier to retrieve the treasure shortly after he was released from prison, but the Oklahoma territorial governor made it clear that he did not want him back in the territory. Whether Cole made a try for the loot when he returned to Oklahoma in 1903 is not known, but in 1910 he made a final attempt at the Robber's Canyon gold.

But by then the country had changed far too much, even for his keen memory. In the 1870's Pryor was not much more than a section house. By 1910 much of Robber's Canyon was fenced, and part of it plowed. But Cole believed that if he could only find the carved rattlesnake luck would turn in his favor. After much hunting—and raising the ire of farmers—he found the snake, badly weathered on the sandstone rock. But it did him no good, though he knew that the buried kettle was near. At least, that is what Cole told his friends in Pryor.[2]

H. W. Kiskaddon, of Tulsa, was sure that the Robber's Canyon treasure was not the only cache Younger failed to retrieve. Although Cole said nothing about it to Oklahomans, he spoke about it to his family in Missouri. A close friend of the family told Kiskaddon the story of the sixty-three thousand dollars that Cole talked about until his dying day.

He had buried the money, Cole said, on the south side of the Arkansas River only a mile downstream from the Sand Springs bridge. When he tried to find it again, the gold had sunk deep in its mucky grave. It would take more than Cole had to retrieve it, which was only a shovel. The old outlaw dared not arouse the citizens by bringing in draft animals to remove the earth, because if he found the money it would be confiscated. It was blood money, and as far as Cole was concerned, it would have to stay there.

Kiskaddon learned all this one evening about 1930, when he was returning home from the oil fields near Claremore.[3] He came upon an old man walking along the road. Kiskaddon recalled the meeting:

He was a giant of a fellow, distinguished in appearance and very courtly in his bearing. Because of his evident refinement, I picked him up and brought him on into Tulsa. On the way into town he told me something of his story. He was eighty-nine years old and his name was O. S. Kelly. He was a brother, he said, of the Kelly tire people of Springfield, Illinois, but he had not seen any of his family for years.

During the Civil War his brothers had fought with the North while he had elected to join the Confederacy. At the close of the struggle he went back to Illinois to find that his family had disowned him. Heartbroken, he started west, and in Missouri near what is now Aurora he traded for 160 acres of woodland. He cleared the

Old-timers of Pryor tell about Cole Younger's return in 1910, when he sought hidden outlaw treasure nearby. Here he appears not long before his death in 1916. Courtesy Western History Collections, University of Oklahoma Library.

land, put in an apple orchard, and lived until the day he started on the trip on which I met him. The thing about Kelly that made people listen with respect to what he had to say was that he was so obviously a man of education and talents. He had been educated in the universities of Germany and his speech and bearing corroborated him.

Kiskaddon said that the four Younger brothers frequently stayed at Kelly's farm and that Cole Younger told him the story of the sixty-three thousand dollars on the Arkansas River and then laughed and said just try to find it. Anyone who dared he wished him luck.

Cole's story was that the gang had held up an express coach conveying the gold and silver northward. They were headed toward Missouri when a

Emmett Dalton, center, was the sole survivor of the Coffeyville fiasco of 1892. Many Sand Springs residents are confident that he retrieved the gang's treasure soon after he was released from prison in 1906. Here Dalton talks with the author Will James, left, and George T. Cole. Courtesy Western History Collections, University of Oklahoma Library.

posse began to catch up with them and they were forced to ditch the loot. The Arkansas River was the final obstacle. At the south bank they jumped from their horses and with some makeshift tools dug a hole for the bags of coins clinging to their horses. Once the hole was filled, they mounted their horses, trampled the fresh sod, and spurred their animals across the river.

Cole Younger told Kelly that he had never retrieved the money and then laughed and added that he was just as sure that no one else had either.

W. H. Reynolds once recalled that Cole spoke in Atoka in August, 1913, on the subject "Crime Doesn't Pay." In his talk Cole mentioned Cat Creek Cave fifteen miles northeast of Stringtown in Atoka County where he and the Jameses had often hidden out. Cole made no mention of hidden booty. But someone had secreted loot there

because Arthur Goad found seven hundred dollars stuffed into the wall behind a large rock.[4]

The Dalton Treasure Map

Emmett Dalton in his book *When The Daltons Rode* did not mention his buried loot. But it has been said that when he appeared in Lawton in 1907 after his release from prison he offered ten thousand dollars to anyone who could show him a certain cave. Many looked for the cave in the Keechi Hills, where Dalton had reputedly stashed seventy-five thousand dollars.[5] It is also believed that Dalton buried some of his loot near Sand Springs. Many area settlers were certain that he recovered some of it after his days of sin were repaid.

Both Grat and Bob Dalton served as deputy United States marshals under "Hanging" Judge Isaac Parker at Fort Smith before launching their outlaw careers. Emmett served as a posseman under his two brothers. Finding it more profitable to be without the law than within, they resorted to horse stealing and fled to California to escape the clutches of Judge Parker.

Later they returned to Indian Territory and for more than a year terrorized banks and trains. Bandits Dick Broadwell and Bill Powers joined their ranks, and together the five pulled successful train robberies at Wharton, Lillietta, Red Rock, and Adair. Rewards amounting to six thousand dollars were placed on their heads. But lawmen failed to find their hideouts—the caves along the Canadian River in the Creek Nation.[6]

The gang's doom came shortly after nine o'clock on the morning of October 5, 1892, when they rode into Coffeyville, Kansas. They planned to rob two banks at once, a feat beyond those of even the Jameses or the Youngers.

From the First National Bank they made off with eleven thousand dollars and from the Condon Bank, another twenty thousand dollars. But they were not to keep it long. A barrage of gunfire cut them down in a battle that lasted only ten minutes. When the smoke had cleared from what witnesses declared were two hundred shots, four bandits and four citizens lay dead in the street. Emmett Dalton, the only survivor, was severely wounded. He was sentenced to life imprisonment

Tim Evens Bob Dalton Grat Dalton Dick Broadwel

Copyrighea by Tackett

The Daltons of the Coffeyville raid 1892.

The Dalton gang met their doom trying to rob two banks at once in Coffeyville, Kansas, on October 3, 1892. Stretched out, left to right, are Bill Powers (mistakenly identified in the photograph as Tim Evans), Bob Dalton, Grat Dalton, and Dick Broadwell. Their deaths ended a long string of bank and train robberies in Oklahoma and Indian territories. Courtesy Glenn Shirley.

in the Kansas State Penitentiary. After serving fourteen years, he gained a pardon, later wrote his memoirs, and died in California in 1937.[7]

"Outlaw treasure is haunted money," Emmett Dalton is reported to have once said after his release from prison.[8] "It lies best where it is, like a shroud for outlaws gone."

But Emmett did not practice what he preached, say old-timers in Sand Springs. Three days after his release from prison he was back at his old hideout, and curious neighbors believed that one of three fresh-dug holes indicated that a round brass kettle might recently have been removed, not far from the caves in the rocky cliffs above Shell Creek. The Dalton gang had often used an old cabin near Sand Springs to hold their secret

meetings and plan their forays. The cabin stood three miles east of the Dalton caves and a mile from the thicket of black-walnut and oak trees where the holes were found.

It had long been rumored that the massive fireplace in the cabin guarded a treasure map, placed there by the outlaws before their departure for Coffeyville. When they found the three holes, the discoverers hurried to the cabin. In the blackened hearth lay a stone that had only recently been removed from the mantel. The treasure map might have been folded and stuffed into the crack behind the stone and retrieved by Dalton.

Years later the cabin was torn down, and today the Sand Springs Home, a haven for orphans and widows, stands on the site. When the Daltons

Nestled in the wooded timber of Younger's Bend on the Canadian River near present Briartown, this cabin was said to have been Belle Starr's home in 1888. Courtesy Glenn Shirley.

roamed the countryside, harboring in caves of the area, Jack Wimberley owned the farm on which they buried their money. Wimberley's wife often cooked for the bandits, and after her meals Jack and the boys would sit around the crackling fire and spin yarns about the days when they had been on the other side of the law as United States marshals. Wimberley never forgot them.

"Uncle" Ed Page often recalled Jack Wimberley and his tales of the Daltons. Page, too, had seen the three holes in the walnut thicket and the hollow in the fireplace mantel from which he was sure Emmett had retrieved the treasure map. On his daily trips over his land Page passed the caves above Shell Creek where the Daltons had often sought refuge. He also passed the old farmhouse and chimney that guarded the aging treasure map. Page recalled in 1931:

We all knew the Daltons had buried some money hereabouts, for Jack Wimberley told us of conversations he had overheard among the boys.

"They used to come to my place," Jack would say, "and my wife and I would feed them, and then they'd sit around and talk and laugh. They used to tell about holdups and bank raids and the like, and laugh about how one fellow acted and another fellow acted. They were always fine and polite, just the nicest gentlemen I ever knew. And their saddle horses were the best I ever saw."

We'd ask him, "Well, Jack, why didn't you turn them in and collect a big reward?"

"Why should I report them?" he'd ask, "I never knew nothing. I'd just hear them talk. How'd I know whether they really did all those things, or were just joking?"

It was Jack who told us that one time he heard the Dalton boys refer to a map or plat that gave the directions to some money they had buried somewhere

near their cave over on Shell Creek. After all the boys had been killed at Coffeyville, all except Emmett, and he had been sentenced to life in prison, the men around here tried to locate the treasure. They searched all through the farmhouse for the map, but couldn't find it. They had a hunch, however, that the money was somewhere near the very thicket it later proved to be, and they dug all around that region, but had no luck.

Then came the news that Emmett had been released. Three days later one of the men who lived near here found the three holes, each dug at the foot of a giant oak tree. At the base of the largest tree was the round

Belle Starr, gunned down by an unknown assassin in 1889, lies buried in the front yard of what was once her home near Briartown on the Canadian River. Courtesy Glenn Shirley.

Robbers Cave, north of Wilburton in Latimer County, was named for its unsavory occupants, who chose the lair because of its superb vantage point over the woodlands. Treasure has been both found and lost in the surrounding hill country. Robbers Cave is now a state park. Photograph by Fred W. Marvel, Oklahoma Tourism and Recreation Department.

impression where a large kettle had sat. In great excitement the fellows spread the news. Some of the boys went up to the farmhouse of Jack's. There they found a stone had been removed from the mantel.

The fireplace was a huge affair, eight feet wide and capable of burning four-foot logs. It was evident the map had been lodged behind the stone in the mantel. It was obvious to us all that Emmett had headed straight down here from Lansing, gone to the house, secured the map, and followed its directions to the black walnut thicket. In the third hole he dug, he found the kettle. Then he left the country and the treasure went with him.[9]

No one knows just how much Emmett recovered. But many think it was no less than seventeen thousand dollars, which the gang had netted from a train robbery at Adair. Whether or not Dalton recovered all of the outlaw loot is anybody's surmise. Emmett, of course, was not telling. But one thing old-timers remember that he did tell concerned his two partners, Bill Powers and Dick Broadwell.

Emmett said that they had buried part of their take from train robberies at Red Rock and Lillietta on the South Canadian River, about sixty miles southwest of Kingfisher. They consisted of several heavy sacks of silver. But they never got to spend it. Emmett did not know just where it was stashed, but he knew that his partners never touched it after it was buried.

284

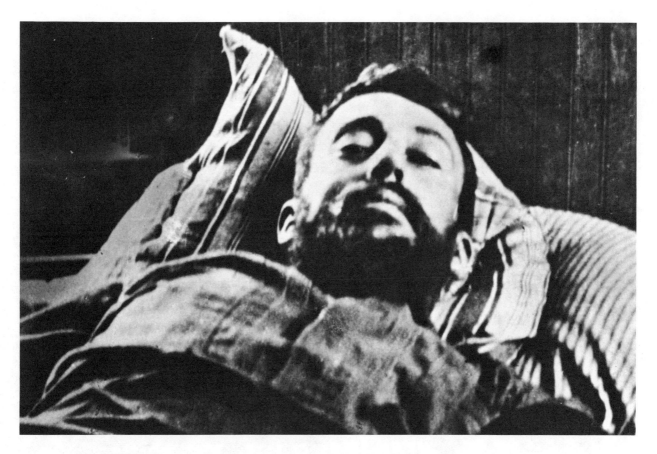

Oklahoma outlaw Zip Wyatt, alias Dick Yeager, was gunned down by a posse in August, 1895. Before he died, he spoke of hidden treasure in the Glass Mountains, where a bandit cave was found in 1903. Courtesy Western History Collections, University of Oklahoma Library.

Robber's Cave

Just north of Wilburton in Latimer County lies Robber's Cave State Park, named for the bandits and desperadoes who found it an excellent hiding place in territorial days.

Near Robber's Cave huge boulders form a labyrinth of long, narrow tunnels. The list of notables who spent time there is long, and in one secret chamber the notorious Belle Starr is credited with hiding part of her plunder. One story has it that "Fiddlin' Jim," one of Belle's lovers, was killed here by a jealous admirer.[10]

Zip Wyatt's Gold

One brisk January day in 1903 a spelunker picked a curious cave to explore in the Glass Mountains of Major County. It was like any other cave in those gyp hills—not spectacular, but large enough to have accommodated a gang of outlaws who holed up here before the turn of the century.

Old-timers remembered that just after Zip Wyatt, alias Dick Yeager, was gunned down by a posse on August 4, 1895, he spoke of hidden money in the hills but failed to tell where it was concealed. The cave found by the spelunker might well have been that undisclosed site of hidden treasure, for while he was exploring the cavern, he happened across a number of moldy greenbacks under a large rock.

The stone was much too heavy to lift, and in trying to free the money, he tore off part of a twenty-dollar bill. He refused to show others the entrance to the cavern, saying only that he had found it near the head of Barney Creek, the very area where the infamous Wyatt and his band were known to have hidden.[11] Perhaps the cave still contains some of Zip Wyatt's plunder—some of it, no doubt, metallic.

Near the confluence of the Grand, Verdigris, and Arkansas rivers, Colonel Matthew Arbuckle established Fort Gibson in 1824 to protect the Five Civilized Tribes from the Plains Indians on the west. Many early writers and artists began their travels westward from this "last outpost of civilization." Here the fort appears partly restored. Photograph by Fred W. Marvel, Oklahoma Tourism and Recreation Department.

17. Lost Indian Treasure

Chief Blackface's Plunder

Early in the 1830's a renegade of Seminole and Negro parentage known as Chief Blackface made his reputation by plundering and terrorizing caravans of homeseekers, Mexican packtrains, traders, and anyone else he and his cutthroats could find to prey on.

Blackface was known to hole up in the pine-timbered hills of both the Cherokee and the Choctaw nations. On one occasion he received word of a party of Mexican traders trailing one hundred gold-laden mules through the Nations bound for St. Louis. Blackface and his men waited patiently for the right moment to strike. When it came, they swooped down on the muleteers. As Chief Blackface had promised, not a trader survived—as far as he knew. He and his crew rounded up the mules and led them to a secret cavern, where the gold was unloaded and then concealed by a select trusted few.

Chief Blackface continued his depredations until finally the day came that he, too, died at the hands of his own kind. Many of his followers were also killed, and the few who survived dispersed throughout the territory.[1]

Indians who knew Blackface were convinced that none of his plunder was removed from the hidden cavern, but the story is well known that one old Cherokee may have stumbled onto part of the treasure in the hills not far from Tahlequah. The Cherokee, who boarded at a local tavern, confided in its owner that he was seeking a treasure his family had told about for generations. After several weeks' lodging the Cherokee had expended his meager funds. He convinced his host that if he could find it, half of the treasure would be his. If he was unsuccessful, nothing would be lost but a few days' lodging and what little food he ate. After thinking it over, the tavern keeper agreed to allow the Indian to stay on for one month. The Cherokee left early each morning just after the sun rose and returned late in the evening. The days passed. Where he searched only the Indian knew.

Late one evening, when he had but a few days remaining, the Indian rushed into the house, waving his host to one side. Sitting down at a corner table, he paused, gasping for breath. It was obvious that he had hurried back. He reported that he had found what his elders had so often spoken about. He would take the innkeeper to the site the following day.

Before leaving the next morning, the Cherokee blindfolded his host and walked him in a large circle. When they left, the innkeeper had no idea in which direction he was being led. About noon they approached the entrance to a cave. The Indian removed a stone from the opening, and the two crawled inside where they could stand up. Carrying a torch and while leading his companion, the Cherokee passed through several underground chambers and then halted, removing the blindfold.

When the Indian held the torch high above his head, the men counted six large receptacles resembling jars or churns. Each was filled with bars of gold—gold enough to load down several animals. Overtaken by the sight of so much treasure, the innkeeper wanted to organize a group of men to remove the gold immediately. He was sure that he knew just the men he could trust. But the Indian refused, saying that something must be done before they could remove the treasure.

The Indian asked for a few more days, muttering something about the old ways. Then, he said, they would be free to take the gold. The innkeeper reluctantly consented, believing that a few more days would make no difference. The Indian again blindfolded the innkeeper and escorted him out of the cavern, stopped long enough to seal the entrance with a few stones, and then led the way through heavy timber—apparently over a different route from the one by which they had come. At the edge of the timber he removed the blindfold, and they continued the short distance to the Tahlequah boarding house, where they arrived late that evening.

When the innkeeper checked on the Cherokee the next morning, the Indian could not be found. Shortly afterward he heard that his boarder had gone into town and knifed a man. The Indian police were searching for him. No one could find the old Cherokee. He had disappeared from the hill country as quickly as he had appeared. No one remembered the name he had used—or perhaps he had not given a name. But his wizened face left a firm imprint in the mind of the Tahlequah innkeeper, and he could never put out of his mind the sight of the gold-stuffed jugs gleaming in the light of the torch.

In February, 1936, the *Tulsa Daily World* reported that certain Tahlequah citizens were making one last attempt to find the old Cherokee.[2] Even today many are convinced that some hidden cavern in the brush-choked hills of the old Cherokee Nation holds the Indian's secret, revealed just long enough for a glimpse of six massive churns filled with gold.

Phillip Usray's Lost Gold

The Civil War in the Indian Nations was as tragic if not as devastating as it was in the South. The Indians were left defenseless when the Union pulled out its troops, leaving the land to be overrun by outlaws and renegades.

At the onset of the war Phillip Usray lived at Sallisaw, in the timbered hills of present Sequoyah County.[3] He was neutral in the conflict and did not want to involve himself with either side. But he had horses and mules that Union forces needed badly, and since they could pay in gold, Usray sold them his stock.

When Usray returned home after the transaction, his young grandson, George, watched him place the gold, along with a fine gold watch and his wife's jewelry, in a tin box, wrap it in a sheepskin rug, and then go to the barn for a shovel. Usray told his grandson that he was hiding the money where it would always be safe. He and the boy walked to the old spring near the house, and he instructed his grandson to wait for him there until he returned. Usray disappeared into the hills and after some time came back without the rug and its contents.

After they had returned home and had finished their evening meal, they heard a loud rapping.

"Open up this door!" someone shouted outside. Instinctively Usray shoved his grandson under

the puncheon floor. Again the men yelled, threatening to break the door down. Usray remained silent.

In moments the door crashed down, and in scrambled three masked men demanding his gold. Usray told them that he had worked hard for his money and was too old to start over. He would not give it away. The outlaws warned him that he would give over the gold or forfeit his life.

"Well, I have only one time to die," sighed the old man, "and if now is the time, I am ready."

The bandits meant what they had said, and, to prove it, they threw a rope around Usray's neck and dragged him outside the house to the spring.

"We'll make you talk or else," one threatened, throwing the rope over a tree limb and pulling him off the ground. Then they lowered him to the ground and asked whether he was ready to give over the gold.

He shook his head and remained silent. They threatened to pull out his toenails, but still he remained silent. And even when they executed the threat, Usray would not give in. And beating him brought no response. Finally they stabbed Usray, pulled his body into the air, and rode off.

Usray's grandson had crawled out from under the house and witnessed everything—and fainted. When he came to, he called out, but there was no response. He ran three miles to the home of his uncle, Tobe Usray. But nothing remained for anyone to do but cut the body down.

Phillip Usray meant what he had said about no one getting his gold, and he died bravely protecting that promise. To this day no one has found his gold, secreted somewhere in the hills about Sallisaw.

Homestead Banks

In the 1860's the nearest banks to the Indian Territory were at Fort Smith, Arkansas, or Sherman, Texas, but few Indians bothered to keep their money in banks. There were at least three who did not, and all lived near Wilburton.

A Choctaw Indian named Kunneotubby lived just north of Wilburton on the creek that now bears his name. The Choctaw had once sold his cattle and had afterward been robbed of the two thousand dollars he received. After that lesson,

Talimena Skyline Drive, near Talihina, in the Ouachita National Forest in southeastern Oklahoma. The region harbors tales of Spanish gold, French explorers, and Indians who secreted their treasure there. Photograph by Mike Shelton, Oklahoma Tourism and Recreation Department.

he always buried his money. He accepted only gold in payment because he could not count silver or paper.

One day Kunneotubby encountered a band of rustlers stealing his cattle, and was overpowered and murdered. His family never knew where he had hidden his money, though they were sure it was not far from the home. It was never found.

Several miles south of Wilburton lived an Indian named Riddle who owned large herds of stock. One morning Riddle called his son from the house and told him that he was burying the family's savings. Young Riddle watched as his father disappeared for a few moments into the woods with a bucket.

The crops had been poor that year, and young Riddle was sent to Texas to buy corn for the stock. During the boy's absence his father died. When young Riddle returned home, he was questioned about the savings, but could only point the direction his father had taken the bucket. A similar ill fate happened to the heirs of Dave Harkins, another nearby settler. His money still reposes where he buried it.[4]

Mrs. Lillie Hicks said that in 1838 her grandfather, Asa Guinn, traveled the Trail of Tears from Georgia and settled near Tahlequah. He buried his savings near his home. Guinn was the only one who knew where he hid it, and when he died, that knowledge went with him.[5]

Mrs. Susan Riley Gott recalled that in 1838 she and her grandfather, John N. Riley, moved from Park Hill to a farm six miles east of Fort Gibson. Shortly before the Civil War her Cherokee grandfather buried their prized possessions, much of it silverware, near the homestead. He, too, died without disclosing its location.[6]

The Lost Cherokee Payment

Just before the Civil War fifty thousand dollars in gold was dispatched to the officials of the Cherokee Nation. The gold was entrusted to four Cherokees, but because of the turbulent conditions in the Nations, they decided to hide the gold before Confederate soldiers could confiscate it, believing that after the war the money could be fairly distributed. They buried the money in kegs.

At the end of the war only one of the four was

still alive, and he lay dying. He tried to direct a Cherokee council member to the hidden gold, but either was misunderstood or failed to tell all. When the council checked his location, there was no sign of the kegs.

Some Cherokees believed that they were hidden half a mile south of the old capitol building (now the Cherokee County Court House), on the bank of Tahlequah Creek. Others believed that it was buried directly behind the capitol, while some believed it had been hidden closer to Park Hill.[7] Today, if you see an old Cherokee keeping a close eye on the grounds around the Tahlequah Court House, you might guess what he is looking for.

Opothleyahola's Gold

It is said that Opothleyahola, the famous Creek chief, received a large annuity from the United States government soon after the outbreak of the Civil War. The annuity, in gold, was intended to be distributed to the Creek Indians, but because of the war many of the tribe had scattered. Some were Confederate sympathizers, but many sided with the Union. Opothleyahola knew that the payment could not be divided equally until the war ended and all his people were brought together once again. He believed that his only alternative was to bury the money until he could pay those who were due their allotments.

D. L. Berryhill, an eight-year-old Creek boy, watched the chief pile the money—twenty-dollar gold pieces—on the kitchen floor of his cabin. With the help of his closest friend the chief placed the money in a large trunk. Opothleyahola and his companion then armed themselves and summoned four Negro slaves to fasten chains around the trunk and carry it to a designated spot. The chest was so cumbersome that the slaves could carry it only a few steps at a time. When they had gone some distance from the house, the chief instructed the slaves to dig a deep hole, into which they lowered the heavy trunk. Opothleyahola then ordered them to remove the chains around the trunk. While they were doing so, the chief's companion shot them.

Young Berryhill, peering around a corner of the chief's cabin, observed these events. His mother discovered him and, fearing for the boy's life, hurried him away.

The Cherokee County Court House in Tahlequah, once the capitol of the Cherokee Nation. The building is a landmark, aged Indians say, to fifty thousand dollars buried for safekeeping during the Civil War. Photograph by Fred W. Marvel, Oklahoma Tourism and Recreation Department.

In November, 1861, Chief Opothleyahola led a band of about two thousand of his tribe to Kansas, where they would be protected by Union soldiers. Many of them planned to enlist in the Union Army. But on the journey Confederate forces overtook the Indians, and three bloody skirmishes were fought. The survivors were scattered during a fierce blizzard. Opothleyahola's trusted friend had been killed, and the chief fell ill in the storm and died shortly after reaching Kansas. The Creeks' tragic journey became known as the Second Trail of Tears. Opothleyahola never revealed where the government payment had been buried. Only the young Creek boy, D. L. Berryhill, knew.

Many years later Joe Grayson, of Okmulgee, Berryhill's grandson, claimed that before Berryhill's death he told him where the treasure was buried. Grayson believed that he could go within fifty yards of it—at a place a few miles south and west of Checotah, just north of Brush Hill where the road forked.

Grayson would not tell anyone his secret except a government search party, for he wanted the money returned to the Creeks. But he died before that search materialized. Many Creeks are sure that somewhere near Brush Hill the large chest—filled to its brim with twenty-dollar gold eagles—remains to be found.[8]

Chief Paseola's Gold

Many historians believe the Battle of Twin Mounds, about eighteen miles east of Stillwater in Payne County, was the first engagement between Union and Confederate forces in Indian Territory. It occurred when a large force of Confederates caught up with Opothleyahola's Union loyalists on November 19, 1861.

In 1887, James Fleming revealed that a Creek named Goab Childers had told him that the Creek chief Paseola had directed two Indians to load sixty thousand dollars on a horse and hide it near the Twin Mounds before the battle. Childers was only fourteen years old at the time, but he saw the two warriors carry the money away. Later in the engagement both were killed.[9] Childers was sure that the Creeks never retrieved the gold.

Many relics have been found at the battle site. Swords and skulls were discovered at Lone Mound

Opothleyahola, chief of the Creeks at the onset of the Civil War. Courtesy Oklahoma Historical Society.

in 1940. A powder flask and guns were found on Salt Creek on the north, and a cannon ball was unearthed southwest of Keystone.[10] No one has reported finding the sixty thousand dollars.

Lacey Mouse and His Gold

Lacey Mouse was a full-blood Cherokee. He had been forced to sell his large North Carolina plantation when the United States government ordered his people to move westward to the Indian Territory. Lacey Mouse took his many slaves with him, although they pleaded to remain behind, for they had heard that the winters were cold in Indian country and they feared that they all might freeze to death.

On the long journey overland the slaves continued their doleful complaints. Finally, at the Mississippi crossing Lacey Mouse halted the caravan. The wealthy Cherokee sensed that he would not have a moment's peace as long as his slaves felt that they were persecuted, and he decided to sell them at the river port.

In the peaceful Spavinaw Hills near Kenwood, in western Delaware County, Lacey Mouse claimed his allotment and built his log cabin. Somewhere on the large tract of woodland he buried the gold he had received for his slaves. Somehow it leaked out that the wealthy Cherokee had hidden his fortune. No one knew the actual amount, but the estimates ran high. He had admitted that he had received good prices for his slaves, and the hill people knew that that meant a thousand dollars or more a slave. Whenever a neighbor ventured a guess at the amount, Lacey Mouse just shrugged and spoke no more of it. But somewhere grim men were conspiring to get it.

One night in 1864 the robbers crept silently to Lacey Mouse's cabin, broke in, and ordered him to take them to the money. But the Cherokee refused, and even when the men threatened his life, he was unmoved. Lacey Mouse's only reply was that they could find the gold themselves. He would never show them.

The leader of the gang became furious and pulled out his pistol, leveling it at the Cherokee. Still Lacey would not budge. If he had to die to protect his gold, no one would get it. The bandit cocked the trigger. Still the Indian stood firm. A bullet through his heart ended his life. The intruders fled Lacey's house, as empty-handed as they had come.

The following morning Lacey's body was found in a pool of blood. The people of Kenwood were determined to catch the men who had killed him, but no clues could be found. When Lacey Mouse was buried, he took two mysteries with him—the identity of his killers, and the location of his gold—something not even his wife knew.

It was never learned who had murdered Lacey, but Albert Zinn, of Tulsa, who spent much of his boyhood days on the Mouse ranch years after the murder, remembered a sequel to the grim story.[11] Several years after Lacey's death, a distant relative of the family who had become gravely ill, said that he had been in Lacey's house on the night he was murdered. When the robbers broke in, he hid in another room and overheard everything that ensued. After Lacey was shot and the killers rode away, the relative saw that Lacey was dead. He was afraid to tell anyone for fear of being blamed for the killing. Too, if the outlaws learned that he might be able to identify them, they might return to kill him too. He confessed that holding back the story all those years had haunted him to his dying day.

Today two more graves lie next to Lacey Mouse's grave, those of members of his family who later hunted for the gold. But Lacey Mouse had concealed it well, so well that no one to this day has unearthed it—at least that is what the hillfolk say.

Baptiste Peoria's Legend

In 1868, Baptiste Peoria, chief of the Peoria Indians, moved his tribe to a location seven miles west of Miami and settled near a large grove of locust trees. In later years, when the moon was full and the campfire burned low, the old chief often delighted in telling a story about the locust grove. It was a tale he earnestly believed, and those who listened believed it, too:

A party of Mexicans were leading a caravan of burros across his land, traveling westward. Three of the little burros were loaded with heavy deerskin sacks of gold and silver. Chief Peoria had heard that the Mexicans had mined the ore in the hills nearby. He believed the rumor to be true, for many old shafts were discovered in the region in later years.

Somehow the Mexicans received word of a patrol of United States soldiers on their trail. No one knew what the soldiers were up to, but the Mexicans were taking no chances. They knew that they could not fight because they were too few in number. Instead, they would bury the ore and return for it later.

"But how can we find our treasure again?" asked one of the men. Their leader remembered that he had brought along a bag of locust seeds.

These they would plant above the treasure. The seedlings would serve as a marker. The hole was dug, and the bags were taken from the burros' backs and dropped into it. After the earth was replaced and trampled, the leader planted the seeds. The locusts would serve as an obvious landmark, for only a few such trees grew in the region.

The Mexicans rode on at a faster pace, and, as far as Chief Peoria knew, the soldiers lost their trail. The locust seeds sprouted and grew, and over the years they, too, shed their seeds and those grew into more trees. In time a large locust grove had grown over the treasure the Mexicans had buried. Baptiste Peoria told his people that no one had ever returned for the "yellow iron."[12]

Lindsay's Gold

In 1873 an Indian named Lindsay was living sixteen miles southeast of Claremore on Scaley Back Mountain, not far from Chouteau. Indians living at Claremore Mound frequently raided his herd of cattle. Finally Lindsay decided to sell out and drove his stock to Denison, Texas. There he sold the cattle and collected more than twenty thousand dollars, most of it in gold.

After Lindsay had paid off his hired hands, he returned to Scaley Back Mountain and buried his money in a ravine. The next morning an uncle from Kansas arrived and found Lindsay dead in his cabin. He may have died in his sleep or someone may have murdered him. No one knows. But to this day the twenty thousand dollars lies where it was placed in 1873.[13]

Ben Marshall's Cache

Among the wealthy Indians in the Nations was one Ben Marshall, known as the Captain Kidd of Indian Territory. His ancestry was both white and Indian. Before the Civil War, Marshall was highly regarded among the Indians of Alabama. He sold his allotment (which became the townsite of Girard) and moved to the Creek Nation, settling in an area known as the Point, a vast region of rich bottomland between the Verdigris and Arkansas rivers. It has been said that five hundred slaves worked his holdings and gathered the yearly harvests.

At that time the closest bank was more than a hundred miles away, and Marshall, leery of banks anyway, converted his money into gold and buried it where it was easily accessible. When the Civil War broke out and the United States Army pulled out of the Indian Nations, the country was overrun with renegades and bandits. Many of the wealthy Indians moved away, Marshall among them.

He traveled south to Stonewall, in the Chickasaw Nation in present Pontotoc County, and there found a new place to settle. Later he returned to his plantation with a farm hand and a wagon and one night unearthed his private bank, placed it in sacks, and rumbled away before morning dawned. His withdrawal amounted to sixty thousand dollars, all in gold.

Marshall returned to Stonewall and secretly reburied his gold. Not even his wife knew where it was hidden. When he died, not a soul had learned his secret. His family made repeated searches to no avail.[14]

Watt Grayson, a Creek who lived west of Eufaula, buried his money and managed to hold onto it throughout the war. But one night in November, 1873, three outlaws broke into his house and demanded his money. The robbers were Myra Belle Reed, who was dressed as a man, her husband, Jim Reed, and Daniel Evans (Myra Belle would come to be known as Belle Starr). Grayson refused to show them where he had buried his savings, and even when the bandits placed a rope around his neck, throwing it over a rafter to pull it tight, he would not talk. They pulled him off the floor and placed lighted candles under his feet. He remained silent.

Finally they seized his wife and proceeded to torture her in the same manner. This Grayson could not bear, and he showed the bandits where his money was hidden. They rode off with thirty thousand dollars in gold. About two years later Judge Isaac Parker sentenced Daniel Evans to hang for murder. Before the trap was sprung, Evans confessed the Grayson robbery, revealing his two accomplices.[15]

The Lost Shipment

An all-out search for $150,000 in government

gold was begun in September, 1904. The treasure was thought to be buried in the Chickasaw Nation on the ranch of J. W. Johnson, who placed guards around his land to keep out trespassers until he had time to conduct his own search.

Johnson had heard the story years before but had no confidence in it until one day he plowed up part of the evidence. Sometime in the late 1800's six men employed by the United States government started out across Indian Territory with $150,000 to pay the various tribes their allotments. Each night when the men made camp, they buried the gold and staked out their horses over the burial site to conceal it.

One night a band of hostiles attacked the government party and tracked those who escaped until all but one were killed. After hiding for days, the survivor returned to find that all his friends had been beheaded. Sometime later he returned with a search party to find the gold but discovered that nothing of their camp remained. The gold was not to be found.

Later the survivor settled near El Paso. Shortly before his death he told the story to a friend, who tried to find the gold, and he in turn told the story to Johnson.

Johnson was little impressed with the story until one day he plowed up five human skulls. He recalled the story of the beheaded victims. He believed that the gold might be found nearby, but if he was any luckier than his predecessors, he never said so.[16]

Old-timers still remember the two sons of a Spaniard who conducted a lengthy search for a lost mine in the Jack Fork Mountains of eastern Oklahoma, where early Indian accounts tell about silver mines in the region. This photograph was taken near Clayton. Photograph by Fred W. Marvel, Oklahoma Tourism and Recreation Department.

18. The Treasure the Spaniards Keep Hunting

Spanish treasure tales have a common ingredient. A lone, aged Spaniard returns to some secluded spot where his ancestors buried a fabulous treasure, usually with the aid of a map laden with so many secret symbols and cryptic signs that—if authentic—must surely have made them the world's foremost experts in subterfuge. Such stories are common all over the Southwest.

Not so common are the stories of the lone Spaniard—or the groups of Spaniards—who appeared time after time over many decades, never giving up the quest for an elusive treasure. Such is the unique story of the rolling hills of eastern Oklahoma close to the Arkansas border. A reputed twelve-million-dollar hoard of gold doubloons and bricks lies secreted in this hilly, densely timbered country. It has been sought by not one but at least a half-dozen or more Spaniards during the last hundred years. And rumors persist that their descendants still haunt the hills—two hills in particular.

Brushy Mountain and Buzzard Hill, both near Spiro, near the banks of the Arkansas River, have been the scene of many a mysterious treasure hunt. Perhaps the first was in 1850. Spaniards from Mexico appeared in the Cherokee Nation with a sheepskin map. The party hired a guide to show them through the wilderness. They were searching for strange symbols to be found on two rivers believed to be the Grand and Cowskin (now Elk River).

In 1916 eighty-one-year-old Ed Carey, the brother of the guide, recalled that the Spaniards revealed that the worn sheepskin had been made two hundred years before and that it described caches of gold bullion deposited by their ancestors. Strange markings were drawn along both rivers where the treasure was buried.[1] The Spaniards spent months exploring the streams for clues but always with little reward. Tired and discouraged, they finally departed and were seen no more.

About thirty years later, sometime in the early 1880's, an old Mexican stopped off at a ranch house near Spiro. He asked permission to bed down for the night, saying that he had walked all the way from his home in Mexico to find something his grandfather had talked about countless times before he died. The rancher invited the Mexican into his home and insisted that he join his family for dinner. Obviously weary, the traveler ate as though he had not had a meal for days. That evening he turned in early, saying little more about the purpose of his journey.

The next day the Mexican talked, but he asked more questions than he gave answers. He was especially interested in landmarks and strange symbols. He asked the rancher whether he knew a place that might be called Buzzard Hill. The cattleman said yes, he knew of such a place. The Mexican asked the rancher to guide him to the hill, for he believed he could show something of interest that his grandfather had talked about recurrently in faraway Mexico. The rancher, intrigued, agreed to do so.

Early the next day the two men rode to Buzzard Hill, a beautiful timbered butte far from the nearest trail, about ten miles east of Spiro. As they rode along, the Mexican explained his purpose for traveling so far: his forefathers had hidden a great store of gold on the hill. The directions to the treasure had been passed down for several generations, and he was the first to be able to travel the long distance.

"Señor, if I can prove to you several things that would make you believe what I say is so, I would like to make a deal with you that will make us both very rich."[2]

The rancher agreed to consider the Mexican's proposition but wanted to see proof that something was buried on the hill before he consented to any agreement. During the days that followed, the Mexican directed the rancher and members of his family as they eagerly dug trenches on the hillside, seeking the clues that the Mexican was sure they would find. First, he directed the workmen to dig several feet down, where they should

On the South Canadian River in Haskell County, near the now-inundated Standing Rock, Wilbert Martin, of Tulsa, found this chunk of pure silver near the base of an ancient oak on which was carved an inverted arrowhead symbol (barely visible in the center of the picture). Courtesy C. L. Packer.

find a cross carved in a rock. After an hour or so they unearthed the stone etched with the cross.

Then he told the men to dig still deeper, where they should find a human skeleton buried standing up with his face pointing down the Arkansas River. After more digging, they unearthed the skeletal remains. Then he moved the hunters to a spot where they would uncover the skeletons of a

woman and a small child buried together in the form of a cross. Again the skeletons were found.

Now the Mexican instructed the party to dig into the side of the hill, where they would find a rock wall carved with Spanish "markings," which only he could read. Hastily they dug away the overburden of soil. Soon their shovels hit the stone ledge. Once the dirt was cleared away, the mysterious symbols appeared. They were peculiar symbols, unlike anything the rancher had ever seen. The Mexican offered no explanation. It was then that he offered his proposal.

The Mexican's story was this: When this land was part of the vast French domain, the Spaniards were working a gold mine here and employed a large force of men. When the miners needed supplies, they ferried some of the gold down the Arkansas River to the Mississippi, thence south to New Orleans, where they sold the precious metal to purchase supplies and then returned upstream.

On the last trip the Spaniards made, one of the miners drank too much and revealed the secret of the mine within French boundaries. After his return to camp the Spaniard confessed his blunder, fearing that the French would quickly investigate. The Spaniards did not need know more. French soldiers would not be far behind. They had to work fast if they were to leave with their lives. Their leader blinded the braggart and buried him alive, standing up, facing down the Arkansas toward New Orleans, where he had betrayed his fellows. The ore and the smelted ingots were hastily dumped into the crude shaft, and the bodies of a woman and small child were buried in the form of a cross. A secret message was hastily chiseled into the rock wall. The mine shaft was filled, and the Spaniards departed swiftly when Indian spies told them of approaching French troops.

The old Mexican showed the rancher and his sons the map, saying that it had belonged to his grandfather, who had inherited it from his father, one of the miners at Buzzard Hill. He told the rancher that he was not a citizen of the United States and was in the country illegally. He could not hope to reclaim the treasure for himself. He would show them to the gold if they would place ten thousand dollars on deposit for him in the bank at Fort Smith, payable only on the day the

Abandoned in 1854 when its garrison moved to Fort Arbuckle, Fort Towson soon fell into ruins. Today little more than stone foundation ruins and fallen chimneys remain. Photograph by Fred W. Marvel, Oklahoma Tourism and Recreation Department.

treasure was recovered. He could easily carry ten thousand dollars back to Mexico, he said, but it would be impossible for him to pack gold bullion on his long journey. If the gold was not found, then the rancher would lose nothing.

The rancher said that ten thousand dollars was much more than he could raise at that time. The Mexican said angrily that the mine shaft held many times that amount and that he would not go a step farther for any amount less than his proposal. The Mexican allowed the rancher ten days to place the money on deposit at Fort Smith.

"If you have not raised the money by sundown on the tenth day," the Mexican warned, "I will return to Mexico and you will never find the treasure!"

In the days that followed, the rancher sold off his cattle in an attempt to raise the cash. But when more than a week had passed and he had raised only six thousand dollars, his hopes ebbed. Even so, he placed the money in the bank at Fort Smith. He returned to the ranch, told the Mexican what

had been done, and pleaded with him to carry on the search, offering a lion's share of the treasure as well.

The Mexican was emphatic. He wanted cash, not bullion. It was to be ten thousand dollars or nothing—for anyone.

On the tenth day the treasure hunters stood on Buzzard Hill before the rock wall etched with the strange Spanish symbols. Once more the Mexican asked the rancher whether he had raised the amount. The rancher's bleak face revealed his answer.

At dusk the Mexican pulled a large silver watch from his pocket. He glanced at it and told the rancher that he had but a few minutes remaining to honor his proposal. As the orange-hued sun sank slowly behind the hill, the Mexican slammed his watch against the stone wall, shattering it. He wheeled around angrily, and walked from the mountain. He would never be seen again.

At the time the rancher believed that he had been shown enough by the Mexican that he would

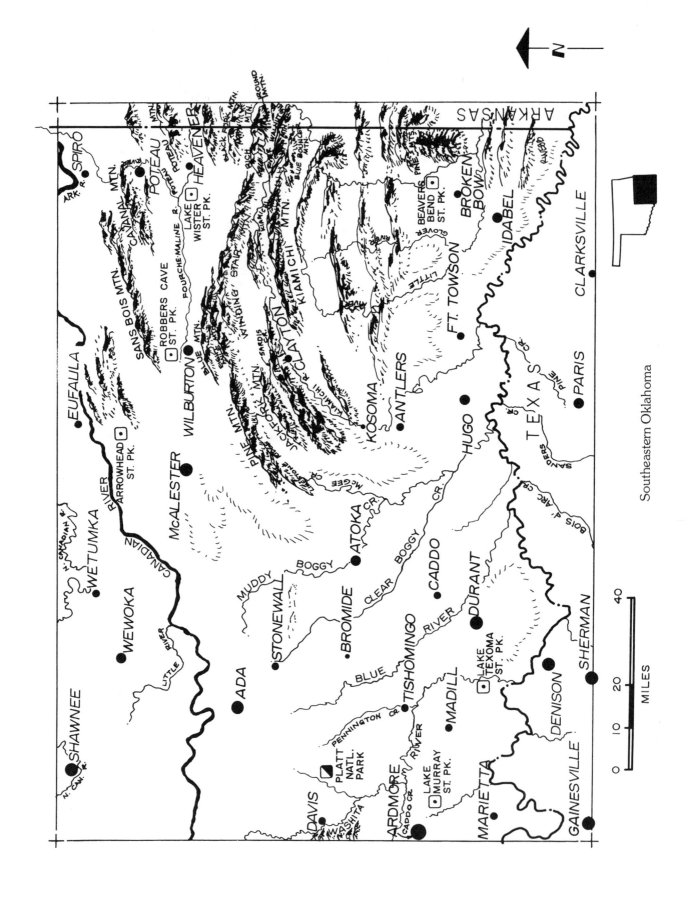

Southeastern Oklahoma

find the hidden mine and the treasure it held without much more work. He was wrong. He and his sons continued the search for months with little success. Once they found the remains of an ancient smelter where the ore had been melted into ingots. Even a few broken crucibles and ladles were uncovered—but no mine.

Over the years the rancher never gave up hope that he would discover the well-concealed shaft somewhere on Buzzard Hill. Trees were uprooted in the belief that one might have grown in the entrance of the mine. A boiler and steam engine were also installed. But nothing unusual appeared, other than fourteen mysterious graves found across a creek from Buzzard Hill.[3] No explanation was given for them.

Several years passed, during which the rancher estimated that he had spent no less than thirty thousand dollars in supplies and equipment.

About a decade later—in 1893—still another party of Spaniards appeared in the vicinity of Brushy Mountain, a few miles northwest of Spiro. This trio also claimed to be descendants of a man who had escaped a massacre. They brought charts that they believed marked the location of the mouth of a cave in which a band of Spanish traders had hidden their gold before Indians attacked the party.

The trio spent months combing the countryside for the lost cave, but, as in the searches before them, nature had played its part well. Finally out of disgust, two of the hunters returned to their native Spain to report their fruitless search. The third Spaniard would not leave, vowing that he would find the gold or never return home. He died of starvation in his relentless quest, and his grave near Brushy Mountain is mute testimony to the vow he made.

The treasure charts the Spaniard attempted to follow so diligently later fell into the hands of a native of eastern Oklahoma and still later came into the possession of a real-estate agent in Muskogee. This man sought the advice of R. D. Clutter, an old prospector and miner from the West.

Clutter began his search in August, 1923.[4] According to the charts, the cave held an estimated twelve million dollars in bullion and doubloons, if

Clutter interpreted them correctly. They led him to a small ravine on the south slope of Brushy Mountain. He was sure he had found the treasure cave, for on the charts appeared "eight places that connected by lines and converged over a point where a small ellipse was drawn."[5]

Clutter believed that the ellipse was the edge of a small oval-shaped cliff that overhung a depression in the hillside. At the edge of the precipice were found what appeared to be drill holes apparently cut into the rock more than a century before. Clutter believed that the Spaniards had drilled the holes, filled them with powder, then blown off the face of the bluff to seal the mouth of the cave.

Another chart showed eight small circles and eight parallel lines that Clutter was sure represented the drill holes he had found on the mountain above the cave. The weathered holes, each about three inches in diameter and four inches deep, appeared to have been dug with a blunt instrument. Clutter was satisfied that another twenty-one lines shown on the map were the grooves that could be seen on a large rock east of the cavern entrance. Each groove pointed toward the mouth of what appeared to be a sealed cave.

Other sketches on the map were drawings of cannons and wagon wheels. It was Clutter's belief that the cave contained not only the gold but wagons, furniture, and supplies the Spaniards had cached in great haste.

Clutter hired a crew of fourteen and four teams of draft animals to dig away the rock and debris. Clutter's workmen ripped more than a hundred cubic yards of earth and stone from the face of the bluff, but they found only grinding stones and pestles, hundreds of arrowheads, and a human skeleton.

What is odd about these searches is that Brushy Mountain and Buzzard Hill are only a few miles apart. Only a few miles west of the peaks is Standing Rock, jutting from the South Canadian River in Haskell County. In *Coronado's Children*, J. Frank Dobie wrote about a Spaniard who had maps to Spanish mines in south Texas and also possessed one to the Lost Standing Rock Mine in Oklahoma.[6] On the east side of the famous landmark was cut a hatchet. At an angle of seventy degrees "east of north," 600 *varas* (about 1,650 feet) away was a cedar tree with a turtle cut on it, pointing to nineteen burro loads of buried bullion.

In later years some treasure was found in the region. Albert Barnhill, of Eufaula, remembered an old Cherokee who would go to Standing Rock periodically and bring back a half-bushel of gold from every trip.[7] While probing the area one day in recent years, Randall Wells, a Tulsa resident, stumbled onto three small silver ingots weighing about half a pound each. Every ingot had a cross molded into it.[8] Wilbert Martin, a Tulsa postman, once found an almost pure chunk of smelted silver near Standing Rock. Once a prominent landmark, the rock bore the carvings of a turtle, a triangle with a handle at one point—perhaps a hatchet—and the date 1851.

Other symbols were found over the years: a turtle pointing to Standing Rock and an etched horse's head and arrowhead at distant sites.[9] Since then, however, the Standing Rock area has been inundated by Lake Eufaula. What mysteries might it have revealed?

Two years after Clutter and his men dug into Brushy Mountain, still another Spaniard appeared in the region. It was in 1925 or perhaps '26 that the foreigner stepped off the train at the Frisco depot in Tahlequah. In the two days that he was in town, he confided in a local merchant that he was seeking a chiseled representation of a horse that should appear on the side of a mountain just south of Tahlequah. A map in his possession showed the horse carving and various landmarks around it.[10]

The merchant had heard that such a carving had been discovered years before and remembered that the etching was of a running horse on the north slope of a hill about seven miles south of Tahlequah. The storekeeper recalled that only a few years before several strangers had been seeking the mysterious carving but that no one

had since found it. The Spaniard thanked the merchant for his information—and never appeared in town again. What he hunted, and where he went, no one knew.

The two sons of an old Spaniard long searched for a mine in the timbered Jack Fork Mountains. Joe White found what he believed to be the mine in Pittsburg County about five miles south of Blanco on Brushy Creek. White protected the mine and carved out a mountain abode on top of a bluff overlooking the old Spanish diggings.

He was sure that he had found the long-hidden mine, for a hundred feet downstream appeared the natural profile of a man's face—looking straight toward the old tunnel. And White found an antiquated Spanish musket in his own digging. By 1938 he had not yet reached the end of the mine.[11]

Once in the 1930's the city fathers of Eufaula were so sure that the low rocky hill half a mile west of town harbored a Spanish treasure that they dislodged part of the hillside with dynamite. They sank deep holes into the mountain but found no treasure.[12] Similar digging occurred on a mountain just northwest of nearby Wetumka.[13]

The residents of Piney, about six miles north of Stilwell, were always convinced that Spanish treasure would be found on nearby Twist Mountain, for numerous cryptic carvings had been found there, and strange stone cairns as much as a mile apart. Then there was the cemetery on the north side of Twist Mountain, filled with graves long before the Cherokees migrated into the country.[14]

Other lone travelers have gone into the hill country of eastern Oklahoma in quest of ancestral riches—always close-mouthed and always disappearing as quickly as they came. Their secrets they always managed to keep to themselves.

Notes

Preface. On the Trail of Lost Treasure

1. J. Frank Dobie (ed.), *Legends of Texas,* 3.
2. *Ibid.,* 6.
3. "Legends of Gold Are Many but None Prove to Exist," *Daily Oklahoman* (Oklahoma City), July 17, 1910.
4. The author's historical treasure map points out this fact. Steve Wilson, *Lost Mines & Hidden Treasures of Southwestern Oklahoma* (map).

1. They Found Buried Treasure

1. "Finds Large Fortune," *Claremore Progress and Rogers County Democrat,* January 3, 1913; "In Digging Ditch, Upturns Fortune," *Daily Oklahoman,* January 4, 1913.
2. Glenn Shirley, *Law West of Fort Smith: Frontier Justice in the Indian Territory, 1834–1896,* 33 (hereafter cited as *Law West of Fort Smith*).
3. The treasure was found at S.4, T.15N., R.2W. "A Pot of Gold," *Daily Oklahoma State Capital* (Guthrie), April 22, 1895; *Edmond Sun-Democrat,* May 3, 1895.
4. *Hennessey Clipper,* January 17, 1895.
5. Hugh D. Corwin, "Spanish Traders Once Bartered with Indians near Tipton," *Lawton Constitution,* May 26, 1963.
6. "Treasure Trove, Gold Was Buried Here," *Daily Oklahoman,* September 30, 1902; "Old Man Finds It," *Alva Review,* November 6, 1902.
7. "Mummified Indian Found by Miners in a Cave in the Wichita Mountains," *Weekly Republican* (Lawton), July 30, 1903. The story was not reported for almost a year.
8. It is probable that Spanish Cave derived its name from this discovery, for soon afterward it was dubbed Mexican Cave.
9. "Lawton Man Purchases Curio, the Skeleton of Young Indian Child Found in the Wichitas," *Daily-News Republican* (Lawton), March 26, 1908.
10. "Found Gold and Skeleton," *Wichita Daily Eagle,* December 11, 1903. See also "Sequoyah or Not Sequoyah?" *Vinita Daily Chieftain,* January 12, 1904; "Where Sequoyah Died," *Mount Sheridan Miner* (Meers), March 3, 1904; "Is Sequoyah Found Again? Skeleton of American Cadmus Still a Mooted Question," *Vinita Daily Chieftain,* April 9, 1904.
11. *Vinita Daily Chieftain,* April 9, 1904.
12. *Washington Evening Star,* January 16, 1904.
13. "Medal Was Chisholm's," *Vinita Daily Chieftain,* January 29, 1904; see also "Cherokee Genealogy of Narcissa Chisholm Owen," *Chronicles of Oklahoma,* Vol. XXIII (Autumn, 1945), 298–300.

14. "Medal Was Chisholm's," *Vinita Daily Chieftain,* January 29, 1904; see also Alvin Rucker, "Bones Found in State Cave May Be Sequoyah's," *Daily Oklahoman,* May 24, 1931.
15. Mr. and Mrs. Omer L. Morgan, of Newhall, California, believed that they found Sequoyah's grave in Coahuila, Mexico. Morgan to the author, February 7, 1965. See also "Sequoyah's Grave Found by Former Residents in Mexico, Removal Sought," *Tahlequah Star-Citizen,* October 2, 1952.
16. "Minutes," *Chronicles of Oklahoma,* Vol. XXIII (Spring, 1945), 90–91, 298.
17. Mrs. Charles A. Paul to the author, February 9, 1972. See also Francis Thetford, "Did Sequoyah Really Lie in Mystery Grave near Snyder?" *Sunday Oklahoman* (Oklahoma City), February 19, 1967.
18. *Temple Tribune,* August 22, 1907; Fred Grove, "The Big Pasture," *Oklahoma Today,* Summer, 1966.
19. Carlos E. Castañeda, *Our Catholic Heritage in Texas,* I, 129–32.
20. Charles M. Cooper, *Temple Tribune* publisher, got in touch with two railroad companies while seeking the tombstone and drew "complete blanks." See Charles M. Cooper, "The Big Pasture," *Chronicles of Oklahoma,* Vol. XXXV (Summer, 1957), 138–39.
21. See Steve Wilson, "Is It True That Dead Men Tell No Tales?" *True Frontier,* October, 1967, pp. 26–27, 52–56.
22. Interview with Mrs. Lola McDaniel, December, 1961.
23. "Buried Treasure Is Found by Negroes," *Wilburton News,* October 27, 1905.
24. *Ibid.,* November 24, 1905.
25. "Gold Buried by Grandmother Found by Grandchildren," *Muskogee Times-Democrat,* August 24, 1906.
26. Muriel H. Wright, "The Collection of Relics and Artifacts from Ferdinandina: Oklahoma's First White Settlement," *Chronicles of Oklahoma,* Vol. XXXIV (Autumn, 1956), 353–56.
27. *Ibid.;* see also Muriel H. Wright, "Pioneer Historian and Archaeologist of Oklahoma," *Chronicles of Oklahoma,* Vol. XXIV (Winter, 1946), 404–11.
28. Wright, "The Collection of Relics and Artifacts from Ferdinandina: Oklahoma's First White Settlement," *Chronicles of Oklahoma,* Vol. XXXIV (Autumn, 1956), 355.
29. Castañeda, *Our Catholic Heritage in Texas,* III, 146–47.
30. George H. Shirk, "Real Estate Deal No. I," *Daily Oklahoman,* August 27, 1950.
31. Henry W. Hamilton, "The Spiro Mound," *Missouri Archaeologist,* Vol. XIV (October, 1952), 56.

32. *Ibid.*, 85.

33. Forrest E. Clements, "Historical Sketch of the Spiro Mound," *Contributions from the Museum of the American Indian*, Vol. XIV (1945), 52.

34. *Ibid.*, 56.

35. *Ibid.*

36. Hamilton, "The Spiro Mound," *Missouri Archaeologist*, Vol. XIV (October, 1952), 24.

37. *Ibid.*, 37.

38. *Ibid.*, 83.

39. Clements, "Historical Sketch of the Spiro Mound," *Contributions from the Museum of the American Indian*, Vol. XIV (1945), 64.

40. Bill Kalb, "Oklahoma's Ancient Culture," *Sunday Oklahoman*, February 28, 1965. See also David A. Baerreis, "The Southern Cult and the Spiro Ceremonial Complex," *Bulletin of the Oklahoma Anthropological Society*, Vol. V (March, 1957), 23–38.

41. Interview with Elmer Craft, June, 1963.

42. James B. Shaeffer, "A Military Burial at Lake Altus," *Chronicles of Oklahoma*, Vol. XXXVI (Winter, 1958), 411–15.

43. George H. Shirk, "Campaigning with Sheridan: A Farrier's Diary," *Chronicles of Oklahoma*, Vol. XXXVII (Spring, 1959), 75, 104–105.

44. John Devine, "Mysterious Night-Riders at Craig County Farm Consult Map While Digging Up Buried Treasure," *Muskogee Daily Phoenix*, February 17, 1935.

45. Indian-Pioneer History, Foreman Collection, Indian Archives Division, Oklahoma Historical Society, Oklahoma City, Vol. 31, p. 450; Vol. 43, pp. 225–26; Vol. 21, p. 481.

46. George H. Shirk, "Report on the Heavener 'Rune Stone,'" *Chronicles of Oklahoma*, Vol. XXXVII (Autumn, 1959), 363–68.

47. Gloria Farley, *The Vikings Were Here.*

48. *Ibid.*; see also Gloria Farley, "Runestones Are Dated at Last," *Sunday Oklahoman*, October 15, 1967.

49. Jim Downing, "Vikings Here in 1006?" *Tulsa Tribune*, October 14, 1965.

50. Farley, *The Vikings Were Here.*

51. Leslie A. McRill, "The Heavener Enigma: A Rune Stone," *Chronicles of Oklahoma*, Vol. XLIV (Summer, 1966), 122–29; Samuel Eliot Morison, *The European Discovery of America: The Northern Voyages, A.D. 500–1600*, 78–79.

52. Gloria Farley, of Heavener, Oklahoma, to the author, April 21, 1973; Farley, *The Vikings Were Here.* For more on Oklahoma's runestones, see Robert H. Hill, "Mystery of the Misplaced Vikings," *Sunday Oklahoman*, November 7, 1965; Frederick J. Pohl, *Atlantic Crossings Before Columbus*; Frederick J. Pohl, *The Viking Explorers*; and Gloria Farley, "Vikings in Oklahoma, November 11, 1012," *East Oklahoma Messenger* (Poteau), April 12, 1973.

53. Bill Mahan, "Buried Treasure Found!" *Gold*, Summer, 1971, p. 7.

54. For anthologies describing Oklahoma's lost treasures, see "Phantom Treasures," *Daily Oklahoman*, December 6, 1936; Bill Burchardt, "Is There Gold in Our Hills?" *Daily Oklahoman*, October 21, 1956; Bill Burchardt, "Lost Loot," *Oklahoma Today*, Winter, 1959, p. 2; C. L. Packer, "Land of Triangles, Turtles and Hatchets," *True West*, August, 1965, p. 14; Robert F. Turpin, "Oklahoma Hot Spots," *Western Treasures Magazine*, August, 1970, p. 34; Robert F. Turpin, "Oklahoma Millions in Buried Treasure," *Treasure*, February, 1971, p. 23. See also Sources for a selection of the author's articles on the subject.

2. The Secrets Spanish Fort Tells

1. Dobie, *Legends of Texas*, 81–84.

2. For evidence in support of this, see Lathel F. Duffield, "The Taovayas Village of 1759: In Texas or Oklahoma?" *Great Plains Journal*, Vol. IV (Spring, 1965), 39–48; W. W. Newcomb and W. T. Field, "A Preliminary Report Concerning an Ethnohistoric Investigation of the Wichita Indians in the Southern Plains" (Austin, Texas, Memorial Museum, December, 1966), Part I, dates 1759 and 1765, mimeographed; Robert E. Bell, Edward B. Jelks, and W. W. Newcomb (comps.), "A Pilot Study of Wichita Indian Archaeology and Ethnohistory," Final Report for Grant GS-964, National Science Foundation, August, 1967, p. 323 and Fig. 26, mimeographed.

3. Leslie A. McRill, "Ferdinandina: First White Settlement in Oklahoma," *Chronicles of Oklahoma*, Vol. XLI (Summer, 1963), 135.

4. For a detailed study of the Taovayas, see Elizabeth Ann Harper, "The Taovayas Indians in Frontier Trade and Diplomacy 1719–1768," *Chronicles of Oklahoma*, Vol. XXXI (Autumn, 1953), 268–89; Part II (1769–79), *Southwestern Historical Quarterly*, Vol. LVII (October, 1953), 181–201; Part III (1779–1835), *Panhandle-Plains Historical Review*, Vol. XXVI (1953), 40–72. See also Llerena Friend, "Old Spanish Fort," *West Texas Historical Association Year Book*, Vol. XVI (October, 1940), 3–27.

5. William Edward Dunn, "The Apache Mission on the San Saba River: Its Founding and Failure," *Southwestern Historical Quarterly*, Vol. XVII (April, 1914), 379–414; see also Robert S. Weddle, *The San Sabá Mission: Spanish Pivot in Texas*, 61–89 (hereafter cited as *The San Sabá Mission*).

6. For detailed accounts of the Parilla expedition, see Castañeda, *Our Catholic Heritage in Texas*, IV, 125–32; Henry Easton Allen, "The Parilla Expedition to the Red River in 1759," *Southwestern Historical Quarterly*, Vol. XLIII (July, 1939), 53–71; Weddle, *The San Sabá Mission*, 118–43.

7. Castañeda, *Our Catholic Heritage in Texas*, IV, 129.

8. *Ibid.*, 130.

9. Weddle, *The San Sabá Mission*, 123–24.

10. Harper, "The Taovayas Indians in Frontier Trade and Diplomacy 1719–1768," *Chronicles of*

Oklahoma, Vol. XXXI (Autumn, 1953), 287. Treviño also told of a middle-aged Frenchman named Antonio who frequently traded with the Taovayas. Well liked by them, he headquartered on Red River about "forty leagues" (just over one hundred miles) away. See W. W. Newcomb, "Eyasiquiche," *Mustang* (newsletter of the Texas Memorial Museum), Vol. VII (December, 1966), 1–5.

11. Herbert Eugene Bolton (ed.), *Athanase de Mézières and the Louisiana-Texas Frontier, 1768–1780*, I, 216, n.318; II, 205–206.

12. For other legends reported in recent years in this region, see Stan Shelton, "Nocona Family Believes Treasure Is Buried in Yard," *Wichita Falls Times*, April 25, 1959; Don James, "Gold Awaits Lucky Finder," *Wichita Falls Times*, December 23, 1962. One legend tells of a Spanish ship that sailed up Red River and foundered near Spanish Fort. See "Wreck of the Pinta on Plum Island Severed Spanish Succession Line," *Daily Oklahoman*, December 6, 1908.

13. James D. Morrison (ed.), "Notes from *The Northern Standard*," *Chronicles of Oklahoma*, Vol. XIX (September, 1941), 281–83. The story of seeking the lost twenty-seven mule loads originally appeared in "The Gold Hunters," *Northern Standard*, June 16, 1849.

14. *The United States Complainant v. The State of Texas in Equity*, II, 1077–96 (hereafter cited as *The United States v. The State of Texas*).

15. This story, "Recovery of Huge Treasure Hidden in Cave near Spanish Fort Related," was reprinted in the *Eagle* (special centennial issue of the Spanish Fort High School), May 10, 1935.

16. Joseph Carroll McConnell, *The West Texas Frontier*, 17.

17. Interview with Mrs. Joe Benton, June, 1963.

18. Jim Koethe, "Spanish Fort Still Cloaks in Mystery Its Real Story," *Wichita Falls Times*, July 12, 1960; James Marler, of Lawton, to the author, February, 1969.

19. Noel M. Loomis and Abraham P. Nasatir, *Pedro Vial and the Roads to Santa Fe*, 171, 265, 267, 351, 388 (hereafter cited as *Pedro Vial*).

20. *Ibid.*, 265; see also Castañeda, *Our Catholic Heritage in Texas*, III, 150–70.

21. Castañeda, *Our Catholic Heritage in Texas*, III, 155; Loomis and Nasatir, *Pedro Vial*, 285–87.

22. Castañeda, *Our Catholic Heritage in Texas*, III, 156; Loomis and Nasatir, *Pedro Vial*, 297.

23. Castañeda, *Our Catholic Heritage in Texas*, III, 157.

24. Loomis and Nasatir, *Pedro Vial*, 315.

25. Castañeda, *Our Catholic Heritage in Texas*, III, 164.

26. *Ibid.*, III, 170.

27. Loomis and Nasatir, *Pedro Vial*, xxi, 416–17.

28. *Ibid.*, xxii–xxiii, 388, 540.

29. *Ibid.*, 538, 540.

3. Quests for Red River's Silver Mines

1. Castañeda, *Our Catholic Heritage in Texas*, III, 255.

2. Bolton, *Athanase de Mézières and the Louisiana-Texas Frontier 1768–1780*, I, 294, 296.

3. *Ibid.*, I, 104, II, 38.

4. Jonathan Daniels, *The Devil's Backbone: The Story of the Natchez Trace*, 102–103.

5. John Sibley, *A Report from Natchitoches in 1807* (ed. by Annie Heloise Abel), 13, 40–42.

6. *Ibid.*, 56–59.

7. *Ibid.*, 74.

8. *Ibid.*, 75–76.

9. John Sibley to General Henry Dearborn, *American State Papers, Indian Affairs*, I, 729–30.

10. Clarence Edwin Carter, *The Territorial Papers of the United States: The Territory of Orleans*, IX, 799–800.

11. W. C. C. Claiborne, *Official Letter Books of W. C. C. Claiborne, 1801–1816* (ed. by Dunbar Rowland), IV, 187–90, 199–200.

12. Julia Kathryn Garrett, "Dr. John Sibley and the Louisiana-Texas Frontier, 1803–1814," *Southwestern Historical Quarterly*, Vol. XLVII (July, 1943), 49–51 (hereafter cited as "Dr. John Sibley").

13. Castañeda, *Our Catholic Heritage in Texas*, V, 283–84.

14. "Copy of a journal from Nackitosh into the interior of Louisiana on the waters of Red River, Trinity, Brassos, Colorado & the Sabine performed between the first of July 1808 & May 1809. By Capt. Anthony Glass of the Territory of Mississippi," manuscript in Silliman Family Papers, Yale University Library, New Haven. All excerpts from the Glass manuscript are quoted by permission of Yale University Library. Glass's misspellings have not been corrected.

15. Loomis and Nasatir, *Pedro Vial*, 499.

16. John Maley, "Journal of John Maley's wanderings in the Red River country of the Southwest, 1811–1813," manuscript in Silliman Family Papers, Yale University Library. All excerpts from the Maley manuscript are quoted by permission of Yale University Library (hereafter cited as "Maley Journal"). Maley's misspellings have not been corrected.

17. Garrett, "Dr. John Sibley," *Southwestern Historical Quarterly*, Vol. XLVII (January, 1944), 321–23.

18. "Maley Journal."

19. John Sibley to Benjamin Silliman, June 2, 1822, Silliman Family Papers.

20. *Ibid.*

21. "Maley Journal."

22. *Ibid.*

23. *Ibid.*

24. Oliver Cummings Farrington, "Catalogue of the Meteorites of North America to Jan. 1, 1909," *Memoirs of the National Academy of Sciences*, Vol.

XIII (1915), 367 (hereafter cited as "Catalogue of the Meteorites").

25. William Johnson to Benjamin Silliman, August 18, 1821, Silliman Family Papers.

26. Sibley to Silliman, June 2, 1822, Silliman Family Papers.

27. Benjamin Silliman, "Notice of the Malleable Iron of Louisiana," *American Journal of Science*, Vol. VIII (1824), 218–25.

28. Farrington, "Catalogue of the Meteorites," *Memoirs of the National Academy of Sciences*, Vol. XIII (1915), 368.

29. J. H. Kuykendall, "Reminiscences of Early Texans," *Texas Historical Association Quarterly*, Vol. VI (January, 1903), 249–50.

30. Daniel Shipman, *Frontier Life*, 23–26.

31. David B. Edward, *History of Texas*, 44–45.

32. James W. Parker, *The Rachel Plummer Narrative,* 111.

33. Farrington, "Catalogue of the Meteorites," *Memoirs of the National Academy of Sciences*, Vol. XIII (1915), 486–90.

34. *Ibid.*, 160–61.

4. Oklahoma's Forgotten Treasure Trail

1. Grant Foreman, *A History of Oklahoma*, 66–67.

2. Grant Foreman, "Sources of Oklahoma History," *Chronicles of Oklahoma*, Vol. V (March, 1927), 44–46.

3. Foreman, *A History of Oklahoma*, 66–67.

4. *The United States* v. *The State of Texas*, II, 1330–39.

5. Walter Prescott Webb and H. Bailey Carroll (eds.), *The Handbook of Texas*, I, 928–29.

6. A. W. Neville, *The Red River Valley: Then and Now*, 251.

7. Bill Thompson, "Are Bars of Mexican Gold Resting on Lake's Bottom?" *Daily Oklahoman*, January 10, 1965.

8. "Texan, 74, Recalls Search for Gold Left by Mexicans," *Daily Oklahoman*, May 15, 1961.

9. *The United States* v. *The State of Texas*, II, 1339–42.

10. *Ibid.*, II, 1320–30.

11. *Ibid.*, II, 1304–14.

12. Josiah Gregg, *Commerce of the Prairies* (ed. by Max L. Moorhead), 334–35.

13. Noel M. Loomis, *The Texan–Santa Fé Pioneers*, 42, n.9.

14. *The United States* v. *The State of Texas*, II, 1255–59.

15. Rex Wallace Strickland, "History of Fannin County, Texas, 1836–1843," *Southwestern Historical Quarterly*, Vol. XXXIII (April, 1930), 267.

16. *The United States* v. *The State of Texas*, II, 1347–56.

17. Strickland, "History of Fannin County, Texas, 1836–1843," *Southwestern Historical Quarterly*, Vol. XXXIII (April, 1930), 267–68.

18. Audy J. Middlebrooks and Glenna Middlebrooks, "Holland Coffee of Red River," *Southwestern Historical Quarterly*, Vol. LXIX (October, 1965), 145–62; Graham Landrum and Allan Smith, *Grayson County: An Illustrated History of Grayson County, Texas*, 1–10; Mattie Davis Lucas and Mita Holsapple, *A History of Grayson County, Texas*, 35–37, 56–57.

19. W. H. Clift, "Warren's Trading Post," *Chronicles of Oklahoma*, Vol. II (June, 1924), 129–40.

20. The trading post may have been on a knoll about four hundred yards east of Cache Creek, a half mile north of Red River in the NE¼ of S.8, T.5S., R.10W. When a man named Todd filed on the land in 1901, he found foundation stones, and while he was breaking sod, he unearthed the remains of charred oak logs. *Ibid.* See also Hugh D. Corwin, "Abel Warren, Area's First Trader, Dealt in Mexican Slaves," *Lawton Constitution*, September 20, 1962.

21. Clift, "Warren's Trading Post," *Chronicles of Oklahoma*, Vol. II (June, 1924), 132.

22. Dobie, *Legends of Texas*, 96–97.

23. For a modern version of this tale, which places the treasure on the Wichita River near a stone carved with a circle, a stream, and mule tracks, see Jim Koethe, "Million Dollar Treasure May Be Buried in Wichita," *Wichita Falls Record News*, November 15, 1956; Jim Koethe, "Iowa Park Man Believes Million Dollar Loot Rests in Wichita River," *Wichita Falls Times*, July 12, 1959.

24. Steve Wilson, "Colonel Snively's Lost Ledge of Gold," *True Frontier*, September, 1968, pp. 14–17, 50–53.

25. *The United States* v. *The State of Texas*, II, 1219–29.

26. *Ibid.*, II, 1211–19.

27. "Gold in Texas," *Northern Standard* (Clarksville, Texas), May 26, 1849; "The Gold Hunters," *Northern Standard*, June 16, 1849.

28. *Northern Standard*, May 26, 1849. At that early date the Clarksville editor reported: "It has been for years, reputed that gold was plentiful in the range of mountains known as the Wichita chain." For excerpts of this story, see Morrison, "Notes from *The Northern Standard*," *Chronicles of Oklahoma*, Vol. XIX (September, 1941), 281–83.

29. *The United States* v. *The State of Texas*, II, 1105–09.

30. *Ibid.*, II, 1066–73.

31. *Ibid.*, II, 1073–77.

32. *Ibid.*, II, 1077–96.

33. Both Lawrence Sullivan Ross and his brother, Peter F. Ross, led Ranger companies in this area before the Civil War. In 1859 Lawrence recaptured Cynthia Ann Parker when his Rangers attacked a Comanche village on the Pease River.

34. *The United States* v. *The State of Texas*, II, 1096–98.

35. Floyd V. Studer, "Archaeology of the Texas Panhandle," *Panhandle-Plains Historical Review*, Vol. XXVIII (1955), 87–95.

36. Alex D. Krieger, *Culture Complexes and Chronology in Northern Texas with Extension of Puebloan Datings to the Mississippi Valley*, 18–26 (hereafter cited as *Culture Complexes*). For a detailed study of the Pueblo ruins, see pp. 17–84.

37. *The United States* v. *The State of Texas*, II, 1176–81.

38. Krieger, *Culture Complexes*, 24–25.

39. Clevy Lloyd Strout, "Flora and Fauna Mentioned in the Journals of the Coronado Expedition," *Great Plains Journal*, Vol. XI (Fall, 1971), 7.

40. A. B. Thomas, "Spanish Exploration of Oklahoma 1599–1792," *Chronicles of Oklahoma*, Vol. VI (June, 1928), 186–213; Castañeda, *Our Catholic Heritage in Texas*, I, 184–94.

41. Loomis and Nasatir, *Pedro Vial*, 499, 501, 535.

42. H. Bailey Carroll (ed.), "The Journal of Lieutenant J. W. Abert from Bent's Fort to St. Louis in 1845," *Panhandle-Plains Historical Review*, Vol. XIV (1941), 49–53, 71.

43. Grant Foreman, *Marcy and the Gold Seekers*, 226–27, n.3.

44. C. Boone McClure, Director, Panhandle-Plains Historical Society, to the author, December 8, 1965.

5. Ghosts of Devil's Canyon and Their Gold

1. Gregg, *Commerce of the Prairies*, 322, 347.

2. Many Oklahoma histories have stated this as fact.

3. Herbert E. Bolton, "The Jumano Indians in Texas, 1650–1771," *Texas Historical Association Quarterly*, Vol. XV (July, 1911), 66–84; Herbert E. Bolton, "The Spanish Occupation of Texas, 1519–1690," *Texas Historical Association Quarterly*, Vol. XVI (July, 1912), 8–22; Castañeda, *Our Catholic Heritage in Texas*, I, 200–207.

4. J. L. Puckett and Ellen Puckett, *History of Oklahoma and Indian Territory and Homeseekers' Guide*, 107. Puckett said that he based his history on old miners' accounts.

5. "Wichita Mountains, Their Mining History Told Briefly," *Purcell Register*, February 16, 1893.

6. John Sibley to General Henry Dearborn, Secretary of War, *American State Papers, Indian Affairs*, I, 725–31.

7. Gregg, *Commerce of the Prairies*, 350–51; see also Joseph B. Thoburn, *A Standard History of Oklahoma*, I, 33.

8. *The United States* v. *The State of Texas*, II, 1347–56.

9. Foreman, "Sources of Oklahoma History," *Chronicles of Oklahoma*, Vol. V (March, 1927), 44–46; Albert Pike, "Narrative of a Journey in the Prairie," *Arkansas Historical Association Publications*, Vol. IV

(1917), 94, 137.

10. George H. Shirk, "Peace on the Plains," *Chronicles of Oklahoma*, Vol. XXVII (Spring, 1950), 2–41; Louis Pelzer, "The Expedition to the Pawnee Pict Village," in *Marches of the Dragoons in the Mississippi Valley*, 34–48.

11. *The United States* v. *The State of Texas*, II, 1042–64.

12. *Ibid.*, II, 1273–82.

13. *Ibid.*, II, 1260–72.

14. *Ibid.*, II, 965–85.

15. J. O. Tuton, "Under Fourteen Flags," *Mangum Daily Star*, October 13, 1937.

16. *The United States* v. *The State of Texas*, I, 186–93, 576–92.

17. "Silver and Gold," *Mangum Star*, February 12, 1892. Twenty months later some mining must have been continuing, for it was reported that "in Greer County several old Spanish silver mines have been reopened." See "Oklahoma Minerals," *Guthrie Daily Leader*, October 17, 1893; *Norman Transcript*, October 20, 1893.

18. *The United States* v. *The State of Texas*, I, 355–67.

19. *Ibid.*, I, 472–85.

20. *Ibid.*, I, 665–76.

21. "Mystery and Romance in Old Diggings, Devil's Canyon, Wichita Mountains, Bears Old Legends of Spaniards," *Daily Oklahoman*, April 23, 1939.

22. Indian-Pioneer History, Foreman Collection, Vol. 29, p. 452.

23. *Ibid.*, Vol. 69, pp. 165–67.

24. J. Frank Dobie, "The Treasure Is Always There," *True West*, September, 1954, p. 35.

25. Tuton, "Under Fourteen Flags," *Mangum Daily Star*, October 13, 1937.

26. *Ibid.*

27. *Ibid.*

28. George A. Frampton to Arthur R. Lawrence, July 10, 1958, Frampton File, Museum of the Great Plains, Lawton, Oklahoma; Frampton to the author, February 7, 1972.

29. "Her Collection Tells About Devil's Canyon," *Kiowa County Star-Review* (Hobart), June 20, 1946.

30. Interview with Jay Winters, Altus, June, 1963.

31. "Nugget at Lawton," *Mangum Star*, April 10, 1902.

32. "Prospecting Party to Locate Wichita Copper Mine," *Daily News-Republican*, August 31, 1907. During the Wichita gold rush many reports were made of Mexican mines and smelters in the mountains. Many of these "ancient" diggings could well have been the work of the prospectors of 1849, but invariably old diggings were "Spanish." See *Mineral Kingdom* (Lawton), June 8, 1905.

33. Interview with Bert Cook, of Phoenix, Arizona, June, 1972.

34. A. C. Greene, *The Last Captive*, xiii.

35. Interview with R. S. Nolan, of Lawton, March, 1958.

36. Interview with Lewis Hankins, of Lawton, November, 1959.

37. Interview with Jack Brown, of Sunset, Texas, June, 1963.

6. Jesse James's Two-Million-Dollar Treasure

1. As recently as June, 1967, Tom O'Hare, of Gibson City, Illinois, spent ten days and twenty-five hundred dollars seeking the James loot in the Wichitas, and left promising to return. *Lawton Constitution*, June 23, 1967.

2. Frank O. Hall and Lindsey H. Whitten, *Jesse James Rides Again*, 25–28.

3. Interview with Slim Dillingham, of Lawton, March, 1958, and on many occasions over the following years.

4. "Younger Visiting," *Daily Oklahoman*, November 17, 1903.

5. "Younger at Lawton," *Daily Oklahoman*, December 1, 1903.

6. "Former Outlaw Will Reside at Fletcher," *Daily News-Republican*, November 18, 1907. Oddly, another erstwhile outlaw appeared in Lawton shortly afterward. The same paper announced on December 22, 1907, that Emmett Dalton, "recently pardoned, . . . is figuring on embarking in the tailoring business."

7. Tom Sharrock, "Frank James' House May Be Moved Soon," *Lawton Constitution*, May 10, 1959.

8. Dobie, *Coronado's Children*, 209–301.

9. Interview with Gordon Ferguson, of Cache, December, 1958.

10. Interview with Jim Wilkerson, of Medicine Park, July, 1959, and subsequent dates.

11. Patrick J. McKenna, "Caches in the Keechi Hills," *Daily Oklahoman*, August 14, 1932.

12. Hall and Whitten, *Jesse James Rides Again*, 26.

13. McKenna, "Caches in the Keechi Hills," *Daily Oklahoman*, August 14, 1932.

14. "Fiction Outdone by Facts in Finding Treasure Buried by James Boys near Cement," *Daily Oklahoman*, May 9, 1920.

15. *Ibid.* McKenna pegged the recovery at five thousand dollars, unearthed in a water hole on the NW¼ of S.24, T.5N., R.9W., on the land of F. J. McKenna.

16. *Ibid.*

17. McKenna, "Caches in the Keechi Hills," *Daily Oklahoman*, August 14, 1932.

18. Buford Morgan, "Treasures of the Wichitas," *Chronicles of Comanche County*, Vol. IV (Spring, 1958), 23–28.

19. Interview with L. A. Owen, of Fletcher, May,

1971.

20. Lindsey H. Whitten, "Lawton Trio Believes End of Trail Is Near in 16-Year Search for Fabulous Treasure in Expansive Wichitas," *Lawton Constitution*, February 29, 1948.

21. Hall and Whitten, *Jesse James Rides Again*, 25.

22. *Ibid.*; interview with Slim Dillingham, a member of that search party.

23. Lindsey H. Whitten, "Joe Hunter Is near End of Rainbow," *Lawton Constitution*, May 19, 1948. I am indebted to Dale Durham, of Elgin, for the full wording of the inscription on the brass bucket.

24. Interview with Wells Blevins, of Medicine Park, June, 1963.

25. *Ibid.*

26. *Ibid.* In a May, 1959, interview Ed Keith, of Lawton, said that he believed Von was a member of the gang. In December, 1959, Fred Huff, of Lawton, said that Von had been with Jesse and Frank when they buried "twenty-two burro loads of Mexican gold" in the Wichitas. Huff confirmed the story that Jesse was planning to kill Von. Slim Dillingham often told a similar story about Von and remembered him as an old man in Lawton.

27. Paul McClung, "Gold Lust Stronger Than Drink," *Lawton Constitution*, April 30, 1950.

28. Interview with Dean Salyer, February, 1958, and on many subsequent occasions.

29. Interview with J. B. Holderbaum, of Lawton, October, 1958, and at subsequent times.

30. James C. White, *The Promised Land: A History of Brown County*, 48, 67–69; Tevis Clyde Smith, *Frontier's Generation*, 32–34.

7. The Last of the Old Prospectors

1. W. Eugene Hollon, "A Spanish 'Arrastra' in the Wichita Mountains," *Chronicles of Oklahoma*, Vol. XXXIV (Winter, 1956), 443–55. See also Sources for a selection of my articles on the Wichita gold rush.

2. [Harry Stroud], "Ison Oldest County Citizen," *Historical Romances*, Vol. I (September, 1931), 15–17. See also Harry Stroud, "George W. Ison Biography," Indian-Pioneer History, Foreman Collection, Vol. 87, pp. 411–26.

3. Interview with Silas Ison, August, 1958, and on many occasions in subsequent years.

4. There appears to be little doubt that George Ison was in the Wichitas as early as 1866. In 1904 he showed reporters "excavations made in the rocks by himself in 1866, and they certainly showed unmistakable evidence of having been dug out many years ago." *Mineral Kingdom*, December 29, 1904.

5. For a similar version of Silas' tales, see Morgan, "Treasures of the Wichitas," *Chronicles of Comanche County*, Vol. VI (Spring, 1960), 34–36.

6. As early as 1905, Silas reported that he had found a lost Spanish mine. *Mineral Kingdom*, January 26, 1905.

7. Stroud, "George W. Ison Biography," Indian-Pioneer History, Foreman Collection, Vol. 87, pp. 411–26.

8. Silas Ison lived to see his one-hundredth birthday. On April 1, 1972, he joined his fellow gold seekers of yore.

8. Skeletons, Jewels, and Platinum

1. Interview with Jim Wilkerson, June, 1960, and on subsequent dates.

2. Jeff Cox, of Lawton, had heard a similar story, in which it was claimed that two pairs of leather chaps of jewels were buried near the outlaw dugout and spring. Interview with Cox, October, 1959.

3. "Dead Man's Bones," *Herald-Sentinel* (Cloud Chief), November 15, 1895.

4. *The United States* v. *The State of Texas*, II, 1077–78, 1082, 1093–94.

5. Tuton, "Under Fourteen Flags," *Mangum Daily Star*, October 13, 1937.

6. Interview with R. S. Nolan, of Lawton, March, 1958, and subsequent dates.

7. *El Reno News*, April 12, 1900.

8. "Was It a Deadly Duel?" *Lawton Weekly News*, December 25, 1902.

9. "Found Man's Bones," *Lawton Weekly News*, April 9, 1903.

10. "Old Gun Barrel," *Weekly Republican*, May 14, 1903.

11. "Skeleton Found in a Dark Cave," *Daily Oklahoman*, December 20, 1903.

12. Walter R. Smith, "Some Legends of Oklahoma," *Chronicles of Oklahoma,* Vol. IV (March, 1926), 52.

13. "Human Form Unearthed in Big Pasture," *Daily News-Republican*, October 18, 1907.

14. "Skeleton in Trunk Found in a Grave," *Daily News-Republican*, October 18, 1907.

15. Interview with Bill Argo, December, 1958, and subsequent dates.

16. Interview with Gordon Ferguson, of Cache, December, 1958.

17. "Story of Plot to Get Hidden Platinum Mine Bared in Murder on Road near Fort Cobb," *Daily Oklahoman*, June 10, 1924.

18. James Depew, of Lawton, always believed that Keown had salted Bat Cave with platinum from Mexico. Interview with Depew, January, 1959, and subsequent dates.

19. Interview with Lloyd Stone, of Meers, August, 1958, and subsequent dates.

20. Cedric Caldwell, "Doan's Crossing on Red River," *Chronicles of Comanche County*, Vol. VI (Autumn, 1960), 78–81.

21. James Mooney, "Calendar History of the Kiowa," in *Seventeenth Annual Report of the Bureau of Ethnology*, Part I, 254–59.

22. Stanley Francis Radzyminski, "Charles Radziminski: Soldier of Two Continents," *Chronicles of Comanche County*, Vol. IV (Spring, 1958), 39–48; see also Colonel W. S. Nye, *Carbine and Lance: The Story of Old Fort Sill*, 18–28.

23. Josh Drake, Jr., "I Still Dig for Buried Treasure," *True West*, April, 1955.

24. Interview with Josh Drake, Jr., of Mangum, July, 1959.

25. J. C. Stratton, letter in *Frontier Times*, Spring, 1958.

26. J. C. Stratton to the author, October 4, 1959.

9. Gold the Stagecoaches Never Delivered

1. Interview with Morris Swett, of Lawton, January, 1958, and subsequent dates.

2. Shorty Shelburne, *Daily Oklahoman*, March 17, 1964, p. 2; and earlier edition of same date, "Dig That Treasure? It's Army's Right," p. 2.

3. Story by Paul McClung, *Lawton Constitution*, April 1, 1964.

4. Story by Paul McClung, *Lawton Constitution*, April 2, 1964.

5. Hobert D. Radland, *The History of Rush Springs*, 23–28, 42–45, 85–88.

6. George Rainey, *The Cherokee Strip,* 137–41.

7. Roscoe P. Conkling and Margaret B. Conkling, *The Butterfield Overland Mail 1857–1869*, I, 130.

8. *Indian Chieftain* (Vinita), June 14, 1894; *Norman Transcript*, August 10, 1894; *Vinita Leader*, July 2, 1896.

9. *Eagle-Gazette* (Stillwater), May 4, 1894; *El Reno News*, August 7, August 21, September 4, 1896.

10. *Edmond Sun-Democrat*, April 6, 1894, April 23, 1897, October 20, 1899.

11. *Edmond Sun-Democrat*, June 29, 1894; *Alva Review*, March 7, 1901.

12. "Buried Stagecoach Loot to Be Sought in Refuge," *Lawton Constitution*, October 12, 1947.

13. Jerry B. Jeter, "Pioneer Preacher," *Chronicles of Oklahoma*, Vol. XXIII (Winter, 1945), 358; see also General R. A. Sneed, "The Reminiscences of an Indian Trader," *Chronicles of Oklahoma*, Vol. XIV (June, 1936), 137–38.

14. Interview with Arthur Henderson, June, 1959, and subsequent dates.

10. The Lost Cave with the Iron Door

1. Interview with Dave Hungerford, June, 1960, and subsequent dates.

2. Morgan, "Treasures of the Wichitas," *Chronicles*

of Comanche County, Vol. III (Autumn, 1957), 93–96.

3. Interview with Silas Lee Ison, August, 1958, and on many occasions in subsequent years.

4. Morgan, "Treasures of the Wichitas," *Chronicles of Comanche County*, Vol. III (Autumn, 1957), 94.

5. Interview with John French, May, 1959.

11. The Frenchmen's Gold at Sugar Loaf Peak

1. Interview with Cy Strong, June, 1966.

2. Tom Bailey, "Oklahoma's Buried Gold Mystery," *True Western Adventures*, August, 1959, pp. 10–13, 60–62.

3. Ralph Emerson Twitchell, *The Leading Facts of New Mexican History*, II, 180.

4. "The Tres Piedras Legend," *Daily Oklahoman*, September 27, 1903. For more on Mike Ryan, see William E. Baker, "A History of Cimarron County," *Chronicles of Oklahoma*, Vol. XXXI (Autumn, 1953), 266.

5. Bailey, "Oklahoma's Buried Gold Mystery," *True Western Adventures*, August, 1959, p. 62.

12. The Mystery of Cascorillo—A Lost City

1. "Hopeful Will the Gold Find Pay?" *Daily Oklahoma State Capital*, June 20, 1895. Only three years before, a silver and lead discovery had been made at Seger, four miles west of Colony in Washita County. *Norman Transcript*, October 21, 1892.

2. "New Gold Find," *Daily Oklahoma State Capital*, June 8, 1895; "Gold! Gold! A Find in Oklahoma," *Daily Oklahoma State Capital*, June 10, 1895; "Special Gold Edition," *Herald-Sentinel*, June 14, 1895. On June 21, 1895, with some reservations the *Edmond Sun-Democrat* reprinted the *Herald-Sentinel* special edition under the head "Three Assays Made," stating: "Its story of a Colorado mining syndicate swooping down on the country is taken to be the throb of an over excited imagination. Otherwise its account is reliable."

3. "Special Gold Edition," *Herald-Sentinel*, June 14, 1895.

4. "From the Gold Field," *Arapahoe Argus*, June 21, 1895.

5. *Arapahoe Bee*, June 28, 1895.

6. "Territorial Round-Ups," *Norman Transcript*, July 12, 1895, reprinted from *El Reno Eagle*.

7. *Herald-Sentinel*, July 19, 1895.

8. "Boggy Mines," *Herald-Sentinel*, July 14, 1895. This was the same E. A. Williams who five years later would found the mining camp of Wildman in the Wichita Mountains, then part of the Kiowa-Comanche-Apache Reservation. It is probable that E. A.'s father, William Williams, a Methodist circuit preacher, was the first to discover gold in the Washita field. See *Edmond Sun-Democrat*, June 28, 1895.

9. I unearthed the Cascorillo story and reported it.

Steve Wilson, "Ghosts Guard Devil's Canyon Gold," *Golden West*, September, 1965; "Was Cascorillo Really There?" *Sunday Oklahoman*, January 9, 1966. As intended, this disclosure prompted some interest. Although the archaeological conclusion appears that "Cascorillo was a figment of Pedro Juangonzales' imagination," the discovery of the Mexican relics, human skeletons, and coins as reported by several sources cannot be disregarded. For the archaeological conclusion, after "regional and national archival repositories were contacted and their materials carefully checked" and an on-site investigation, see Harold N. Ottaway, "Cascorillo: Archaeological Fact or Romantic Fantasy?" *Chronicles of Oklahoma*, Vol. XLIX (Spring, 1971), 100–104.

10. *Guymon Herald*, July 1, 1909.

11. Walter R. Smith, "Some Legends of Oklahoma," *Chronicles of Oklahoma*, Vol. IV (March, 1926), 51–52.

13. Cartloads, Jack Loads, and an Aztec Sun God

1. "Legends of Gold Are Many," *Daily Oklahoman*, July 17, 1910.

2. Nat M. Taylor, *A Brief History of Roger Mills County*, 22–23.

3. Interview with Lost Creek residents, June, 1960.

4. Muriel H. Wright, *The Story of Oklahoma*, 23.

5. *Indian-Pioneer History*, Foreman Collection, Vol. 5, p. 28.

6. *Edmond Sun-Democrat*, February 15, 1895.

7. "Buried Treasure Story, Oklahomans Believe They Have a Clew to $500,000 of Spanish Gold," *Hennessey Clipper*, June 4, 1896.

8. Claude E. Hensley to Morris Swett, Morris Swett Collection, Fort Sill Museum, Fort Sill, Oklahoma.

9. Dobie, *Coronado's Children*, 296–97.

10. Interview with Jock Thomas, of Lawton, April, 1957, and subsequent dates.

11. Interview with Comanche residents, April, 1963.

12. Howard F. Van Zandt, "The History of Camp Holmes and Chouteau's Trading Post," *Chronicles of Oklahoma*, Vol. XIII (September, 1935), 316–37.

13. *Ibid.*, 333.

14. D. B. Hamilton, "Legend Says Gold Lies Beneath Tulsa Soil," *Tulsa Daily World*, January 1, 1933.

14. The Treasures the Arbuckles Guard

1. "Lost Spaniard Mine Discovered," *Daily Oklahoman*, September 18, 1912.

2. "Thirteen Jack Loads," *Daily Ardmoreite*, March 15, 1896.

3. Mrs. Naomi A. Hintze, of Salisbury, North Carolina, to the author, December 6, 1961. See also Naomi A. Hintze, *Buried Treasure Waits for You*, 174.

4. "Arbuckle Mountains Are Rich in Mineral Wealth," *Daily Oklahoman*, November 27, 1910.

5. Van Zandt, "The History of Camp Holmes and Chouteau's Trading Post," *Chronicles of Oklahoma*, Vol. XIII (September, 1935), 331.

6. Indian-Pioneer History, Foreman Collection, Vol. 71, p. 416.

7. Interview with O. J. Testerman, of Springer, June, 1963.

8. Indian-Pioneer History, Foreman Collection, Vol. 16, pp. 489–90.

9. Interview with Morris Swett, of Lawton, January, 1958, and subsequent dates.

10. Ralph L. Evans, *Frontier Days of Love County*, 10–11.

11. Muriel H. Wright, "A Spanish *Arrastra* in McClain County," *Chronicles of Oklahoma*, Vol. XXXIV (Winter, 1956), 484.

12. *El Reno News*, November 9, 1899.

13. "May Locate Booty of James Gang in Indian Territory," *Muskogee Times-Democrat*, November 6, 1907.

14. Jim Koethe, "Wichita [Arbuckle] Mountains Treasure Trove," *Wichita Falls Times*, August 9, 1959.

15. Tales of the Indian Nations

1. H. B. Hutchinson, "Daddy of Lead Zinc Mines Tells His Story," *Daily Oklahoman*, May 11, 1930; La-Vere [Shoenfelt] Anderson, "Adventurous Prospector Seeking Fabled Spanish Gold Discovered Oklahoma's Rich Lead and Zinc District," *Tulsa Daily World*, April 19, 1931; Velma Nieberding, "Old Peoria: A Mother of Mining Camps," *Chronicles of Oklahoma*, Vol. L (Summer, 1972), 142–55.

2. A[rrell] M. Gibson, "Early Mining Camps in Northeastern Oklahoma," *Chronicles of Oklahoma*, Vol. XXXIV (Summer, 1956), 193–202.

3. *Ibid.*, 199–200; see also Arrell M. Gibson, *Wilderness Bonanza: The Tri-State District of Missouri, Kansas, and Oklahoma*, 39 (hereafter cited as *Wilderness Bonanza*).

4. Gibson, "Early Mining Camps," *Chronicles of Oklahoma*, XXXIV (Summer, 1956), 195; Gibson, *Wilderness Bonanza*, 16–17.

5. Gibson, "Early Mining Camps," *Chronicles of Oklahoma*, Vol. XXXIV (Summer, 1956), 196–98.

6. "Old Mystery Mine, Sunk by Spaniards 200 Years Ago, Caused Opening of District," *Daily Oklahoman*, April 22, 1923.

7. "Mexican Mine Is Late Discovery," *Daily Oklahoman*, December 6, 1908; Indian-Pioneer History, Foreman Collection, Vol. 93, p. 184.

8. S. W. Ross, "Tales of Hidden Treasure Along the Illinois, Cherokees and Spaniards Have Left a Rich Lore in Hill Tradition," *Tulsa Daily World*, June 28, 1931.

9. John Sibley to General Henry Dearborn, Secretary of War, *American State Papers, Indian Affairs*, I, 729.

10. Anna Lewis, "La Harpe's First Expedition in Oklahoma, 1718–1719," *Chronicles of Oklahoma*, Vol. II (December, 1924), 331–49. For an excellent work on La Harpe, see Mildred Mott Wedel, "J.-B. Bénard, Sieur de la Harpe: Visitor to the Wichitas in 1719," *Great Plains Journal*, Vol. 10 (Spring, 1971), 37–70.

11. Bolton, *Athanase de Mézières and the Louisiana-Texas Frontier, 1768–1780*, II, 83–84.

12. Indian-Pioneer History, Foreman Collection, Vol. 80, p. 297.

13. B. L. Phipps, "Lost Gold Mines of Oklahoma," *Chronicles of Oklahoma*, Vol. VII (September, 1929), 341–42; "Treasure Hunts Again Starting near Durant," *Tulsa Daily World*, April 16, 1934.

14. La-Vere Shoenfelt Anderson, "When There Was Gold in 'Them Thar Hills,'" *Tulsa Daily World*, March 22, 1931.

15. *Ibid.*

16. La-Vere Shoenfelt Anderson, "Seeking the Pot of Gold at Rainbow's End," *Tulsa Daily World*, March 29, 1931.

17. La-Vere [Shoenfelt] Anderson, "Buried Treasure in the Devil's Promenade," *Tulsa Daily World*, June 14, 1931.

18. Walter R. Smith, "Some Legends of Oklahoma," *Chronicles of Oklahoma*, Vol. IV (March, 1926), 53.

19. Arthur H. Lamb, *Tragedies of the Osage Hills*, 9–12.

20. S. W. Ross, "Tales of Hidden Treasure Along the Illinois," *Tulsa Daily World*, June 28, 1931.

21. *Ibid.*

22. *Ibid.*

23. *Ibid.*

24. *Ibid.*; see also Indian-Pioneer History, Foreman Collection, Vol. 42, pp. 444–46.

16. Gold the Outlaws Never Spent

1. "Hunt for Hidden Money Proves Not So Fruitful," *Blackwell Morning Tribune*, September 15, 1932.

2. La-Vere Shoenfelt Anderson, "Buried Treasure Left by Oklahoma Outlaws," *Tulsa Daily World*, March 15, 1931.

3. La-Vere [Shoenfelt] Anderson, "When the Bold Youngers Rode in Oklahoma," *Tulsa Daily World*, April 12, 1931.

4. Indian-Pioneer History, Foreman Collection, Vol. 82, pp. 19–22.

5. McKenna, "Caches in the Keechi Hills," *Daily Oklahoman*, August 14, 1932.

6. Shirley, *Law West of Fort Smith*, 100–101.

7. *Ibid.*, 102.

8. La-Vere [Shoenfelt] Anderson, "Caves of the Dalton Gang on Cliff Above Shell Creek Still Hold Lure for Those Seeking Hidden Bandit Gold," *Tulsa Daily World*, April 26, 1931.

9. *Ibid.*

10. Debo and Oskison, *Oklahoma: A Guide to the Sooner State*, 300.

11. "Yeager's Plunder Found, Money Believed to Have Been Hidden by Dick Yeager Found in a Cave," *Daily Oklahoman*, January 15, 1903.

17. Lost Indian Treasure

1. "Buried Treasure Is Found by Negroes," *Wilburton News*, October 27, 1905; "Buried Treasures Were Never Found," *Wilburton News*, November 24, 1905.

2. S. W. Ross, "'Old Nation' Indians Seek Lucky Cherokee," *Tulsa Daily World*, February 23, 1936.

3. Indian-Pioneer History, Foreman Collection, Vol. 33, pp. 65–68.

4. "Buried Treasures Were Never Found," *Wilburton News*, November 24, 1905.

5. Indian-Pioneer History, Foreman Collection, Vol. 5, p. 71.

6. *Ibid.*, Vol. 4, p. 126.

7. Ross, "Tales of Hidden Treasure Along the Illinois," *Tulsa Daily World*, June 28, 1931.

8. Indian-Pioneer History, Foreman Collection, Vol. 13, p. 439; Vol. 20, pp. 459–62; Vol. 26, pp. 392–94.

9. *Ibid.*, Vol. 29, p. 272.

10. Angie Debo, "The Location of the Battle of Round Mountains," *Chronicles of Oklahoma*, Vol. XLI (Spring, 1963), 70–104.

11. La-Vere [Shoenfelt] Anderson, "Death Haunts Trail of Buried Slave Gold," *Tulsa Daily World*, June 21, 1931.

12. Anderson, "Buried Treasure in the Devil's Promenade," *Tulsa Daily World*, June 14, 1931.

13. Walter R. Smith, "Some Legends of Oklahoma," *Chronicles of Oklahoma*, Vol. IV (March, 1926), 52–53.

14. "'Capt. Kid' of Indian Territory," *Daily Oklahoman*, May 1, 1904.

15. Shirley, *Law West of Fort Smith*, 88.

16. "Search for Treasure," *Lawton Constitution*, September 15, 1904.

18. The Treasure the Spaniards Keep Hunting

1. "Ed Carey Has Drunk from Spring Eighty-one Years," *Daily Oklahoman*, July 30, 1916.

2. Jim Koethe, "Abandoned Mine Object of Hunt," *Wichita Falls Times*, August 23, 1959.

3. "Old Story About Buzzard Hill Gold Mine North of Spiro Continues to Thrive," *Daily Oklahoman*, August 30, 1959.

4. "Lost Treasure Lures Hunters into Mountain," *Daily Oklahoman*, August 26, 1923.

5. *Ibid.*

6. Dobie, *Coronado's Children*, 40.

7. Indian-Pioneer History, Foreman Collection, Vol. 13, pp. 464–65.

8. Interview with Randall Wells, of Tulsa, December, 1966.

9. C. L. Packer, "Buried—and Drowned—Treasure," *Tulsa World*, July 19, 1964; C. L. Packer, "Land of Triangles, Turtles and Hatchets," *True West*, August, 1965, p. 14.

10. Ross, "Tales of Hidden Treasure Along the Illinois," *Tulsa Daily World*, June 28, 1931.

11. Indian-Pioneer History, Foreman Collection, Vol. 94, p. 52.

12. *Ibid.*, Vol. 31, p. 185.

13. *Ibid.*, Vol. 14, p. 395.

14. *Ibid.*, Vol. 30, p. 245.

Sources

Manuscripts

Bell, Robert E., Edward B. Jelks, and W. W. Newcomb, comps. "A Pilot Study of Wichita Indian Archeology and Ethnohistory." Final Report for Grant GS-964, National Science Foundation, August, 1967. Mimeographed.

Frampton, George A. Letter to Arthur R. Lawrence, July 10, 1958. Frampton File, Museum of the Great Plains, Lawton, Oklahoma.

Glass, Anthony. "Copy of a journal from Nackitosh into the interior of Louisiana on the waters of Red River, Trinity, Brassos, Colorado & the Sabine performed between the first of July 1808 & May 1809. By Capt. Anthony Glass of the Territory of Mississippi." Silliman Family Papers, Yale University Library, New Haven.

Hensley, Claude E. Letter to Morris Swett, April 10, 1957. Morris Swett Collection, Fort Sill Museum, Fort Sill, Oklahoma.

Indian-Pioneer History. 112 vols. Foreman Collection, Indian Archives Division, Oklahoma Historical Society, Oklahoma City.

Johnson, William. Letter to Benjamin Silliman, August 18, 1821. Silliman Family Papers, Yale University Library, New Haven.

Maley, John. "Journal of John Maley's wanderings in the Red River country of the Southwest, 1811–1813." Silliman Family Papers, Yale University Library, New Haven.

Newcomb, W. W., and W. T. Field. "A Preliminary Report Concerning an Ethnohistoric Investigation of the Wichita Indians in the Southern Plains." Austin, Texas Memorial Museum, December, 1966. Mimeographed.

Sibley, John. Letter to Benjamin Silliman, June 2, 1822. Silliman Family Papers, Yale University Library, New Haven.

Books

American State Papers, Indian Affairs. 2 vols. Washington, D.C., Gales & Seaton, 1832.

Bell, Robert E. *Oklahoma Archaeology: An Annotated Bibliography.* Norman, University of Oklahoma Press, 1969.

Bolton, Herbert Eugene, ed. *Athanase de Mézières and the Louisiana–Texas Frontier, 1768–1780.* 2 vols. Cleveland, Arthur H. Clark Co., 1914.

Breihan, Carl W. *The Complete and Authentic Life of Jesse James.* New York, Frederick Fell, 1953.

Carter, Clarence Edwin, comp. and ed. *The Territorial Papers of the United States: The Territory of Or-leans, 1803–1812.* Vol. IX. Washington, D.C., 1940.

Castañeda, Carlos E. *Our Catholic Heritage in Texas, 1519–1936.* 7 vols. Austin, Von Boeckmann-Jones Co., 1936–58.

Claiborne, W. C. C. *Official Letter Books of W. C. C. Claiborne, 1801–1816.* Ed. by Dunbar Rowland. 6 vols. Jackson, Miss., State Department of Archives and History, 1917.

Conkling, Roscoe P., and Margaret B. Conkling. *The Butterfield Overland Mail 1857–1869.* 2 vols. Glendale, Arthur H. Clark Co., 1947.

Daniels, Jonathan. *The Devil's Backbone: The Story of the Natchez Trace.* New York, McGraw-Hill, 1962.

Debo, Angie, and John M. Oskison, eds. *Oklahoma: A Guide to the Sooner State.* American Guide Series, Works Projects Administration. Norman, University of Oklahoma Press, 1941.

Dobie, J. Frank. *Coronado's Children.* New York, Grosset & Dunlap, 1930.

———, ed. *Legends of Texas.* Publications of the Texas Folklore Society, No. III. Reprint of 1924 edition. Hatboro, Penn., Folklore Associates, 1964.

Edward, David B. *The History of Texas.* Cincinnati, J. A. James & Co., 1836.

Evans, Ralph L. *Frontier Days of Love County.* Marietta, Okla., Marietta Monitor Publishing Co., 1966.

Farley, Gloria. *The Vikings Were Here.* Heavener, Okla., Heavener Ledger Print, August, 1968, January, 1972.

Foreman, Grant. *A History of Oklahoma.* Norman, University of Oklahoma Press, 1942.

———. *Marcy and the Gold Seekers.* Norman, University of Oklahoma Press, 1939.

Gibson, Arrell M. *Wilderness Bonanza: The Tri-State District of Missouri, Kansas, and Oklahoma.* Norman, University of Oklahoma Press, 1972.

Greene, A. C. *The Last Captive.* Austin, Encino Press, 1972.

Gregg, Josiah. *Commerce of the Prairies.* Ed. by Max L. Moorhead. Norman, University of Oklahoma Press, 1958.

Hall, Frank O., and Lindsey H. Whitten. *Jesse James Rides Again.* Lawton, Okla., LaHoma Publishing Co., 1948.

Hintze, Naomi A. *Buried Treasure Waits for You.* Indianapolis, Bobbs-Merrill Co., 1962.

Krieger, Alex D. *Culture Complexes and Chronology in Northern Texas, with Extension of Puebloan Datings to the Mississippi Valley.* Austin, University of Texas Publication No. 4640, October 22, 1946.

Lamb, Arthur H. *Tragedies of the Osage Hills.* Paw-

Oklahoma Treasures and Treasure Tales

huska, Okla., Osage Printery, n.d.

Landrum, Graham, and Allan Smith. *Grayson County: An Illustrated History of Grayson County, Texas.* 2d ed. Fort Worth, Historical Publishers, 1967.

Loomis, Noel M. *The Texan–Santa Fé Pioneers.* Norman, University of Oklahoma Press, 1958.

———, and Abraham P. Nasatir. *Pedro Vial and the Roads to Santa Fe.* Norman, University of Oklahoma Press, 1967.

Lucas, Mattie Davis, and Mita Holsapple Hall. *A History of Grayson County, Texas.* Sherman, Texas, Scruggs Printing Co., n.d.

McConnell, Joseph Carroll. *The West Texas Frontier.* Jacksboro, Texas, Gazette Press, 1933.

McReynolds, Edwin C. *Oklahoma: A History of the Sooner State.* Norman, University of Oklahoma Press, 1954.

Marcy, Captain Randolph B., and Captain G. B. McClellan. *Adventure on Red River: Report on the Exploration of the Headwaters of the Red River.* Ed. by Grant Foreman. Norman, University of Oklahoma Press, 1938.

Morison, Samuel Eliot. *The European Discovery of America: The Northern Voyages A.D. 500–1600.* New York, Oxford University Press, 1971.

Morris, John W., and Edwin C. McReynolds. *Historical Atlas of Oklahoma.* Norman, University of Oklahoma Press, 1965.

Neville, A. W. *The Red River Valley: Then and Now.* Paris, Texas, North Texas Publishing Co., 1948.

Nye, W. S. *Carbine and Lance: The Story of Old Fort Sill.* Norman, University of Oklahoma Press, 1937.

Parker, James W. *The Rachel Plummer Narrative.* Reprint of 1839 edition. Palestine, Texas, 1926.

Pelzer, Louis. *Marches of the Dragoons in the Mississippi Valley.* Iowa City, Iowa, State Historical Society of Iowa, 1917.

Pohl, Frederick J. *Atlantic Crossings Before Columbus.* New York, Norton, 1961.

———. *The Viking Explorers.* New York, Thomas Y. Crowell Co., 1966.

———. *The Viking Settlements of North America.* New York, Clarkson N. Potter, 1972.

Puckett, J. L., and Ellen Puckett. *History of Oklahoma and Indian Territory and Homeseekers' Guide.* Vinita, Okla., 1906.

Radland, Hobert D. *The History of Rush Springs.* Rush Springs, Okla., Gazette Publishing Co., 1952.

Rainey, George. *The Cherokee Strip.* Guthrie, Okla., Co-Operative Publishing Co., 1933.

Shipman, Daniel. *Frontier Life.* Houston, 1879.

Shirk, George H. *Oklahoma Place Names.* Norman, University of Oklahoma Press, 1965.

Shirley, Glenn. *Law West of Fort Smith: Frontier Justice in the Indian Territory, 1834–1896.* Reprint of 1957 edition. New York, Collier Books, 1961.

Sibley, Dr. John. *A Report from Natchitoches in 1807.* Ed. by Annie Heloise Abel. New York, Heye Foundation, 1922.

Smith, Tevis Clyde. *Frontier's Generation.* Brownwood, Texas, 1931.

Taylor, Nat M. *A Brief History of Roger Mills County.* n.p., 1947.

Thoburn, Joseph B. *A Standard History of Oklahoma.* 2 vols. New York, American Historical Society, 1916.

Thomas, Alfred B. *After Coronado: Spanish Exploration Northeast of New Mexico, 1696–1727.* Norman, University of Oklahoma Press, 1935.

Twitchell, Ralph Emerson. *The Leading Facts of New Mexican History.* 2 vols. Reprint of 1912 edition. Albuquerque, Horn & Wallace, Publishers, 1963.

The United States Complainant, v. The State of Texas in Equity. 2 vols. Supreme Court of the United States, October Term, 1894, No. 4, Original. Washington, D.C., Judd & Detweiler, 1894.

Webb, Walter Prescott, and H. Bailey Carroll, eds. *The Handbook of Texas.* 2 vols. Austin, Texas State Historical Association, 1952.

Wedel, Robert S. *The San Sabá Mission.* Austin, University of Texas Press, 1964.

Wedel, Waldo R. *Prehistoric Man on the Great Plains.* Norman, University of Oklahoma Press, 1961.

White, James C. *The Promised Land: A History of Brown County.* Brownwood, Brownwood Banner Publisher, 1941.

Wright, Muriel H. *The Story of Oklahoma.* Oklahoma City, Webb Publishing Co., 1929–30.

Young, Otis E, Jr. *Western Mining: An Informal Account of Precious-Metals Prospecting, Placering, Lode Mining, and Milling on the American Frontier from Spanish Times to 1893.* Norman, University of Oklahoma Press, 1970.

Articles

Allen, Henry Easton. "The Parilla Expedition to the Red River in 1759," *Southwestern Historical Quarterly*, Vol. XLIII (July, 1939), 53–71.

Anderson, La-Vere Shoenfelt. "Adventurous Prospector Seeking Fabled Spanish Gold Discovered Oklahoma's Rich Lead and Zinc District," *Tulsa Daily World*, April 19, 1931.

———. "Buried Treasure in the Devil's Promenade," *Tulsa Daily World*, June 14, 1931.

———. "Buried Treasure Left by Oklahoma Outlaws," *Tulsa Daily World*, March 15, 1931.

———. "Caves of the Dalton Gang on Cliff Above Shell Creek Still Hold Lure for Those Seeking Hidden Bandit Gold," *Tulsa Daily World*, April 26, 1931.

———. "Death Haunts Trail of Buried Slave Gold," *Tulsa Daily World*, June 21, 1931.

———. "Seeking the Pot of Gold at Rainbow's End," *Tulsa Daily World*, March 29, 1931.

———. "When the Bold Youngers Rode in Okla-

314

homa," *Tulsa Daily World*, April 12, 1931.

_____. "When There Was Gold in 'Them Thar Hills,'" *Tulsa Daily World*, March 22, 1931.

Baerreis, David A. "The Southern Cult and the Spiro Ceremonial Complex," *Bulletin of the Oklahoma Anthropological Society*, Vol. V (March, 1957), 23–38.

Bailey, Tom. "Oklahoma's Buried Gold Mystery," *True Western Adventures*, August, 1959.

Baker, William E. "A History of Cimarron County," *Chronicles of Oklahoma*, Vol. XXXI (Autumn, 1953), 266.

Bolton, Herbert E. "The Jumano Indians in Texas, 1650–1771," *Texas Historical Association Quarterly*, Vol. XV (July, 1911), 66–84.

_____. "The Spanish Occupation of Texas, 1519–1690," *Texas Historical Association Quarterly*, Vol. XVI (July, 1912), 8–22.

Burchardt, Bill. "Is There Gold in Our Hills?" *Daily Oklahoman*, October 21, 1956.

_____. "Lost Loot," *Oklahoma Today*, Winter, 1959.

Caldwell, Cedric. "Doan's Crossing on Red River," *Chronicles of Comanche County*, Vol. VI (Autumn, 1960), 78–81.

Carroll, H. Bailey, ed. "The Journal of Lieutenant J. W. Abert from Bent's Fort to St. Louis in 1845," *Panhandle-Plains Historical Review*, Vol. XIV (1941).

Clements, Forrest E. "Historical Sketch of the Spiro Mound," *Contributions from the Museum of the American Indian, Heye Foundation*, Vol. XIV (1945).

Clift, W. H. "Warren's Trading Post," *Chronicles of Oklahoma*, Vol. II (June, 1924), 129–40.

Cooper, Charles M. "The Big Pasture," *Chronicles of Oklahoma*, Vol. XXXV (Summer, 1957), 138–39.

Corwin, Hugh D. "Abel Warren, Area's First Trader, Dealt in Mexican Slaves," *Lawton Constitution*, September 20, 1962.

_____. "Spanish Traders Once Bartered with Indians near Tipton," *Lawton Constitution*, May 26, 1963.

Debo, Angie. "The Location of the Battle of Round Mountains," *Chronicles of Oklahoma*, Vol. LVI (Spring, 1963), 70–104.

Devine, John. "Mysterious Night-Riders at Craig County Farm Consult Map While Digging up Buried Treasure," *Muskogee Daily Phoenix*, February 17, 1935.

Dobie, J. Frank. "The Treasure Is Always There," *True West*, September, 1954.

Downing, Jim. "Vikings Here in 1006?" *Tulsa Tribune*, October 14, 1965.

Drake, Josh, Jr. "I Still Dig for Buried Treasure," *True West*, April, 1955.

Draper, W. R. "A New Gold Field." *Scientific American Supplement* No. 1352 (November 30, 1901), 21669–70.

Duffield, Lathel F. "The Taovayas Village of 1759: In Texas or Oklahoma?" *Great Plains Journal*, Vol. 4 (Spring, 1965), 39–48.

Dunn, William Edward. "The Apache Mission on the San Sabá River: Its Founding and Failure," *Southwestern Historical Quarterly*, Vol. XVII (April, 1914), 379–414.

Farley, Gloria. "Runestones Are Dated at Last," *Oklahoma's Orbit*, October 15, 1967.

_____. "Vikings in Oklahoma, November 11, 1012," *East Oklahoma Messenger* (Poteau), April 12, 1973.

Farrington, Oliver Cummings. "Catalogue of the Meteorites of North America to Jan. 1, 1909," *Memoirs of the National Academy of Sciences*, Vol. XIII (1915), 160–61, 366–71, 486–90.

Foreman, Grant. "The Lore of Devil's Canyon," *Daily Oklahoman*, February 17, 1935.

_____. "Oklahoma's Greatest Law Suit," *Daily Oklahoman*, November 25, 1934.

_____. "Sources of Oklahoma History," *Chronicles of Oklahoma*, Vol. V (March, 1927), 44–46.

Friend, Llerena. "Old Spanish Fort," *West Texas Historical Association Year Book*, Vol. XVI (October, 1940), 3–27.

Garrett, Julia Kathryn. "Dr. John Sibley and the Louisiana-Texas Frontier, 1803–1814," *Southwestern Historical Quarterly*, Vol. XLVII (July, 1943), 48–51, Vol. XLVII (January, 1944), 319–24.

Gibson, A. M. "Early Mining Camps in Northeastern Oklahoma," *Chronicles of Oklahoma*, Vol. XXXIV (Summer, 1956), 193–202.

Gould, Charles N. "Legends of Gold Are Many but None Prove to Exist," *Daily Oklahoman*, July 17, 1910.

Grove, Fred. "The Big Pasture," *Oklahoma Today*, Summer, 1966.

Hamilton, D. B. "Legend Says Gold Lies beneath Tulsa Soil," *Tulsa Daily World*, January 1, 1933.

Hamilton, Henry W. "The Spiro Mound," *Missouri Archaeologist*, Vol. 14 (October, 1952), 17–88.

Harper, Elizabeth Ann. "The Taovayas Indians in Frontier Trade and Diplomacy." Part I (1719–68), *Chronicles of Oklahoma*, Vol. XXXI (Autumn, 1953), 268–89; Part II (1769–79), *Southwestern Historical Quarterly*, Vol. LVII (October, 1953), 181–201; Part III (1779–1835), *Panhandle-Plains Historical Review*, Vol. XXVI (1953), 40–72.

Hill, Robert H. "Mystery of the Misplaced Vikings," *Oklahoma's Orbit*, November 7, 1965.

Hollon, W. Eugene. "A Spanish 'Arrastra' in the Wichita Mountains," *Chronicles of Oklahoma*, Vol. XXXIV (Winter, 1956), 443–55.

Hutchinson, H. B. "Daddy of Lead Zinc Mines Tells His Story," *Daily Oklahoman*, May 11, 1930.

Jeter, Jerry B. "Pioneer Preacher," *Chronicles of Oklahoma*, Vol. XXIII (Winter, 1945), 358–68.

Kalb, Bill. "Oklahoma's Ancient Culture," *Oklahoma's Orbit*, February 28, 1965.

Koethe, Jim. "Abandoned Mine Object of Hunt," *Wichita Falls Times*, August 23, 1959.

———. "Spanish Fort Still Cloaks in Mystery Its Real Story," *Wichita Falls Times*, July 12, 1960.

———. "Wichita [Arbuckle] Mountains Treasure Trove," *Wichita Falls Times*, August 9, 1959.

Kuykendall, J. H. "Reminiscences of Early Texans," *Texas Historical Association Quarterly*, Vol. VI (January, 1903), 249–50.

Landsverk, O. G. "Norsemen in Oklahoma," *Oklahoma Today*, Summer, 1970.

Lewis, Anna. "La Harpe's First Expedition in Oklahoma, 1718–1719," *Chronicles of Oklahoma*, Vol. II (December, 1924), 331–49.

McClung, Paul. "Army Starts Digging for Sill's Treasure," *Lawton Constitution*, April 1, 1964.

———. "Gold Lust Stronger Than Drink," *Lawton Constitution*, April 30, 1950.

———. "Sorry, Folks, There Isn't Any Treasure," *Lawton Constitution*, April 2, 1964.

McKenna, Patrick J. "Caches in the Keechi Hills," *Daily Oklahoman*, August 14, 1932.

McRill, Leslie A. "Ferdinandina: First White Settlement in Oklahoma," *Chronicles of Oklahoma*, Vol. XLI (Summer, 1963), 126–59.

———. "The Heavener Enigma: A Rune Stone," *Chronicles of Oklahoma*, Vol. XLIV (Summer, 1966), 122–29.

Mahan, Bill. "Buried Treasure Found!" *Gold*, Summer, 1971.

Middlebrooks, Andy J., and Glenna Middlebrooks. "Holland Coffee of Red River," *Southwestern Historical Quarterly*, Vol. LXIX (October, 1965), 145–62.

Mooney, James. "Calendar History of the Kiowa," in *Seventeenth Annual Report of the Bureau of Ethnology*. Part I, 254–59. Washington, D.C., Government Printing Office, 1898.

Morgan, Buford. "Treasures of the Wichitas," *Chronicles of Comanche County*, Vol. III (Autumn, 1957), 93–96.

———. "Treasures of the Wichitas," *Chronicles of Comanche County*, Vol. IV (Spring, 1958), 23–28.

———. "Treasures of the Wichitas," *Chronicles of Comanche County*, Vol. VI (Spring, 1960), 34–36.

Morrison, James D., ed. "Notes from *The Northern Standard*," *Chronicles of Oklahoma*, Vol. XIX (September, 1941), 281–83.

Newcomb, W. W., Jr. "Eyasiquiche," *Mustang* (newsletter of the Texas Memorial Museum), Vol. 7 (December, 1966), 1–5.

Nieberding, Velma. "Old Peoria: A Mother of Mining Camps," *Chronicles of Oklahoma*, Vol. L (Summer, 1972), 142–55.

Ottaway, Harold N. "Cascorillo: Archaeological Fact or Romantic Fantasy?" *Chronicles of Oklahoma*, Vol. XLIX (Spring, 1971), 100–104.

Packer, C. L. "Land of Triangles, Turtles and Hatchets," *True West*, August, 1965.

———. "Buried—and Drowned—Treasure," *Tulsa World*, July 19, 1964.

Phipps, B. L. "Lost Gold Mines of Oklahoma," *Chronicles of Oklahoma*, Vol. VII (September, 1929), 341–42.

Pike, Albert. "Narrative of a Journey on the Prairie," *Arkansas Historical Association Publications*, Vol. IV (1917).

Radzyminski, Stanley Francis. "Charles Radziminski: Soldier of Two Continents," *Chronicles of Comanche County*, Vol. IV (Spring, 1958), 39–48.

———. "Charles Radziminski: Patriot, Exile, Pioneer," *Chronicles of Oklahoma*, Vol. XXXVIII (Winter, 1960), 354–68.

Ross, S. W. "'Old Nation' Indians Seek Lucky Cherokee," *Tulsa Daily World*, February 23, 1936.

———. "Tales of Hidden Treasure along the Illinois, Cherokees and Spaniards Have Left a Rich Lore in Hill Tradition," *Tulsa Daily World*, June 28, 1931.

Rucker, Alvin. "Bones Found in State Cave May Be Sequoyah's," *Daily Oklahoman*, May 24, 1931.

Shaeffer, James B. "A Military Burial at Lake Altus," *Chronicles of Oklahoma*, Vol. XXXVI (Winter, 1958), 411–15.

Sharrock, Tom. "Frank James' House May Be Moved Soon," *Lawton Constitution*, May 10, 1959.

Shelburne, Shorty. "Army to Dig for Treasure If Any's Done," *Daily Oklahoman*, March 17, 1964.

Shirk, George H. "Campaigning with Sheridan: A Farrier's Diary," *Chronicles of Oklahoma*, Vol. XXXVII (Spring, 1959), 68–105.

———. "Real Estate Deal No. I," *Daily Oklahoman*, August 27, 1950.

———. "Report on the Heavener 'Rune Stone,'" *Chronicles of Oklahoma*, Vol. XXXVII (Autumn, 1959), 363–68.

Silliman, Benjamin. "Notice of the Malleable Iron of Louisiana," *American Journal of Science*, Vol. VIII (1824), 218–25.

Smith, Walter R. "Some Legends of Oklahoma," *Chronicles of Oklahoma*, Vol. IV (March, 1926), 50–54.

Sneed, General R. A. "The Reminiscences of an Indian Trader," *Chronicles of Oklahoma*, Vol. XIV (June, 1936), 137–38.

Stratton, J. C. Letter in *Frontier Times*, Spring, 1958.

Strickland, Rex Wallace. "History of Fannin County, Texas, 1836–1843," *Southwestern Historical Quarterly*, Vol. XXXIII (April, 1930), 262–98.

Stroud, Harry. "Ison Oldest County Citizen," *Historical Romances*, Vol. I (September, 1931), 15–17.

Strout, Clevy Lloyd. "Flora and Fauna Mentioned in the Journals of the Coronado Expedition," *Great Plains Journal*, Vol. XI (Fall, 1971), 5–40.

Studer, Floyd V. "Archeology of the Texas Panhandle,"

Panhandle-Plains Historical Review, Vol. XXVIII (1955), 87–95.

Thetford, Francis. "Did Sequoyah Really Lie in Mystery Grave near Snyder?" *Sunday Oklahoman,* February 19, 1967.

Thoburn, Joseph B. "The Prehistoric Cultures of Oklahoma," *Chronicles of Oklahoma*, Vol. VII (September, 1929), 211–41.

Thomas, A. B. "Spanish Exploration of Oklahoma, 1599–1792," *Chronicles of Oklahoma*, Vol. VI (June, 1928), 186–213.

Thompson, Bill. "Are Bars of Mexican Gold Resting on Lake's Bottom?" *Daily Oklahoman,* January 10, 1965.

Turpin, Robert F. "Oklahoma Millions in Buried Treasure," *Treasure,* February, 1971.

———. "Oklahoma Hot Spots," *Western Treasures Magazine,* August, 1970.

Tuton, J. O. "Under Fourteen Flags," *Mangum Daily Star,* October 13, 1937.

Van Zandt, Howard F. "The History of Camp Holmes and Chouteau's Trading Post," *Chronicles of Oklahoma,* Vol. XIII (September, 1935), 316–37.

Whitten, Lindsey H. "Joe Hunter Is near End of Rainbow," *Lawton Constitution,* May 19, 1948.

———. "Lawton Trio Believes End of Trail Is near in 16-Year Search for Fabulous Treasure in Expansive Wichitas," *Lawton Constitution,* February 29, 1948.

Wilson, Steve. "A. J. Meers: The First of the Gold Seekers," *Prairie Lore,* Vol. I (October, 1964), 40–45.

———. "Colonel Snively's Lost Ledge of Gold," *True Frontier,* September, 1968, pp. 14–17, 50–53.

———. "The Door That Guards $11,000,000," *Treasure World,* February–March, 1970, pp. 28–33.

———. "Early Pioneer Recalls Gunfights of Lawton's Youth," *Chronicles of Comanche County,* Vol. VI (Spring, 1960), 41–43.

———. "Economic Possibilities of Mining in the Wichita Mountains," *Proceedings of the Oklahoma Academy of Science,* Vol. XLIII (1963), 160–63.

———. "Ghosts Guard Devil's Canyon Gold," *Golden West,* September, 1965, pp. 20–21, 60–63.

———. "Gold Rush," *Oklahoma Today,* Winter, 1961–62, pp. 8–10.

———. "The Great Oklahoma Gold Rush," *Golden West,* Part I, November, 1964; Part II, January, 1965; Part III, March, 1965.

———. "Gunfight at Cutthroat Gap," *True West,* March–April, 1970, pp. 14–19, 61–63.

———. "Is It True That Dead Men Tell No Tales?" *True Frontier,* October, 1967, pp. 26–27, 52–56.

———. "Meers: Frolicking Gold Camp in the Wichitas," *Oklahoma Today,* Winter 1972–73, pp. 20–23.

———. "The Mine with the Iron Door," *Artifact,* January, 1967, pp. 6–9.

———. "Mystery of the Disappearing Gold," *West,* May, 1964, pp. 40–41, 50–52.

———. "The Mystery of the Tres Piedras Gold," and "The Bloody Doom of Mission San Sabá," *True Frontier,* November, 1967.

———. "Oklahoma's Greatest Gold Rush," *Proceedings of the Eighth Biennial Geological Symposium,* March, 1963, pp. 149–60.

———. "Oklahoma's Missing Army Payroll," *True Treasure,* March–April, 1971, pp. 24–25.

———. "Oklahoma's Treasure Trails," *Saga,* June, 1967, pp. 16–21, 79–84.

———. "Outlaw Gold of Oklahoma," *True Treasure,* May–June, 1968, pp. 28–33.

———. "Secret Code to the Jesse James Treasure," *Argosy,* October, 1965, pp. 50–51, 102–105.

———. "Secrets of Devil's Canyon and Its Gold," *True Treasure,* January–February, 1969, pp. 54–65.

———. "Spanish Treasure: Finders Keepers!" *True Frontier,* March, 1968, pp. 26–29, 55–57.

———. "Tales of an Oklahoma Prospector," *Uranium Prospector and American Outdoorsman,* May, 1960, pp. 2–3.

———. "The Treasure Spaniards Keep Hunting," *West,* March, 1966, pp. 14–15, 54–56.

———. "Was Cascorillo Really There?" *Sunday Oklahoman,* January 9, 1966.

Wright, Muriel H. "The Collection of Relics and Artifacts from Ferdinandina: Oklahoma's First White Settlement," *Chronicles of Oklahoma,* Vol. XXXIV (Autumn, 1956), 353–56.

———. "Pioneer Historian and Archeologist of Oklahoma," *Chronicles of Oklahoma,* Vol. XXIV (Winter, 1946), 404–11.

———. "A Spanish *Arrastra* in McClain County," *Chronicles of Oklahoma,* Vol. XXXIV (Winter, 1956), 484.

Newspapers

Alva Review, March 7, 1901; November 6, 1902.

Arapahoe Argus, June 21, 1895.

Arapahoe Bee, June 28, 1895.

Arkansas State Gazette (Little Rock), August 14, 1839.

Blackwell Morning Tribune, September 15, 1932.

Claremore Progress and Rogers County Democrat, January 3, 1913.

Daily Ardmoreite (Ardmore), March 15, 1896.

Daily News-Republican (Lawton), August 31, October 18, November 18, December 22, 1907; March 26, 1908.

Daily Oklahoma State Capital (Guthrie), April 22, June 8, June 10, June 20, 1895.

Daily Oklahoman (Oklahoma City), September 30, 1902; January 15, September 27, November 17, December 1, 20, 1903; May 1, 1904; December 6, 1908; November 27, 1910; September 18, 1912; January 4, 1913; July 30, 1916; May 9, 1920;

April 22, August 26, 1923; June 10, 1924; December 6, 1936; April 23, 1939; August 30, 1959; May 15, 1961.

Eagle (Spanish Fort, Texas), Special Centennial Issue of the Spanish Fort High School, May 10, 1935.

Eagle-Gazette (Stillwater), May 4, 1894.

Edmond Sun-Democrat, April 6, June 29, 1894; February 15, May 3, June 21, 28, 1895; April 23, 1897; October 20, 1899.

El Reno News, August 7, 21, September 4, 1896; November 9, 1899; April 12, 1900.

Guthrie Daily Leader, October 17, 1893.

Guymon Herald, July 1, 1909.

Hennessey Clipper, January 17, 1895; June 4, 1896.

Herald-Sentinel (Cloud Chief), June 14, July 14, 19, August 30, November 15, 1895.

Indian Chieftain (Vinita), June 14, 1894.

Kiowa County Star-Review (Hobart), June 20, 1946.

Lawton Constitution, September 15, 1904; October 12, 1947; June 23, 1967.

Lawton Weekly News, December 25, 1902; April 9, 1903.

Mangum Star, February 12, 1892; April 10, 1902.

Mineral Kingdom (Lawton), December 29, 1904; January 26, June 8, 1905.

Mount Sheridan Miner (Meers), March 3, 1904.

Muskogee Times-Democrat, August 24, 1906; November 6, 1907.

Norman Transcript, October 21, 1892; October 20, 1893; August 10, 1894; July 12, 1895.

Northern Standard (Clarksville, Texas), May 26, June 16, 1849.

Purcell Register, February 16, 1893.

Tahlequah Star-Citizen, October 2, 1952.

Temple Tribune, August 22, 1907.

Tulsa Daily World, April 16, 1934.

Vinita Daily Chieftain, January 12, 29, April 9, 1904.

Vinita Leader, July 2, 1896.

Washington Evening Star, January 16, 1904.

Weekly Republican (Lawton), May 14, July 30, 1903.

Western Independent (Fort Smith, Arkansas), August 28, 1873.

Wichita Daily Eagle, December 11, 1903.

Wilburton News, October 27, November 24, 1905.

Interviews

Bill Argo, Cache, Oklahoma, December, 1958.
Mrs. Joe Benton, Nocona, Texas, June, 1963.
Wells Blevins, Medicine Park, Oklahoma, June, 1963.
Jack Brown, Sunset, Texas, June, 1963.
Dayne Chastain, Seminole, Oklahoma, August, 1973.
Bert Cook, Phoenix, Arizona, June, 1972.
Jeff Cox, Lawton, Oklahoma, October, 1959.
Elmer Craft, Eldorado, Oklahoma, June, 1963.
James Depew, Lawton, Oklahoma, January, 1959.
Slim Dillingham, Lawton, Oklahoma, March, 1958.
Josh Drake, Jr., Mangum, Oklahoma, July, 1959.
Gordon Ferguson, Cache, Oklahoma, December, 1958.
John French, Lawton, Oklahoma, May, 1959.
Lewis Hankins, Lawton, Oklahoma, November, 1959.
Arthur Henderson, Cold Springs, Oklahoma, June, 1959.
J. B. Holderbaum, Lawton, Oklahoma, October, 1958.
Fred Huff, Lawton, Oklahoma, December, 1959.
Dave Hungerford, Faxon, Oklahoma, June, 1960.
Silas Lee Ison, Wichita Mountains Wildlife Refuge, August, 1958.
Ed Keith, Lawton, Oklahoma, May, 1959.
Mrs. Lola McDaniel, Lawton, Oklahoma, December, 1961.
William Mahan, Dallas, Texas, July, 1963.
R. S. Nolan, Lawton, Oklahoma, March, 1958.
L. A. Owen, Fletcher, Oklahoma, May, 1971.
Dean C. Salyer, Lawton, Oklahoma, February, 1958.
Lloyd Stone, Meers, Oklahoma, August, 1958.
Cy Strong, Boise City, Oklahoma, June, 1966.
Morris Swett, Lawton, Oklahoma, January, 1958.
O. J. Testerman, Springer, Oklahoma, June, 1963.
Jock Thomas, Lawton, Oklahoma, April, 1957.
Randall Wells, Tulsa, Oklahoma, December, 1966.
Jim Wilkerson, Medicine Park, Oklahoma, July, 1959.
Jay Winters, Altus, Oklahoma, June, 1963.

Correspondence

Mrs. Gloria Farley, Heavener, Oklahoma, April 21, 1973.
George A. Frampton, Lincoln, Nebraska, February 7, 1972.
Mrs. Naomi A. Hintze, Salisbury, North Carolina, December 6, 1961.
C. Boone McClure, Canyon, Texas, December 8, 1965.
James Marler, Lawton, Oklahoma, February 8, 1969.
Omer L. Morgan, Newhall, California, February 7, 1965.
Mrs. Charles A. Paul, Lubbock, Texas, February 9, 1972.
J. C. Stratton, El Paso, Texas, October 4, 1959.

Maps

Johnson, Henry D., Jr. *Oklahoma's Buried Treasures.* N.p., 1960.
Wilson, Steve. *Lost Mines & Hidden Treasures of Southwestern Oklahoma.* Oklahoma City, Semco Publishing Co., 1961.

Index

Abert, Lieut. James W.: 104–105, 237
Abrams, Alfred: 4
Ada, Okla.: 243, 244
Adair, Okla.: 281, 284
Adair County, Okla.: 28
Adams, Corwin: 4, 98
Afton, Okla.: 251
Alexander (leader of wagon train): 99, 190
Alexander, William C.: 69–71, 76
Alexandria, La.: 91
Allen (outlaw): 201, 203–204
Alligators: 78, 84
Alonso, Friar: see Terreros, Father Alonso Giraldo de
Altus, Okla.: 98
Amangual, Capt. Francisco: 71, 104
Amarillo, Texas: 104
American Journal of Science: 86
Anadarko, Okla.: 194, 236
Andrews, H. A.: 251
Antelope Hills: 61, 235
Antonio (French trader): 305n.
Apache, Okla.: 132, 135
Apache Indians: 45–46
Arapaho, Okla.: 227
Arapahoe Argus: 227
Arapahoe Bee: 227
Arbuckle Mountains: 241–47
Arcadia, Okla.: 206
Archer County, Texas: 113
Ardmore, Okla.: 130, 243
Argo, Bill: 192–93
Arkansas River: 12, 78, 94, 238, 280, 281, 297, 298; mounds on, 16, 24; Vikings on, 28; German colonists on, 34
Arkansas State Gazette: 93
Arkansas Technological College Geology Museum: 34
Artillery Mound: 274
Atlantic Crossings Before Columbus: 31
Atlas (mine): 181
Atoka, Okla.: 281
Atoka County, Okla.: 281
Augusta, Okla.: 206
Aurora, Mo.: 280
Austin, Texas: 118

Bailey, Dr. (of Choctaw County): 28
Baines, Blunt: 131
Baker, Ed: 31
Baker, Joe: 198–99
Bald Mountain: 269
Barnett, Bill: 5
Barney Creek: 285
Barnhill, Albert: 301
Barnsdall, Okla.: 279
Barren Fork River: 276
Barry, James Buckner "Buck": 99
Bartlesville, Okla.: 25
Bat Cave (in Slick Hills): 193–95, 309n.
Battle of San Jacinto: 94
Battle of Twin Mounds: 292
Baumgarner Hollow: 275
Baxter, Roy: 139
Bean, William: 115
Bears: 78, 81; black, 40; oil from, 79
Beaver Creek: 49, 59
Beavers: 78, 79, 81
Beef Creek (Maysville), Okla.: 205
Bee, Hamilton P.: 96–97

Beeswax: 79, 84
Belknap Creek: 92
Bell, Preston: 99
Beltchamber, Dan: 241
Bennett, Holsey Green: 132
Benton, Mrs. Joe: 49
Bent's Fort: 104
Berryhill, D. L.: 290, 292
Bevel, Jim: 140–41
Big Beaver Creek: 236
Big Pasture: 191
Big Wichita River: 92
Bird's Fort: 94
Bison: see buffaloes
Black Bear Creek: 236
Blackface (renegade Seminole chief): 287
Black Mesa: 215, 224
Blanco, Okla.: 301
Blevins, Wells: 141, 143–45
Blue River: 81, 205
Blum (attorney): 194
Bobb, Jim: 275–76
Bobb, Robin: 275–76
Boggy Creek: 227
Boggy Depot, Indian Terr.: 205
Bois d'Arc Bayou: 71, 76
Boise City, Okla.: 215, 217
Bonanza Mine: 125
Bonham, Texas: 190
Bonilla, Francisco Leyva de: 101
Boone, Capt. Nathan: 117, 237
Boone, Daniel: 237
Boren, Richard: 92–93
Borger, Texas: 106
Boulanger, Joe: 274
Bowie County, Texas: 91, 92
Boyles, Mrs. Frank: 225
Braden, Ross: 91
Bradley (Maley's companion): 78–81, 84, 85
Brazos River: 72, 74–76, 86, 87
Brevel (French trader): 70, 111; discovers silver mines, 84; finds silver mines in Wichitas, 113
Brewer, E. C.: 5
Briggs, George W.: 98–101
Broadwell, Dick: 281, 284
Bromide, Okla.: 241
Brown, Earl Abner: 243
Brown, Jack: 127
Brown, Rachel: 16
Brownwood, Texas: 146–47
Brush Hill: 292
Brushy Creek: 301
Brushy Mountain: 297, 300, 301
Bryan, E.: 124
Buck (with Baker gang): 198–99
Buck Creek: 117
Buehge Springs: 199
Buffaloes: 40, 78, 80, 81, 82, 84; observed by Glass, 75; tallow of, 79; hides of, 115; hunters of, 117; bones of, 119
Buffalo Hump (Comanche chief): 197
Bull Dog Hill: 33
Bullion Hole: 241
Buried City (Pueblo ruins): 101
Burkburnett, Texas: 49
Burleson, Gen. Edward: 118
Burlington, Okla.: 206
Burnett, R. H.: 93
Burns (miner): 227

Burns City, Texas: 39
Busse, Rub: 139
Butler, Okla.: 230
Butterfield, John: 206
Butterfield Overland Mail: 205
Buzzard Hill: 297–300
Buzzard Roost: 134, 138, 192

Cable, Joe: 136
Cache, Okla.: 123, 141, 190, 192
Cache Creek: 93, 94, 97, 129, 132, 135, 236, 306n.
Caddo, Indian Terr.: 205
Caddo County, Okla.: 193
Caddo–Fort Sill Road: 205
Caddo Indians: 79, 197, 260
Caine, Ed: 191
Caldwell, Kans.: 205
California Trail: 274
Camel Back Mountain: 122
Camp Augur: 101
Camp Cooper: 118
Camp Doris: 149
Camp Holmes: 237
Camp Radziminski: 197–98
Canadian River: 24, 49, 61, 71, 89, 101, 104, 196, 237, 238, 243, 281
Caney River: 274
Cañon Diablo: see Devil's Canyon
Canute, Okla.: 230
Canyon, Texas: 106
Capps, Luther: 28
Cardin, Indian Terr.: 251
Carey, Ed: 297
Carmack, Thomas K.: 97, 100
Carrizzo Creek: 101
Carter, Okla.: 99, 190
Carter County, Okla.: 243
Cascorillo (Spanish town on Turkey Creek): 34, 98, 310n.; discovered, 229–30
Casey, Tim: 11–12
Cashotoo Indians (on Red River): 78–79
Castañeda, Carlos E.: 60
Castillo, Capt. Don Diego del: 111
Castillo, Lee: 99, 190
Cat Creek Cave: 281
Catlin, George: 115
Cedar Top Mountain: 98–100
Cement, Okla.: 134, 192
Century, Indian Terr.: 251
Champion, Mrs. Alfred N.: 204
Chandler, Okla.: 206
Charleston, S.C.: 78
Charley Crossing (on Red River): 206
Charons Gardens Mountain: 183
Charons Gardens Wilderness: 182
Chastain, Dayne: 266
Cheadle Crossing (on Blue River): 205
Checotah, Okla.: 292
Cherokee, Okla.: 206
Cherokee County Court House: 290
Cherokee Indians: 241, 263, 269, 301
Cherokee Nation: 275, 276, 287, 290, 297
Cherokee Outlet: 12
Cherokee Town, Okla.: 205
Cherubin, Col. Stanley J.: 204
Cheyenne, Okla.: 206
Cheyenne-Arapaho Agency: 233
Cheyenne-Arapaho Indian Reservation: 227, 230

Cheyenne Indians: 235
Chicago, Rock Island & Pacific Railroad: 205
Chickasaw Indians: 241
Chickasaw Nation: 113, 244, 294, 295
Chihuahua, Mexico: 129, 216
Chihuahua traders: 92–93
Chihuahua Trail: 93–94
Childers, Goab: 292
Chimney Rock: 276
China Creek: 92
Chisholm, Alfred: 9
Chisholm, Jesse: 237
Chisholm, Thomas: 9
Chisholm Trail: 147, 201
Choctaw Bayou: 94
Choctaw-Chickasaw Nation: 97
Choctaw County, Okla.: 28
Choctaw Indians: 16, 28, 84, 258, 260; see also Choctaw Nation
Choctaw Nation: 91, 205, 287
Chouteau, Col. Auguste Pierre: 237
Chouteau, Okla.: 294
Chouteau Creek: 237, 238
Ciboleros: 111
Cimarron County, Okla.: 215, 224
Cimarron River: 101, 215, 224
Circle K Ranch: 194
Civil War: 206, 210, 242, 249, 275, 280, 288, 290, 294
Claiborne, William C. C.: 70
Claremore, Okla.: 269, 280, 294
Claremore Mound: 294
Clarendon, Texas: 106
Clark, J. C.: 235
Clark, Margaret: 184
Clarksville, Texas: 97, 99, 190
Clark, William: 61
Clay County, Texas: 39, 190
Clayton, N.Mex.: 224
Clayton, Okla.: 259, 260
Clear Boggy River: 205
Clear Fork of the Brazos: 45, 92
Cleo, Okla.: 206
Cleo Springs, Okla.: 4
Cleveland, Okla.: 206
Cleveland County, Okla.: 237
Cloud Chief, Okla.: 227, 229
Cloud Chief Herald-Sentinel: 227, 229
Clutter, R. D.: 300, 301
Coal: 79
Coal Creek: 260
Cochran, John: 76
Cockrell, Rep. Jeremiah V.: 113
Cockrell, Sen. F. M.: 113
Cockrell, Simon N.: 93, 113, 115, 117, 120
Cody, William F. "Buffalo Bill": 134
Coffee's Fort: 94
Coffee, Colonel Holland: 92–94, 113
Coffee's Trading House: 94, 115
Coffeyville, Kans.: 281–83
Coggin Brothers and Ford Bank: 147
Coker, Charles: 34
Colbert's Ferry (on Red River): 206
Cold Springs, Okla.: 207
Cole, W. F.: 47
Colony, Okla.: 310n.
Colorado River: 75
Colville, Silas: 93, 113
Comanche, Okla.: 237
Comanche County, Okla.: 123, 124, 145, 195, 196
Comanche Indians: 39–40, 44–45, 49, 58, 61, 69, 71, 91, 98, 99, 113, 115, 190, 196–98, 235, 243; chief of, tells of silver ore, 70; Glass trades with, 72, 74, 75; meet Maley, 81; worship meteorite, 86–87; sought for peace treaty, 96; traders with, 104–105; meet dragoons in Devil's Canyon, 117

Comancheros: 104–105, 111, 118
Comanche Springs: 118
Commerce, Okla.: 251
Commerce of the Prairies (Gregg): 113
Concho River: 111
Conchos River: 104
Confederates: grave of, 10–11
Conley (with James gang): 146–47
Connelly, Dr. Henry: 93
Conner, John: 96
Contrabanding: 58
Cook, Bert: 125
Cook, Everett: 135–36
Cook (old outlaw): 137
Cooke, Col. William G.: 92, 94
Cooke, Lieut. Phillip St. George: 117
Cooke County, Texas: 39, 46
Cooperton, Okla.: 211
Copper: 80
Coronado, Francisco Vásquez de: 9, 101
Coronado's Children (Dobie): 300
Cortés, Juan: 71
Cossatot Mountains: 34
Cotton County, Okla.: 93
Cottrell, G. W.: 201, 203–204
Courtney, Okla.: 28
Couthat, Indian Terr.: 251
Cowan, I. E.: 123
Cow Creek: 205
Cowskin (Elk) River: 251, 297
Cox, Jeff: 309n.
Cox, William: 78–81, 84, 85
Craft, Elmer C., Jr.: 25, 28
Crain (farm on Red River): 91
Crain, Walton: 47
Cramer (miner): 227
Crater Lake: 141, 144
Craterville, Okla. (mining camp): 149
Crawford, Okla.: 235
Creek Indians: 196, 251, 290, 292
Creek Nation: 281, 294
Croix, Teodoro de: 46
Cross Timbers: 40, 86, 237
Crowder, Mrs. Edna: 203–204
Crystal Cave: 247
Cummins, W. F.: 118–19
Cusher, Simeon: 260
Custer, Gen. George: 27
Custer County, Okla.: 227
Cut-Off-Head Mountain: 196
Cutthroat Gap: 34, 145–47, 149, 196–97, 207, 211

Daily News-Republican: 191
Daily Oklahoman: 194, 204
Dallas, Texas: 130, 191, 199
Dallas County, Texas: 93
Dalton, Bob: 281
Dalton, Bud: 139
Dalton, Emmett: 192, 281–84, 308n.
Dalton, Grat: 281
Dardanelle Rapids: 34
Davenport, Kate: 28
Davis, James: 71, 76
Davis, John: 71, 76
Davis, Lieut. Jefferson: 117
Davis, Okla.: 241, 245
Davis, Samuel H.: 245–47
Dead Man's Cave: 247
Dean, Ray B.: 206
Dearborn, Henry (secretary of war): 70
Deep Fork, Canadian River: 260
Deer: 40, 78; among Wichita Indians, 72
Deer Creek: 12, 16
Delaware County, Okla.: 293
Denison, Texas: 94, 294
Denton County, Texas: 87
Depew, James: 309n.
Devil's Canyon: 98, 230; Mexican mining set-

tlement in, 34; Maley finds gold in, 83–84; Mexican town in, 99; location of, 111; Mexican miners living in, 115; cave in, 117; ruins investigated by Cummins in, 118–19; silver rush near, 120; story of massacre in, 121; Spanish carving in, 122; artifacts found in, 123; gold found in, 124; mysterious landmark in, 125–26
Devil's Den: 243
Devil's Promenade: 273
Dexter, Texas: 39
Dilling, E. W.: 136
Dillingham, Slim: 140–41, 308n.
Doaksville, Indian Terr.: 91
Doan, C. F.: 120
Doan's Store: 99, 120, 195
Dobie, J. Frank: 300
Dodge, Col. Henry: 115, 117
Dodge City, Kans.: 101, 147, 195, 197
Doolin, Bill: 189
Doolin gang: 206
Dorchester, R. S.: 205
Double Mountain Fork, Brazos River: 58
Downs, Jeremiah: 69
Drake, Josh M.: 198–99
Drake, Josh M., Jr.: 198–99
Draper, W. R.: 149
Driftwood, Okla.: 206
Duncan, Okla.: 181, 184, 205
Dungeon, Jourdon: 76
Durant, Okla.: 206
Durham, Dale: 308n.
Dutisné, Claude-Charles: 12

Eagle Mountains: 96
Easterwood, H. J.: 229
Eastland County, Texas: 198
Edmond, Okla.: 206
Edward, David: 86–87
Edwards, Forrest: 124–25
Eight Mile Creek: 241
El Comercio de los Franceses (French post): 58
Eldorado, Okla.: 25
El Dorado, Texas: 147
Eldredge, Col. J. C.: 96
Elk Creek: 98
Elk Mountain: 125, 210, 212
Elk River: 251, 297
Elledge, W. N.: 235
Ellis County, Okla.: 230
Elm Creek: 98, 190
Elm Springs: 125, 187
El Paso, Texas: 129, 199
El Paso Stage Company: 205
El Reno, Okla.: 190, 235
Emerson, Okla.: 191, 192
Emet, Indian Terr.: 205
Erick, Okla.: 199
Erin Springs, Okla.: 205
Estep, Jim: 34
Esterville, Va.: 181
Estes, Dick: 189
Eufaula, Okla.: 24, 294, 301
Eustice, Samuel (secretary of war): 75
Evans, Daniel: 294

Fancher, Erwin E.: 7–9
Fancher, Logan: 7, 9
Fannin County, Texas: 71, 76, 92, 94, 99, 190
Farley, Mrs. Gloria: 31, 34
Faulkenberry, J. R.: 31
Fawn Creek: 125
Faxon, Okla.: 209
Fayetteville, Ark.: 25
Ferdinandina (French trading post): 12, 16, 39
Fernández, Santiago: 59

"Fiddlin' Jim" (Belle Starr's lover): 285
First Regiment of the United States Dragoons: 115, 117, 124
Flag Spring: 215, 216, 224
Flat Top Mountain: 111, 198, 199
Fleener, George: 229
Fleetwood, Okla.: 59
Fleming, James: 292
Fletcher, E. R.: 101
Fletcher, Okla.: 131, 135, 136
Ford, Col. Henry: 147
Foreman, Grant: 89
Foresman, Bill: 238–39
Forest Chappel, Texas: 91
Forrester, Okla.: 34
Fort, J. M.: 91–92
Fort Arbuckle: 205, 244, 247
Fort Belknap: 87, 197
Fort Cobb: 193, 194
Fort Coffee: 16
Fort Davis: 118
Fort Elliott: 101, 207
Fort Gibson: 9, 12, 115, 117, 197, 206, 290
Fort Griffin: 45
Fort Johnson: 94
Fort Leavenworth: 244
Fort Sill: 27, 147, 149, 189, 192, 201, 203–207, 236, 273
Fort Smith: 16, 34, 93, 113, 115, 249, 281, 288, 298, 299
Fort Towson: 91, 94
Fort Washita: 94, 241
Fort Worth, Texas: 9, 47, 249
Fort Worth & Denver Railroad: 205
Fourteen Mile Creek: 276
Fragoso, Francisco Xavier: 59–60, 101
Fraley (treasure hunter): 238
Frampton, George H.: 123
Freeman, G. R.: 91
Freeman, Thomas: 71
French: trading posts of, on Red River, 12; trade with Wichitas, 39–40; counted among Wichitas, 45; post of, found by José Mares, 58; search by, for silver mine, 69; accompany Spanish soldiers seeking mine, 69; traders massacred on Red River, 91; traders in Black Mesa, 215; and silver mines on Kiamichi, 259–60; trader Gaignard tells of silver mines, 260; trader Antonio liked by Taovayas, 305n.
French, John: 211–12
Fryer, Jim: 101
Fulton, Ark.: 79, 92

Gaignard, J.: 260
Gainesville, Texas: 47, 60, 97
Gálvez, Bernardo de: 46
Gates, W. E.: 98
Gazette (Fort Worth, Texas): 47
G (Custer) County, Okla.: 227
Germans: 34
Geronimo, Okla.: 191, 192
Gilbert, Father: 113
Gilbert Creek: 190
Gillespie, John: 191
Girard, Ala.: 294
Glass, Anthony: 82, 84, 87; plans silver-mine expedition, 69; is granted license to trade, 70; reaches Wichita villages, 71–72; finds venerated metal, 74; returns to Wichita villages, 75; returns to Natchitoches, 75
Glass, Antonio: *see* Anthony Glass
Glass Mountains: 4, 285
Glen Eden (Coffee's home): 94
Goad, Arthur: 281
Goff, J. M.: 190
Gold: discovered by Maley, 83–84; bullion sold by Chihuahua traders, 93; sought in Wichita Mountains, 97; found near Santa Fe, 216; discovered in Washita County, 227; discovered in Roger Mills County, 229; in Wichitas, 306n.
Gold Bell Mine: 149
Golden (mining camp): 227
Golden Pass (mining camp): 149
Goldie, Capt. (leader of wagon train): 273–74
Gott, Mrs. Susan Riley: 290
Grandfield, Okla.: 9, 59, 101
Grand River: 24, 263, 268, 270, 297
Granite, Okla.: 123, 149, 195
Granite Mountain: 98
Grant, Ulysses S.: 94
Grayson, Joe: 292
Grayson, Watt: 294
Grayson County, Texas: 94
Great Plains: 39, 111, 233
Great Spanish Road to Red River: 89
Great Temple Mound: *see* Spiro Mound
Great Western Trail: 120, 195
Green, Dr. F. R.: 124–25
Greer County (Texas and Oklahoma): 89, 93, 98–100, 117–20, 195, 196, 199, 307n.
Greer County Court Case: 89, 92, 96–99, 113, 117
Gregg, Josiah: 113, 237
Grey Horse Stage: 206
Griffeth, Mike: 33
Griffs, George: 233
Griswold, Gillett: 236
Gruber, Pvt. William: 27
Guess, George: 8; *see also* Sequoyah
Guinn, Asa: 290
Guthrie, Okla.: 4
Guthrie National Bank: 4

Half Moon (mine): 182
Hallett, Henry: 7
Hammon, Okla.: 233
Happy, Texas: 106
Hardsook, George: 3
Hardys (trappers on Red River): 79
Harkins, Dave: 290
Harris, John: 115
Harrold, Texas: 92
Hartshorne, Okla.: 260
Haskell, Okla.: 260
Haskell County, Okla.: 300
Hattonville (Commerce), Indian Terr.: 251
Haystack Mountain: 199
Headquarters Mountain: 123
Heavener, Okla.: 28, 31, 34
Heavener Runestone: 28, 31, 33–34
Hedlund, Mrs. Belle: 134, 136–38
Hemphill County, Texas: 101
Henderson, Arthur: 207
Hennessey, Okla.: 206
Hennessey Clipper: 4
Henrietta, Texas: 205, 206
Hensley, Claude E.: 236
Herrera, Simón de: 71
Herring, Bob: 198–99
Hickory Creek: 243
Hicks, Mrs. Lillie: 290
Hicks, Tom: 263
Hietans: *see* Comanche Indians
Higgins, Texas: 233
High Top Peak: 31
Hills, J. M.: 11
Hobart, Okla.: 99, 120, 212
Hockerville, Indian Terr.: 251
Holderbaum, J. B. "Burt": 147
Holibaugh, John R.: 251
Holmes, Stephen: 71
Honey Grove, Texas: 92
Hopkins County, Texas: 100
Horne, G. W.: 120
Horse and Saddle Cave: 140
Horseshoe Lake (on Red River): 91

Horse Thief Corral: 146–47
Horton, Mo.: 206
Hot Springs, Ark.: 85
Houston, Sam: 94, 96, 115
Huff, Fred: 308n.
Hugo, Okla.: 28, 34
Humaña, Antonio Gutiérrez de: 101
Hungerford, Dave: 209–10
Hunter, Joe: 136–39, 141
Huntsville, Texas: 199
Huntsville State Prison: 201
Hurtado, Juan Paez: 101
Hutchinson, Kans.: 233
Hyatan (Comanche): 81; *see also* Comanche Indians

Illinois Bend (of Red River): 82
Illinois River: 24, 275, 276
Independence, Mo.: 134
Indiahoma, Okla.: 210, 211
Indian Nations: 249, 288
Indian Rock: *see* Heavener Runestone
Indian Territory: 3, 205, 249, 279
Ingram, Okla.: 206
Iron Ore: 74, 79, 80
Ison, Bob: 184
Ison, George W.: 181–84, 186–87, 308n.
Ison, Silas Lee: 149, 180–82, 184, 186–87, 211, 308n., 309n.
Ivey, Jack: 92

Jack Fork Mountains: 301
James, Ann: 131
James, Frank: 34, 129ff., 192, 211, 244, 279; settles near Fletcher, 131; looks over old haunt, 134; niece of, seeks treasure, 135; name of, on brass bucket, 139; meets Ison in Wichitas, 182–84
James, Jesse Woodson: 129ff., 211, 279; treasure of, found in Keechi Hills, 138; name of, on brass bucket, 139; believed to be Ford, 147; meets Ison in Wichitas, 182–83; gang of, 196; treasure of, 209; loot of, 244; caves named for, 247; loot of, sought, 308n.
Jefferson, Pres. Thomas: 9, 69
Jefferson County, Okla.: 49
Jennings, Okla.: 273
Jester's Cave: 196
Johnson, E. B.: 241
Johnson, J. W.: 295
Johnson, Montford: 241
Johnson, M. T.: 93
Johnson, William: 78
Johnston County, Okla.: 241
Jones, Charlie: 139
Jones, Hiram: 250
Jones, Sherman: 47
Jonesborough, Texas: 91, 93
Juangonzales, Pedro: 230
Juirk, Edward: 76

Kansas, Oklahoma & Gulf Railroad: 263
Kansas State Penitentiary: 282
Kansas Volunteers: 27
Kaskarado Creek (in Roger Mills County): 229
Kay County, Okla.: 12, 39
Kearney, Lieut. Col. Stephen W.: 117
Keechi Hills: 134–37, 140, 147, 192, 281, 308n.
Keith, Ed: 308n.
Kelley, A. E.: 191
Kelly, O. S.: 280, 281
Kenton, Okla.: 101
Kenwood, Okla.: 293
Keown, A. S.: 193–95, 309n.
Kerr Museum: 34
Ketch, Frank: 194
Ketcher, Laura B.: 28

Keys, Mrs. Lucy: 8
Keystone, Okla.: 292
Kiamichi Mountains: 258, 260
Kiamichi River: 79, 92, 259–60
Kinder, James: 192
Kingfisher, Okla.: 284
King Mountain: 121
Kiowa, Kans.: 206
Kiowa County, Okla.: 7, 111, 195, 197, 199
Kiowa-Comanche-Apache Reservation: 4, 113, 118, 131, 149, 181, 189, 190, 201, 205, 236
Kiowa Indians: 98, 99, 117, 120, 196, 198, 233
Kiser, W. B.: 101
Kiskaddon, H. W.: 280
Kitchen Canyon: 31
Knee, Dr. L. C.: 131–32
Knowlton, William: 76
Kohlmeyer, H.: 279
Kosoma, Okla.: 260
Kunneotubby, Mr.: 288, 290
Kyle, William: 117–18

Lacey, Okla.: 206
LaFarge, Pierre: 216
La Harpe, Bénard de: 259–60
Lake Altus: 25, 28
Lake Eufaula: 301
Lake Spavinaw: 262
Lake Texoma: 94
Lamar County, Texas: 91, 92
Lamberson, Judge H. A.: 230
Lance, Fred: 236
Landsverk, O. G.: 33
La Rivière la Mine (Mine River): 259
Larsh, Mayor D. L.: 235
Larter, Capt. Harry C., Jr.: 236
Las Vegas, N.Mex.: 224
Latimer County, Okla.: 285
Lawton, Okla.: 5, 130, 131, 140, 181, 191, 192, 211, 212, 236, 281, 308 n.
Lawton Constitution: 204
Lawton Daily News-Republican: 124
Lawton Weekly News: 190
Leavenworth, Brig. Gen. Henry: 117
Lee, A. J.: 28
Lee, Fitzhugh: 94
Lee, Robert E.: 94
Lee's Summit, Mo.: 130
Le Flore County, Okla.: 16, 28
Lehmann, Herman: 124–25
Levelland, Texas: 201
Lewis, John S.: 69
Lewis and Clark Expedition: 61
Lexington, Okla.: 238
Lightning Gulch (mining camp): 149
Lillietta, Okla.: 281, 284
Lincolnville, Indian Terr.: 251
Lindsey, Bunt: 236
Lipan Apache Indians: 40; visit Glass's camp, 75
Lipscomb County, Texas: 233
Litchfield, Joe: 4
Litchfield, John: 4
Little River: 79
Little Wichita River: 39, 46, 97, 99
Llano Estacado: 96; Spanish artifacts found on trail across, 101, 104–106
Lloyd, Rev. W. J. B.: 260
Lone Mound: 292
Lone Wolf (Kiowa chief): 99
Long, Maj. Stephen H.: 89
Longest Site: *see* San Bernardo
Long Horn Cave: 195
Long Horn Mountain: 195
Lopat, Angelina: 225
Lopat, Emanuel: 216, 225

Lopat, José: 215, 216, 224, 225
Lost Canyon: 237
Lost Cave with the Iron Door: 209–13
Lost Creek: 235
Lost Standing Rock Mine: 300
Louisiana Territory: 215
Love County, Okla.: 28, 93
Loving (gold seeker): 97
Low, Jacob: 71, 76
Lower Hietans: *see* Comanche Indians
Lower Pine Creek: 91
Lucas, George: 192
Lucas, Joseph: 69, 71
Lugert, Okla.: 120

McBride, Henry: 33
McCall, Ezra: 71, 76
McClestar, William: 76
McCoy, Wooster: 263
McCurtain County, Okla.: 260
McDaniel, L. B.: 91
McDaniel, Mrs. Lola: 11
McDaniel, W. M.: 10
McElroy, N. J.: 122
McFail, Robert: 97
McKinney, Texas: 87
McNaughton, John Patrick: 249–51
McNeal, Joseph: 4
McNott Ranch: 49
Madill, Okla.: 204
Madison, James (secretary of state): 70
Major County, Okla.: 285
Maley, John: 113; arrives in Natchitoches, 78; discovers a sugar-loaf peak, 79; discovers Spanish silver mine and smelter, 80–81; trades with Wichitas, 82; discovers gold in Wichita Mountains, 83–84; disappears in Nashville, 85
Mangum, Okla.: 99, 119, 123, 199, 206
Mangum Star: 124
Marcy, Capt. Randolph B.: 71, 92, 105
Mares, José: 58, 101
Marietta, Okla.: 242
Marino Valley, N.Mex.: 216
Marshall, Ben: 294
Martín, Alejandro: 58
Martín, Capt. Hernán: 111
Martin, Wilbert: 301
Martínez, José: 118
Mason, Samuel: 69
Mayes County, Okla.: 261, 269
Maysville, Okla.: 205
Meadows gang: 268
Medicine Creek: 149
Medicine Park, Okla.: 141, 189
Meers, A. J.: 119–20
Meers (mining camp): 10, 127, 149, 193, 195
Melton, Grandpap: 275
Menard, Texas: 42
Mennonite (mine): 182
Mershom, Edward: 230
Mesquite: 92, 118
Meteorites on Red River: 69; described to Glass, 72; visited by Glass, 74; expeditions to retrieve, 75–76; interest Maley, 78; Wichita Indians show to Maley, 83; reports published on, 85–86; retrieved by Neighbors, 87
Mexican Cave: 303n.
Mexicans: traders, 91; traders on Red River trail, 92; dragoons of, with Connelly, 93; traders with Comanches, 104–105; call Wichitas Sierra Jumanos, 111; as miners in Devil's Canyon, 115; and silver mine, 117–18; as traders on Pecos River, 118; seek lost mine, 124
Mexican War: 93, 96
Mézières, Athanase de: 46, 69

Miami, Okla.: 250, 251, 273, 293
Mill Creek: 205, 244–47
Mill Creek, Okla.: 205
Miller, Frank: 139
Miller County, Ark.: 91
Mineral Kingdom: 149
Mine (Kiamichi) River: 79, 259, 260
Mission Santa Cruz de San Sabá: 42
Missouri, Kansas & Texas Railroad: 205
Missouri, Oklahoma & Gulf Railroad: 241
Missouri River: 61
Mobeetie, Texas: 98, 101
Molina, Fray Miguel de: 44
Monge, Alf: 33
Monroe, La.: 84–85
Montague County, Texas: 39, 92
Monument Camp: 227
Mooney, James: 120
Moore, Andy: 266–70
Moore, Bert: 12
Moore, B. F.: 191
Moore, T. C.: 191
Moore, T. D.: 241
Morgan, Col. John: 182
Morgan, Mr. and Mrs. Omer L.: 303n.
Morgan's Inn: 270
Mormons: 261, 262
Morris, Capt. W. A. "Bud": 39, 49
Morris, T. V.: 31
Morris Creek: 31
Moscoso, Luis: 9
Moseley, G. W.: 251
Mosquitoes: 79
Mound Builders: 16–25
Mountain Park, Okla.: 124, 197
Mount Magazine: 34
Mount Pinchot: 147, 211, 212
Mount Roosevelt: 10
Mount Scott: 34, 83, 113, 132, 190–93
Mount Sheridan: 127, 149, 190
Mount Sheridan Miner: 149
Mouse, Lacey: 292–93
Mud Creek: 237
Murray, Dove: 181, 186, 187
Murray, Gov. William H. "Alfalfa Bill": 181
Museum of the American Indian: 25
Museum of the Great Plains: 49
Museum of the Lyceum of New York: 86
Muskogee, Okla.: 24, 206, 300
Muskrats: 79
Mystery Mining & Milling Company: 241

Nacogdoches, Texas: Treviño escorted to, 46; visited by Vial, 60; expedition from, for sacred metal, 76; Spanish road leading to, 115; mineral carried to, 230
Nail's Crossing (on Blue River): 205
Narrows (on Otter Creek): 98, 118, 207
Nashville, Tenn.: 85
Natchez, Miss.: 69, 75, 84, 85
Natchez Trace: 69
Natchitoches, La.: reached by Vial and Fragoso, 60; Spaniard defects to French at, 69; Wichita and Comanche Indians go to, 70; Glass departs from, 70; Glass returns to, 75; sacred metal weighed at, 76; Maley returns to, 84; Red River trail to, 89; Spanish road leading to, 115; Gaignard explores Red River from, 260
National Science Foundation: 49
Navajoe, Texas: 120
Navajoe Mountain: 83, 84, 98, 117–18
Navajoe Trail: 207
Neighbors, Robert S.: 87
Nest Egg Mountain: 149
Neville, Judge A. W.: 91
Newcombe, George W.: 250
Newkirk, Okla.: 12, 39

New Madrid: 71
New Orleans, La.: 76
New Potosí (silver mine): 81
New York City, N.Y.: 25
New York State: 78
New York Times: 149
Nichols, A. J.: 244
Nocona, Texas: 49
No Man's Land: 215
Norman, Okla.: 25, 235
Norsemen: 28, 31–34
Norteños (Nations of the North): 40
North Canadian River: 34
Northern Standard: 97
Northfield, Minn.: 130
North Fork of Red River: Spanish trail down, 4; explored by Maley, 83; Spanish road on, 89; Texas Regulars travel up, 92; trading post at mouth of, 93; considered headwaters of Red River, 97; Spanish trail on, 98; stone fortifications on, 99; Devil's Canyon tributary of, 111; trading post at mouth of, 113, 115; mine found near, 117; wagon train up, 190; Otter Creek tributary of, 197

Oakdale, Okla.: 206
Occonostota (Cherokee chief): 9
Ochiltree County, Texas: 101
Oglesby, Okla.: 3, 279
Ohampett, G. W.: 229
O'Hare, Tom: 308n.
Okeene, Okla.: 206
Oklahoma City, Okla.: 194, 213, 235, 236
Oklahoma Historical Society: 9, 12, 24, 235
Oklahoma Panhandle: 215
Okmulgee, Okla.: 292
Oldham County, Texas: 101
Old Maid (mine): 182
Oñate, Juan de: 101
Opothleyahola (Creek chief): 290, 292
Oreana (mining camp): 149
Osage County, Okla.: 206, 279
Osage Hills: 273
Osage Indians: 16, 83, 91, 196, 274; raids of, on Wichita Indians, 72; attack Maley, 84
Osage Nation: 274
Osburn, T. J.: 227
Ottawa County, Okla.: 250, 251
Otter Creek: 98, 118, 124, 190, 196–98, 207
Otter Creek Miner: 149
Otters: 78, 79, 81
Ouachita Post: 84
Ouachita River: 84, 85
Overton, George: 139
Overton, Will: 139
Owen, L. A.: 136
Owen, Mrs. Narcissa: 8–9
Owen, Sen. Robert L.: 8–9

Page, "Uncle" Ed: 283
Palmer Lake (on Red River): 91
Palo Duro Canyon: 58, 59, 106
Palo Duro Creek: 106
Panhandle-Plains Museum: 106
Panis Indians: *see* Wichita Indians
Panis Nation: *see* Wichita Indians
Panis Noirs: *see* Wichita Indians
Panis Piqués: *see* Wichita Indians
Panther Creek: 189, 206
Panthers: 79
Parilla (Parrilla), Col. Diego Ortiz: 12, 49; erects fort, 42; investigates mission ruins, 44; commands punitive expedition, 44–46
Paris, Texas: 91, 92, 93
Paris News: 91
Parker, Cynthia Ann: 306n.
Parker, Judge Isaac: 281, 294
Parker, Quanah: 98, 191

Parker Creek: 101
Park Hill, Okla.: 274, 275, 290
Parmer, Allan: 147
Parmer, Susan James: 147
Paseola (Creek chief): 292
Passmore, John M.: 120
Patterson, Joseph: 229
Paul, Mrs. Charles A.: 9
Pauls Valley, Okla.: 205
Pawhuska, Okla.: 273
Pawnee, Okla.: 206
Pawnee County, Okla.: 273
Pawnee Indians: 273, 274
Pawnee Picts: *see* Wichita Indians
Payne, Joe: 251, 257–58
Payne, "Uncle" George: 139
Payne County, Okla.: 292
Peabody, W. S.: 251
Peabody Museum of Natural History: 86
Pease River: 92, 93, 98, 99, 306n.
Peavine, Okla.: 28
Pecan Creek: 192
Pecan Point, Texas: 91
Pecan trees, found by Glass: 75
Peck, Lieut. William: 237
Pecos River: 118
Peoria, Baptiste: 293–94
Peoria, Okla.: 250, 251
Peoria Indians: 249, 293
Peoria Mining Company: 250
Perdue, Mr.: 263, 266
Perry, Okla.: 206, 236
Petersburg, Tenn.: 249
Piankashaw Indians: 273
Picher, Okla.: 251
Pike, Albert: 115
Piney, Okla.: 301
Piper, William: 76
Pinhook (Paris), Texas: 93
Pittsburg County, Okla.: 301
Platinum: *see* meteorites
Plum (Pease) River: 92
Plummer, Mrs. Rachel: 87
Pocola Mining Company: 23
Pohl, Frederick J.: 31
Pollard, James T.: 99–101, 190
Ponca City, Okla.: 34
Pontotoc County, Okla.: 294
Porter (miner): 227
Porter Hill, Okla.: 195
Post Oak (Emet), Okla.: 205
Post Trader's Store, at Fort Sill: 201, 204
Poteau, Okla.: 206
Poteau Mountain: 28, 31, 34
Poteau River: 24, 34
Pottawatomie County, Okla.: 244
Poverty Gulch (mining camp): 149
Powers, Bill: 281, 284
Prairie Dog Town Fork, Red River: 58, 92, 93, 97, 190
Presidio San Luis de las Amarillas: 42
Preston, Texas: 94
Prince (finder of Iron Door): 210
Pryor, Okla.: 261, 267, 279, 280
Pryor Creek: 268
Pryor Creek, Okla.: 12
Pueblo culture: 101
Purcell, Okla.: 237
Purcell Register: 113
Pushmataha County, Okla.: 259

Quantrill, William: 147, 183
Quapaw, Indian Terr.: 251
Quapaw Indians: 251
Quartz Mountain State Park: 25

Raccoons: 78, 79
Radziminski, Lieut. Charles: 197

Ragsdale, Martin H.: 91
Ragtown, Texas: 91
Ralston, Okla.: 34
Ranball, J. E.: 229
Randolph, Elmo: 11–12
Randolph, Robert: 11–12
Rattlesnake Mine: 7
Rattlesnakes: 84
Red Fork, Okla.: 4
Red River: 39; Wichita village on, 12; cave on, 28; Lipan Apaches on, 40; twin Wichita villages on, 42; Wichita fortification on, 45; fort on, 46; cave on, 47; artifacts found on, 49; Glass plans silver-mine expedition up, 69; Maley explores, 78–84; traders on Spanish trail on, 91 ff.; Coffee's Fort on, 94; copper mine on, 100; silver mines found on, 113; wagon train up, 190; explored by Gaignard, 260
Red River County, Texas: 91
Red Rock, Okla.: 281, 284
Reed, Jim: 294
Reed, Myra Belle: *see* Belle Starr
Reed, Sam: 191
Reed, Okla.: 196
Remer, Sam: 191
Reynolds, W. H.: 281
Riley, John N.: 290
Ringgold, Texas: 49, 99
Río Colorado de Natchitoches (Red River): 118
Río Grande: 96
Ripps, Fred: 191
Robber's Canyon: 279, 280
Robber's Cave State Park: 285
Roberts, Thomas F.: 92
Robinson, Edward: 76
Rock Bluff (on Red River): 94
Rock Creek: 273
Roger Mills County, Okla.: 229, 233, 235
Roosevelt, Okla.: 149
Rose, Okla.: 269
Ross, Lawrence Sullivan "Sul": 118, 197, 306n.
Ross, Peter F.: 306n.
Ross's Rangers: 99
Royce, "Uncle" Billy: 134–36
Runyan, Art: 123
Rush Springs, Okla.: 136, 137, 197, 205
Rutherford, Judge (farm on Red River): 91
Ryan (leader of wagon train): 99, 190
Ryan, Michael: 224
Ryan, Okla.: 59

Sac and Fox Agency: 206
Saddleback Ruin: 101
St. Geneviève, Mo.: 61
St. Joseph, Mo.: 130, 245
St. Louis, Indian Terr.: 251
St. Louis, Mo.: 205, 206; reached by Vial, 61
Salas, Fray Juan de: 111
Salcedo, Gov. Manuel María de: 71
Saline, Okla.: 269
Sallisaw, Okla.: 288
Salt Branch (perhaps Blue River): 81
Salt Creek: 292
Salt Lake City, Utah: 249
Salt licks: 81
Salyer, Dean C.: 145–47
San Angelo, Texas: 111
San Antonio, Texas: 87; distance from Spanish outpost to, 44; cannons removed to, 46; visited by Vial, 60
San Augustine, Texas: 60
San Bernardo (Taovaya village on Red River): 34, 46, 49, 72
Sand Springs, Okla.: 279, 280, 281, 282
Sand Springs Home: 282
San Fernando, Mexico: 8

San Francisco, Calif.: 205, 206
San Sabá Mission: 44
San Sabá River: 42
Santa Fe: reached by Vial and Santos, 49; reached by Mares, 58; Vial leaves for Natchitoches from, 59; Vial returns to, 60; Vial dies in, 65; trail from Natchitoches to, 89ff.; traders with silver specie from, 196; placer mining near, 216; stone markers between Las Vegas and, 224
Santa Fe–Natchitoches Trail: 89ff.; revealed in court testimony, 89; known to Marcy's Comanche guide, 92; Mexican traders on, 93; known to Delaware guide, 96–97; through Wichita Mountains, 98; through Hopkins County, 100; across Texas Panhandle, 101, 104–106; Coffee post built near, 113, 115; past Navajoe Mountain, 117
Santa Fe Trail: 61, 215, 217, 224, 237
San Teodoro (Taovaya village on Red River): 46, 49, 72
Santiesteban, Fray José de: 44
Santos, Cristóbal de los: 49, 58
Sauerberg, Mark: 120–21
Saule, A. M.: 191
Savage, John: 235
Scaley Back Mountain: 294
Schamp, George: 71, 76, 86
Schoolcraft, Henry: 251
Schurz, Carl (secretary of the interior): 250
Scientific American Supplement: 149
Second-eye, Jim: 96
Seger, Okla.: 310n.
Seminole County, Okla.: 266
Seminole, Okla.: 266
Seneca, Mo.: 249, 251
Sequoyah County, Okla.: 288
Sequoyah: tomb of, 7–9; grave of, in Mexico, 303n.
Settles, J. C.: 117, 118
Shackelford, William: 47
Shaeffer, James B.: 25
Shaw, Jim: 96–97
Shawnee, Okla.: 34, 244
Shawnee Indians: 249
Shell Creek: 282, 283
Sherman, Texas: 249, 250, 288
Shipley, Jim: 33
Shipman, Daniel: 86
Shreveport, La.: 260
Shrock, John: 47
Sibley, Dr. John: 69–70, 113, 259; describes metal found by Glass, 75; takes charge of magic stone, 76; offers Maley free license, 78
Sierra Jumanos (Wichita Mountains): 111, 113; see also Wichita Mountains
Silliman, Benjamin: 85–86
Silver: Wichita Indians tell Maley about, 82; mines discovered by Maley, 84; found in Wichita Mountains, 113; mine near Navajoe Mountain, 117–18; rush near Devil's Canyon, 120; discovered in Roger Mills County, 229; mines on Kiamichi, 259–60; mines found in Greer County, 307n.
Silver Mine Expedition: 70
Silverton (Greer County mining camp): 120
Simonson, Maj.: 118
Sioux Indians: 233
Sisney (treasure hunter): 233
Sivells Bend (on Red River): 39
Six Toes (with Baker gang): 198–99
Skeletons: found in Wichita Mountains, 190–91; unearthed in Keechi Hills, 192; found in Washita County, 227, 229; found near Union City, 235
Skinner, William: 76

Skullyville, Okla.: 206
Slick Hills: 195
Smith, John: 76
Smith, Zack: 139
Snider, Mr. and Mrs. Duncan: 28
Snively, Col. Jacob: 94–96
Snyder, Okla.: 7, 197
Soldier Spring Mountain: 111, 122, 195
South Canadian River: 236, 284, 300
Southern Methodist University: 49
Southern Stage Company: 205
South Fork of Red River: 97–99
South Mud Creek: 47
Spaniards: trail of, 4; cavalry of, attack Tonkawas, 45; attack Wichita fortification, 45–46; hire Vial, 49, 59; soldiers and civilians seek mine, 69; silver mine discovered, 80–81; gold placer workings of, 83; abandoned silver mines of, 84; discover sacred metal, 87; trail of, down Red River, 89; trail of, through Wichita Mountains, 98; grave of, on Otter Creek, 98; trail of, across Texas Panhandle, 101, 104–106; swords and artifacts of, found in Panhandle, 106; as captives among Comanches, 117; artifacts of, found, 235; mines of, found in northeastern Oklahoma, 249, 251; silver mines of, in Greer County, 307n.
Spanish Canyon: 5
Spanish Cave: 5, 303n.
Spanish Crossing (on Canadian River): 104
Spanish Fort, Texas: 39, 45, 46, 47, 70, 82, 92, 93, 100, 243, 305n.
Spanish Fort Bend (on Red River): 39
Spanish Peaks: 235
Spavinaw, Okla.: 262, 263
Spavinaw Creek: 261
Spavinaw Hills: 261, 262, 293
Spearman, Texas: 106
Spiro, Okla.: 16, 24, 297, 300
Spiro Mound: 16–25
Spring Creek: 98, 99, 101, 268
Spring Draw: 106
Springer, Okla.: 242
Springfield, Mo.: 249
Spring Mountain: 34
Spring River: 249, 251, 273
Standing Rock: 35, 300–301
Stanfield, Texas: 46
Starr, Belle: 209, 211, 268, 285, 294
Starr, Henry: 269
Stephens (Iron Door finder): 211
Stephens County, Okla.: 237
Stillwater, Okla.: 292
Stilwell, Okla.: 301
Stinnett, Mrs. Billy: 275
Stinnett, "Uncle" Billy: 274–75
Stockwell, H. O.: 233
Stone, Lloyd: 195
Stonewall, Okla.: 294
Stonewall County, Texas: 58
The Story of Cole Younger (Younger): 279
Stovall Museum: 25
Stratton, J. C.: 199
Stringtown, Okla.: 281
Strong, Cy: 215, 217, 224, 225
Stroud, Okla.: 206
Studley, Theo E.: 138
Sublett, Capt. Dave: 118
Sugar Loaf Peak: 215, 217, 224
Sulphur Springs (Sulphur), Okla.: 205
Sunnyside, Indian Terr.: 251
Sunset, Texas: 127
Suttenfield, Sophia: 94
Swedish: 34
Swett, Master Sergeant Morris: 201, 203–204

Tahlequah, Okla.: 24, 206, 251, 274–76, 287, 288, 290, 301
Tahlequah Creek: 290
Talley, Olin: 120
Talley, S. C., Sr.: 99
Taloga, Okla.: 236
Taos, N.Mex.: 115, 216
Taovaya Indians: see Wichita Indians
Tarbone Mountain: 129–31, 139, 140
Tar River, Indian Terr.: 251
Tascosa, Texas: 101
Tatesuck (Spanish captive): 72, 75
Tawehash: see Wichita Indians
Tejas Indians: 44
Temple, Okla.: 94
Temple Tribune: 9
Tennessee Cavalry: 182
Tepee Creek: 118
Tepee Mountain: 122, 195, 196
Terral, Okla.: 46
Terreros, Fray Alonso Giraldo de: 44
Territory of Orleans: 70
Terry Hill: 33
Testerman, O. J.: 242–43
Texan–Santa Fe Expedition: 96
Texas Boundary Commission: 105
Texas Memorial Museum: 87
Texas Panhandle: 34, 49, 61, 71, 89, 98, 101, 104–106, 130, 196, 207, 233
Texas Rangers: 95, 118, 198, 199
Texas Regulars: 92
Texas Republic: 94
Texas State Prison: 199
Thoburn, Joseph B.: 12
Thomas, Charley: 236
Thomas, Deputy Marshal Heck: 184
Thomas, George (ranch): 193
Thomas, Jock: 236
Thomas, Wes: 31
Thompson, Joe C.: 123
Tillman County, Okla.: 9, 93, 113
Tipton, Okla.: 4, 98, 197
Tishomingo, Okla.: 204, 205, 243
Tittle, L. H.: 123
Tom Patton Cave: 28
Tonkawa Indians: 44–45, 197
Toyash (Wichita Mountains): 111
Toyash: see Wichita Indians
Trail of Tears: 290
Travis, Capt. Charles E.: 118
Treasure Lake: 5, 209, 210, 212
Treaty of Medicine Lodge: 189
Treviño, Lieut. Antonio: 46, 305n.
Trinity River: 69, 94
Tucumcari, N.Mex.: 233
Tulsa, Okla.: 4, 206, 238, 262, 280, 293, 301
Tulsa County, Okla.: 33
Tulsa Daily World: 288
Turkey Creek: 227, 229, 230
Turkey Mountain: 4–5
Turkeys: 78, 79, 84
Turley, Okla.: 33
Twin Hills: 273
Twin Mountains (near Devil's Canyon): 121
Twist Mountain: 301

Unassigned Lands: 237
Union City, Okla.: 235
United States Geological Survey: 251
The United States v. The State of Texas: 89, 113, 230
University of Arkansas Museum: 25
University of Oklahoma: 24, 49; Department of Anthropology of, 25
University of Texas: 49, 87
Uselding, Ray: 106
Usray, George: 288
Usray, Phillip: 288

Usray, Tobe: 288
Ute Creek: 104

Vaca, Alonzo: 101
Valeréz, Don Juan: 9
VanCloor, J.: 199
Van Dorn, Brev.-Maj. Earl: 197–98
Vernon, Texas: 195, 198
Vial, Pedro: 65, 89, 101, 104; explores route to Santa Fe, 49, 58; explores route from Santa Fe to Natchitoches, 59–60; explores from Santa Fe to St. Louis, 60–61; meets Amangual on Canadian River, 71
Viana, Francisco: 71
Vici, Okla.: 230
Vikings: 28, 31–34
Villasur, Pedro de: 101
Vinita, Okla.: 28, 249
Von, John: 143–45, 308n.

Waco, Texas: 124
Waggoner, Dan, and Sons: 98
Walkingstick, Ed: 28
Walnut Bayou: 93
Walnut Bend (on Red River): 39
Warren, Abel: 93–94
Warren's Camp: 227
Warren's Trading House: 97; post, 94; location of, 306n.
Washington Evening Star: 8
Washita County, Okla.: 227, 229, 310n.
Washita River: 118, 204
Watonga, Okla.: 206
Wauhillau, Okla.: 276
Webb, Van: 203–204
Wells, Randall: 301
West, "Uncle" Johnny: 262–63, 266
Western Independent (Fort Smith, Ark.): 3
Wetumka, Okla.: 301
Wewoka, Okla.: 34
Wharton, Okla.: 281
Wheeler County, Texas: 98
When the Daltons Rode (Dalton): 281
White, James: 76

White, Joe: 301
White, Joseph: 71
White Bead Hill, Okla.: 205
White Eagle (Comanche chief): 117
White Shields Creek: 233
Whittaker, W. T.: 261–62
Wichita, Kans.: 274
Wichita County, Texas: 87
Wichita Daily Eagle: 124
Wichita Falls, Texas: 9, 191
Wichita Indians: 39, 46, 49, 58–59; village of, on Deer Creek, 12; on Red River, 12; settle on Red River, 40, 42; attack Spanish mission, 44; fight from fortification, 45–46; visited by De Mézières, 46; sites of, excavated by museums, 49; visited by Vial, 49; visited by Mares, 58; visited by Vial, Fragoso, and Fernández, 59; mineral deposits reported near, 69; go to Natchitoches, 70; visited by Glass, 71–72; revere metallic mass, 74; Glass returns to, 75; show Schamp sacred metal, 76; visited by Maley, 82–83; Santa Fe Trail past villages of, 92; village of, southeast of Wichita Mountains, 97; village of, in Devil's Canyon, 111; met by United States Dragoons, 115, 117; ruins of village of, 120; with Ross, 197
Wichita Mountains: 189, 191, 193, 206; mummy found in, 5; gold seekers in, 7; Sequoyah's death in, 8; skeletons discovered in, 9–11, 25; sighted by Vial and Fragoso, 59; explored by Maley, 83–84; Snively's expedition past, 94; Eldredge seeks Comanches in, 96–97; Texans seek gold in, 97; Spanish trail through, 98; Texas Rangers in, 99; known as Sierra Jumanos, 111; silver reported in, 113; United States Dragoons in, 115, 117; search for silver in, 118; gold rush in, 124; Jesse James in, 129ff.; gold rush in, 149; skeletons found in, 190–91; Cave with Iron Door in, 209–13; gold in, 306n.; gold rush in, 307n.

Wichita Mountains Wildlife Refuge: 5, 125, 180, 206, 209, 210
Wichita River: 94, 96, 97, 306n.
Wicker, Henry: 190
Wilbarger County, Texas: 92
Wilburton, Okla.: 12, 285, 288, 290
Wilburton News: 12
Wild boars: 40
Wild cattle: 78
Wild Horse Creek: 205
Wild horses, found by Glass: 75
Wildman (mining camp): 149, 310n.
Wild Woman Cave: 247
Wilkerson, Jim: 134, 189, 195
Williams, E. A.: 229, 230, 310n.
Williams, William: 310n.
Williams, William M.: 76
Williams, William Y. "Buffalo Head": 275
Williams' Camp: 227
Wilson, Ed: 31
Wilson, Gene: 49
Wimberley, Jack: 283
Winding Stair Mountain: 34
Winters, Lee: 122–24
Winters, Mamie: 124
Wister, Okla.: 34
Wolf, Negro Squire: 205
Wolf Creek, stone ruins in brakes of: 101
Woolaroc Museum: 25
Wright, George W.: 91
Wyatt, Zip: 285

Yale University: 86
Yeager, Dick: 285
Yewed, Okla.: 206
Yoder, Harvey: 135
Young, Peter: 71, 76
Young County, Texas: 87, 99
Younger, Cole: 130, 139, 147, 183, 279–81
Yukon, Okla.: 235

Zaldivar, Vicente de: 101
Zinn, Albert: 293
Zorger, C. E.: 131